God, Jews and the media

In order to understand contemporary Jewish identity in the twenty-first century, one needs to look beyond the synagogue, the holy days and Jewish customs and law to explore such modern phenomena as mass media and their impact upon Jewish existence. This book delves into the complex relationship between Judaism and the mass media to provide a comprehensive examination of modern Jewish identity.

Covering Israel as well as the Diaspora populations of the US and UK, the author looks at journalism, broadcasting, advertising and the Internet to give a wide-ranging analysis of how the Jewish religion and Jewish people have been influenced by the media age. He tackles questions such as:

- What is the impact of Judaism on mass media?
- How is the religion covered in the secular Israeli media?
- Does the coverage strengthen religious identity?
- What impact does the media have upon secular-religious tensions?

Chapters explore how the impact of Judaism is to be found particularly in the religious media in Israel – Haredi and modern Orthodox – and looks at the evolution of new patterns of religious advertising, the growth and impact of the Internet on Jewish identity, and the very legitimacy of certain media in the eyes of religious leaders. Also examined are such themes as the marketing of rabbis, the 'Holyland' dimension in foreign media reporting from Israel, and the media's role in the Jewish Diaspora.

An important addition to the existing literature on the nature of Jewish identity in the modern world, this book will be of great interest to scholars of media studies, media and religion, sociology, Jewish studies, religion and politics, as well as to the broader Jewish and Israeli communities.

Yoel Cohen is on the faculty of the School of Communication, Ariel University Center of Samaria, Israel (School Chairman 2009–11).

Routledge Jewish Studies Series
Series editor: Oliver Leaman, University of Kentucky

Studies, which are interpreted to cover the disciplines of history, sociology, anthropology, culture, politics, philosophy, theology, religion, as they relate to Jewish affairs. The remit includes texts which have as their primary focus issues, ideas, personalities and events of relevance to Jews, Jewish life and the concepts which have characterised Jewish culture both in the past and today. The series is interested in receiving appropriate scripts or proposals.

MEDIEVAL JEWISH PHILOSOPHY
An Introduction
Dan Cohn-Sherbok

FACING THE OTHER
The Ethics of Emmanuel Levinas
Edited by Seán Hand

MOSES MAIMONIDES
Oliver Leaman

A USER'S GUIDE TO FRANZ ROSENZWEIG'S STAR OF REDEMPTION
Norbert M. Samuelson

ON LIBERTY
Jewish Philosophical Perspectives
Edited by Daniel H. Frank

REFERRING TO GOD
Jewish and Christian Philosophical and Theological Perspectives
Edited by Paul Helm

JUDAISM, PHILOSOPHY, CULTURE
Selected Studies by
E. I. J. Rosenthal
Erwin Rosenthal

PHILOSOPHY OF THE TALMUD
Hyam Maccoby

FROM SYNAGOGUE TO CHURCH: THE TRADITIONAL DESIGN
Its Beginning, its Definition, its End
John Wilkinson

HIDDEN PHILOSOPHY OF HANNAH ARENDT
Margaret Betz Hull

DECONSTRUCTING THE BIBLE
Abraham ibn Ezra's Introduction to the Torah
Irene Lancaster

IMAGE OF THE BLACK IN JEWISH CULTURE
A History of the Other
Abraham Melamed

FROM FALASHAS TO ETHIOPIAN JEWS
Daniel Summerfield

PHILOSOPHY IN A TIME OF CRISIS
Don Isaac Abravanel: Defender of the Faith
Seymour Feldman

JEWS, MUSLIMS AND MASS MEDIA
Mediating the 'Other'
Edited by Tudor Parfitt with Yulia Egorova

JEWS OF ETHIOPIA
The Birth of an Elite
Edited by Emanuela Trevisan Semi and Tudor Parfitt

ART IN ZION
The Genesis of National Art in Jewish Palestine
Dalia Manor

HEBREW LANGUAGE AND JEWISH THOUGHT
David Patterson

CONTEMPORARY JEWISH PHILOSOPHY
An Introduction
Irene Kajon

ANTISEMITISM AND MODERNITY
Innovation and Continuity
Hyam Maccoby

JEWS AND INDIA
History, Image, Perceptions
Yulia Egorova

JEWISH MYSTICISM AND MAGIC
An Anthropological Perspective
Maureen Bloom

MAIMONIDES' *GUIDE TO THE PERPLEXED*: SILENCE AND SALVATION
Donald McCallum

MUSCULAR JUDAISM
The Jewish Body and the Politics of Regeneration
Todd Samuel Presner

JEWISH CULTURAL NATIONALISM
David Aberbach

THE JEWISH-CHINESE NEXUS
A Meeting of Civilizations
Edited by M. Avrum Ehrlich

GERMAN-JEWISH POPULAR CULTURE BEFORE THE HOLOCAUST
Kafka's Kitsch
David Brenner

THE JEWS AS A CHOSEN PEOPLE
Tradition and Transformation
S. Leyla Gürkan

PHILOSOPHY AND RABBINIC CULTURE
Jewish Interpretation and Controversy in Medieval Languedoc
Gregg Stern

JEWISH BLOOD
Reality and Metaphor in History,
Religion and Culture
Edited by Mitchell B. Hart

JEWISH EDUCATION AND HISTORY
Continuity, Crisis and Change
*Moshe Aberbach; Edited
and translated by
David Aberbach*

JEWS AND JUDAISM IN MODERN CHINA
M. Avrum Ehrlich

POLITICAL THEOLOGIES IN THE HOLY LAND
Israeli Messianism and
its Critics
David Ohana

COLLABORATION WITH THE NAZIS
The Holocaust and After
Edited by Roni Stauber

THE GLOBAL IMPACT OF THE PROTOCOLS OF THE ELDERS OF ZION
A Century-Old Myth
Edited by Esther Webman

THE HOLOCAUST AND REPRESENTATIONS OF THE JEWS
History and Identity in the Museum
K. Hannah Holtschneider

WAR AND PEACE IN JEWISH TRADITION
From the Biblical World to the Present
Edited by Yigal Levin and Amnon Shapira

JESUS AMONG THE JEWS
Representation and Thought
Edited by Neta Stahl

GOD, JEWS AND THE MEDIA
Religion and Israel's Media
Yoel Cohen

God, Jews and the media
Religion and Israel's media

Yoel Cohen

LONDON AND NEW YORK

First published 2012
by Routledge
2 Park Square, Milton Park, Abingdon, Oxon OX14 4RN

Simultaneously published in the USA and Canada
by Routledge
711 Third Ave, New York, NY 10017

Routledge is an imprint of the Taylor & Francis Group, an Informa business

© 2012 Yoel Cohen

The right of Yoel Cohen to be identified as author of this work has been asserted by him in accordance with sections 77 and 78 of the Copyright, Designs and Patents Act 1988.

All rights reserved. No part of this book may be reprinted or reproduced or utilised in any form or by any electronic, mechanical, or other means, now known or hereafter invented, including photocopying and recording, or in any information storage or retrieval system, without permission in writing from the publishers.

Trademark notice: Product or corporate names may be trademarks or registered trademarks, and are used only for identification and explanation without intent to infringe.

British Library Cataloguing in Publication Data
A catalogue record for this book is available from the British Library

Library of Congress Cataloging in Publication Data

ISBN: 978-0-415-47503-7 (hbk)
ISBN: 978-0-203-12334-8 (ebk)

Typeset in Times New Roman
by Taylor & Francis Books

Printed and bound in the United States of America by Publishers Graphics, LLC on sustainably sourced paper.

Contents

Preface: Israel Television interviews God   ix

PART 1
Mediated Judaism   1

1   Media, Judaism and Culture   3

2   The Jewish Theory of Communication   15

PART 2
Media culture wars   33

3   Constructing religion news: the religion reporter decides   35

4   News values, ideology and the religion story   48

5   Mikva news   77

6   Dual loyalties: the modern Orthodox dilemma   96

7   Identity, unity and discord   108

PART 3
Issues in mediated Judaism   133

8   www.techno-Judaism   135

9   Kosher advertising   156

10   The marketing of the rabbi   172

11 At bay in the Diaspora 186

12 From out of Zion shall come forth
    foreign news 205

PART 4
Conclusion 219

13 Judaism in the information age 221

   Notes 235
   Selected bibliography 241
   Index 252

Preface: Israel Television interviews God

Normally, the head of Israel's broadcasting authority would see the Chief Rabbi only on key dates such as when the latter was invited to appear on television at the Jewish New Year. So when a somewhat nervous, if not frantic, Chief Rabbi called the authority head at his home at the end of the Sabbath, it was clear something unusual had occurred.

The Chief Rabbi related that during his sleep on the Holy Sabbath he had had a vision from Almighty God, in which God told the learned rabbi that He wished to speak to the Jewish people, indeed to mankind, through an interview on Israel Television.

Considering that God had not spoken directly to humans since the end of the age of the Jewish prophets in the fifth century BCE, it was highly unusual that He should now return to a more direct relationship. After the age of prophecy, God's relationship with the Jewish people was based upon belief (*emunah*). So now, God's decision represented a revolutionary change. True, God spoke to each generation in terms that they understood, so it was not so surprising that in the information age, when much appeared to be determined by broadcast media – from the fireside chats or 'meet the press' encounters of the US president downwards – God decided to use a similar framework to communicate His message. However, the fact of the State of Israel, re-established after a gap of nearly two thousand years since the destruction of the Second Jewish Temple in 70 CE, must also have played a part in His decision to communicate directly after so much time.

There were a number of messages that God sought to convey. With the yet unresolved Arab–Israeli conflict, and against the background of growing nuclearisation of Arab states, there was a need to reassure the Jewish people of God's uncompromising commitment to Israel's security and to the Jewish people's future. Moreover, in the age of globalisation, there was a need to strengthen the uniqueness of the Jewish identity, particularly in light of rampant intermarriage in Jewish communities abroad. Yet, the interview was to be directed not only to Israel but rather to humanity as a whole, in particular to the other monotheistic faiths like Islam and Christianity. One theme of God's message to the entire world was the need to deal with poverty in the developing world – where over three-quarters of the world's population lived – by redistributing economic resources between the developed and developing worlds. Another was the need to find peaceful means towards resolving conflicts.

An international and historic scoop was just the ploy to get the somewhat staid Channel 1 back on its feet, after the more popular second television channel had drawn so many viewers away from it since the latter's establishment in the mid-1990s. The first channel wisely resisted pressure from the second channel that the channels should combine broadcasting for the historic interview. The international media were aghast that one country should be given 'the exclusive' and in a language not known by many outside Israel. But Hebrew was the holy tongue. For the Muslim and Christian worlds it was a reminder of Israel's 'election' as God's chosen ones. But undoubtedly the interview would be broadcast simultaneously on television stations worldwide with subtitles.

God's decision to speak aroused no less controversy at home. For the modern religious in Israel, or *dati leumi* population, which believed that the creation of the state of Israel alluded to the messianic age, this was just one further confirmation of this. But the ultra-Orthodox Haredim – who rejected the idea that the messianic age had come and saw the State of Israel as being distant from being a truly Torah-observing entity – had a dilemma with regard to God's decision to address the Jewish people through the very medium, television, which Haredim had for years delegitimised as morally decadent.

God is non-corporeal. What would viewers see – apart from the interviewer? According to the strict rules of journalism, the interview ought to be done on radio rather than television, given the latter's need for visuals. But it was too spectacular an event not to do on television.

The broadcasting authority head set up a steering committee to deal with a host of logistical and related questions. The first question concerned the date of the interview. Clearly the High Holy Day period, which falls in September, or the Jewish month of Tishrei, was the most appropriate time. One person suggested Yom Kippur, the Jewish Day of Atonement, regarded as the holiest day in the Jewish calendar. But one participant in the steering committee, Israel television's head of religious broadcasting – or Jewish tradition department, as it is known formally – remarked that observant Jews do not watch television on this the holiest day of the Jewish calendar when they are in synagogue at prayer. A compromise was fixed and the date set for the evening after the New Year holiday, or Rosh Hashanah – which would be an appropriate time, with the build-up in a spiritual sense to the Yom Kippur finale a week later.

Another key question was who would do the interview? If it would be a male interviewer, should he don a skullcap out of respect? Could a woman anchorperson interview the Almighty? The head of dama – a declared feminist – argued that God had certain female attributes. But the authority head settled what had become a lively theological debate by saying that God was above any gender.

Yet another question was that of the studio décor: given God's non-corporealness, instead of showing the interviewee, all that the cameras could show – in addition to the interviewer – would be a blank screen. One idea that was mooted was a memorial flame – but that conveyed pessimism. Another was the menorah, part of the symbol of the Jewish state. Yet another suggestion was a picture of the famous Western Wall in Jerusalem. Yet given that the interview was not just directed to the Jewish people, it was decided that the studio would have a neutral, if obvious, background of sky and clouds. Nevertheless, it would be interwoven with brief cuts to the other, more Jewish themes – a reminder of Israel's exclusive interview.

As the day approached, there was heavy pressure from potential advertisers who sought to buy space, but as a public television channel, Channel 1 did not carry commercial advertising. Haredi reservations about television were solved by the decision to carry the interview on Israel Radio simultaneously. An invited studio audience would, in addition to the Chief Rabbi himself, include the Israeli Minister of Religious Affairs as well as representatives of the faiths in the Holyland. The interview would be carried in a live satellite link-up on numerous television stations around the world – even on stations in Islamic countries which did not have diplomatic ties with Israel.

All was set. The studio clock ticked to the hour. The interviewer began: 'Welcome to what can only be described as a truly historic interview of profound significance. Before we start on substantive questions, I would like to ask you, Almighty God, a question which many, many of our viewers are intrigued by: "Why have You decided to speak to mankind now, and through a channel which You have never used before?"' There was silence. More silence. The silence went from seconds to minutes. Something had gone awfully wrong. God did not answer.

Had God changed His mind and decided not to speak? Was there a technical hitch? Or had the Chief Rabbi erred? The broadcasting authority head began to ask himself if the Chief Rabbi had misinterpreted on that fateful Sabbath what he thought to be a vision of God; perhaps, in fact, it was no more than a dream. Or perhaps the Chief Rabbi had erroneously believed, even if only subconsciously, that he had a superior spiritual status, with a direct 'line of communication' to the Almighty.

The non-interview created a crisis. The rabbis of the modern Orthodox community were at pains to explain that what was billed as one further manifestation of the final redemption had not occurred. But for the Haredi rabbinical leadership it was another opportunity to ridicule the state Chief Rabbinate. After all, the Chief Rabbi, a state appointment, was elected by rabbis and town mayors, with the winning candidate chosen less for his spiritual standing or his erudition and more because of his political connections and media savviness. And for the secular community, the whole incident served as further reason to doubt God's existence. Jews in the Diaspora felt particularly uneasy, and some even feared an outburst of anti-Semitism.

Not only did Israel Television and the Chief Rabbinate have egg on their faces, but it was highly embarrassing to the State of Israel and the Jewish people as a whole that, after the massive build-up, the interview failed to occur. While there was some sympathy for the Chief Rabbi in some quarters, the question was asked: why had the broadcasting chief – a professional journalist – failed to carry out some checking standard in journalism to verify that the Chief Rabbi had indeed had a vision and that God would 'go live'? Heads had to roll. The broadcasting chief resigned.

Clearly, had the interview with God actually occurred, it would have underlined how mass media and Jewish identity have become intertwined today. An interview with God would have been one more way for God to communicate with the Jewish people, in addition to those He has employed over the centuries. Undoubtedly, an interview with God would also have been the news story of the year. The contrasting reactions to an interview with God from the modern Orthodox, or *dati leumi*, community and the ultra-Orthodox Haredi community would have been reported and commented upon in different ways in each sector's religious media. For some Haredim, curiosity with God's interview would mean some would follow the interview on the Internet – challenging the authority of their rabbis' ban on the Internet. The very decision of God to use mass media channels would have raised again the question of the impact of mass media inside the synagogue. Jews abroad would have been no less enthusiastic about the interview with God than Israeli Jews. There would have been very widespread interest in the interview among international public opinion, particularly in countries where monotheistic religions like Christianity and Islam are dominant.

While the interview never happened, the scenario put forth above does illustrate nevertheless how mass media and Jewish religious identity intertwine today and is a clue to some of the questions to be discussed in the pages of this book. In order to understand contemporary Jewish identity in the twenty-first century, one needs to go beyond the synagogue, Jewish customs and law (*halakhah*) and the holy days to incorporate such modern phenomena as mass media and their impact upon Jewish existence. That is what *God, Jews and the Media: Religion and Israel's Media* does. It examines how the Jewish religion and the Jews of Israel have been influenced by the media age.

Under the Jewish Theory of Communication, Chapter 2 discusses the variegated aspects of God's relationship with Israel, in particular Jewish religious communication law (*halakhah*).

Chapters 3 and 4 discuss factors that determine which religion-related events 'pass the news threshold' in order to be defined as news. How is religion covered in the secular press and public broadcasting? Coverage of major events can also have an influence on Jewish identity itself. News interest in religion raises a number of questions, to be discussed in Chapter 7, from the exposure of audiences to religion-related news, to whether religion coverage impacts on their Jewish identity, and to such related questions like the impact of the media upon secular–religious relations. If media coverage of religion is determined by news values, and if most, non-strictly religious Israeli Jews draw much of their religious identity today from the mass media, the fact that much religion does not fit news criteria has important implications. A 'media-orientated

Jewish identity' is produced rather than one reflecting centuries of Jewish tradition and religious culture.

The role of the media in religious identity is felt differently in the religious media in Israel – Haredi and modern Orthodox, as discussed in Chapters 5 and 6. And while both communities draw their religious identity from extra-media sources like religious instruction, the religious media still have a role. For the Haredi community the religious press and radio provide an alternative – and regulated – source to secular media, one that does not threaten the cultural ghetto view which Haredism fosters. The modern Orthodox, while preferring to reconcile the modern and Torah worlds, have also developed their own media – not only to provide a somewhat more supervised media but also to give expression to much in their own society that fails to get reported by the secular media.

The dilemmas of the Haredim have never been felt more than in the contemporary challenges from advanced technology like the Internet. While, as Chapter 8 describes, the Internet plays a huge role in hosting data bases of Jewish educational software, which contribute to strengthening religious identity, the Internet also poses a spiritual threat for many in the religious communities, and the Haredim in particular – a far greater threat than earlier media forms like the press, radio and television.

The marketing of Judaism has moved well beyond traditional frameworks like the synagogue pulpit to media channels, as discussed in Chapter 10. The marketing of religion takes its cue from the world of advertising – which itself has become a subject of controversy in Israel. As discussed in Chapter 9, advertising is a subject of scrutiny by public bodies, with particular emphasis on matters of sexual exposure. A separate question is how advertisers market their products for the ultra-Orthodox Haredi market.

Jewish identity is not found in Israel alone but has an important international dimension. Israel is a focus of national identity not just for Israelis but also for Diaspora Jews. The Israel centredness goes back to early Biblical times when the Holy Land was the setting for the religion's evolution. But as discussed in Chapter 11, the news from Israel is not only followed by Jews abroad avidly but has become an element in their Jewish identity, in an age where conventional forms of religious identity like synagogue attendance have been declining. This is particularly true in the case of the United States. In terms of international public opinion, the Holy Land is perceived through a special prism in the international media, including in Christian and Muslim media – as discussed more widely in Chapter 12.

The book concludes, in Chapter 13, by suggesting likely future trends for Judaism in the information age.

I am grateful to the many individuals associated with the media who have shared their thoughts and impressions with me in researching media and religion. My thanks go to the staff of the following libraries for assistance during my visits: The Jewish and National Library, The Hebrew University, Jerusalem; The Lifshitz Religious College of Education, Jerusalem; The Jewish Theological

Seminary, New York; The Gottesman Library, Yeshiva University, New York; Union Theological Seminary, New York; The University of Colorado at Boulder; The University of Louisville, Kentucky; The University of Toronto; The University of Uppsala, Sweden; Bosphorus University, Istanbul; and The School of Divinity, Edinburgh University. My dedication is to Srif whose natural scepticism and critique has made media watching only more intellectually challenging and stimulating.

YOEL COHEN
JERUSALEM, 2012

Part 1
Mediated Judaism

1 Media, Judaism and Culture

> Thanks to the mike the congregation and the speaker merge in a kind of acoustic bubble that encompasses everyone, a sphere with centres everywhere and margins nowhere. Without a microphone, the orator is located in a single spot; with the mike, he comes at you from everywhere at once. These are the real dimensions of acoustic oneness.
> (Marshall McLuhan, *The Medium and the Light: Reflections on Religion*)[1]

Mass media play an important role in public life in Israel including in aspects of Jewish religious life. There is considerable coverage of certain aspects of religion in the general media notwithstanding the media's preoccupation with defence and military matters. With Israel defined as the Jewish state, and Judaism the official religion, religion becomes 'centrefold' in the Israeli consciousness, and this, in turn, becomes expressed in the media agenda. Religion is often a subject of discussion given the nature of Israeli coalition politics with religious political parties often kingmakers of the coalition, with government budgeting of religious educational institutions the subject of political infighting, as well as with rabbis having an influence in Israeli public life.

Contrasting perceptions among the Israeli population about the nature of mass media – for the non-religious a western-style free media; for the religious, a media which are subservient to Jewish values – have had an impact on the media marketplace in Israel. A divided society, different religious streams – ultra-Orthodox and modern Orthodox – have developed their own separatist media. The ultra-Orthodox, or Haredi, sector has a broad spread of institutional print media, daily newspapers and weekly magazines, reflecting both Ashkenazim and Sephardim, as well as hassidic and European Lithuanian sub-streams, and more recently commercial weekly magazines. There are also Haredi radio stations, some officially approved, others pirate. Certain institutions such as talmudical colleges (*yeshivot*) today run their own websites playing a role in strengthening Jewish religious identity.

The study of media and religion

To examine the media–Judaism interface, one needs to examine two questions: first, the impact of Judaism upon mass media; second, the impact of mass media upon Judaism. In the latter, in examining the relationship of Judaism and mass media, the book examines how the Jewish religion and the Jewish People have been influenced by the media and the media age.

The impact of Judaism on mass media is in particular in the religious sectors where the very legitimacy – or non-legitimacy – of mass media in the eyes of religious leaders is questioned. The superior status of traditional Jewish religious values in these religious communities means that media have less influence and are rebuffed by the community as it seeks to maintain at all costs its true religious identity. The book examines the positive role in strengthening religious identity played by legitimised content of religious media, and how other media are rejected by the community. One chapter discusses the ethics of advertising and marketing and the extent to which these principles have been implemented by religious news organisations. Another chapter examines the impact of such mass media as the modern phenomenon of synagogue bulletins.

In the second question, about the impact of mass media upon Judaism, one needs to go beyond the synagogue, Jewish customs and law (*halakhah*) and the holy days to such modern phenomena as mass media and their impact upon contemporary Jewish life. The Internet, for example, has accentuated the mediating process within Judaism, irrespective of whether they belong to physical communal structures linking Jews into a virtual worldwide Jewish community. The search for God has become an Internet surf of spiritual discovery; already by December 1998 a 'search for God' produced 3.9 million answers, and just a month later 4.5 million.[2] Moreover, Lynch (2010) argued that some of the deepest controversies around contemporary religion are bound up with the content and uses of the media. Public broadcasting in Israel on the Sabbath, for example, became part of the debate inside the country regarding Sabbath observance and the attempts of religious groups to impose their patterns of behaviour upon Israeli public life. Yet another example concerns the mutual images and stereotypes which the Haredi media have about secular Israelis, and which the general media construct about Haredim – adding to the religious–secular divide which characterises Israeli society. Haredim blame the media for the negative image they enjoy inside Israel.

Another example of how current controversies are often media-related is the threat felt by Haredim that cultural ghettos or walls play a vital role in staving off non-religious influences, and to preserve their purist standards of religious life After banning secular newspapers and creating their own presses, Haredi rabbis successfully imposed a ban on television for expressing values anathema to the Haredi view of Torah, and reflecting the community's qualifications about entertainment as a standard. More latterly, Haredi rabbis took a similar approach towards the Internet, where the existence of websites like pornography was seen as a greater threat than all earlier media forms. But the centrality of the Internet in twenty-first century life, including at the workplace, has left these rabbis in a major quandary in 'tackling' the Internet danger. Even Haredi websites and commercial weeklies have challenged the exclusivist monopoly which Haredi rabbis enjoyed among their followers.

The media–religious nexus in Israel also requires taking into account the nature of the relationship of the new state to the Jewish religion. The question of the state's relationship to the Jewish religion has occupied leaders on both sides of the Israeli political spectrum – the non-religious and the religious – since Israel's establishment in 1948 as each sought to impose their own mould on the national fabric. Much of the religious-versus-secular debate takes place on the pages and across the airwaves of the news media. The non-religious wish to create a modern, secular, social democratic state. They see Israel as a national home for Jews, serving a vital role for those fleeing from persecution. For the 'religious', the state–religion dilemma should be reconciled in the form of a democratic theocracy of sorts. The 'religious' are broken into two main groupings: modern Orthodox and ultra-Orthodox or Haredim (Hebrew for pious ones). Both religious communities wish the Jewish state to be Jewish in substance, and not just in symbolic nature. For the modern Orthodox, the creation of the state of Israel is seen as a positive juncture on the path towards Jewish messianic redemption. To them there is no conflict between modernity and Jewish goals. Their members participate at all levels, including doing national army service and engaging in university study. The new state entity should be run along democratic lines as long as this does not clash with Jewish Law. The question of Jewish thinking about mass media has therefore taken on practical relevance in the modern state of Israel.

Communication in Israel and for Jews living in the Diaspora (which today exists mainly in the US and Western Europe) is characterised by Western rather than Jewish values. Any impact of a model of Jewish social communication upon mass media behaviour inside Israel has shown little fruit; only the small religious media gives expression to Judaism as a code of social communication. The influence of Judaism is limited to matters of Jewish civil law comprising issues like who is a Jew, family law and national symbols like holydays. The breathless speed of nation-state building, against a background of external military threat, and the task of absorbing immigrants bringing to the Jewish homeland different, even sometimes clashing, cultural values, has not produced a single unified Jewish socio-cultural code. To the extent that any Israeli socio-cultural code has evolved, it is heavily Americanised. This may change in the long term as demographic patterns point to larger birthrate patterns among the Haredi and modern Orthodox religious communities and as members of these communities play a greater role in the country's political, economic and educational strata – as well as media. The ultra-Orthodox Haredi population has a more fundamentalist approach to Jewish social communication but still remains somewhat removed from mainstream Israeli society. The modern Orthodox, though less fundamentalist in social communication, are more involved in mainstream Israeli society.

Whatever the consequences of the respective secular and religious populations for media and religion in Israel, there is much in religion and much in mass media which does not appear to affect the other. The two worlds – the world of religion and the world of mass media communication systems – each function with little or scant attention to the other.

The relationship of religion to media in Israel is necessarily influenced by mass media inputs and by the market forces of news values. Journalists are not very interested in religion as a news story. Much in religion is not newsworthy, and does not involve such newsworthy elements as social conflict or elites. Religious belief, often drawing upon the sub-conscious, does not fit such criteria of newsworthiness. Religion-related items that do get defined as news do not stay for long upon the news agenda but are replaced by what else is happening in the news agenda at any particular time.

Moreover, Judaism is by its very nature different from the media. Religion is about faith, a moral code, religious law, liturgical worship, and religious holidays. The Jewish religion comprises faith and a code regulating behaviour between man and God, and man and man. Information is the opposite of faith, being verifiable.

Birth of a sub-discipline

The media–religion nexus in Israel is required study for anybody examining the place of contemporary religion in Israel. A variety of approaches for studying media and religion exist. The media literacy approach predates the modern state of Israel, and the theological or historical approaches predate even the age of mass communications. Strictly theological and historical approaches preceded social scientific approaches for studying media and religion. A theological approach comprises rulings and other Bible-related content touching on media and theology. While the Bible itself and latter works like the Mishna, Talmud, and latter Geonic literature was prepared hundreds and thousands of years before the modern age of communications, a Jewish view about mass media may be extrapolated. In so far as the Bible offers not only a code of life but even more a theory of life – of which communication is one facet – Judaism offers a 'theological view' about communications. Included are communication-related matter such as the prohibition on the divulging of private information, the religious obligation of modesty and the obligation of Sabbath observance. Yet, the Jewish theological theory of communication is not merely the sum total of these and other parts, but also an all-embracing theory about communication among people, and between the individual and God.

A historical approach describes Jews and Jewish communication through the ages to the present day, how the Jewish people communicated from the early days when the Israelites, after the exodus from Egypt, travelled through the Wilderness to the Promised Land, to the first and second Jewish Commonwealth, to the Jewish Expersion and communication among different communities, following the destruction of the second Jewish Temple in 70 CE, and finally the return in the modern state of Israel. The approach is a broadly descriptive-journalistic one rather than being analytical, or generating broad principles of patterns of behaviour.

A religious media literacy approach examines how the rabbi and the synagogue have dealt with the threats to religious identity presented by literature, television, cinema and the Internet. A range of techniques have been used by different religions to block 'unsuitable' materials by the Church including, in the Roman Catholic case, the Index of Forbidden Books and latter ban on Disney, and delegitimising specific persons, such as the case of Galileo who was placed under house arrest by the Catholic Church for teaching the theory of heliocentrism, or the idea that the planets revolve around the Sun or bans on literature such as the Roman Catholic Church's (Stout, 2002). The Protestant Church sought to educate the individual to be selective and ban undesirable content. The contrasting Catholic and Protestant approaches to media literacy also characterise how the Haredi and modern Orthodox have fought their culture wars with the wider media social environ.

With the discipline still being defined, the scientific study of the media–religion relationship is in its early days. There has been a tendency over the years to study the media and religion in isolation from one another, with a resulting oversimplification of reality – with the media taken as an absolute by sociologists of religion, and religion taken as an absolute by sociologists of media. There was a need for an interdisciplinary approach that takes into account the surrounding media and religion cultures, which examines effects among religion, media and culture at the individual, institutional and societal levels. The *Journal of Media and Religion*, the *Journal of Communication and Religion*, published under the auspices of the Religion Newswriters Association of the USA, the *Journal of Religion and Film*, *Communication Research Trends* published by the Center for the Study of Communication and Culture, the series of Media, Religion and Culture conferences, and *Religion in the News*, published by the Center for the Study of Religion in Public Life, Trinity College, Hartford, a professional journalism review, have each contributed to recording the vicissitudes of the new discipline – albeit with a strong American perspective.

The correct way to examine the Israeli and Jewish media–religion experience is to compare it to media and religion in other religions and societies. Given the common behavioural patterns of media and religion in different faiths and societies, the study of the Jewish and Israeli case must be informed by research about the media–religion nexus in other religions and societal contexts. By corollary, the Israeli and Jewish case could provide fruitful input into media and religion research in other religions and societies notwithstanding certain differences and specific characteristics of each case. In this sense, the study of media, Judaism and culture is a sub-discipline to the wider discipline of media, religion and culture. Given that media, religion and culture is itself is in an evolutionary phase the Israeli and Jewish case has much to offer researchers of media and religion elsewhere as the media, religion and culture undergoes the inevitable birth pangs in its evolutionary period of defining the parameters of the new discipline.

No single dominant tradition has emerged, but like all evolving disciplines, a number of competing approaches to media and religion exist today. An early analytical approach is textual analysis. Texts of reports in the media are examined chiefly regarding the accuracy and balance in reporting. In one sense textual analysis has religious roots, with much of the study of Judaism involving the analysis of biblical and latter Jewish texts like the Mishna. This is a valuable means for examining the role of the media in the secular–religious divide in Israel. Silk (1995) argues that media texts reflect the values of religious institutions. Thus, Baumel (2005) examined the Haredi press through linguistic tools in order to generate the Haredi outlook on the social role of media inside the Haredi community. Heilman (1990) examined the coverage of one Israeli election in the secular media.

The sociological approach measures behavioural patterns in media and religion providing a more precise picture (Buddenbaum, 2002) than descriptive journalistic studies like those relating to the Haredi press by Levi (1990) and Ilan (2000). The sociological approach includes analysis of the content of news reporting on religion, or journalistic behaviour as reflected in surveys of reporters and editors (Buddenbaum, 1988; Dart and Allen, 1993), and surveys of religious clergy regarding their attitudes to the media and their exposure to, and usage of, news media channels (Cohen, 2011b).

Notwithstanding the value of the sociological approach, such as producing a quantitative picture, it lacks such variables as feeling, inspiration and identity (Roof, 1999) which are clearly essential in any examination involving religion. It calls for an all-embracing approach. The cultural studies approach goes beyond sociology to recognise that religion is multilayered and incorporate a range of models such as the effects of media exposure upon religious identity, and social structures like religious organisations. Some have gone further taking on a Durkheiman view that the media themselves are religious, generating religious feeling and experience. While it is a radical instance in the case of an organised religion like Judaism to suggest that media forms have replaced institutional forms of worship like the synagogue service, newer media forms like television and the Internet are supplementing communal institutional ties to reach unaffiliated Jews.

Another approach to the study of media and religion focuses on media technology. Whereas technology is generally seen as value free or neutral with society choosing how to deploy it, Christians argues that technology is value concerned, with a perspective on the sacredness of human life. Quoting Jacques Ellul, Christians (2002) critiques contemporary society for allowing the power of machines to define social institutions like politics and medicine – with their technological progress becoming a social goal in itself – and calls on humanity to seize control and channel technological means towards human goals. Thus technological means like printing, video and computers should be channelled to religious organisations towards religious educational tools.

The book reflects a continuation of the different approaches. It begins by examining Jewish theological rulings on thinking about mass media (Chapter 2).

Media, Judaism and Culture 9

The sociological approach is the basis for examining news content and the image of religion in the general media (Chapters 3 and 4), and the examination of foreign media coverage of the Holyland (Chapter 12). A culturalist approach to examining the impact of media coverage, both positively in religious identity and negatively in secular–religious relations, is discussed in Chapter 7. Both the sociological and culturalist approaches underline how the Haredi and modern Orthodox respectively have developed the media and how it contributes to their sectors (Chapter 5 and 6), and how the media impacts upon the Israeli–Diaspora connnection (Chapter 11).The two approaches are also appropriate in examining Jewish aspects of advertising (Chapter 9) and the application of PR in the synagogue (Chapter 10). The technological element in media and religion gets expression in Chapter 8.

Media and religion studies in Israel

Writings about media and Judaism were mostly among rabbis and a few educators from the modern religious sector and were of two kinds going back to the 1970s. The first type comprised philosophical discussions about media and religion. The introduction of Israeli television in 1968 raised a debate about its pluses and minuses as a medium. In 1997 the Ministry of Education organised a conference of rabbis and journalists on the subject. The second type concerned narrow Jewish law rulings about practical questions such as the functioning of the electronic media on the Sabbath. Yet, the extent to which media-related questions have preoccupied contemporary rabbinical writings should be not be exaggerated. For example, *Tehumin,* a leading law annual which deals with current applications of Jewish law, and comprising some 50 articles in each issue, has not once in its 30 years addressed broader media-related questions – as distinct from a narrow spread of practical issues mostly concerning copyright and the media functioning on the Sabbath.

Occasional writings appeared much earlier. The classic, the *Hofetz Hayyim*, or Israel Meir Ha-Cohen (1873), was a ground-breaking exploration of the implications for interpersonal communication of the Book of Numbers verse prohibiting the divulging of information which negated the public image of a person. The Hofetz Hayyim's interpretation of the verse as banning the publication of information previously known – giving overwhelming weight to the right of privacy – had implications for the rise of newspapers and, subsequently, the electronic media and for the principles of the right to know, and freedom of the press. His widely accepted rulings led Haredi rabbis to ban exposure to the press if only because they were conduits of social gossip. But the reality of Jewish nation-state building raised questions about the Hofetz Hayyim's rulings. At the time of the Jewish *yishuv* in Palestine in the 1920s and 1930s, for example, the then Chief Rabbi Avraham Kook recognised the growing presence of modern mass media and the need to recognise that modern journalism drew upon interesting and related matter. Latter day rabbis (Chwat, 1995) have debated the Hofetz

Hayyim rulings. Ariel developed the concept of 'constructive gossip' to justify the media's watchdog role (Ariel, 2001).

With the virtual absence until the late-1980s of mass communications teaching in Israel's universities, media and religion generally failed to arouse the attention of the small core of academics engaged in mass communications research. Even by the turn of the millennium, such other questions as media and politics, children and the media, security and the media were frequent subjects of research. With a secular, anti-religious bias in Israeli social science, there was little demand or wish of Israeli media scholars to deal with media and religion questions – notwithstanding the role which religion clearly plays in the country's life. An early study of leisure patterns also examined religious activity as a 'leisure' pattern (Katz and Gurevitch, 1976). Latterly, a handful of academics, some of whom identified with the modern religious sector, began to teach and research media and religion. Those identified religiously are required to bring to bear academic objectivity in, for example, dealing with non-Orthodox Judaism. A number of doctorates, as well as master's theses, mostly at Bar-Ilan University, Israel's religious university, were the subject of religion-related questions including Jewish ethics in journalism, Haredi media and advertising. Questions of research addressed included the coverage of religion in the Israel media (Cohen, 2005, 2006a, 2006b); Haredi media (Amran, 2006; Baumel, 2002, 2005; Micolson, 1990; Neriah Ben-Shahar, 2008; Sela, 2004; Tsarfaty, 2009); the modern religious sector and the media (Gabel, 2006); and Israeli rabbis and the media (Cohen, 2011b). Certain questions of Jewish theological attitudes concerning the social role of traditional media forms were discussed by Chwat (1995), Cohen (2001, 2006d), Korngott (1993), Rakover (2006), Rashi (2008) and Warhaftig (2009). Schwartz (2005) presents an early Jewish law discussion of the computer, and Cohen (2012) of the Internet. Blum Kulka, Blondheim and Hacohen (2002) examine the usage of speech in the synagogue and yeshiva.

Jewish theological questions about the mass media have not been addressed more reflecting in part that social scientists are ill-trained to deal with Jewish theology or comparative religion. Research and teaching of media and religion was almost exclusively concerned with writing on Israeli aspects of media and religion, failing to incorporate some of the research done on media and religion in other countries and religions, notwithstanding the comparative value. It failed to recognise that media, Judaism and culture was a sub-discipline of the wider, evolving one of media, religion and culture. Rosenthal examined Protestant responses to the growth of television in the US (Rosenthal, 2008). Greater involvement of Israeli scholars in groups like Media, Religion and Culture would tie Israeli research findings more with the ongoing research dialogue abroad. Research was even bereft of the status of the coverage of non-Jewish religions inside Israel and failed to be addressed.

Professional organisations like the Israel Journalists Association through its professional annual, the Israel Advertising Association in its journal *Otot*, and the *Seventh Eye*, a monthly critique of Israeli journalism, have occasionally raised the coverage of religion-related subjects. Occasional surveys of media exposure among the religious population have shed light on media consumer patterns. The Maale School of Film, which is identified with the modern religious sector, taught film under the guidelines of rabbis regarding such matters as concerning sexual related content. One company Shophar offered individuals identified with the Haredi sector professional courses in journalism, and advertising and public relations.

The last 20 years have produced greater demand in the schools in the modern religious educational sector for media-related studies. The Ministry of Education produced a media studies curriculum suitable for the educational sector. Teacher training colleges, like the Lifshitz and Orot teacher training colleges, offer degrees for education in mass communication. By 2010, over 80 schools in the modern religious sector had film tracks. Media education proved to be well-timed, preceding the invention and spread of the Internet. If media education produced greater understanding among the modern religious about the working of the media, the Haredi educational sector remains bereft of media education, notwithstanding an urgent need to generate understanding of the media aspects of democracy in a community where democracy and media are regarded as in conflict with Torah values.

Review of the literature

Reflecting the low priority which religion enjoys among mass communications researchers in Israel, little applied research has been carried out concerning the interplay of media and religion in the Israeli Jewish context. The question of Jewish theological attitudes concerning the social role of the media was discussed by Korngott (1993), Chwat (1995) and Cohen (2001, 2006c). Schwartz (2005) examines the computer from a Jewish religious law perspective. The Haredi press has been described (Baumel, 2002, 2005; Levi, 1990; Micolson, 1990) but the coverage of religion in the secular media has received almost no attention (Heilman, 1990). Religion content in different Israeli news media forms, religious and secular, was examined (Cohen, 2005) but the coverage of religion on Israeli websites, secular and religious, has received no attention. The Haredi sector is estranged from the general population, with their own separatist media, raising important anthropological and socio-psychological questions. There is little research on religion as a subject of international news, most research on religion having been carried out in the domestic context. The Israeli case is useful in examining the place of religion in international news flows because religion news in the Holyland would, it might be postulated, be more pronounced than in most other countries. There is virtually no research on media aspects of the Jewish Diaspora. While there have been a number of research articles addressing one aspect or another of media and religion in Israel, there is no single study interweaving the manifold aspects, and examining how one impacts on the other. Research interest in the Internet generated interest also among Israeli researchers in media and religion. Horowitz (2000) and Cohen (2011a, 2006c) describe early Haredi rabbinical attitudes to the Internet. Barzilai-Nahon and Barzilai (2005) examine how the Internet has been adapted to Haredi community needs, and Tydor Baumel-Schwartz (2009) analysed Orthodox Jewish women's Internet forums.

Most research on religion and media has been carried out in the US context (Abelman and Hoover, 1990; Buddenbaum, 1990; Ferre, 1980; Garrett-Medill Center for Religion and the News Media, 1999; Hoover, 1998). Israel provides a contrasting case from the US experience as, unlike in the US, religion and the Jewish state are, by nature, interwoven. The synagogue–state relationship in Israel has been the subject of wide attention (Abramov, 1976; Liebman and Don-Yehiya, 1983; Sharansky, 2000). Less attention in research about state–religion relations inside Israel has been given to non-official actors like news media, notwithstanding popular street-level discussion inside Israel about the media's coverage of religion. There are also certain theological differences between Judaism's and Christianity's perceptions of mass media and their social role – which make the Israeli model a contrasting case from the US model.

References

Abelman, R. and Hoover, S. M. (1990) *Religious Television: Controversies and Conclusions.* Norwood, NJ: Ablex.

Abramov, S. (1976) *Perpetual Dilemma: Jewish Religion in the Jewish State.* Rutherford, NJ: Fairleigh Dickinson University Press.

Amran, M. (2006) *The Media in the Service of Ultra-Orthodox Community: The Use of Audiotapes as Indicators of Continuity and Change in the Ultra-Orthodox Community* [Hebrew], Ph.D thesis. Jerusalem: The Hebrew University.

Ariel, A. (2001) 'Loshon HaRah B'Maarekhet Tziburi Democrati' [Hebrew: The Place of Social Gossip in the Public Democratic System], *Tzohar,* 5–6.

Barzilai-Nahon, K. and Barzilai, G. (2005) 'Cultured Technology: The Internet and Religious Fundamentalism', *The Information Society,* 21.

Baumel, S. (2002) 'Communication and Change: Newspapers, Periodicals and Acculturation among Israeli Haredim', *Jewish History,* 16(2).

——(2005) *Sacred Speakers: Language and Culture among the Haredim in Israel.* Oxford and New York: Berghahn.

Blum Kulka, S., Blondheim, M. and Hacohen, G. (2002) 'Traditions of Dispute: From Negotiations of Talmudic Texts to the Arena of Political Discourse in the Media', *Journal of Pragmatics,* 34.

Buddenbaum, J. (1988) 'The Religion Beat at Daily Newspapers', *Newspaper Research Journal.*

——(1990) 'Network News Coverage of Religion', in J. Ferre (ed), *Channels of Belief: Religion and American Commercial Television.* Ames, IA: Iowa State University Press.

——(2002) 'Social Science and the Study of Media and Religion: Going Forward by Looking Backward', *Journal of Media and Religion,* 1.

Christians, C. G. (2002) 'Religious Perspectives on Communication Technology', *Journal of Media and Religion,* 1.

Chwat, A. (1995) 'Itonim V'Hadashot Mitzva O Isur' [Hebrew: Newspapers and News: Religious Obligation or Prohibition], Elkana, *T'lalei Orot.*

Cohen, Y. (2001) 'Mass Media in the Jewish Tradition', in D. Stout and J. Buddenbaum (eds), *Religion and Popular Culture: Studies on the Interaction of Worldviews*. Ames, IA: Iowa State University Press.

——(2005) 'Religion News in Israel', *Journal of Media and Religion*, 4(3).

——(2006a) 'Israel' entry, in D. Stout (ed) *Encyclopedia of Religion, Communication and Media*, New York and London: Routledge.

——(2006b) *The Religion-News Media Nexus is Israel*, Sociological Institute for Community Studies, Bar-Ilan University.

——(2006c) 'Judaism' entry in D. Stout (ed) *Encyclopedia of Religion Communication and Media*, New York and London: Routledge.

——(2006d) 'Communication in Jewish Perspective', in F. J. Eilers (ed) *Social Communication in Religious Traditions in Asia*, Manila: Logos Publications. First published in 2006 as 'Social Communication, Mass Media and the Jewish Tradition', *Religion and Social Communication*, Asian Research Center for Religion and Social Communication (Bangkok: St John's University), 4(2).

——(2011a) 'Haredim, the Internet: A Hate–Love Affair', in M. Bailey and G. Redder (eds) *Mediating Faiths: Religion and Socio-Cultural Change in the Twenty-First Century*, Farnham: Ashgate.

——(2011b) 'Rabanim V'HaTikshoret: Maarekhet Yahasim Mesuchsachot' [Hebrew: Rabbis and the Media: A Conflictual Relationship], in M. Rachimi (ed), *Amadot (3): Etgarim V'Yaadim* [Hebrew: Positions (3): The Media: Challenges and Goals]. Elkana and Rehovot (Israel): Orot Academic College.

——(2012) 'Jewish Cybertheology', *Communication Research Trends*, 31.

Dart, J. and Allen, J. (1993) *Bridging the Gap: Religion and the News Media*. Nashville, TN: Vanderbilt University, Freedom Forum.

Ferre, J. (1980) 'Denominational Biases in the American Press', *Review of Religious Research*, 21.

Gabel, I. (2006) *Ha-tzibur ha-dati leumi v'hu-Tikshoret: Yahasei ahava-sinaa* [Hebrew: The Modern Religious Community and the Media: A Love-Hate Relationship]. Tel Aviv: Herzog Institute, Tel Aviv University.

Garrett-Medill Center for Religion and the News Media (1999) *Media Coverage of Religion, Spirituality, and Values*. Evanston, IL: Northwestern University.

Ha-Cohen, I. M. (1873) *Chofez Hayim*. Vilna. For an English edition: Z. Pliskin (1975) *Guard Your Tongue: A Practical Guide to the Laws of Loshon Hara Based on the Chofez Hayim*. Jerusalem: Aish HaTorah.

Heilman, S. C. (1990) 'Religion Jewry in the Secular Press: Aftermath of the 1988 Elections', in C. Liebman (ed), *Conflict and Accommodation Between Jews in Israel*. New York: Avi Foundation.

Hoover, S. (1998) *Religion in the News*. Thousand Oaks, CA: Sage.

Horowitz, N. (2000) *'Haredim, Vha-Internet'* [Hebrew: Haredim and the Internet], *Kivunim Hadashim*, 3.

Ilan, S. (2000) *Haredim Ltd*. Jerusalem: Keter.

Katz, E. and Gurevitch, M. (1976) *The Secularisation of Leisure: Culture and Communication in Israel*. London, Faber.

Korngott, E. M. H. (1993) *Or Yehezkel* [Hebrew: The Light of Ezekiel: Contemporary Issues in Jewish Law]. Petach Tiqva: Or Yehezkel Institute.

Levi, A. (1990) 'The Haredi Press and Secular Society', in C. Liebman (ed), *Conflict and Accommodation between Jews in Israel*. Jerusalem: Keter–Avi Chai.

Liebman, C. and Don-Yehiya, E. (1983) *Civil Religion in Israel*. Berkeley, CA: University of California Press.

Lynch, G. (2010) 'Religion, Media and Cultures of Everyday Life', in J. Hinnells (ed), *The Routledge Companion to the Study of Religion*. London and New York: Routledge.

Micolson, M. (1990) *Itonut Haredit B' Yisroel* [Hebrew: the Haredi Press in Israel]. Tel Aviv, *Kesher*, 8.

Neriah Ben-Shahar, R. (2008) *Haredi Women and Mass Media in Israel – Exposure Patterns and Reading Strategies* [Hebrew], Ph.D thesis. Jerusalem: The Hebrew University.

Rakover, N. (2006) *Protection of Privacy in Jewish Law*. Jerusalem: The Jewish Legal Heritage Society.

Rashi, T. (2008) '"Zkhut Ha-Tzibbur Ladaat" B'takanenei Haetika Haitonaut Leumat "Hovat Hatzibur Ladaat", B'mishpat Ha-Ivri' [Hebrew: '"The Right to Know" in Journalism Ethics Contrasted with "The Obligation to Know" in Hebrew Law'], in T. Rashi and M. Zaft (eds), *Tikshoret V'Yahadut* [Hebrew: Media and Judaism]. Petach Tiqva: Keter HaZahav.

Roof, W. C. (1999) *Spiritual Marketplace: Baby Boomers and the Remaking of American Religion*. Princeton, NJ: Princeton University Press.

Rosenthal, M. (2008) *American Protestants and TV in the 1950s: Response to a New Medium*. London and New York: Palgrave-Macmillan.

Schwartz, Y. (2005) *Idan Hamakhshev Velekhav* [Hebrew: The Computer Era and What We Can Learn From It]. Jerusalem: Yeshivat, Dvar Yerushalayim Zichron Tvi. See also: No author stated (2005) *Hamakshev le'or hahalakha* [The Computer in the Light of Halakha]. Talmud Vehalakha Institute.

Sela, P. (2004) *Sociolinguistic Factors in Ultra-Orthodox Newspapers*. Ph.D thesis. Ramat Gan: Bar-Ilan University.

Sharansky, I. (2000) *The Politics of Religion and the Religion of Politics: Looking at Israel*. Lantham, MD: Lexington.

Silk, M. (1995), *Unsecular Media: Making News of Religion in America*. Urbana, IL: University of Illinois Press.

Stout, D. A. (2002) 'Religious Media Literacy: Toward a Research Agenda', *Journal of Media and Religion*, 1.

Tsarfaty, O. (2009) 'Alternative Identity and Memory in Ultra-Orthodox Newspapers', *Journal for Semitics*, 19(1).

Tydor Baumel-Schwartz, J. (2009) 'Frum Surfing: Orthodox Jewish Women's Internet Forums as a Historical and Cultural Phenomenon', *Journal of Jewish Identities*, 2(1).

Warhaftig, I. (2009) *Tzin'at Adam: Hazhut l'prutiut l'or halakhah* [Hebrew: The Right to Privacy in Jewish Law]. Ofra: Mishpetei Eretz.

2 The Jewish Theory of Communication

> O God, guard my tongue from evil
> And my lips from speaking evil
> Let my soul be silent to those who curse me
> And may my soul be as dust to all.
> (Prayer of Mar, the son of Ravina, Babylonian Talmud,
> Tractate Berakhot, 17a)

Infinite God as communicator

Language, speech and communication play a central role in Judaism. This is because Judaism views God as infinite, and therefore the only knowledge of God that humanity enjoys is through his acts and messages. This led Gruber (1999) to conclude that 'language, particularly Hebrew, had a theological significance in Judaism not associated with language in another religion'. Hebrew is coined the 'holy language'. It is the language of creation and of revelation. The Biblical account of the world's being called into existence through mere divine utterance gives emphasis to this. Until Babel, Hebrew – God's language – was spoken by all; after Babel there was an intended confusion of languages.

The two-way communication with God has been of a number of layers: informational, emotional and command. It is noteworthy that almost every command to Moses is accompanied by the word 'to say', i.e. to pass on, or communicate, to others.

The informational is from God to mankind, the revelation as recorded in the Bible, detailing statements and events. The Bible is not, as some think, just a book of laws and ethics, but rather the seeds of a 4,000-year-long relationship between God and his chosen people; the entire Book of Genesis does not contain one law.

In chronicling often-dramatic events such as the early Israelite history in Egypt, the crossing of the Red Sea, the giving of the Ten Commandments at Mount Sinai, and the capture of the Promised Land of Canaan, the Bible is not very different from the news media. It may be considered one of the earliest journals.

God's messages were transmitted through the prophet. He was a spokesman 'selling' God's Word. Yet the prophet was more than a messenger; he was a participant standing in the presence of God (Jeremiah 15:19). His communication was not neutral but comprised ethical monotheism or a religion of morality, raising the spiritual standards and moral fibre. Yet the manner of persuasion in communication in Judaism is uncertain. Zulick argues that the absence in biblical Hebrew for the word 'to persuade' suggests that the leading figure in the rhetorical act is the hearer rather than the orator. 'Words carry weight. They convince they are the right words, the authoritative words, and not because of the persuasive art of the orator' (Zulick, 1992).

Since the end of Jewish prophecy in the fourth century BCE the hidden divine meaning to events cannot be extrapolated. Prophecy was replaced by faith as the staple ingredient of the relationship between the Jewish People and God. The creation of the State of Israel together with such later events as a series of dramatic wars, the reunification of Jerusalem, and historic peace agreements suggest to some a divine force. But in the absence of prophecy, any Jewish theological study of media events is reduced to belief ('*emunah*').

The second layer in the God–man communication is the emotional, such as the binding of Isaac, the Crossing of the Red Sea, the capture of the Promised Land. In chronicling such dramatic events, the Bible is not very different from the news media. It develops an embracing relationship between God and his people. As in any media event, the spectator – or, in this case, the reader of the Bible event – becomes a participant in the event itself – from the serenity of the pew (Dayan and Katz, 1992).

A more active role is played by man through speech; the oral recognition of God, of monotheism, remain staple elements of the relationship between God and his people. The daily prayers end with the 'Aleinu' prayer, a call for monotheism.

Speech also has an important role in the annual Jewish life cycle. It is a key means for fulfilling the command 'to remember the Sabbath day' (Exodus 20:8). The Sabbath is sanctified at its onset by reciting the *kiddush* prayer. Similarly, the Sabbath is concluded by the verbal recital of the *Havdalah*. And while each of the major Jewish holidays have specific characteristics – the Jewish New Year, the blowing of the ram's horn; Yom Kippur, the 25-hour-long fast of atonement; Passover, the eating of unleavened bread (*matzot*); Sukkoth, dwelling, and more specifically eating, in tabernacles – oral prayers fulfil important roles also, enabling the congregant to become a participant in man's relationship to God. The prayer service expresses penitence on the Jewish New Year and Yom Kippur, and expresses praise for the Exodus on the Passover and for the Giving of the Ten Commandments on Shavuot. On Sukkoth the thanksgiving is for God's protection in the Sinai desert on the way to the Promised Land.

Oral prayers have taken on added importance since the destruction of the Second Jewish Temple in Jerusalem in 70 CE. Until then, Temple worship – with its sacrificial order of communal and individuals offerings, obligatory and free-will – played a central role in the God–Jew relationship. Following the destruction of the First and Second Temples, synagogue prayer took centre stage, as a substitute for the sacrificial service.

The third layer of communication by God are the values or (*mitzvot*) positive and negative commands in the Bible, providing a code of spiritual and social behaviour. For example, the first three of the Ten Commandments command belief in God's oneness. But as an ethical religion, Judaism regulates not only man's relationship with God but also with his fellow man. Judaism does not preach asceticism or social isolation but encourages social participation, and, therefore, communication between men makes a Jewish theory of communication important. Judaism provides a code for regulating communication. In other words, this seeks to extrapolate a view of the nature and social role of mass media from the Jewish Tradition. While not rejecting the 'good life', the Jewish *weltanschauung* is that Man should use his free choice to raise his stature to emulate the characteristics of the Infinite God. To do this, it draws upon God's revelation to the Patriarch Abraham and his sons, and the giving of the Torah at Mount Sinai.

While as a multifaceted book, the Old Testament interlaces belief and history with norms and ritual, it is as a code of norms that its presence is most felt today. Given that the Torah and later Jewish law works like the Mishnah, Talmud, and such codifiers as Maimonides necessarily predated the mass media age, it is necessary, in determining the Jewish view of media, to locate points of overlap between Judaism and mass media behaviour. The very extent to which Judaism should intrude into social life is unclear. Some Jewish theologians argue that with the exception of specific subjects including family law, and the Sabbath, Judaism has nothing to say about much of human activity. But others define Judaism as an entire way of life with something to say about all spheres of human conduct. Where there is a confluence of interests between Judaism and mass media – such as the provision of information about events and societies, which contributes to understanding and reduces conflict – it is not generally identified as a peculiarly religious goal (Cohen, 2001). However, whether narrowly or widely interpreted, much of the overlap between media behaviour and Judaism appears conflictual. Areas of conflict that will be discussed in this chapter include sexual exposure in the media, Biblical prohibitions on social and political 'gossip', and the functioning of the electronic media on the Sabbath day.

Jewish law draws upon the written law and the oral law. The oral law enables a full understanding of the written law. In applying ancient tests to such modern problems like media ethics, the oral law provides an important key for interpreting the written law.

Jewish laws of communication

One problem in determining the 'Jewish view of mass media' is that the media is changing so rapidly that the rabbinic literature does not have all the answers. As Alfred Cohen, editor of the *Journal of Halacha and Contemporary Society* (2005), noted in discussing a Jewish view of the Internet:

> Since use of the Internet is such a new practice, there has scarcely been time for a body of broadly accepted halakhic literature or rabbinic comment to develop. Consequently, much of our study will involve trying to find cognate situations discussed in earlier generations, to identify the appropriate categories of activities discussed in rabbinic literature which could guide us in the current situation.
>
> (Cohen, 2005)

Each media form brings with its unique characteristics. The subjects where Judaism and the media form under examination in some cases are identical, raising the same issues, reactions and solutions, in others are different. In some cases the level of conflict between Jewish theology is greater with one media form than with earlier media forms; in other cases, the opposite is true.

Sexual modesty

Judaism, in contrast to Christianity, has said little about the pictorial portrayal of violence. The focus is on portrayal of sex and physical immodesty. The Israelite camp in the Wilderness in 'which God walked shall be holy ... that God should not see anything unseemly and turn Himself away from you' (Deuteronomy 23:15) is an allusion to nudity being looked on negatively. Moreover, the unseemliness results in the withdrawal of the divine presence (*shekhinah*).

Different branches of Judaism interpret sexual modesty differently. Orthodox Judaism forbids a man to look on a female immodestly attired; in the ultra-Orthodox community this includes the uncovered hair of a married woman. Similarly, a man is forbidden to listen to a woman singer, lest he be sexually aroused; the modern Orthodox community permits listening to a female voice if the song is prerecorded. Conservative and Reform rabbis are critical of sexual freedom as expressed, for example, on Internet websites, the latter taking a stand on media sexploitation of women.

The prohibitions that Orthodox rabbis impose on men regarding modesty are not imposed on women. One rabbinical concern stated in Jewish sources regarding a man's exposure to immodest matter is that as a result of his exposure to images alluding to sex, a man could be sexually aroused to masturbation or 'improper emission of seed' (onanism) [Genesis 38]. These restrictions raise profound artistic questions of how love can be portrayed and expressed in a manner which is religiously acceptable. And the rabbis have failed to distinguish between being in the physical presence of an immodestly dressed woman and simply seeing her on a television or Internet screen.

The question of sexual content on Internet websites generated widespread concern in Haredi circles, resulting in a blanket ban on the Internet, as will be discussed in Chapter 8, because of its uncontrolled access to sexual-related matter. The 'Eda Haredit' (or Committee of Torah Sages), the umbrella group of Haredi rabbis in Israel, established a special *bet din* (or religious law court) to deal with questions concerning communication-related matters. The Internet was regarded by them as a far worse moral threat than television: whereas television was supervised, the Internet enabled free access to pornographic sites. The *bet din* banned the Internet.

A separate question concerns interactive media. The specific question of extramarital romantic relationships on the Internet has been addressed by rabbis, with the question of whether it is tantamount to adultery. According to one rabbi, Yair Lerner (2005), while a couple in which one partner carried out an on-line romantic relationship is not obligated to divorce (which would be the case, for example, where one partner has had extramarital relations), the rabbis regard such a deed as a profound breach of Jewish values and would recommend that the pair divorce. Lerner would not, however, see a marital cancellation because of an Internet relationship as grounds for not giving the woman her dowry, detailed in the original marital contract between the two.

Tzeniut, or modesty, is discussed at length in Jewish sources, in rather vivid and technical terms concerning appropriate dress code – such as the amount of skin or hair (the latter in the case of married women) that may be revealed, size of hemlines, and the lengths of skirts and sleeves. By distancing oneself from illegitimate sensuality, one achieves personal sanctity. The Jewish concept of holiness is not one of exposure or revelation but rather modesty.

Although the Jewish Tradition is critical of sexual exposure in the news media, this is less obvious than it appears. Physical pleasure from sexual relations within marriage is regarded in a positive light in Judaism. To be true, modesty as a motif in Judaism is an ethical value less about physical exposure and more about the manner of a person's behaviour in his social relations. The human body in Jewish terms, argues Lamm (1997), is not an object of beauty, as it was in Greek culture, in an aesthetic sense, but rather in sacred terms – and that which is sacred needs to be hidden. *Tzeniut* has to do with honour, self respect, or an awareness of one's self worth. Just like the dignity of God is its very concealment, the dignity of the human individual – created in God's image – is in his obscurity. However, obscurity is not just in physical terms but in every sense, including a person's talent and wealth, amongst others.

The right to know – or not

While there are no clear rules in ancient Jewish texts about democracy, there is a strong tradition of public accountability. As the Book of Numbers 32:22 writes. 'And you shall be clean (or innocent) before God and before the people of Israel'. For example, the Temple tax, the half shekel, which was used for the purchase of sacrifices in the First and Second Jewish Temples, was kept in a special office in the Temple. The kohen, or priest, who worked in that office had his clothes checked on entering and departing from the room. Some rabbis today have raised the question of the disclosure of information of corruption or sexual improprieties committed by rabbis. Such disclosures defame the religion and even God. While over the years rabbis have generally favoured covering up rather than disclosure, even if it may be in the social interest for people to know, yet the Bible was not averse to publishing details of the sins of the righteous as a means towards moral teaching. The dilemma, one rabbi, David Stav (1997) argued, is between disclosure and silence. Disclosure would cause a defamation of God's name – because once a rabbi is defrocked it not only reflects upon the whole community but also may discourage other people from coming closer to religion – but silence would suggest that we tolerate this behaviour. A strong society is one that thrives even after it is self-critical and discloses. Otherwise the information will come out in a less controlled way from anti-religious sources.

The idea of accountability is also expressed in the need to take measures against those who infringe laws. As Leviticus 19:17 says: 'You shall admonish your fellow and do not bear a sin because of him'. The Bible itself discloses Moses's sin in smiting the Rock instead of speaking to the Rock to bring forth water, which would have otherwise publicised a miracle and have been a means towards moral teaching. The Torah is saying that it is not only permitted to publish information which if kept unpublished would damage society but obligatory. Biblical commentators have noted that the same verse which prohibits the disclosure of secret information continues ' ... do not stand idly by the blood of your neighbour', suggesting that if somebody, including a journalist, hears of information that is deleterious, such as corruption committed by a government minister or an official, he has an obligation to take steps to rectify the situation. The Bible appears to acknowledges the fourth estate role, or societal watchdog, fulfilled by the media (Korngott, 1993).

Notwithstanding this, the major innovation of Jewish theology in mass media behaviour concerns the divulging of previously unknown information. Leviticus (19:16), in warning against not being 'a talebearer among your people, or standing idly by the blood of your neighbour', imposes substantial limits on the passage of information. The *Hofetz Hayim* (Ha-Cohen, 1873) interpreted these verses in ways which limited interpersonal conversation. He divided types of information into a number of categories. Most severe is the divulging of secret information to the wider public that is intended or has the effect of damaging someone's reputation (*lashon hara*). When Miriam spoke ill of Moses for 'the Cushan woman he married', she was smitten with leprosy [Deuteronomy 12]. Also forbidden, but with lesser severity, is the disclosure of even positive information about somebody (*rehilut*). These deeds are, in fact, intrusion of the privacy of the individual.

While in modern society, the right to privacy is subservient to the right to know, in Judaism the right to know is subservient to the right to privacy. In

Judaism the only right to know is the right to know Jewish knowledge, i.e. the Torah, national laws, and information which if kept secret would cause damage to someone. Modern society permits everything to be published apart from that which personally damages someone's reputation. This includes a large middle category of information which is not of vital importance to know. Judaism does not acknowledge an automatic right to this middle category of information. Thus, Judaism distinguishes between the large flow of otherwise interesting information disclosed by the media which does not come under this category, disclosure of which it prohibits, and the much smaller category of information of social value (Chwat, 1995).

These restrictions in Judaism profoundly affect the work of the professional journalist in disclosing previously unpublished information. The journalist draws much of his information from sources who disclose selectively, often in order to weaken a political opponent. Thus, the laws of evil gossip (*lashon hara*) have a particular relevance at times of elections and the disclosure is a tactic in electioneering. Yet, if information about a candidate which could raise serious questions about his suitability is not available, it may result in someone not suited to the public office being elected. When a person has information incriminating someone who is a publicly elected or appointed official, how can he bring it to public attention? The Talmud has decided that once the information is known to three people it is no longer forbidden. As the Talmudic Tractate *Erachin* (16a) notes, 'once the information is known to three people, it is the same as announcing it to the world'. Information, therefore, takes on a relative value. The journalist and his informant have carried out a most heinous act in making the information public, but that same information may be heard by other people.

However, even if something is known, one may not disclose more information about the same subject without incurring the penalty of the transgression. And something which was previously known to the public but has 'disappeared from the headlines', with the public having forgotten about it, may also not be disclosed. In order to allow such disclosure, one rabbi, Ariel (2001), has developed the concept of 'evil gossip by consent'; individuals in public office understand that they necessarily expose themselves to publicity. Judaism recognises the right of the population to know about actions taken on their behalf, particularly regarding misdeeds or dangers to the public. One way during elections to avoid the transgression, according to Ariel, would be to present the discriminating information as about the party, its organisation, rather than about the candidate. Another category where information could be disclosed concerns the sins in the eyes of Jewish law committed by Jews not observing the commandments.

Disclosure of information which the discloser feels must reach the public presupposes that the facts are correct and the deed is indeed illegal. Sometimes it is ambiguous whether the deed is indeed wrong. The discloser has to know firsthand about the crime. He has to attach his name to the claim and cannot disclose behind an unattributable leak. Rumours are not enough to base it on unless the danger to the public is very great. If a rumour, it has to be reported in the media in a manner in which it is qualified as 'according to rumours' and not as if it is proven information. But the tendency for the latter condition to be overlooked after a period of time when rumours become general knowledge is a problem in the eyes of Jewish Law.

A key question is the motive of the discloser. The disclosure should be 'out of a sense of love', to achieve societal correction. If the discloser had a self-interest – such as during elections – the disclosure is forbidden. This raises the question of the role of the media. If the media's goal is the public goodwill this is justified by Jewish Law, but it is not if the goal is 'ratings', or the journalist seeks to ingratiate himself with his editor or the owner who expect him to locate exclusive information. It led rabbis to prefer that the disclosure be to the police or the state comptroller since they have the public interest at heart. Yet, one Jewish journalist has argued that reporters seek to pursue the truth. Moreover, they evaluate the motives of news sources who speak to them (Wertheimer, 2001). But for the Hofetz Hayim – who lived in the second half of the nineteenth century when the press was more ideological and therefore more inclined to attack people – this was not enough. He argues that one should only disclose to the public after all avenues through private channels to seek correction have been exhausted. Thus, only if police channels are not responsive, or themselves corrupt, should one go public. Indeed, public disclosures in the media go in different directions, producing different reactions and counter-reactions, making it difficult to ensure that the desired outcome – societal correction – will be achieved (Ariel, 2001).

Taken liberally, there are certain similarities between the modern journalist today and the Jewish laws of disclosure, but the Hofetz Hayim's other criteria fail to be met by the media, such as his preference to correct through private, non-media channels. Moreover, whereas disclosure à la Hofetz Hayyim is subservient to the rule of Jewish law, the fourth estate in Western society is by its very watchdog nature an independent organ.

Where a journalist has erred and besmirched somebody's good name unjustifiably, given the news organisation's influence, one rabbi, Efraim Korngott, argues, it needs to apologise publicly and, if demanded, even pay damages (Korngott, 1993, p. 359). And this will generate a sense of caution among the media in checking and ensuring that only accurate information is published.

The sanctity of communication

Knowledge and information also possess Jewish ethical dimensions in terms of copyright ownership, accuracy, advertising, and the printing of God's holy name.

God's Name. The prohibition in Jewish law against pronouncing the Holy Name of God, the Tetragrammaton, is an acknowledgement that no word can capture the awesome, infinite power of the creator. As an extension of this, Jewish law regards as sacrilegious the destruction of texts with other names of God. To overcome the problem, texts such as prayer books are by tradition buried in a cemetery. Some religious newspapers print sermons and other religious material. The preferred means of the religious media is to use God's name in an abbreviated form (for example, G-d). Some rabbis limit the prohibition to the printing of full Scriptural verses in Hebrew and not to other types of references to God such as in the media. With the introduction of computers and the Internet, rabbis have addressed the question of the name of God appearing on screen and have ruled that the prohibition on erasing God's name occurs in print, not when in electronic form since, in contrast to paper, electronic forms are not permanent; electrons fired at the inside of the screen form light patterns that cannot be seen from the front of the screen. They are constantly being refreshed but at a rate the human eye cannot see. Rabbi Shlomo Zalman Auerbach, a leading rabbinical authority in the Haredi community, ruled that since no complete letter actually exists, this does not constitute writing. Rabbi Ovadiah Yosef ruled that erasing on a CD is an indirect act of erasing. Moreover, there is no specific intention to write in God's name permanently. However, Rabbi Moshe Feinstein, a leading authority on *halakhah* (Jewish Law) in the US, ruled that one should nevertheless refrain from removing God's name because it appears as if one is erasing (Brueckheimer, 2003).

Copyright ownership. Jewish Law recognises a prohibition of stealing knowledge. Material, such as a book or song, which is the exclusive property of one person may not be copied without their permission. News coverage of events which are publicly known cannot claim copyright ownership. But investigative journalism in which one news organisation is the exclusive source of the information may claim exclusivity. 'News borrowing' of information in the latter category is, therefore, only permitted where such permission has been obtained. In the case of Bible-related material – such as sermons and related material in religious media – some rabbis argue that since the Bible is not the exclusive property of one party, no copyright stipulation exists for Bible-related materials.

Rabbis have begun to consider the question of whether copying texts is regarded as stealing. The question of copyright has received renewed attention in light of the proliferation of the computer and that downloading and copying texts is regarded by many people as acceptable practice. One rabbi, Dov Lior, allowed it, quoting a basic principle in Jewish law that once an owner has given up possession of an object which has gone missing, somebody in whose possession it falls does not have to return it to him.[1] Other rabbis have ruled differently; one rabbi, Ram Cohen of Otniel Yeshiva, ruled that since some people do pay for downloaded texts and other downloaded materials, the owner has not 'given up hope of receiving it back'. Jewish law cannot be different from national law, and copying texts unauthorised is therefore forbidden.

Accuracy. Information reported in the media has to be accurate to avoid the audience being deceived. The question of complete and honest reporting is related to the Bible. For example, the sin of the Biblical spies was that they coloured with their own opinions the report of their mission to spy out the Promised Land (Liebes, 1994). Reflecting that truth is regarded as a foundation of the world, the Book of Proverbs (12.19) states, 'Truthful lips shall be established forever, but a lying tonge is only for a moment'. So important is truth that lying is tantamount to idol worship. The requirement for accuracy is problematic when a news organisation, under tight deadlines, faces news sources which do not wish to give their account of events. The provision of information about events and societies which contribute to understanding and reduce conflict – while not generally identified as a peculiarly religious goal – is endorsed by Judaism. One of the sins of the 10 out of the 12 spies about the Promised Land was that they added their own ideological views to their factual report.

Advertising. The problem of deception is acute in advertising, where a customer is persuaded to buy a product which he or she would not otherwise do if they knew all the facts. Judaism, therefore, places limitations on modern advertising. While advertising plays a positive role in providing customers with information regarding different brands of products, there are moral limits to what may be done. Drawing upon the Biblical verse 'In selling. … do not be distortionate' (Leviticus 25:17), Judaism prohibits the trader, in promoting his products, from creating a false impression or *'genevat daat'*. A trader is required to divulge to a prospective customer all defects in his product. A trader is permitted to draw the buyer's attention to the good features of a product as long as these are accurate. Levine (1981) argues that projecting the quality of a good or service is regarded positively in Judaism. But goodwill obtained deceptively through a false impression is forbidden. However, a trader is not obligated to correct an erroneous impression that is the result of self-deception. Showing the defects of the opponent's products is forbidden – as distinct from pointing out the positive aspects of one's own products – and is tantamount to slander and falsehood.

E-commerce

E-commerce raises important questions. In Jewish law an acquisition (*kinyan*) occurs when someone performs some sort of physical action that demonstrates his ownership, such as lifting up the object. In e-commerce, the item advertised on the screen exists only 'virtually'. Does an acquisition take place if the object has not yet come into the possession of the seller? To be true, acquisition was widely discussed in the Talmud. According to one rabbi, Shlomo Dickovsky (2002), '"Virtual" acquisition is not regarded as an obstacle to a sale, since the object does exist even if at that point in time it is not in the physical possession of the seller, and it is still considered a sale'. Nevertheless, a secondary type of acquisition in Jewish law is the signing of an agreement, or *kinyan situmqa* [Babylonian Talmud: Babba Metzia 74a]. Acquisition with a computerised signature is regarded as a signature and the deal is a deal to all intents and purposes.

Media functioning and the Sabbath

The prohibition of work on the Sabbath Day, as enjoined by the fourth of the Ten Commandments (Exodus 20:8), has implications for the exposure of Jews (Orthodox and Conservative) to electronic media on the Sabbath and other holy feasts. (Reform Jews interpret the obligation to rest on the Sabbath more liberally.) Given the prohibition on activating electricity on the Sabbath, television, radio (Auerbach, 1996) and the Internet cannot be used. The subject of Sabbath observance in the modern technological age is one that occupies rabbis today. A couple of research institutions have been established over the years to research technological developments from a Jewish law perspective with special reference to their functioning on the Sabbath. The Jerusalem-based Institute of Science and Halakha comprises some rabbis, engineers and scientists. Another organisation is Zomet, which has invented practical solutions to the application of technology in the modern state.

Moreover, a Jew may not benefit, even after the Sabbath, from media work which was produced by other Jews on the Sabbath. In Israel while newspapers are not published on the Sabbath, the electronic media functions on the Sabbath and other holy days, with the single exception of Yom Kippur. A question is raised whether newspapers published on Sunday may be benefited from if they contain news gathered by Jewish journalists on the Sabbath. Amongst other media-related questions addressed by rabbis are whether a religious Jew may give an interview to a broadcast journalist on the weekday in the knowledge that it will be broadcast on the Sabbath, and whether a Jew living in Israel may listen to or see a rebroadcasting of a programme first broadcast by Jews on the Sabbath.

The focus of rabbis' legal discussions concerning the Internet has concerned the Sabbath. Whereas the Sabbath functioning was an issue which occasionally came up in earlier media forms, it became centre stage in *halakhah* discussions of computers and the Internet. The prohibition of work on the Sabbath day has implications for the Internet given both that the Internet operates simultaneously across time zones and that the Sabbath – the period commencing at sunset on Friday and continuing for 25 hours to Saturday eve – falls at different times in different parts of the globe. Questions raised by the rabbis include: Is it permitted to receive e-mail in your mailbox when it is the Sabbath or if sent from a country where it is the Sabbath? May one send e-mail to an address in a country where it is currently the Sabbath? Is it permitted for a Jew to enter a website in a foreign country where it is currently the Sabbath? According to Yuval Sherlo (2002), who heads a talmudical college (*yeshiva*) in the Israeli city of Petach Tiqva, the obligation to observe the Sabbath is for the surfer himself, and therefore one can send mail to a site where it may be the Sabbath. Illustrating the lack of consensus among rabbis about the Internet medium is that other religious Jewish authorities recommend that one should not visit a website in a time zone where it is currently the Sabbath.

The Sabbath has special implications for e-trading. Stores are closed on the Sabbath, given the prohibition to benefit from trading on the day of rest. So may one leave one's own trading website open, including in a time zone where it is the Sabbath, and thereby chance that a Jew there may breach the Sabbath law? Or should a site which engages in on-line trading be closed by the owner on the Sabbath? One website, *Babbakamma*, is a list of Sabbath-observing websites for those strictly observant. Reflecting the ongoing discussion about Internet within rabbinical circles, one US rabbi, Rabbi Moshe Heinemann initially wrote that a site should be closed because the owner's property, his website, is making money for him on Sabbath. The rabbi had assumed that clicking a button automatically caused a charge to be registered against the buyer's credit card and instantaneously transfers the funds to the seller. Subsequently, the rabbi learnt that credit card processors and banks never actually transferred funds on Saturday or Sunday (Cohen, 2005). And, with regard to midweek holy days like the New Year, he recommended that a website be built in such a way as to defer credit transfers until after the holy day falling mid-week. One solution for a Jewish trader is to go into partnership with a non-Jew and in a fictitious manner give over ownership of the business at the commencement of the Sabbath to receive it back after the end of the Sabbath.

Is leaving open a trading website on the Sabbath tantamount to placing a 'stumbling block before the blind' (Leviticus 19:14)? And may one purchase from a Jewish-owned website functioning in a time zone where it is currently the Sabbath? According to Eretz Hemdah, a Jerusalem-based centre for training rabbis, a payment for an on-going weekly or monthly service to a data base is not regarded as trading on the Sabbath, yet a one-time transaction would be. Is a trader obligated or not to close his website in a specific time zone where it is the Sabbath? One programme, www.shomershabes, automatically closes a website for the duration of the Sabbath according to different time zones; thus, in two places in the world, one in which it is the Sabbath and one in which it is not, the programme enables the website not to be accessible to the former but to be accessible to the latter. But according to the Eretz Hemdah Institute, it is not necessary to close down the website in time zones where it is the Sabbath, since other websites are available. It is thus not considered a violation of the biblical command 'not to place a stumbling block before the blind'. Moreover, the Torah does not require a Jew to go to the financial expense of closing down the website when 'the cause of the stumbling block is a passive agent rather than an active one' (Eretz Hemdah, 2003).

The Sabbath day is not only characterised by restrictions on work but also as a spiritual experience of prayer, study and rest on the holy day. Mundane activities such as media exposure, including newspapers, arguably take away from the Sabbath atmosphere. The Talmudic codes show two schools of opinion on newspaper reading on the Sabbath. Some medieval rabbinical authorities, including Nachmanides, Rashi, Rosh and Rashba ban only certain types of information in newspapers, such as advertisements or economic and other articles directly related to an individual Jew's work, lest he come to make even a mental decision regarding work. But others, including Maimonides, Meiri and the Ritva, ban secular reading altogether, lest it take away from religious study, which ought to characterise the Sabbath (Apfel, 2007). Thus, some Haredi daily newspapers publish separate *kodesh* sections, comprising Torah-related content alone for this stricter school, even though rabbis allow information to be read that is vital to the Jewish community – as long as it does not cause concern and reduce the festive Sabbath atmosphere.

Technically, electronic media, like the Internet, television and radio, could be left on prior to the Sabbath or pre-programmed beforehand to begin functioning at a pre-arranged time on the Sabbath. But Orthodox rabbis are not inclined to allow this – even though they are inclined to allow similar exposure to the written press. Even if the broadcast or on-line content is religious in nature, rabbis are not inclined to allow the functioning of the electronic media.

Even if it would be a creative way of enhancing the spiritual quality of the Sabbath, in prohibiting on-line, television and radio transmissions on the Sabbath, Rabbi Avraham Yosef, son of the former Sephardi Chief Rabbi of Israel, Rabbi Ovadiah Yosef, has argued that the voice and echoes of a person's voice have an effect upon the functioning of an electrical circuit, raising and lowering the volume, in effect an 'act of work on the Sabbath'. However, Waldenberg, who was rabbi of the Shaare Zedek hospital in Jerusalem, allowed the shofar on Rosh Hashanah to be broadcast by loudspeaker or radio or television, begging the question why the Orthodox rabbis are vehemently against, for example, listening to a video cassette on the Sabbath, set up before the commencement of the Sabbath. Reflecting the Conservative nature of Orthodox rabbis, David Lau, rabbi of the Israeli city of Modiin, remarked: 'The Sabbath clock is not a solution for all matters', and Yosef ruled that no electricity network may function on the Sabbath except that which is necessary for regular living, like heating and eating.

But just like after the early invention of electricity, certain rabbis were hesitant to allow it to be used on the Sabbath even if it was preprogrammed before the beginning of the Sabbath, lest its functioning result in others suspecting that the electricity was manually turned on, and yet today it is accepted practice, so it is argued that it is only a matter of time until Orthodox rabbis allow the computer or videocassette, comprising religious matter like a shiur or religious songs, to function on the Sabbath itself if preprogrammed prior to the Sabbath – thereby adding to the Sabbath or festival atmosphere. In wartime, rabbis have allowed usage of the electronic media. In the Gulf War 1990–91, when Iraq launched 39 missiles towards Israeli territory, radio and television became the primary channels through which the Israel Army informed the civilian population about missiles launched seconds earlier from Iraq and of the need for the population to enter secure rooms – lest the missiles have nonconventional warheads. On the first Sabbath of the war religious Jews left the radio on the regular channel in the event of the siren, but they also heard, as a result, the regular broadcasts. By the second Sabbath the broadcasting authorities had allotted a special band which had no broadcasts except the siren, thereby not spoiling the Sabbath atmosphere of religious households, which the news updates on the regular channels did.

The virtual 'minyan'

Communal 'virtual prayer' has been incorporated into Reform synagogual structures with on-line Internet services held by a number of Reform congregations. But virtual communal services (the '*minyan*') have been rejected by the Orthodox and Conservative streams, given that they are bound by *halakhah*. A fundamental criterion for communal prayer for the Orthodox is the physical presence of ten men. This is similarly true with Conservative Judaism (with the exception that some communities recognise that women may also form the *minyan*). According to the Jewish law code, *Shulkhan Arukh*, Orah Hayyim 55, 'the ten men (who constitute the *minyan*) must be in one place and the prayer leader (*chazan or shaliah zibbur*) with them'.

While much of the Jew's thrice-daily prayer service may be said by an individual praying alone, some aspects of the prayers may be said only in a *minyan*. The most relevant prayer concerns the *Kaddish* mourning prayer said by relatives of the deceased in the 11-month period after death. So central is the place of the *Kaddish* prayer in the Jewish religious psyche as a familial obligation that even some Jews who are not generally observant make a point of attending services to recite the *Kaddish* – raising the question of whether a mourner, unable to reach a synagogue, may fulfil his commitment in a virtual type of *minyan*, in which the individual situated at a separate location is connected on-line to a physical *minyan* of ten. There are other key parts of the service that must be recited communally (including the Bible reading on the Sabbath).

Orthodox rabbis reject the possibility that a Jew at another location from a *minyan* – whether for reasons of bad weather, or ill health, or physical danger such as wartime – may fulfil his prayer obligations by going on-line to an existing *minyan* prayer service. Given the *Shulkhan Arukh* dictum that the ten-man *minyan* must be in one place and the *chazan* or *shaliah zibbur* with them, someone who is outside the room is not regarded as part of the *minyan*. According to Yosef, a *minyan* based merely upon hearing or sight is not a *minyan*. According to Sherlo, Jewish law is focused upon the physical reality, not the media reality that humans have succeeded in creating.[2] To be true, rabbis over the years have been concerned about the need to strengthen the community-orientated nature of Jewish life. Yet it seems likely that, even if a solution to the Net *minyan* were found within the limits of Jewish law, most people would prefer – rather than pray at home – to come together for a group religious experience in a physical setting, as they have done for centuries.

The Conservative Movement also rejected the 'virtual *minyan*'. In a detailed response prepared in 2001 by the movement's Committee on Jewish

Law and Standards, Rabbi Avram Israel Reusner similarly argued against such a *minyan*, drawing also upon the *Shulkhan Arukh* principle that a minyan requires a physical proximity. Drawing an analogy with physical space as a motif in Judaism, Reisner referred to ten levels of territorial spirituality. These ten levels start from outside the Holy Land to inside the Holy Land, outside Jerusalem to inside Jerusalem, and so on, culminating in the Holy of Holies chamber, which, according to Jewish tradition, is entered by the High Priest on Yom Kippur. Reisner draws from the laws of the Temple against the possibility of a virtual *minyan*. He argues that if a person who was in a physically impure state could be brought electronically within the precincts of a rebuilt Temple, he would not be guilty of trespassing on holy ground – which normally would require an atonement sacrifice (Reisner, 2001).

Yet, there are circumstances according to some Orthodox rabbis, as well as Conservative rabbis, where one may link up virtually to an off-line *minyan* service. Notwithstanding the *Shulkhan Arukh* dictum that ten men must be physically in one location, there is a clause in the Jewish tradition for a person who is unable to reach the synagogue to pray at home at the same time as the *minyan* is in prayer. According to Dr Itzhak Arusi, the chief rabbi of Kiryat Ono, the prayer of a person not present at a *minyan* would be strengthened were he to pray with his heart directed towards a *minyan* at prayer. Both Arusi and Yosef[3] agree that certain parts of the prayers only said in communal service could be recited by someone praying in a virtual manner and not physical manner. However, a mourner may not say the Kaddish prayer, given the rule that the prayer leader has to be physically present with the *minyan*.

A related Jewish legal question in considering the Internet concerns the transmission of prayer through electronic circuits. Many Orthodox rabbis have said that if parts of the service that should be heard in a *minyan*, like the Bible reading or Book of Esther on the Purim festival, are recited in an electronic form, one has not fulfilled his obligation. Yet, not all rabbis agree. For many years Israel Television has broadcast the Book of Esther. Waldenberg (1998) allowed patients at the Shaare Zedek Hospital to fulfil their obligation by listening to this broadcast. Rabbi Feinstein notes that the obligation of visiting the sick may be performed by telephone if there is no other way for a person to reach the sick (Feinstein, 1959).

May this be a precedent for linking up virtually to a physical *minyan*?

For Conservative Judaism, there is a point of departure here from the Orthodox stream. Reisner argues that where there is a two-way on-line audio voice connection between a mourner and the physical *minyan*, *Kaddish* could be said since the *Kaddish* is generic praise, neither constituting a benediction nor including God's name. However, even Reisner admits that an individual not party to the *minyan* should not be the sole reciter to which the *minyan* responds, but indeed someone who is praying in the physical *minyan* is in practice the prayer leader.

Another question concerns praying from an electronic device like an iPod or mobile phone, which are able to include among their many features also the daily Jewish prayers. One scholar, Abraham Lifshitz (2010) has argued that it is inappropriate to pray from an electronic *siddur*, or prayer book, drawing upon an edict that a Jew in the midst of prayer should not hold anything lest his concentration be interrupted by that object. Lifshitz suggests that thoughts concerning the value of the phone itself – such as the possibility of its loss – or perhaps some other features – receiving text messages, for example – might interfere with the individual's concentration in prayer.

Conclusion

The impact of Judaism on modern mass media behaviour has been limited to a number of themes only. Major issues like copyright, accuracy and advertising have not been influenced by specifically Jewish values, while issues of great importance in Judaism like sexual modesty or social gossip have not been subject to change. In contrast, religious media have been affected by these religious mores – as well as other questions, including media functioning on the Sabbath and writing the holy name of God. But the extent to which the strictures regarding political gossip has been respected by the religious media – which exist in a competitive framework, and a source-reporter environment – is questionable.

It is difficult to precisely assess the influence of Judaism's view of social communication. On the one hand, Judaism influenced the growth of monotheism. Noahide laws have become widely accepted. Yet those areas where Judaism has influenced other religions do not involve communication in the main. This is perhaps because, as Falk argues, in contrast to Greek rhetoric, Jewish rhetoric calls for polite and pleasant speech (Falk, 1999).

Nevertheless, the impact of Jewish ideas also regarding communication may be identified. The 13 principles of faith, as enunciated by Maimonides, overlap with latter-day functions carried out by the media in Western societies. For example, the belief that God rewards the righteous and punishes the wicked is not dissimilar to media criticism and media exposure of corruption and evil by officials.

The strictures on gossip and the right of privacy were taken up, and expanded, by Prophet Mohammed to become fundamental principles of Islam, namely the principle of the personal honour of the individual as well as grace in interpersonal relations. No less important is the Jewish value of accuracy in reporting and the importance of the truth in Islam.

The impact of Judaism on Christianity concerning communication is felt most in matters concerning sexual modesty – even if the hardline Catholic sinful view of sexual pleasure even within the family framework does not reflect the true Jewish view. Therefore, the influence of the subdiscipline of media, Judaism and culture upon the larger discipline of media, religion and culture can be traced.

References

Apfel, H. D. (2007) 'Reading Options on Shabbat', *Journal of Halakhah and Contemporary Society,* 44, Fall.

Ariel, A. (2001) 'Loshon HaRah B'Maarekhet Tzibnori Democrati' [Hebrew: The Place of Social Gossip in the Public Democratic System], *Tzohar,* 5–6.

Auerbach, S. Z. (1996) 'Shidurei Radio B'Shabbat' [Hebrew: Radio Broadcasts on the Sabbath], Alon Shevut, *Tehumin,* 16.
Brueckheimer, A. (2003) 'Halakha and Technology: Erasing G-d's Name from a Computer', *Journal of Halacha and Contemporary Society,* XLV, 49.
Chwat, A. (1995) 'Itonim V'Hadashot Mitzva O Isur' [Hebrew: Newspapers and News: Religious Obligation or Prohibition], Elkana, *T'lalei Orot.*
Cohen, A. (2005) 'Internet Commerce on Shabbat', *Journal of Halacha and Contemporary Society,* L, 38.
Cohen, Y. (2001) 'Mass Media in the Jewish Tradition', in D. Stout and J. Buddenbaum (eds), *Religion and Popular Culture: Studies on the Interaction of Worldviews.* Ames, IA: Iowa State University Press.
Dayan, D. and Katz, E. (1992) *Media Events: The Live Broadcasting of History.* Boston: Harvard.
Dickovsky, S. (2002) 'Internet B'Halakha' [Hebrew: Internet and Jewish Law], Alon Shevut, *Tehumin,* 23.
Falk, E. (1999) 'Jewish Laws of Speech: Toward Multicultural Rhetoric', *The Howard Journal of Communications,* 10.
Feinstein, M. (1959) *Igeret Moshe,* New York: Section 208.
Gruber, M. (1999) 'Language(s) in Judaism', in J. Neusner and A. J. Avery Peck (eds), *The Encyclopaedia of Judaism.* New York: Continuum.
Ha-Cohen, I. M. (1873) *Chofez Hayim,* Vilna. For an English edition: Z. Pliskin (1975) *Guard Your Tongue: A Practical Guide to the Laws of Loshon Hara Based on the Chofez Hayim.* Jerusalem: Aish HaTorah.
Eretz Hemdah (2003) Mishar B'Internet Ushmirat Shabbas [Hebrew: Trade on the Internet and Sabbath Observance], *Shut B'Bmarei Habazak,* 5, 89.
Korngott, M. H. (1993) *Or Yehezkel* [Hebrew: The Light of Ezekiel: Contemporary Issues in Jewish Law]. Petach Tiqva: Or Yehezkel Institute.
Lamm, N. (1997) 'Tzeniut: A Universal Concept', in M. D. Angel (ed), *Haham Gaon Memorial Volume.* New York: Sepher-Hermon Press.
Lerner, Y. (2005) 'Kesher Romantic B'Internet' [Hebrew: A Romantic Relationship on the Internet], Alon Shevut, *Tehumin,* 25.
Levine, A. (1981) 'Advertising and Promotional Activities as Regulated in Jewish Law', *Journal of Halakha and Contemporary Society,* Spring, 2(5).
Liebes, T. (1994) 'Crimes of Reporting: The Unhappy End of a Fact-finding Mission in the Bible', *Journal of Narrative and Life History,* 4.
Lifshitz, A. (2010) 'Tefila Mitoch Siddur Electroni' [Hebrew: Praying from an Electronic Prayer Book], Alon Shvut,*Tehumin,* 30.
Reisner, A. I. (2001) *Wired to the Kaddosh Barukh Hu:. Minyan via Internet.* New York: Rabbinical Assembly [OH 55:15 2001].
Sherlo, Y. (2002) 'Questions and Answers', *Moreshet,* 23 June.
Stav, D. (1997) 'Publicising the Sins of the Rabbis', *Nekuda,* October.
Waldenberg, E. (1998) *Tzitz Eliezer,* Jerusalem VIII, II.
Wertheimer, D. (2001) 'Letter', *The Journal of Halakha and Contemporary Society,* Fall, XLII.
Zulick, M. (1992) 'The Active Force of Hearing: The Ancient Hebrew Language of Persuasion', *Rhetorica,* X, 4.

Part 2
Media culture wars

3 Constructing religion news: the religion reporter decides

> I had only met one Haredi in my life before I began covering the beat, my uncle's neighbour. The real story is beyond politics. The Haredim fascinated me.
> (Amnon Levi, religious affairs reporter, *Hadashot*)[1]

News media are primary sources for learning about religion. While there are other options like literature and religious institutions, the news media is an important source for following up-to-date developments. Israelis are well served with different news media. There are four major daily newspapers: the quality *Haaretz*, a politically left-wing progressive paper but which favours a free economic market, and three other mass-circulation popular daily newspapers, *Yediot Aharonot, Yisrael Hayom* and *Maariv*.

Until the mid-1970s, the mid-market and politically right of centre *Maariv* was the most widely circulated daily in Israel. A cooperative, *Maariv* was created after a fight with the *Yediot Aharonot* owner resulted in the journalists leaving to create their own newspaper. By 2011, *Maariv*'s circulation had dropped so that 13 per cent of the Israeli population saw *Maariv* newspaper daily, and 16 per cent at weekends, according to the 2011 TGI readership survey, the country's independent survey of the public's exposure to print and broadcast media.[2] Despite downmarketing the paper, from mid-market to a popular paper, in order to compete with *Yediot Aharonot* and also changing editors in rapid succession, the paper failed to sustain itself economically.

For over 30 years since the mid-1970s, *Yediot Aharonot* was the biggest selling newspaper in Israel. Thirty-five per cent of the Israeli population saw the newspaper daily, and 43 per cent at weekends, according to the 2011 TGI readership survey. Owned by the Mozes family, it ran under the banner of 'the country's paper', and, while popular in layout with provocative headlines and human interest stories, it also engaged in more serious reporting.

Yisrael Hayom is a newcomer to Israel's newspaper scene, owned by an American Jew Sheldon Anderson, and right-wing. Distributed free, in its short existence it competed to be the biggest circulation newspaper in Israel. By 2011 it achieved this, with 37 per cent of the Israeli population seeing *Yisrael Hayom* daily (and 30 per cent at weekends), according to the TGI readership survey. However, with its comprehensive coverage of politics, economics, art and social affairs news, both Israeli and foreign, *Haaretz* was recognised as the country's leading quality newspaper, read by decision-makers and leaders in the political, economic and artistic sectors. Seven per cent of the Israeli population saw *Haaretz* daily (and 8 per cent at weekends), according to the TGI readership survey; it was a mainly subscription delivered paper rather than obtained at kiosks like *Yediot Aharonot* and *Maariv*. It sees human rights as a supreme value, from which developed its belief in the separation of religion and state. *Globes* is a daily financial newspaper and enjoyed a circulation of 4.4 per cent according to the TGI survey.

With no newspapers published on Saturday, the Sabbath, Friday issues have the fatter weekend Sabbath eve issues. A local weekly newspaper market has also developed, many of which are owned by the three major newspapers – *Haaretz, Yediot Aharonot* and *Maariv*.

Israel's once flourishing ideological media has died, with the exception of the Haredi or ultra-Orthodox newspapers: *Yated Neeman, Hamodia, Hamevaser* and a weekly oriental Sephardi newspaper, *Yom LeYom*, each of which are published by political movements. An independent newspaper, *Mekor Rishon* is identified with a right-wing nationalist population and is read widely among the modern religious population. In one sense it replaced the daily *Hatzofe* newspaper which was for over 60 years the organ of what was the National Religious Party. Independently published, the widely read weekend edition is distinguished for its quality of writing.

Geared towards a state with many immigrants, Israel had a foreign language press, which has all but died as the immigrants and their children became fully absorbed and were exposed to the main Hebrew language press. One exception is the English language *Jerusalem Post* and the more recently founded *Haaretz* edition in English. In addition, the mass immigration in the 1980s from Russia created a number of Russian-language newspapers, reviving for a generation, until the children are exposed fully to the Hebrew-language culture, the foreign-language press.

Israel's three television channels (the higher standard Channel 1, created in 1968, the popular Channel 2, created in 1993, and a newer, Channel 10, established in 2000) are – notwithstanding an array of cable and satellite channels – the major television channels, given that these broadcast in the Hebrew language and reflect Israeli cultural tastes. Each station possesses news departments for the nightly news programme. Since shortly after its founding, the second television channel succeeded in winning the ratings war to become the country's most popular station.

Israel Radio, the main public radio channel (it and television Channel 1 belong to the same public broadcasting authority), and Galei Zahal, the military radio station financed by the Ministry of Defence, have been the primary radio stations. The public broadcasting model requires broadcasters to have broadcasts with religious content. In the case of radio, a specific radio channel, 'Moreshet' (Tradition) is devoted to programmes with Jewish religious cultural content. A large proliferation of pirate radio stations, many religious, has lessened the exposure of Kol Yisrael and Galei Zahal. Their impact was further dented in the mid-1990s, when the Knesset (the Israeli Parliament) approved the creation of regional radio to cater to local tastes. It included sectoral radio, two of which are religious stations, Radio Kol Chai and Radio Be'Ramah, geared today towards the religious Haredi population, and a station, Radio Galei Yisroel, geared towards the settler population of the West Bank or Judea and Samaria, many of whom are identified with the modern religious population.

Two of the major internet news websites are Y-Net and NRG – owned by *Yediot Aharonot* and *Maariv* respectively. Another is Walla. Each website has a site focusing on Judaism and Israeli religious developments. Given that the Internet is less limited by space considerations, they have increased coverage of religious news developments.

The Israeli media is characterised by a considerable amount of religion-related matter. With a fifth of the Knesset's 120 seats being held by religious political parties – whether from the Haredi or modern Orthodox religious sectors – these sometimes become the kingmakers in the coalition-style of government, and consequently religion politics is a daily feature of news agendas. But while certain politically related questions like 'who is a Jew' have become the subject of wide coverage, many other topics regarding religion are not newsworthy – producing an imbalanced and incomplete picture of religion.

Research on news has produced a variety of theories on how news is produced. Most fundamental is the mirror theory, according to which the media reflects what happens. But most research on news suggests that the media's portrayal is not an identical image of what happens. By contrast, organisational theories like Tuchman explain the news as the outcome of a routine process in which news organisations produce a newspaper or broadcast bulletin according to a specific time or drawing upon specific manpower resources of newsgathering – the news reflecting these limitations. An event which occurs close to edition time is necessarily covered less comprehensively than that occurring much earlier than edition time, enabling reporters to cover the event more comprehensively with background features and analysis (Tuchman, 1973). Another approach to analysing the construction of news is occupational theory; Tunstall discusses whether the biographical background of reporters and editors influences how the news is reported and edited (Tunstall, 1971). Reporters covering religion have a background store of professional knowledge about the subject, which contributes to a more accurate and comprehensive coverage. A variation on the organisational approach as a means to analysing the news is to examine the relations between reporters and editors (Argyris, 1974; Gans, 1980). The story, however well-researched, will not pass the 'filter' and be defined as news if the editor, faced with many other competing stories for the limited space or airtime, does not share the same enthusiasm as his erstwhile or intrepid reporter. Yet another approach (Nimmo, 1964) is that the news – defined as the output of governmental media relations or source–reporter relations – reflects the sum total of interactions between news sources and reporters. Information which becomes defined by reporters as news comprises interesting information, which news sources knowingly leak or disclose in order to influence public opinion and the public agenda.

Ostgaard (1965) theorises that news output is a conglomeration of access for reporters to news events, occupational factors about reporters, the impact of editors and proprietors, and a selection of psychological factors such as whether the event generates feelings and emotions of excitement and entertainment. Thus, religion news is the outcome of journalists' evaluations of the newsworthiness of the story, reporter–religion source relations, and the psychological questions of which religions, which events and which aspects of religion are regarded by editors as important and interesting for the news organisations. Among factors to be examined are editors' evaluations regarding the newsworthiness of religion-related news, background knowledge about the religion of reporters, the level of understanding of reporters covering the religion beat, reporters' access to news sources like rabbis, and whether religion itself has an ethical influence upon whether to publish or broadcast certain matter. Religion competes for the limited space and airtime with other categories of news, like political or military news, which editors may evaluate are of greater interest than religion. The impact of ideology (Hall, 1982) cannot be ignored even with the general media, but its major impact on religion news coverage in Israel will be discussed later in the context of the religious media, and in particular the Haredi media.

The religion affairs reporter

Most key Israeli news organisations have specialist reporters covering religion. There are full-time religious affairs reporters on the key daily newspapers including *Haaretz, Yediot Aharonot, Yisrael Hayom* and *Maariv*. The broadcasting organisations Channel 1, 2, 10, Israel Radio and Galei Zahal have reporters covering the 'beat' on a part-time basis; for example, in one case the television reporter covering the Knesset also covered the Haredim, given that so much is the political story of the Haredi political parties. The news websites Y-Net and NRG each have religion portals, with their own religious reporters. In practice, the vast majority of religion writing is done by a handful of individuals which gives them immense responsibility and influence – a phenomenon which characterises specialist correspondents throughout contemporary news journalism. The religion affairs reporter in Israel has covered invariably only the Jewish religion – in contrast to the religious affairs reporter in other countries where the reporter covers the gamut of religions. That Islam-related developments are not covered by the religion reporter in Israel but instead by the staff reporter responsible for covering Israel's Arab population has important implications because the religious dimensions of Israel's Arab population fail mostly to be covered and, if covered, fail to receive the interpretative analysis which a religion affairs reporter brings to his work. And Christianity does not fall into anybody's brief in the Israeli newsroom, notwithstanding the significance that key shrines important to Christianity are situated in Jerusalem, Bethlehem and Nazareth.

The focus for some of the reporters has been the Haredi community. Two leading cases who covered the 'beat' for many years were Shahar Ilan of *Haaretz* and Amnon Levi of the defunct *Hadashot*. Each had his emphasis. Ilan's was the political clout of Haredim, and in particular the government's financial and budgetary subsidies that the community receives. Ilan's investigative work here produced a long running series 'Haredim '98'. By contrast, Levi believed that the real story was beyond politics and concerned the lifestyles of Haredi society.[3]

The level of a reporter's background knowledge impacts upon his work. The small number of religion reporters in Israel makes it difficult to produce any generalised patterns. In terms of background knowledge, both Ilan and Levi came to their jobs with little personal acquaintance with Haredim.

In contrast, Nadav Shragai, who was the religious affairs correspondent at *Haaretz* in the 1980s, came from a modern religious background. The grandson of Shlomo Zalman Shragai who had been mayor of Jerusalem and member of the National Religious Party, Shragai benefited from the religious studies which are integral in the state religious education system. Yehuda Schlesinger, the religious affairs reporter of *Yisrael Hayom*, grew up in the Haredi city of Benei Berak. Benny Lis, who covered the modern religious sector at Israel Television's Channel 1 – within his mandate of covering the settlements in the West Bank, many of whose members belonged to the modern religious community – came from a modern religious background.

His colleague, Nitzan Chen, the channel's Knesset correspondent – like *Haaretz*'s Shahar Ilan – covered the Haredim from the vantage point of Haredi political parties. He too grew up in a modern religious home. However, while studying Contemporary Jewry at the Hebrew University he moved from the Orthodox wing of Judaism to the Conservative movement, including studying at its rabbinical seminary, the Schechter Institute, with a view to being ordained as a Conservative rabbi. Later he even considered running to become the head of Israel Radio's 'Moreshet' Jewish tradition channel. Over the years the channel had been in the pocket of the modern religious political parties and drew only a small listening audience, overwhelmingly from within the religious population. Chen wanted to open up the channel to a broader agenda beyond traditional content, to such questions as Jewish identity.

In examining the religion background of religious affairs reporters in the US, a distinction has been drawn between background knowledge about theology – such as academic study of the subject – and religious involvement. In terms of religion knowledge, Ranly's study (1979) found that half of the religion affairs correspondents in the US media had taken courses in religion or theology. Twenty-nine per cent of religion affairs reporters surveyed by Buddenbaum had studied theology or religion. Buddenbaum (1988) found that reporters from larger circulation papers were three times more inclined to have studied religion or theology than reporters from smaller circulation papers. Thirteen per cent of reporters surveyed said that a religion reporter should have a degree in religion or theology, but 26 per cent disagreed. Thirty-seven per cent said that the 'good' religion reporter required knowledge of religion. Dart and Allen's Freedom Forum study found even greater support for a religion knowledge background: 76 per cent of the religion reporters whom they surveyed said that religion studies were helpful in covering the religion beat; another 14 per cent said it was essential. Only 10 per cent said that it was not necessary for the job (Dart and Allen, 1993).

In terms of religious activity, many religion reporters in the US are active religiously. Only 15 per cent of Buddenbaum's survey were not active at all religiously. Between two-thirds to 80 per cent of religion reporters (depending on newspaper circulation size) said they were very active or somewhat active religiously. It needs to be questioned whether a journalist so personally involved in one religion, which by implication might delegitimise other religious options, can be objective. In Israel, these options might include, for example, covering the struggle by non-Orthodox streams like Conservative or Reform Judaism for Israeli official recognition, or covering other religions – like Christianity or non-monotheistic faiths – which may be theologically problematic from a Jewish Orthodox viewpoint. By 2000 Channel 1 and Channel 2 had two returnee Jews to Judaism. Sivan Rahav-Meir, a former army radio reporter who became ultra-Orthodox and was Channel 2's religion reporter, would appear on screen dressed modestly with a wig and long sleeves, a manner adopted by Haredi women. Uri Revach, a formerly secular Israeli, became a Haredi Jew while working at Channel 2. He later worked as the spokesman in 2001–3 for the Religious Affairs Minister, Asher Ohana of the Shas Party. Revach, who identified with the Habad sect of hassidim, later joined Channel 1 and turned his office at the Broadcasting Authority into a small synagogue for a prayer *minyan* and organised religious lessons (*shiurim*) in the office of the head of radio. He even encouraged fellow workers to 'lay tefillin', i.e. perform the daily religious obligation of donning phylacteries used by Jewish males in the morning religious service. He also – in accord with religious tradition – affixed *mezuzot,* containing text of the holy *Shema* prayer, to the doorposts of some 40 rooms in the broadcasting building where they were absent. Already while working earlier at Channel 2, he was allowed by the station director not to work on the Sabbath. Visibly religious on the screen, he has an unruly beard and a Conservative dark jacket without tie, as worn by Haredi men. He does not, in his words, 'thank God, surf the Internet or have e-mail'. While he still covers the religion beat for the main news channel, much of his work today is on the Jewish tradition channel of Israel radio, *Moreshet*. He says that his goal is to reach 'not just religious listeners but all who thirst to hear Judaism'.[4] He hopes for the day when journalists who define themselves as left-wing and antireligious will broadcast as full returnees from the yet-to-be-rebuilt Jewish Temple in Jerusalem.

There is limited support among US reporters on whether it is desirable or not that a religious person should cover the 'beat'. Only a quarter of reporters surveyed by Dart and Allen (1993) said that a religious person should cover the religion beat, a quarter disagreed, and the rest were neutral. None favoured that a member of the clergy should cover religion news, 27 per cent were neutral, and the rest opposed the idea of clergy journalists.

Source–reporter relations

The news flow is determined also by the access that reporters enjoy to news events and to news sources. Religion affairs reporters gather news from official spokesmen; given that one of the foci of the religion reporter is coverage of the Haredi sector, much time is spent drawing upon sources in the Haredi world and from the Haredi media. But in practice the religious beat is characterised by limited access because religious communities are inclined to be closed and suspicious of outsiders, such as the media, and not to invite journalists to events. The spokespersons of official institutions like the Chief Rabbinate and Ministry of Religious Affairs are relevant for only certain types of religion stories such as religious conversion. Given the lack of formal source-media channels in, for example, the Haredi world, the work of the religion affairs reporter is to locate the centres of power within communities – the key rabbis, whether measured by the size of their flock or by their influence – and to develop a network of tipsters, aides, cronies, religious teachers and students close to rabbis. Haredi rabbis have unclear lines of contact with journalists, many viewing the non-religious media as 'treifah' (the term used for non-kosher food) – yet some do recognise the need to nevertheless talk to the 'devil'. An important source for reporters is the Haredi media, particularly the institutional Haredi media like *Hamodia, Yetad Neeman* and *Hamevaser,* in order to gauge the reaction of rabbis to inter-religious and national developments.

Rabbi Ovadiah Yosef: sparring with the press

Illustrating the difficulties encountered by the media in covering the religious world is the case of Rabbi Ovadiah Yosef, the undisputed head of religious Oriental or Sephardic Jewry in Israel and former chief rabbi of Israel. Born in Baghdad in 1920, he was brought to Palestine at the age of three, wrote his first religious treatise at 17, and became a rabbi at the age of 19, holding rabbinical positions in Cairo and Tel Aviv. As the mentor of the Shas political party, which has been a kingmaker of the coalition system of government, his political influence was undeniable. If, for years, Yosef struggled politically for equality for Sephardic Jews – for example, the acceptance of Sephardi children in Ashkenazi-controlled schools and *yeshivot* – theologically, he saw Sephardism as the true Judaism of the land of Israel, and Ashkenazim as merely an import from Diaspora European communities of old (Kedem and Meizlich, 2002).

He has a love–hate relationship with the media. He is clearly aware of the importance of media and the public. Yosef's weekly sermon on Saturday night, after the termination of the Sabbath, at the Yatzchim Synagogue in Jerusalem's Buhkarian Quarter, is broadcast on satellite to followers in Israel and abroad and is widely quoted including in the secular media. There is a vast difference between his writing style and the language of his weekly *shiur* on Saturday nights, which is delivered in a colloquial style understood by the flock, with 'the language of the street shaping the spiritual leader's rhetoric rather than the reverse'.[5] His invective not infrequently raised media eyebrows. Thus, after the Israeli media in July 1997 discussed his reference, in a speech, to a rabbinic ruling prohibiting a man from walking between two women, the rabbi lashed out at the media as 'hating the Torah. This was the only thing you can pick from my religious lesson!! May God send us another media, one which loves the Torah and its teaching'.[6]

That a religious movement exists around a key personality merely strengthens the news interest. Buddenbaum, in examining US television network coverage of religion, argued that the fact that the Pope is an easily identifiable, charismatic figure caused the Catholic stream of Christianity to receive wide coverage (Buddenbaum, 1990, p. 77).

Yet Yosef has given only four sit-down interviews over a period of 40 years. He is 'above' the media, declining to conduct a 'dialogue' with them. This superciliousness gives Yosef an aura of holiness, of being above public criticism. He is surrounded by a coterie of political cronies, aides, and family including his daughter, daughter-in-law, and some of his sons, who vet individuals seeking to meet or speak to Yosef. He has held meetings or 'briefings' to the media, but the attending journalist is warned not to ask the rabbi questions. Channel 2's Matti Cohen, who dared to ask the respected rabbi for his view on the rule of (secular) law in Israel, found himself ignored for months by Shas party politicians, and tips and leaks were passed to the reporter's rival channel. The same occurred later to Cohen's rival at Channel 1, Nitzan Chen, who after one such briefing asked Yosef a provocative question and was then thrown out of the meeting. 'Get out, this iniquity,' snapped the rabbi. 'We won't answer him. Let him be cursed,' the rabbi added. It took Chen two days to recover from the rabbi's remarks; Chen even contemplated ceasing to cover the Shas party. For months he was scooped by Channel 2's Cohen.[7] As David Landau, then editor of *Haaretz* and an author of a biography of Yosef, remarked:

> that a journalist covering religion day after day, cannot exchange one word with a key source does not exist in any other sphere of journalism. Even the Mossad gives briefings. Nobody would consider covering a beat in any other area of journalism through messages or spokesmen of one sort or another rather than access to the source himself.[8]

When some reporters sought to change the rules by uniting and not covering the Shas, 'this was impossible, irresponsible', as *Maariv*'s former reporter on

Haredim, Shlomo Tzenaya, put it: 'A boycott by the media of Shas appears to me to be impossible. The rabbi is just not interested in being interviewed. Anyone who suggests a media boycott of Shas just does not understand the language which they in Shas speak.'[9]

Source–reporter relations in the religion 'beat' are characterised by pressures of one sort or another well beyond the Yosef case. After the *Jerusalem Post*'s religious affairs reporter, Judy Siegel, published a scoop which embarrassed Ashkenazi Chief Rabbi Shlomo Goren, the latter cut off all ties with the reporter. 'In 1974, the year after the Yom Kippur war, I learnt that Rabbi Goren had "planted" a question on a radio phone-in programme in which he appeared. The question was about whether the Israeli Army's chaplaincy corps [which Goren had previously headed] was right in "leaving the bodies" of soldiers on the battlefield on the Sabbath and religious holidays' (when there is generally a religious prohibition of work). 'Acting on a tip', Siegel said, 'I managed to track down the caller, who, contrary to what Goren said on the radio, had never been in the army and never seen any bodies on the battlefield. The chief rabbi refused to comment when I called him, giving him the name of the person, one of his own proteges, who had placed the question.' Siegel's scoop made the front pages of the following day's newspapers, and the controversy was even raised as a parliamentary question to the defence minister in the Knesset. When Siegel called the chief rabbi the following day, he angrily took the phone, snapping, 'You wrote *lashon hara* [a religious prohibition for speaking ill of somebody]. People like you lose their place in the Next World.' Goren refused to speak to Siegel for over a year – forcing her to resort to Goren's colleague and opponent, Rabbi Ovadiah Yosef. Relations soured once again when the newspaper published a news report by Siegel concerning kosher food, and one of the newspaper's sub-editors placed as a headline to the story, 'Goren Surrenders Kashrut Authority to Zolti' (a reference to Rabbi Zolti, the chief rabbi of the city of Jerusalem). Goren understood the phrase 'the chief rabbi surrenders' to mean 'to give up out of weakness' rather than merely 'to turn over'. Since he and Zolti had not spoken to one another for years, the headline infuriated him. Goren cut off all contact again to Siegel for many months.[10]

Threats and pressures take on a variety of forms. When Shahar Ilan, then a young religious affairs reporter at *Kol Ha'ir*, the Jerusalem local weekly, published a piece which aroused the angst of European Haredim of the Lithuanian faction, an advert appeared in the Lithuanian Haredi daily *Yated Neeman*. Under the heading 'Wanted: a *shidduch* [marriage partner] for a widow. Possible under age 40 groom from Sephardi oriental background,' the advert added Ilan's telephone number. Ilan was inundated by potential suitors for his wife, represented by marriage introduction agencies.[11] In another case, when *Hadashot*'s Amnon Levi covered inter-Haredi tensions between different rival factions inside the Vishnitz hassidic Haredi community, he and his photographer were pelted with etrogim (or citrus fruit) after they came to hear a sermon (*derasha*) of a Vishnitz rabbi, Yerahmiel Domb. Avi Pozen, another *Kol Ha'ir* reporter, who in 1990 penned an article claiming that the Belze rabbi, Issachar Dov Rokach, was out of favour in his own community, was beaten up two years later when he turned up to cover the marriage of Rokach's son and was left with a broken nose and other wounds.[12]

A tendency in Israeli journalism to take a more critical stance regarding officials also had implications for coverage of religious leaders and religious institutions. While the media were inclined to be circumspect in criticising those in authority during the period from state independence in 1948 to the mid-1970s, including deferring both to religious authorities and to rabbinical leaders, after the military intelligence surprise on the eve of the 1973 Yom Kippur war, the Israeli media became more critical, more questioning, a 'coming of age', showing in some cases scant regard and expressing open criticism of those in office and, in the case of religion coverage in the 1950s to the 1970s, of an inclination of the Israeli media intelligentsia – left-wing and secular – to be scornful and contemptuous for religious leaders, whom they regarded as primitive.

By the 1980s, some policymakers, politicians and officials realised the need to ingratiate themselves with reporters in order that their messages reach the public. But few rabbis did so until the turn of the twenty-first century. One exception was Ashkenazi Chief Rabbi Israel Meir Lau, whose warm and humane appearances on television and radio contributed towards generating understanding for religious positions and thereby helped to reduce secular–religious tensions. But many rabbis, particularly from the Haredi community, clung to their spiritual pedestals. More recently, a younger generation of rabbis identified with the modern religious, including the stricter '*hardal*' sub-stream – and not characterised by the stiffness and coldness of their predecessors, or the Conservative black attire of the Haredim – have appeared in the electronic media – lessening the distance between men of the cloth and the public. Of late, a trend for the entry into Israeli journalism of the modern religious has brought with it sympathy towards Jewish tradition, and the background knowledge has contributed towards more serious coverage of religion.

The religion beat presents its special challenges for the woman reporter. As the *Jerusalem Post*'s first woman to cover the religion beat in the 1970s, Judy Siegel found that she 'didn't have an easy time being taken seriously, especially by those in the religious establishment. Chief rabbis, *dayanim* (religious court judges), and others were at first aghast that a woman had come to interview them, partly because it meant sitting alone in the same room together. They almost seemed to prefer having a non-observant male interviewer over a religious female one. But gradually I won their confidence, and they sought me out when they wanted their views printed, "forgetting" that I was a woman.' The most uncomfortable assignment for Siegel was attending an assembly of delegates of the Agudath Yisrael movement from around the world. The invitation sent to the *Jerusalem Post* was addressed to 'Mr Judy Siegel'. 'Sitting at the press table, I was the only female among over 2,000 mostly black-coated men.'[13]

In 1997 women reporters were barred from covering a festive event marking the completion of the tenth cycle of the *Daf Yomi* (a popular study project among the Orthodox of learning a page of the Talmud daily). A woman reporter who dressed up as a man to win entry was identified – 'I won't reveal the means by which we discovered her. They're secret,' said one of the organisers later – and the woman reporter watched the event from a segregated area for women where the event was broadcast simultaneously on a huge screen. Likewise in 2010 women reporters were barred from a mass demonstration with tens of thousands of Haredim, who were protesting the gaoling of fathers who were running a school in the town of Emanuel which was found by the courts to be discriminatory toward Sephardi girls. The women reporters had to cover the event from outside.[14]

Reporter–editor relations

No less important than the role of reporters is the role in news construction played by sub-editors on the editorial desk, because they control the final flow of what is printed, broadcast or placed on the Net. The reporter is inclined to give greater importance to the news value of certain events than editors who are limited by space or airtime. The role of the sub-editor is to decide what will be in the front page or top of the bulletin, whether the story reporting is accurate or requires additional information or elucidation, whether related reports should be combined into a single report.

While the reporter–editor dependency exists in all specialisms, it is particularly evident in the religion beat. Religion is secondary to other subjects regarded as more important including political and military issues, and while the religion affairs reporter may regard it as important, the editor – with an eye on what will interest the audience – may not regard it with the same amount of import. All reports go through a filtering process, with sub-editors deciding which are important, and which are less important, all competing for the limited space or broadcast time. The Internet, is, by nature, less limited by space considerations.

When there is a religion affairs reporter who is active religiously, it needs to be asked whether there is a gap between his religious outlook and that of his editor or publisher, and what the consequences of this would be. For example, Nadav Shragai was removed from his post on the religion beat on *Haaretz* in 1987, which he had held for five years, during a public controversy over a Meretz political party initiative to allow cinemas in Jerusalem to be open on the Sabbath. The young reporter had covered the news story, but Shragai, who is religious, also wrote an op-ed piece in which he denounced the change in the secular–religious status quo which would result from the opening of the cinemas on the Sabbath. It contrasted with the paper's editorial position, which favours freedom from religious coercion. He was admonished by a senior editor and moved to another desk job.[15] In another case, Haim Zisovitch, a candidate for the plum post of Washington reporter almost lost the job because he was religious. Shulamit Aloni, the left-wing Culture Affairs minister, who had ministerial responsibility for the Broadcasting Authority, objected to the appointment on the ground that Zisovitch would not work on the Sabbath. The case raises the broader question of employment for all reporters from a religious or traditional background who do not work on the Sabbath; the problem can be acute in the case of broadcasting or the Internet which function on the Sabbath. But in the Zisovitch case the equally left-wing director-general Mordechai Kirchenbaum came to Zisovitch's defence.[16]

But the expectations of editors and the management also result in the religious affairs correspondent making himself amenable to the former. For example, Nitzan Chen – though personally religious, praying daily, observing kashrut and the Sabbath – removed his *kippa*, or skullcap, which he was accustomed to wear. 'The *kippa* limits me, categorises me as belonging to a specific stream. I don't want to be categorised because I am not the representative of any stream.' However, religious symbols may help a reporter on the religious beat to reach sources which would otherwise be closed or limited to a secular reporter. When a Shas minister saw him *kippa*-less he remarked to him, 'Nitzan, you really have disappointed me. You have fallen in with the elite.' Chen added: 'I have feelings of guilt about it. One day I may put it back – if only for my child'.[17] But to suggest that owners or editors oppose employing religious journalists on principle is inaccurate. Thus, Yehuda Mozes – then mythical proprietor of *Yediot Aharonot*, whose father had been a religious court judge in Kalish, in east Europe – even kept a Torah scroll in a cupboard in his office.[18] Moreover, notwithstanding the paper's anti-cleric stance, Gershom Schocken, editor and publisher of *Haaretz*, maintained a Jewish cultural identity. According to his daughter, Raheli Edelman (and publisher of the Schocken book publishing house), 'We used to be taken by our father to the synagogue on the High Holidays. On the Sabbath eve he would pronounce the kiddush at the evening meal. And, on *Sukkot* (Feast of the Tabernacles), we would go to the market to buy the *arba minim* for the holiday. Dad was not religious but had respect for religious tradition and wanted his children to know the sources.'[19] Gershon's father, Zalman, who lived in Germany prior to moving to Palestine, identified with the Reform movement and sought to strengthen Jewish culture through publishing texts on Jewish theology and culture in the publishing house which began in Germany as Schocken Verlag.

Conclusion

News output is a conglomeration of factors including the access of reporters to news events, occupational factors about reporters, and the impact of editors and owners. But news output is also a product of several psychological factors, which generate news interest – to be discussed in Chapter 4 – such as feelings and emotions of excitement generated by events.

References

Argyris, C. (1974) *Behind the Front Page*. San Francisco: Jossey Bass.

Buddenbaum, J. (1988) 'The Religion Beat at Daily Newspapers', *Newspaper Research Journal*, Summer.

——(1990) 'Network News Coverage of Religion', in J. Ferre (ed), *Channels of Belief: Religion and America Commercial Television*. Ames, IA: Iowa State University Press.

Dart, J. and Allen, J. (1993) *Bridging the Gap: Religion and the News Media*. Nashville, TN: The Freedom Forum First Amendment Center, Vanderbilt University.

Gans, H. (1980) *Deciding What's News*. New York: Vintage.

Hall, S. (1982) 'The Rediscovery of Ideology: Return of the Repressed in Media Studies', in M. Gurevitch, T. Bennett, J. Curran and J. Woollacott (eds), *Culture, Society and the Media*. London: Methuen.

Kedem, R. and Meizlich, S. (2002) *HaRav Ovadiah* [Hebrew: Rabbi Ovadiah Yosef]. Tel Aviv: Hemed.

Nimmo, D. (1964) *Newsgathering in Washington*. New York: Prentice-Hall.

Ostgaard, E. (1965) 'Factors Influencing the Flow of News', *Journal of International Peace Research*, 2.

Ranly, D. (1979) 'How Religion Editors of Newspapers view their Jobs and Religion,' *Journalism Quarterly* 56: 4, Winter.

Tuchman, G. (1973) 'Making News by Doing Work: Routinizing the Unexpected', *American Journal of Sociology*, 79.

Tunstall, J. (1971) *Journalists at Work*. London: Constable.

4 News values, ideology and the religion story

> That freedom of expression includes freedom of pornographic expression is not self-evident. There are several levels of expression – political, artistic and commercial. Not each is eligible for the optimal legal protection.
> (Judge Michael Heshin, in a minority opinion in the Supreme Court ruling in 1994 on Playboy's appeal to broadcast on Israeli cable television)

While in newsgathering the religion affairs reporter has a major role to play, no less important in examining the construction of religion news are psychological and ideological news values. Such other factors as reporter–editor relations and background training of religion reporters are subservient to psychological factors of newsworthiness. However intensive the efforts of news sources to spin the news, if the subject is not newsworthy it will not pass the barrier of newsworthiness. Galtung and Ruge (1965) explained news as events which comprise at least one of three criteria: news about conflict or social breakdown; news about elites; and news which is culturally proximate to an audience.

This is also applicable to religion news. Crises involving religion are defined as news. Religious elites – whether defined as individuals like leading rabbis or institutions like the chief rabbinate or yeshivot – are more likely to be defined as newsworthy than lesser souls or less significant institutions. Religions which are closer or more 'proximate' to Israeli audiences, notably Judaism, or subjects which are 'proximate' to them, like the enforcement of the Sabbath, will have a greater chance of being defined as news than less proximate ones. An example of a less proximate event is religious conversion. Religious conversion does not affect the overwhelming number of Israelis apart from Russians, in contrast to the Jewish diaspora, where there is far greater number of cases of intermarriage and conversions, particularly in the non-Orthodox streams.

Religion events which pass the news barrier and are defined as news may reflect a constellation of criteria. An example of a religion-related event that possessed all the ingredients of a news story with broad appeal concerned a love affair over the Internet in 2005 involving Ayala, the 17-year-old daughter of Israel's Sephardi Chief Rabbi Shlomo Amar, and the subsequent trial of Amar's son, Meir, for kidnapping his sister's boyfriend. In Haredi circles marriages – or at the very least, dates – are arranged. The story had the ingredients of love, an Internet-born relationship – with the Internet itself forbidden in Haredi circles – violence involving the kidnapping and beating up a suitor and a court trial in which the kidnapper was sentenced to two and a half years imprisonment. In addition the media's curiosity was aroused as to the extent, if any, of the involvement of the Chief Rabbi's wife and of perhaps the Chief Rabbi himself. These were questions the media failed to answer.

The media not only construct the reality but may even contribute to creating it. Dayan and Katz (1992) have argued that major television-covered events like sports, coronations and state funerals result in the audience itself becoming involved as a 'participant' in an event. Thus, a funeral of a leading rabbi or the consecration of a new *sefer Torah* (scrolls of the Law) broadcast on the Internet or radio are followed avidly by members of the community.

A content analysis of religion

In order to produce a fuller picture of trends in religion coverage in the Israeli media, coverage of religion in the Israeli press, radio and television was analysed by the author for a two-month period in 2000: religion-related content in *Yediot Aharonot,* the secular mass-circulation popular newspaper*; Haaretz,* the quality elite newspaper; *Hatzofe,* a now extinct daily reflecting the modern Orthodox sector; *Hamodia,* the Haredi daily; Israel Radio's morning newsreel; 'Ha-Kol Dibburim' ('It's All Talk'), a politics-orientated radio interview programme; Israel television's nightly *Mabat* news programme; Israel Television's post-Sabbath religion-orientated programme; the second channel's current-affairs programme, 'Five with Gadi Sukenik'; and the daily mid-day news diary programme of Radio Kol Chai, the Haredi radio station. The study examined the following motifs of religion coverage: religious political parties, public personalities associated with religion, rabbis, religious institutions (such as *yeshivot* [talmudical academies of higher religious learning], burial societies, religious schools), religious youth movements (a feature of community life in Israel and abroad providing a range of semi-educational activities held mostly on the Sabbath) and God. (This survey did not include the regular column on the weekly Bible reading which appears in *Yediot Aharonot, Maariv* and *Haaretz,* or the special *kadosh* or 'holy' supplement section dealing with wholly theological dimensions of the religion which appear in the Haredi and modern Orthodox weekend papers and which in some cases comprise entire supplements.)

Quantitatively, religion received wide coverage. Ten per cent of editorial content in secular, non-religious media surveyed comprised religion. Zecharya, examining the secular *Haaretz* in a 1988 study, found there was 4 per cent on religion (Zecharya, 1989). It was comparable to the 1999 Garrett-Medill study of US media coverage of religion, spirituality and values (Garrett-Medill Center for Religion and the News Media, 1999). Yet, while the author's study on the Israeli media found that television had relatively more religion-related stories than newspapers, the reverse was true with the Garrett-Medill study on the US media; 9 per cent of national television news concerned religion, spirituality and values in contrast to 30 per cent of the press. It is much higher than the Buddenbaum (1990) ten-year long study (1976–86) of US religion coverage of network television, which found that an average of only 4 per cent of television news content mentioned or discussed religion.

The centrality of religion in Israeli public life was reflected in the fact that 22 per cent of all religion reporting in the study was on the front page or beginning of broadcast programmes. This was relatively high. In the Garrett-Medill study 14 per cent of religion on US television news was the first item; 8 per cent of religion in newspapers made it to the front page. The latter could be explained due to the intense television coverage which religion-rated developments generated (Shepherd, 1995). In the Israeli case, the explanation is the political significance of these developments, for example, the impact of the religious political parties upon Israel's coalition-style government. It should be noted that only 27 per cent of news reports in the author's survey were accompanied by photographs – lower than the Garrett-Medill study of US media in which 49 per cent of all newspaper reports were accompanied by a photo.

The conflict orientation in news is reflected in the Israeli media, such as institutional infighting within the religious world; religious political parties comprised 15 per cent of all religion reporting in the Israel study. This was even truer in the US: 47 per cent of religion-rated reports on television had a conflict dimension, as did 24 per cent and 25 per cent of newspaper and news magazine coverage. (The Garrett-Medill study included international conflict news with a religion dimension, whereas the Israel study did not have an international news dimension but focused wholly on domestic conflict.)

God – the ultimate, elite symbol of religion – accounted for only 0.3 per cent in the news pages. Alternatively, only 10 of the 3,618 items on religion comprising the data base concerned God. Similarly, the Garrett-Medill US study found that only 3 per cent of religion coverage on television, 11 per cent in newspapers and 11 per cent in news magazines concerned God. And, Mowery (1995), in examining the citation of the word God in reporting in *The New York Times* in the month of January 1994, found that many were in contexts which trivialised God, such as in references to the weather, political news intoning God, or expressions of hopes and fears of people, and that only comparatively few were spoken by clergy (Mowery, 1995). This illustrates graphically how distant much in religion is from meeting the criteria of newsworthiness.

Moreover, Judaism has a different time-span from the media. Judaism's time-span does not meet criteria of event-types in terms of occurring between the appearance of two editions of two newspapers, or the broadcast of two consecutive bulletins. If past events in Jewish history – the Exodus from Egypt, the Receiving of the Ten Commandments at Mount Sinai, for example – fulfil criteria for dramatic media interest, this is no longer true today. The incorporeal, which cannot be felt by time or space, underlines this distance.

To be true, the absence of content on God is compensated, in part at least, by the weekly column on the Torah reading in the Friday Sabbath eve newspaper issue. The weekly religious broadcast programmes on the Sabbath eve and after the end of the Sabbath on radio and television include interviews with rabbis on a range of theological issues. In the Garrett-Medill US study only 2 per cent of religion-related news on television, 5 per cent of newspapers and 3 per cent of news magazines concerned spirituality as opposed to religion and values. And 4 per cent of religion-related content on television, 12 per cent of newspaper content, and 19 per cent of news magazine content on religion in the Garrett-Medill study concerned prayer (Garrett-Medill Center for Religion and the News Media, 1999).

The news sections of the media are the main framework through which Israeli audiences receive information from media about religion. Most of the daily press coverage of religion came in news reporting as distinct from the feature pages: 70 per cent as opposed to the inner sections, including the second section of news features like '24 Hours' of *Yediot Aharonot* and *Maariv*'s 'Today' section. This clearly has implications for the information flow received by audiences, with an emphasis on day-by-day – often disconnected – developments, with an inclination for conflict-ridden religion developments, in contrast to features and commentaries comprising longer-term trends that characterise a newspaper's inner sections. No significant difference quantitatively in newspaper coverage was found in the Israeli press between the daily issue of newspapers (17 per cent) and the weekend issue published on the Friday eve of the Sabbath (15 per cent), which are fatter with supplements providing more background articles and features.

Despite the expectation that religion would occupy the quality media more – particularly in the case of *Haaretz*, which advocates separation of synagogue and state – in overall terms of newspaper space, the mass circulation *Yediot Aharonot* gave a similar amount (5 per cent) to *Haaretz* (5 per cent). It reflects the interest in religion even for downmarket audiences. However, each media form covers religion differently. Some religion news is more newsworthy for the quality serious newspapers than for popular newspapers. The quality *Haaretz* carries more news reports than the popular headline-winning *Yediot Aharonot*; *Haaretz* had 613 religion reports in the two-month period as opposed to *Yediot Aharonot*'s 453 reports. Theological discussions and longer-term religious trends, for example, are of greater interest to the quality press. The reverse is also true, and some stories, such as religious scandals particularly involving rabbis and sex, draw greater interest among the popular press than the quality press.

Religion is politics

Religion subjects may be divided between those subjects which possess a higher propensity to become defined as news and those less likely to cross the threshold. Religion stories with public or political dimensions are the most covered subjects. Over 28 per cent of religion content was related to public or political matters; the biggest single category was found to be the religious political parties (15 per cent). This was not dissimilar to the American experience. 'Religion in American politics' was found by Hoover (1998) to be high (fifth out of 16 popular categories of religion news). And Ferre's study of the *New York Times* and the *Washington Post* (Ferre, 1980) found church and state the biggest category (21 per cent) – above church liturgy, religious education, evangelicism and church unity. The dominance of religious parties in the study on the Israeli media was notable in particular in television (27 per cent) and radio (35 per cent) as opposed to 12 per cent with newspapers. The 'Five with Gadi Sukenik' show in particular had 45 per cent of its religious content on religious political parties. The secular papers' preoccupation with the religious political parties reflected a general preoccupation with the influence of the parties on the makeup of the coalition-style of government and their lesser concern with internal developments within the religious community.

Elitism – whether defined as elite institutions or elite individuals – is relevant to religion coverage. As a religion characterised by hierarchy, the Jewish religion fulfils criterion of involving elites: important people such as Chief Rabbis and heads of hassidic courts ('*admorim*'), and institutions like religious political parties. The biggest category of religion news was religious political parties (15 per cent), followed by religious public figures (13 per cent), reflecting the public and elite dimensions of the news. Rabbis, another elite, comprised 8 per cent. When the data is broken down, rabbis accounted for 5 per cent in the daily secular press in contrast to 10 per cent in the religious daily press. Rabbis take up a larger percentage of coverage in the Haredi media, which is not surprising given the manifold roles that a rabbi fulfils in community life as, amongst others, mentor, Jewish law instructor, spiritual leader, family adviser and marriage guidance counsellor. Religious institutions comprised 3 per cent (2 per cent in the daily secular press in contrast to 4 per cent in the daily religious press) and religious youth movements 0.6 per cent. But public figures got relatively more attention in the general secular daily press than the religious daily press: 14 per cent compared to nearly 12 per cent. Major rabbinical personalities get covered in the event that they make an important pronouncement, but they are also covered if they make or relate to eccentric Jewish law rulings, for example, a ruling by the Sephardi Chief Rabbi Ovadiah Yosef on whether a Jew may pick his nose on the Sabbath or another that forbade a man from walking between two women.

Religious experience and patterns, including the festival experience, tend to get reported. In the period examined, only the one-day Shavuot holiday occurred, and accounted for 5.3 per cent of all reporting.

Haredim rule the airwaves

There is no proportionate relationship in coverage between the amount of coverage which different Jewish religious streams receive and their size in the population. Haredim, or ultra-Orthodox, account for 43 per cent of total religious coverage even though they account for only 9 per cent of the Israeli Jewish population. Television was even more preoccupied with Haredim (59 per cent) than newspapers. One notable exception was Israel Radio: coverage of Haredim dropped to 10 per cent. For the secular media, there was a preoccupation with Haredim and their impact on Israeli politics and society, and their coverage of the Haredi sector reached 54 per cent in both *Yediot Aharonot* and *Haaretz*. The Haredim are media stars both because of their visibility, with their distinct black garb, and because of their political clout.

The centrality of the Haredi coverage reflects a number of factors. If in the past Haredim withdrew from Israeli public life and delegitimised the creation of the modern secular state of Israel – since they condition it on the arrival of the Messiah – the Haredi parties today are active both at the parliamentary level in encouraging their members to vote – thus assuring governmental budgeting for religious and educational Haredi institutions – and at the governmental level in accepting portfolios in Israel's coalition-style government. The oriental Sephardic Haredi party 'Shas' which originated as a protest both against the dominant European establishment in Israeli public life as well the Ashkenazi or European Haredi 'Agudat Israel' party, which in 2012 has 11 Knesset seats, enjoys a considerable support base among the modern Orthodox and even merely 'traditional' non-strictly religious Jews from an oriental background.

The 16 per cent of press coverage in the content analysis of the modern Orthodox was mostly accounted for by the small circulation *Hatzofe*, which, until the newspaper was later absorbed by the *Mekor Rishon* independent newspaper group, reflected the modern Orthodox viewpoint and was read by that population. About 76 per cent of the total coverage on modern Orthodox appeared in *Hatzofe*. In the two non-religious newspapers, modern Orthodox accounted for 7 per cent (*Yediot Aharonot*) and 12 per cent (*Haaretz*). The proportionately lower amount of religion content concerning modern Orthodox may be explained by the fact that since the 1967 war the modern Orthodox community has become increasingly identified with the nationalist task of settling the Biblical territories of Judea, Samaria and Gaza captured in the war. Its main political parties, the 'Jewish Home' and 'Israel Is Our Home', are taken up today a little less with specifically religious issues like 'who is a Jew' or other legal matters concerning synagogue–state relations. Given that other political parties to the Right, including the ruling Likud, are also taken up with settlement activity – including the implications of an Israeli–Palestinian peace for the existing settlement activity – media focus on specifically the modern Orthodox parties has faded somewhat.

Israeli coverage of religious groups contrasts with the American case. Noteworthy is that, whereas mainline Christians (Roman Catholic and Anglican) received proportionately more coverage in the US elite press than fundamentalists and evangelicals (Ferre, 1980), the reverse is true with Israel, with the modern Orthodox proportionately less covered by media than the

Haredim. The Reform and Conservative communities accounted for only 0.2 per cent and 0.1 per cent respectively. (Twenty-eight per cent of reports examined in the study did not verify which religious stream; 12 per cent comprised more than one stream.)

A focus upon one religious stream was less found in the weekend round-up which is characterised by a lot of background features to the news of the previous week and beyond. The weekend issues found only 21 per cent of weekend content dealt with Haredim as opposed to 42 per cent in daily papers. The contrast between daily and weekend coverage was particularly marked with the non-religious newspapers – 48 per cent of the religion content on the daily issues concerned Haredim in contrast to only 8 per cent in their weekend issues. While the media cover the daily, seemingly repetitive, developments in Haredi politics, it is natural that they do not merit constant in-depth pieces in the weekend issues.

Religion content in the Israeli media is Israel-centred; 78 per cent concerned Israel. Only 5 per cent of religion coverage dealt with Jewish religion overseas (17 per cent undefined). Religion coverage in Israel is, therefore, geographically proximate. Notwithstanding the ties between Israelis and the Diaspora, and in particular with the Jewish communities of North America and West Europe, Israeli audiences are taken up with their own concerns and generally fail to follow the happenings in the Diaspora communities, with possible exception of such 'conflictual' news as antisemitic incidents.

Jews are news

The focus is overwhelmingly with coverage of the Jewish religion. A correlation has been suggested between the size of particular religious communities existing in a particular place and the size of media coverage which the group receives (Ferre, 1980; Hart, Turner and Knupp, 1980). Thus, Buddenbaum (1986) found that Jews comprised 7.1 per cent of religion content in the *New York Times* in contrast to 3.5 per cent in the *Minneapolis Star* and 4.2 per cent in the *Richmond News-Telegraph*, Virginia. Similarly, nearly half of the coverage of *Minneapolis Star* concerned Lutherans and just over a fifth of the *Times-Despatch* concerned Baptists, reflecting that Minneapolis was the headquarters of the American Lutheran Church and that Jerry Fallwell, a Baptist, had his headquarters in Virginia. In the Israel study, Islam and Christianity were regarded as far less newsworthy; 0.4 per cent of content comprised Christianity and 1 per cent comprised Islam. Non-monotheistic religions like Buddhism and Hinduism were beyond the Israeli media's periscope.

It is nevertheless surprising that Islam received such a low figure given that out of Israel's total population of 6,370,000 (Central Bureau of Statistics) Muslim Arabs account for 970,000 and represent a significant section of the Israeli population – with its attendant political implications. Although the Christian community amounting to 135,000 souls is relatively small and declining, the low figure for media coverage of Christianity is also surprising given that Israel and the Palestinian Authority are home to key places of Christian faith in Jerusalem, Nazareth and Bethlehem. Most of the limited non-Jewish coverage occurred in the newspapers (1.6 per cent). Christianity and Islam featured even less in radio (1 per cent) or television (0.4 per cent). With the exception of Judaism, the Garrett-Medill US study also found that the press were incrementally inclined more than television to cover minority religions: 64 per cent of television religion content comprised Christianity in contrast to 59 per cent of newspaper coverage. Similarly, Islam received 9 per cent in television in contrast to 14 per cent in the press, where also Buddhism and Hinduism each received 2 per cent. In the aftermath of 9/11, Islam received more attention in the US media.

The findings about the non-Jewish religions in Israeli media content contrast with the Garrett-Medill study where the dominant Christian faith comprised only 52 per cent of religion content, compared to 19 per cent Judaism, 15 per cent Islam, 2 per cent Buddhism and 1 per cent Hinduism (other 11 per cent). The dominant place of the Jewish religion in media coverage reflects the ethnocentrism which characterises Israeli-Jewish discourse, and the religious origins of the modern state of Israel.

The Israeli media is therefore lacking in coverage of religion particularly for Israeli Arabs, for whom interest in religion content concerns Islam. Jemayel (2006, p. 133), examining Israeli Arab readership patterns, found that of the 36 per cent of Israeli Arabs who read Israeli Hebrew newspapers only 17 per cent read them on a regular basis. Forty-five per cent of Israeli Arabs who do not read the Israeli Hebrew press do not do so because of lack of interest. It was not surprising that regarding religion content, Jemayel found that only 20 per cent of Israeli Arabs are interested in religion content in the Israeli Hebrew media, with 80 per cent expressing no interest. It contrasts with 82 per cent, 79 per cent, 79 per cent, 74 per cent and 65 per cent of Israeli Arabs who expressed interest in reading Israeli Hebrew media content on politics, society, health, economics and culture, respectively.

Given the limited and selective coverage of non-Jewish religious news, it needs to be asked whether Israeli editors are correct in the low estimate of interest of their audiences. Hoover (1998) found that interest of audiences in 'religions other than your own' scored in ninth place (4.01) out of 16, higher than such other topics as ecumenism, faith experiences and American religious movements.

Israel's religious media are even less interested in non-Jewish religions. There was a higher percentage in the secular press (2.4 per cent), particularly in the quality paper *Haaretz,* than in the religious press (1.5 per cent), underlining an exclusivist Jewish undercurrent which pervades the religious media. Indeed, the religious media believe that it is inappropriate to be seen to be giving recognition to non-Jewish religions. Similarly, the Haredi media also fail to relate to the non-Orthodox streams like Conservative or Reform except to denigrate them.

The perpetual threat of a change in the secular–religious status quo in a country where religious parties seek to impose certain standards such as

Sabbath observance or matters of personal status including marriage and divorce and conversion is good copy, particularly given the inbuilt conflict element in the story. But media proprietors and editors feel that too much attention to religion may alienate audiences.

Ethical constraints

There is a long history of pressures upon the Israeli media. There is no tradition of complete freedom in Israel to the extent that there is, for example, in the United States. The media are susceptible to restraint whether imposed from above such as from public or official institutions, or ethical restraints and societal influences. Most visible are institutional restraints since, and even prior to, state independence, in 1948. Against the background of the threats to Israel from neighbouring Arab states – with Egypt becoming the first Arab state to recognise Israel only in 1976 – Israeli editors were inclined to accept not only the stringencies of Israeli military censorship regarding the non-publication of sensitive military information but also to accede requests from the senior political echelon, including the Prime Minister and Defence Minister, not to publish certain matters. For example, oil supplies from Iran in the period of the Shah, even though not a narrowly military subject, could not be disclosed lest it embarrass the Shah in the Arab world, and result in Iran being pressured to cut oil supplies. But since the military intelligence surprise which preceded the outbreak of the 1973 Arab–Israeli war, the Israeli press has become critical and independent from external pressures. The Israel Press Council acts as a forum for debate including on certain religion-related questions. Israeli broadcasting is more inclined than the press to ethical pressures. Until 1965 Israel Radio was a department within the Prime Minister's Office. Since then, radio and later television adopted the BBC-type public broadcasting model, implying that broadcasting fulfils a social responsibility role. A public board comprising representatives of political parties (including religious parties) and public figures supervises broadcasting policy at the first and second television channels and Israel radio. With the growing political clout over the last 30 years of religious parties, their influence is felt. Notwithstanding this, the so-called Nakdi Guide – a collection of guidelines produced for the Broadcasting Authority by journalist Nakdimon Rogel – shows little concern with religious matters.

But ethical constraints are embedded within the Israeli society including the country's journalistic profession. Underwood (2001), examining Canadian journalists, found that moral and ethical values are closely connected to the wider Christian Tradition. While restraints in the Israeli general media – as distinct from the religious media – do not originate from narrow Jewish legal rulings halakhah, in a wider sense Jewish solidarity does exist. For example, the Israeli media are hesitant to publish news which may endanger the emigration of Jews from closed countries like Iran, Syria and Yemen. To be true, the media, with the exception of the Haredi media, function in accordance with Western democratic values – as distinct from Jewish values. And, for example, religious figures like rabbis come under the scrutiny of the media within the framework of the right to know. Yet, Western ethical conduct has been influenced by the monotheistic faiths, and the standards of behaviour for interpersonal relations discussed in biblical literature, including such questions as the public image of the individual. More specifically, religious related ethical concerns which impact on media behaviour include, for example, the broadcasting of pornography, blasphemous matters about God and religious symbols, and the question of broadcasting on the holy Sabbath.

The balance between the freedom of expression and the right to privacy has emerged also in the case of matters concerning the presentation of religion and religious people. When Dor Zadik, a religious-looking Haredi man, was photographed by *Haaretz*'s chief photographer, Alex Levac, with a stand with religious books in the Dizengoff shopping mall in Tel Aviv against a poster of a woman in a sexually suggestive pose wearing close fitting pants and standing with legs apart, the man sued *Haaretz* saying that the photo contradicted his world view and was tantamount to an invasion of privacy.[1] Accepting that it was an invasion of privacy, the Judge said 'he shows a man in a setting – not a particularly religious setting – in contrast to, say, were it to show him at the Western Wall or at a religious wedding. It could be said', the judge added, that 'the photo shows somebody who, while caring about religious matters at home, does not both in secular settings about the laws of modesty'. But while he would have awarded him 30,000 shekels, the judge only awarded Zadik 20,000 shekels because the man failed to choose a respectable background against which to set up his stand to distribute his religious books. However, *Haaretz*, appealing the verdict argued that the public interest in the photo justified any infringement of privacy. 'The photo crossed the hurdle of public interest and served to document Israeli social reality,' said the judges. The photo expresses co-existence between different social sectors in Israel society when these are diametrically opposite world views and when one side strenuously objects to the public expression of the views of the other. In accepting *Haaretz*'s appeal, the court also ordered Zadik to pay *Haaretz*'s legal costs of 15,000 shekels.[2]

The case for the right to know is more acute in the case of individuals who hold public office, given the public's basic right to be informed in order to make decisions. By virtue of putting themselves forward for public office individuals become subject to public scrutiny. The media thus fulfil a social responsibility role. If a rabbi, who by definition has exhorted his followers to a higher spiritual standard, fails to live up to that standard, it becomes a matter of public interest. Three cases of rabbis – each of which produced contrasting media spin – will be examined. The allegation by a *Maariv* investigation that Rabbi Shlomo Aviner, a leading modern Orthodox rabbi who headed a leading yeshiva, had sexually molested two women was widely dismissed as journalistic invention. But when not dissimilar charges came up with another widely esteemed rabbi, Rabbi Motti Elon, greater credibility was attached partly because the charges were levelled by a forum of rabbis rather than a newspaper. And when a newspaper revealed that the country's chief rabbi, Rabbi Yonah Metzger, had stayed at hotels at widely reduced charges, the rabbi who generated little public respect – the allegations were accepted by the public.

1. In October 2005 the Second television Channel reported that Ashkenazi Chief Rabbi Yonah Metzger and his family stayed at a Jerusalem hotel for the religious holidays including Passover at a symbolic price 'covering the meals, and the rooms were free'. As a state religious judge (*dayan*) there was the fear of a clash of interests by somebody who had taken favours. After the police investigation found a basis on which to bring charges against Metzger, the Attorney General suggested that, while there was no legal basis to forcing him to dismiss himself unless he was found guilty, it would be appropriate that Metzger should dismiss himself until the completion of the court proceedings. Said the attorney-general, 'the position of chief rabbi should broadcast absolute integrity. Any stain or suspicion to a person of this post is very sensitive. The more senior and serious a position of somebody who is also suspect of criminal deeds, the more he should voluntarily dismiss himself from his position, and by definition the role of chief rabbi fits this definition'. But he refused. Metzger was a controversial appointment as chief rabbi. The support base of the chief rabbinate was the modern Orthodox – which sought to endorse the Zionist state with its spiritual religious appendage. The state rabbinate was neither the darling of the secular or ultra-Orthodox population. The secular opposed the interventionist behaviour of religious authority in civil matters in Israel, and the ultra-Orthodox had their own rabbinical leaders. To be true, Metzger had been the candidate of the ultra-Orthodox in the elections for chief rabbi – a process involving public figures and religious figures voting him in – which sought, successfully, to abort the selection of another candidate of the modern Orthodox sector. Yet, further media embarrassment followed. In July 2008 *Maariv* disclosed that Metzger was accustomed to taking numerous private trips abroad to numerous countries which were sponsored by Jewish businessmen to advance their local political and commercial interests – sometimes in collision with those of the local Jewish community. Following an investigation by the Attorney-General of the exposé, Metzger was instructed to fly only with the approval of the Prime Minister's Office. Just a month earlier, the same newspaper reported that while attending a conference, Metzger asked a French photographer to go to his hotel room and lie naked on his bed.

2. A contrasting case was that of Rabbi Shlomo Avener, the charismatic head of a leading Jerusalem yeshiva, 'Ateret Cohanim'. A cover story of its weekend magazine, entitled '*Yetzer Hora*', or 'Evil Inclination', *Maariv* claimed that Aviner – who counselled hundreds of women over the year regarding religious and personal matters – had allegedly molested two women. The five-page story – which drew on taped testimony of the two women – began: 'Many years they kept to themselves the secret ... they turned to almost every important rabbi they knew. But when the rabbis

joined together in a wall of silence, the two women concluded that exposure will deliver.' One headline read 'Intimate relations that had sexual molestation'. The article described how the rabbi, who is known for his conservative views on any contacts between men and women outside of marriage, was reported to have sat physically close to the women he counselled, in one case opposite the Western Wall plaza. He would ask the women to describe her intimate experiences and feelings to her husband; at one occasion he said 'Tonight you will be together, and I will come to inspect'. In another case, one of the women said that 'when I had sexual intercourse with my husband, he wanted to know. When I declined, he persisted, "What are you ashamed of me?"' He would call her after 10 at night, saying, she said, 'I love to hear your childish voice'. He would sign letters to them with 'your love'.[3]

Public reaction was one of amazement. The newspaper's claims were rejected by his immediate followers and more widely in the modern religious camp. Aviner's home settlement imposed a ban on the *Maariv* newspaper. The rabbi's standing in the modern religious population withstood the media storm – which speaks as much about the media standing in the religious population as about Aviner himself. The newspaper subsequently published an independent examination which refuted the original allegations. And, in 2010 a senior religious court in Jerusalem, chaired by Chief Rabbi Yonah Metzger, turned down an appeal by one of the women who had made the original allegations, accepting Aviner's explanations that his references to 'lover' were meant as to how she was seen in her husband's eyes, and that when he appeared to sit touching her it was unintentional 'while he had tried to reach a certain object'.[4] When later asked for his reaction, Aviner declined to react to the newspaper's allegations, saying merely that to do so would itself amount to a transgression of the religious law. This was not surprising since Aviner had written an essay years earlier in *Iturei Cohanim* (No. 81), the monthly journal of his yeshiva, in which he concluded that it was forbidden to read newspapers given that they infringed Jewish religious law by publishing gossip for motives of self-profit rather than primarily for the public good.

3 A similar case which had a different ending from the Aviner case was that of Rabbi Motti Elon, who had allegedly molested students or even had a homosexual relationship. An educator in the modern religious sector, Elon had headed a leading Jerusalem yeshiva, Yeshiva Hakotel, where his charismatic personality drew thousands to hear his weekly *shiurim* on the weekly Bible reading. Beforehand he was principal of the elite private Horev boys' high school in Jerusalem. The scion of a leading family – his father had served as deputy president of the Israel Supreme Court, and a brother was a Knesset member – he had been tipped as a future chief rabbi.

What differentiated the Aviner and Elon cases was that while the Aviner case was the result of a secular newspaper disclosure, the allegations about

Elon came to light by an unofficial clearing house comprising leading rabbis and educators in the modern religious sector – named Takana – which had been set up to deal with sexual molestation in the modern religious sector.

In 2006 Takana took up the allegations privately with Elon. He subsequently left public life, moving from Jerusalem to a northern Israeli village. To Takana's credit, it was surprising that no rumour about the allegations reached out to the public or the media. However, Elon continued later with some of his *shiurim* from his new habitat, and Takana as a result decided to go public with their allegations. When Takana went public the story filled newspapers from the mainstream Israeli media for days. One headline rang, 'An earthquake in the modern religious community'. As more details came out after the first reports, *Yediot Aharonot* ran with a headline: 'The rabbi requested that I strip. I trembled.'[5]

The allegations created a crisis in the modern religious sector. That Takana included leading rabbis like Rabbi Aaron Lichtenstein and Rabbi Yaacov Ariel added to the legitimacy of the body and its standing. The matter became more complicated after a feminist religious group, Kollek, which belonged to Takana, resigned from the body, claiming that Takana ought to have acted more vigorously earlier as well as stop Elon's teaching activities from his new habitat in the north of the country. The fact that the allegations came from a body which included leading rabbis meant that the allegations were taken seriously. One problem was that Takana refused to disclose the details of the complaints they had received, but simply stated that Elon had been asked not to give *shiurim*, and after Elon did not carry out this, Takana went public to reveal the ban it had placed on Elon. But it failed to respond to calls to provide information justifying its ban on Elon. 'We have our style,' Yehudit Shilat, a Takana member, said in a *Mekor Rishon* interview.[6] 'We are people who abide by Jewish law [an apparent reference to the religious prohibition of *loshon hara* – of disclosing information defamatory on a person – YC]. We are not media people. We have a language that is difficult. What can we do?' Clearly Takana did not evaluate the public and media outcry which would result from its seemingly nebulous announcement – which was intended to warn the public by saying that Elon failed to adhere it its calls. 'We never realized the noise and mess the disclosure caused,' Shilat admitted. 'So it took one or two days until the public was able to listen to us and we were able to speak. We did not have public relations advisers. Perhaps we ought to have had.'[7] Elon himself – like Aviner earlier – did not respond and take the public relations offensive, citing a religious prohibition of causing a *hilul hashem* (or damaging the image of the entire religious community in the eyes of the wider Israeli public) which could be caused were he to respond to Takana's announcement. Press commentators, such as Dan Margalit of *Yisrael Hayom* and compère of a daily evening news television show, questioned Takana's standing and said that only the police had the right to investigate such allegations. There were even calls for the government's legal adviser to order a police inquiry. Indeed, months later the police brought charges against Elon.

Youngsters in the modern religious sector did not believe the allegations about the mythical rabbi figure and went through a process of self-denial of the news. The two newspapers identified with the modern religious sector handled the crisis in different ways. *Mekor Rishon* took a liberal stance, covering the story in its varied manifestations. It spent over ten pages on the subject in its weekend edition after the affair broke out. This included a column from the Minister of Science, who headed one of the modern religious political parties. Yet, intimate details of how a yeshiva student was allegedly asked by the rabbi to lower his underpants, which was covered in the general media, was not covered by *Mekor Rishon*. Moreover, it was subsequently disclosed by the paper that *Mekor Rishon* had known about the allegations before the affair exploded, as did a couple of other religious journalists such as Yifat Erlich.[8] By contrast, *BaSheva*, the weekly identified with stricter sub-stream, *hardal* or Haredi leumi, covered the allegation with a single report, relating to it with a sense of embarrassment and underriding scepticism about the allegations.

While the allegations concerning Aviner, Elon and Metzger are in the public interest, it may be asked how far may the media go in disclosing the lives of public officials. What – if any – of their lives is sacred? That they have chosen to 'inject' themselves into the public sphere implies a commitment to undergo public scrutiny. It was wholly unjustified to disclose the juicy romance of the Chief Rabbi Amar's daughter Ayala – with the exception, which was ignored, of whether the chief rabbi, a public appointee, knew about or was involved in his son kidnapping his daughter's suitor or was present when he was subsequently brought to his the rabbi's house? Janaway (1993, p. 50) argues that there is confusion regarding the rights and rules of privacy. For many journalists the conflict between the right to know and the right to privacy becomes simply a question of what is newsworthy. There is little about the lives of public people that remains sacred. When Barack Obama, then a US presidential candidate, visited the Middle East during his electioneering campaign in 2008 and placed a prayer message – as many do – in the 'Kotel', the Western Wall in Jerusalem, its contents were subsequently disclosed by *Maariv* – after a yeshiva student removed the message from the Wall and gave it to one of the paper's reporters. It read, 'Lord – protect my family and me. Forgive my sins, and help me guard against pride and despair. Give me the wisdom, to do what is right and just. And, make me an instrument of your will.'[9] The rabbi of the Western Wall, Rabbi Shmuel Rabinowitz described as 'sacrilegious the removal of the note. Notes placed in the Kotel are between the person and his Maker. Heaven forbid that one should read them or use them'. Obama said it was private conversation between him and God. Before the Attorney-General could decide whether or not to open a police investigation, the yeshiva student returned the prayer note to the Kotel. *For Maariv*, it was newsworthy because it was interesting. But was there a public interest in disclosing Obama's private beliefs? Or do the American public not have a right to know what influences an American presidential candidate, which includes the nature of his religious beliefs? If not, was *Maariv*'s disclosure an infringement of Obama's privacy?

The media have a legitimising role in society and the public trusts the media to set norms. Yet, Olen argues that if journalists are our representatives then their moral rights are no greater than our own (Olen, 1988, p. 71). The lack of clarity about the media's rights and obligations in this regard reflects not only confusion within the media but also confusion and weakness in the audience – which ought to reject journalists' criteria that what is of interest is itself enough to justify the media writing about something.

Rabbis and scandals – a poll

Rabbis – often the subject of media attention – not only reject the media's appetite for scandal but even legitimate coverage of these. In order to generate a picture of rabbis' attitudes to the publication in the media of information about scandals involving rabbis, a survey of rabbis from different streams was carried out by the author (300 filled responses).[10] There is no consensus between rabbis whether information about scandals should be published: Haredi rabbis opposing most, and non-Orthodox rabbis favouring most. All rabbis thought that it was less desirable that such disclosure should be done in the religious media than in the general media. But while rabbis feared that such information caused a *hilul hashem*, they did acknowledge that it had a deterring effect on other rabbis.

Rabbis were questioned on whether immoral deeds by rabbis should be reported in the media. The media was broken between the general media and the religious media. Wide differences were found among rabbis from different religious streams regarding whether scandals should be published in the general media. While only 10 per cent, 8 per cent and 5 per cent of Haredi rabbis 'strongly agreed', 'agreed a lot' or 'agreed' that these should be published, 25 per cent, 22 per cent and 12 per cent of modern Orthodox rabbis did. Yet modern Orthodox rabbis were broken down between mainstream modern Orthodox and the stricter Haredi leumi or *hardal* substream. Wide differences were found to the point where *hardal* was much more near to Haredi than to modern Orthodox. Thus, 46 per cent of mainstream modern Orthodox favoured strongly or very strongly that such matters should be covered in the general media as opposed to 14 per cent of hardal substream (Haredi 13 per cent). Twenty-five per cent of hardal did not agree at all in contrast to 12 per cent of modern Orthodox, and 35 per cent of hardal agreed to only a little extent in contrast to 18 per cent of modern Orthodox.

Fifty-seven per cent, 30 per cent and 13 per cent of non-Orthodox rabbis 'strongly agreed', 'agreed a lot' or 'agreed' that scandals involving rabbis should be reported by the general media. Little difference was found between Reform and Conservative.

Asked whether these matters should only be published in religious media, and not in the general media, in order to avoid a *hilul hashem* rabbis were not inclined to favour publication of these matters even in the religious media. Rather, they thought that, given the religious media's role in community-building and more specifically as the media were suitable for the Jewish family, these disclosures should not appear in the religious media. Fifty-four per cent and 33 per cent of Haredi and modern Orthodox rabbis 'definitely disagreed' and 14 per cent and 24 per cent of Haredi and modern Orthodox rabbis 'disagreed to a great extent' that news about such deeds should be reported in the religious media.

There was a greater consensus between mainstream modern religious and hardal rabbis that these matters should not be limited to only 'religious media'. Thus only 10 per cent of modern Orthodox 'favoured strongly' and none 'very strongly' to publicise these matters only in religious media (in contrast to 46 per cent who favoured publishing it in the general media). Thirty-eight per cent of mainstream modern religious opposed publishing these in religious media (as opposed to 12 per cent who opposed in general media). There was a trend for Reform rabbis to favour more than Conservative rabbis not to publish this information in religious media.

Thirty-three per cent and 15 per cent of Haredi and modern Orthodox rabbis agreed to 'a very great extent' and 'to a great extent' that the reporting of immoral deeds committed by rabbis besmirched the image of the entire religious community in the eyes of the wider Israeli public. *Hardal* rabbis were increasingly less inclined than mainstream modern Orthodox to think that publicity of such deeds reflects badly on the entire religious community – which suggests that the *hardal* are less apologetic and cared less about their image. The mainstream modern Orthodox were more sensitive to the image of religion and religious groups among the wider public: 58 per cent of mainstream modern Orthodox believed 'strongly' or 'very strongly' that such coverage reflects badly on the whole community in contrast to 35 per cent of hardal.

Eighteen per cent and 20 per cent of non-Orthodox rabbis believed so 'to a very great extent', and 'to a great extent'. Conservative rabbis (58 per cent) were more inclined than Reform rabbis (36 per cent) to think that such publicity 'strongly' or 'very strongly' harmed the image of religion among the broader public. Yet even the Reform rabbis (40 per cent) thought that it damaged it (Conservative 15 per cent).

All rabbis believe that such publicity contributes to deterring rabbis from carrying out such deeds. Seventy-six per cent of Orthodox rabbis and 62 per cent of non-Orthodox rabbis believe such publicity deterred other rabbis 'to some extent', 'to a great extent' or 'to a very great extent'. Reform rabbis (56 per cent) were incrementally more inclined than Conservative rabbis (36 per cent) to say that such publicity strongly or very strongly damaged. Rabbis born in Arab countries were less inclined (35 per cent) than other groups to believe that such publicity strongly or very strongly deterred Rabbis.

Ideology, consensus and censorship

Through legislation, ethics have become concretised to enjoy legal binding force. Censorship may be seen as the institutionalised ethical norms. In practice, ethics is also subject to the political whims and ramifications of government and political party policy-making. This is particularly so in a country like Israel where government does not comprise one party but a coalition bloc of parties. Moreover, what is considered acceptable behaviour is subject to different interpretations – by the Knesset, political parties and the public and the Supreme Court. Whereas decisions by the Knesset are the sum total of pressures of different political parties, the Supreme Court stands by the statute book. Three varying examples of censorship show how the outcomes varied according to different constellations. The following examples of decisions and pressures at the legal, political and public spheres contrast between political interference in the public broadcasting concerning media broadcasting on the Sabbath, religious pressures on irreverence at religion in broadcast content, and how the Israeli Supreme Court approaches broadcasting pornography and the Knesset.

At a primitive level, certain Haredi groups have sought to stop the secular media from appearing on the streets. Rabbi Ovadiah Yosef termed the secular media 'licentious and using inappropriate language' and forbade his followers from exposing themselves to secular media.[11] Accordingly, in a strict sense, one who sells newspapers are causing others to sin. In one case Avigdor Nebentzahl, the rabbi of the Jewish Quarter of Jerusalem's Old City – a stone's throw from the Kotel, the Western Wall – asked stores in the Quarter not to sell secular newspapers – some heeded, others did not.[12] In another case, a Haredi group, 'Keshet', attempted to set on fire in 1990 two stores in the religious city of Benei Beraq which sold secular papers.[13] Another instance was when the Israel Broadcasting Authority moved its management to a new renovated building in 1992, which was situated near to the hassidic Belze community, community leaders applied pressure abortively against the move. In another instance, a programme on a Jerusalem radio station dealing with sexual related matter, and presented by a leading sexologist from the city's main Hadassah Hospital, was cancelled after the city's religious affairs council threatened to withdraw the kashrut certificate from a hotel, in whose premises the radio station was based.[14]

Damaging a religion or religious figures is a breach of Israeli law. Going back already to the British mandate, and the Abuse and Vilification Order, passed in 1929 following Arab riots, there is a one-year jail sentence for a person who 'publishes an advertisement that blatantly offends the faith or religious sensitivities of others' or 'states in public and within range of a given person a word or sound that blatantly offends his faith or religious sensitivities of others'.

In one sense greater sensitivity has sometimes been shown towards non-Jewish religions than the Jewish religion which is regarded as home territory or open game. For example, a person was sentenced to a two-year jail term in 1977 after carrying a flyer depicting a pig wrapped in a *kaffiyeh* and treading on an open book, with the word Mohammed written on the pig and Koran on the book.

Ironically, when the affair involving the Danish cartoon of Prophet Mohammed erupted, the Israeli media and public were not unduly concerned – either at the insult to Mohammed or to the question of the right of self-expression. Rather, the focus of the Israeli media in the Danish cartoon episode concerned the extremities of the protests in the Islamic world and on hatred of Israel. After all, Jews were often targets of anti-Semitism in the Arab press. For example, the religious *Hamodia* newspaper, in an editorial, 'Behind Cartoon Anger', opined that

> perhaps an irresponsible and dangerous act was committed by the Danish newspaper. At the same time, the behavior of the mobs, who torched Scandinavian embassies in certain Arab capitals cannot be defended in anyway. These protests are clearly not the spontaneous reactions of an aggrieved people. They are the result of a well-planned, determined effort by individuals and governments bent on fomenting violence.[15]

Yet there have also been cases where attacks on Judaism and Jewish figures are generated vehement reactions inside the country. For example, a stand-up comic Gil Kopatch had a regular spot in the late-1990s on Friday nights with a high ratings show with Yair Lapid, broadcast on the first television channel, in which he gave the weekly Bible reading in the synagogue an irreverent and contemporary social interpretation, bringing out the human foibles of the Biblical character. In one case, the matriarch Sarah was presented by Kopatch as light headed, and humour laden, who makes the life of her Egyptian maid, Hagar, a misery before firing her. In another programme in 1996, drawing upon the Biblical verse that 'Noah drank the wine, and was drunken; and he was uncovered within his tent', Kopatch said that Noah was 'not only bombed out of his mind, he probably danced in his tent and did a striptease. Ham saw his father's nakedness. Apparently, Noah was a bit of an exhibitionist. He liked dancing with his willy hanging out. The amazing thing in this is that he was about 600 years old. Ham saw and got a shock. You ask yourself, what's so shocking about the willy of a 600-year-old man? And Ham, of all people, who was the ancestral father of the blacks.'

Religious members of the Knesset called for Kopatch's weekly segment to be cancelled from the programme. The Knesset's Education Committee held a discussion. 'Kopatch is trampling with arrogance and contempt on every Jewish feeling, everything sacred,' Shlomo Benizri, a Knesset member for the Shas religious party, fumed. Religious parties lobbied the Prime Minister's Office, which is responsible for appointing the director-general of the broadcasting authority; its director-general, Avigdor Lieberman, said that while he liked satire, this crossed the boundaries of expression. Imagine what would happen if such a skit was made about the *Koran* or Christian beliefs.[16] To be true, a 1965 Knesset law gave the broadcasting authority control over editorial content. But secular politicians responded that the religious bloc was robbing them of the right of self-expression. Responding to his critics Kopatch said that 'religion is the bureaucracy of faith. It is my right to comment in the way I want to. Nobody can tell me what to think. God wants thinking people, not those who follow their rabbi without asking questions. God exists among us – but not exactly – because God is ultimately humanity plus one.'[17] To be true, Lapid's programme was broadcast on the Sabbath when Orthodox Jews refrain from watching television, so the slight was less hurtful. But religious defenders would counter that the fact that Kopatch's remarks are broadcast on the holy Sabbath added salt to the wound. Rather, the Kopatch affair became another ball in the secular–religious battlefield in Israel. A public opinion poll found wide differences existed among Israeli Jews about the Kopatch spot: 49 per cent of religious Israelis, 27 per cent of traditional Israeli Jews and 17 per cent of secular Israeli Jews said that the spot should be cancelled from the programme, whereas 70 per cent of secular Israeli Jews, 60 per cent of traditional Jews and 24 per cent of religious Jews said there was no need to cancel the segment.[18]

Two case studies – the question of Sabbath broadcasting and access to pornography on cable television in Israel – are policy questions which periodically return to the public agenda in Israel, and are illustrative in examining the reactions and pressure of the various sides to the respective dispute.

Thou shall not broadcast on the Sabbath

The broadcasting of radio and television on the Sabbath in the Jewish state has come up at different times in the country's history. In light of the public controversy over Sabbath broadcasting, it is useful to examine Israeli public behavior on the subject. 65% of Israeli Jews in 2009 watched television or listened to the radio on the Sabbath.[19] The Haredim (95%) and the *hardal* substream (87%) of modern Orthodox never watch television or listen to radio on the Sabbath. In addition, the overwhelming number of modern orthodox or *dati leumi* are estimated to also never look at television or listen to radio on the Sabbath. Men were slightly more inclined (27%) than women (23%). And, oriental Sephardi were more inclined to reply never (34%) than Ashkenazim (7%) – an allusion to the oriental Jew's conformity to tradition.

For many the watching of television or listening radio is not regarded by them as an infringement of the Sabbath. Thus of those who always light candles on the Sabbath eve or recite the *kiddush* blessing over the wine at the Friday night festival meal only 43% and 47% never watch television or listen to radio on the Sabbath. In contrast to 65% who television watching or radio listening, for example, surfing the Internet on the Sabbath was done by 52%.

The religious political parties – in particular the modern religious parties rather than the ultra-Orthodox ones – have addressed the issue, regarding public broadcasting on the Sabbath as an infringement of Jewish religious law. In accord with the biblical prohibition against work on the Sabbath, *halakhah* (Jewish religious law) prohibits the usage of electricity on the Sabbath, including electronic media like radio and television. Theoretically, broadcasting could be permitted if the radio or television were preset with a time device to function on the Sabbath, and programmes themselves are produced prior to the Sabbath.

The difference between the modern religious parties and the Haredi parties is that the latter oppose television in its entirety – coining it 'the impure vessel' – and have even organised street demonstrations outside television headquarters in Jerusalem. As much effort was made by Haredi rabbis into ensuring that fellow Haredim did not fix up to television antennas than to the question of television broadcasting for the general population. The large antennas which characterised television installation in the 1960s and 1970s on roof tops enabled Haredi leaders to locate 'transgressors' inside their communities; lists of Haredim who had installed television were published and they were lobbied to remove them otherwise they would be exorcised from the community. By contrast, the modern religious – which seek to synthesise religious values with modernity as well as disciplined exposure to the entertainment media – are not against television per se but address specific issues like broadcast content and Sabbath broadcasting. They regard broadcasting on the Sabbath as inappropriate to the religious face of the Jewish state. The question of Sabbath observance in public places was a bandwagon of the now extinct National Religious Party (NRP) in its platform to stamp a Jewish religious imprint on the Jewish state. According to its party programme, it sought to cancel television on the Sabbath and religious holidays – a decision which ignores traditional Jewish values, the heritage of the majority. To be true, the NRP, like other religious parties, objected not only to television broadcasting but also to radio on the Sabbath, but their clout was more limited given that radio began already during the British Mandate, and had garnered for itself an important position for Israelis as a supplier of information in a country at conflict.

In addition to the political parties, various religious individuals and extra-parliamentary groups have over the years lobbied in various ways against Sabbath broadcasting, including in the Israeli courts to the level of the Supreme Court, in the governing councils of the broadcasting authorities, on the pages of religious media and even street demonstrations. For example, in 1993, after Israel Education Television – a public channel – began broadcasting on the Sabbath eve and Saturday, an NRP MK petitioned the Supreme Court arguing that religious audiences would be discriminated against by not being able to view certain programming which was broadcast during the Sabbath, and demanded that broadcasts be moved to weekdays. In 2010 a group petitioned the Supreme Court that the military radio station, Galei Zahal – which belongs to, and is financed, by the Ministry of Defence – should desist from broadcasting for the 24 hours of the Sabbath, from Friday eve to the termination of the Sabbath on Saturday night. The group argued that Galei Zahal should cease its Sabbath broadcasts since General Staff regulations allow only for military operations on the Sabbath in the Israeli Army deemed essential to the security of the state to be carried out. In the end, the Galei Zahal commander and the group discussed ways to limit Sabbath desecration such as by not using soldiers, but civilians, on the Sabbath and by recording programmes prior to the Sabbath. In 2002 a religious party MK demanded that a popular foreign news magazine programme 'Seeing the World', which was broadcast on Channel 1 on Saturday night, be moved from its time slot which in summer time fell prior to the termination of the Sabbath, to a time after the Sabbath in order to enable also the religious population to watch the programme. When the Eurovision Song Contest was held in Israel in May 1999, religious MKs protested that final rehearsals were held on the Sabbath. Over the years, a number of live interviews scheduled with prime ministers for Friday night – peak viewing time in Israel – were moved following pressure from religious party MKs. And, in 2001 a group of four religious people who were interviewed for a programme which was scheduled to broadcast in the Sabbath unsuccessfully appealed to the Supreme Court against its broadcast time during the Sabbath. The court president, Judge Sharon Barak, argued that hurting the religious sensitivities of the four did not undermine the boundaries of mutual tolerance and that it was a price to be paid for living in a democratic society where religious and secular live side by side. But in a minority opinion, Judge Dalia Dorner said that the four would be directly affected by being parties to Shabbat desecration, against their will.[20]

The inauguration of Israel Television

Two major struggles for and against Sabbath broadcasts occurred in 1968 shortly after the founding of Israel Television, and following the 1990 Gulf War, during which emergency broadcasting was introduced for the duration of the war. Ahead of the opening of regular television broadcasting in Israel in 1969, the National Religious Party conditioned joining the Labour coalition government, headed by Prime Minister Golda Meir – which sought the party's support after Labour failed to win an overwhelmingly majority in the November 1969 general election. Anxious to win the support of the National Religious Party, Meir acceded to the party's demands and turned to the broadcasting authority requesting that the Friday night broadcasts scheduled after the beginning of the Sabbath be broadcast earlier in the evening prior to the Sabbath commencement, and that Saturday broadcasts be later after the termination of the Sabbath. But broadcasting authority heads said that only its governing council – and not the government – were empowered to make such a decision. With the exception of council members representing religious parties, the council, comprising 31 members from different political parties and from the wider public, threw out Meir's request. The broadcasting authority chairman threatened to resign if Sabbath broadcasting was banned. A debate among the Israeli public and media ensued. 'The key constitutional question is whether in taking into account coalition-building, a government has a right to limit the individual's freedom without having received an express permit to do so from the Knesset,' opined a *Haaretz* editorial.[21] The majority of the public favoured Sabbath broadcasting; a straw poll of 100 people conducted by *Haaretz* found that 77 per cent of people surveyed favoured broadcasts on the Sabbath, 16 per cent opposed them and 7 per cent abstained.[22] The entire matter was determined when one Israeli, Adi Kaplan, and his lawyer Yehuda Resler appealed a Supreme Court Judge Zvi Berenson – on Friday night at the judge's home, who was the Supreme Court judge on weekend roster – for a court order requiring the broadcasting authority to broadcast on the Sabbath. The broadcasting authority was inundated with telephone calls praising the citizen's deeds. Resler was profiled and became a media personality overnight. 'The authority's decision is a decision for common sense. If there is a decision not to broadcast television, one should also ban radio on the Sabbath,' *Haaretz* opined in an editorial printed on the newspaper's front page.[23] A court appeal by the government law adviser to overturn Berenson's ruling – arguing that the weekend injunction was unjustified since such court appeals are really for emergency matters only – was rejected.

The NRP charged that it was a breach of the status quo in religion–state relations. 'The implication of the court's decision is the cancellation of Judaism in the Jewish state,' said an editorial in *Hatzofe*,[24] the NRP's organ. In an op-ed piece in the same paper, Sephardi Chief Rabbi Itzhak Nissim said that there was an intrinsic difference between television and radio. Whereas radio was broadcast immediately, television required considerable preparation, causing desecration of the Sabbath. Nissim attempted to draw a difference between news on radio and the performance of plays on the Sabbath which, Nissim claimed, destroyed the religious spirit of the Sabbath.[25] The NRP, by conditioning its joining the government upon the Sabbath broadcast issue, lost out on an electoral issue of even greater import to that sector: Jewish settlement in the West Bank, regarded by the party as biblical Israeli territory.

Wartime television on the Sabbath

The roles of pro- and anti-Sabbath television were reversed in 1991 when in the aftermath of the Gulf War an opportunity arose – which would bear fruition – for pro-Sabbath television supporters. During the war, when Israel was targeted by 39 Iraqi missiles, the government had used the electronic media as channels to inform the Israeli public of an impending missile attack and of the need for the Israeli population to enter protected areas. With the end of the war, so ended all day Saturday broadcasting, with the exception of the Friday eve and Saturday evening broadcasts. With Saturday the only rest day, the secular majority had over the years felt discriminated in that they were unable to enjoy the full range of public entertainment including television. In an effort to continue all-day broadcasting, the broadcasting authority sought to get around the renewed ban by approving broadcasts for the Israeli Arab population – the justification being that otherwise this population would be exposed to broadcasts from neighbouring Arab countries – which had inciteful content.

But the Communication and Education ministers, Raphael Pinhasi and Zevulun Hammer, who possessed legal powers to approve broadcasting policy changes, refused to approve these broadcasts. The ministers, who each were from religious political parties, Shas and the NRP respectively, suspected that the broadcasts to the Arab populations – programmes which also had Hebrew subtitles – were in fact a camouflage for a range of broadcasts to the Israeli Jewish population as well. The broadcasting authority's director-general, Aryeh Mekel, was anxious that in the growing competition which included the new second television channel, as well as the introduction of cable television, this would lose viewers from the authority's first channel. Left-wing MKs appealed the Supreme Court for an injunction instructing Pinhasi and Hammer to implement the broadcasting authority's decisions to broadcast on the Sabbath 'for the Arab populations'. But Pinhasi and Hammer, in countering the court's action, took the controversial step of persuading members of the broadcasting authority's council management to undo its earlier decision permitting broadcasting for Arab viewers. Finally, in 1993, following general elections in Israel, the new Communications Minister, Moshe Shahal, who belonged to the secular Labour Party, opened the way for broadcasting 'to the Israeli Arab populations', from 10 am on Saturday mornings.

The outcome strengthened the secular interpretation of the day of rest, as including entertainment such as television. The Sabbath television wars deepened the secular–religious divide in Israel. The religious population felt alienated from the majority secular population as something sacred to their identity was desecrated. But the secular had been alienated by the religious coercion, and by the consequent limits on cultural and entertainment on Saturday, their only day of rest. Even if the Sabbath television war was ultimately won by the secular, that religious political parties had deployed coercion – rather than, for example, educational and informational means towards enhancing and generating respect for religious values – widened the secular–religious gap yet further.

There are signs of greater Sabbath observance in Israel. The 2009 Gutman survey reported that 28 per cent of Israelis observe the Sabbath more than in the past (59 per cent no change, 13 per cent less so). This was not only those who said they belonged to the Haredim or modern orthodox: even 32 per cent of Israeli Jews who described themselves as 'traditional' (non-strictly religious) said that they observe the Sabbath more today (56 per cent replied no change, and 12 per cent less). The 65 per cent figure of Israeli Jews who in 2009 watched television or listen to the radio was a decline from 71 per cent in the previous survey of Israeli Jewish religious behaviour carried out ten years beforehand. Of those who said that they were 'much more religious' or 'more religious than in the past', 75 per cent and 41 per cent said that they they never looked at television or listened to the radio on the Sabbath.

Those aged 29–30 were incrementally less likely to watch television or listen to radio on the Sabbath than their peers; 30 per cent in this age group which did not is a gradual increase from, for example, the 71–78 age group in which 19 per cent alone said that they did not.[26] This raises the possibility in the long-term that a majority of Jews may favour no broadcasting on the Sabbath.

No sex please

The differences between the Knesset as a value-setter and decider of standards and that of Courts were found in the controversy over the question of whether pornography should be broadcast on cable channels. With the expansion of cable television in Israel in 2000, pornographic channels arrived in Israel; 30 per cent to 50 per cent of cable subscribers in Israel bought cable packages which also included pornographic channels. A 2001 Nielsen poll found over a quarter of the 13 per cent of all Israelis who visit sex sites on the Internet were aged between 12 and 17.[27] The Knesset in 2001 passed a law under which cable and satellite channels would not be allowed to broadcast sex channels; however, the door was left open to channels of which only a small part of their programming comprised sex programmes. The law was passed easily by 52:10 – not only did the religious political parties vote in favour of the bill but so did Arab parties, which also oppose pornography, as well as feminist Knesset members who backed the bill. The law reduced the number of cable customers for pornography in 2002 by 50 per cent.[28] A year later, in 2002, a law proposal by Zevulun Orlev of the National Religious Party sought to close the loopholes and prohibit all pornographic broadcasting including even channels of which only a part of the programming comprised sexual content. 'I am concerned,' Orlev said, 'about the social effects of the broadcasts on violence against women. This is not a religious law but a law reflecting cultural values, traditional values.' Haredi politicians were less introspective: Quoting the biblical passage of the story of Sodom and Gomorrah, a Shas member of the Knesset said the country is 'full of violence'. 'The country degenerates to new depths and the court allows everything. We do not need to scream but rather women should. Instead of exposing the woman's honour, or external personality, we are exposing her flesh for saturation', he said. With the new law, he added, 'we have saved the youth. It is a pity that all that is left of the Left's liberal values is protecting the right to pornography.' The opponents of the law, including the left-wing Meretz, argued that the campaign against pornography should be via education and public discussion, not censorship. 'Israel', Meretz Abraham Poratz remarked, 'had joined "enlightened" nations like Iran and Afghanistan'.

The same year, 2002, saw that the law was further amended to even include the Playboy channel as also being pornographic. It was passed by 44:20, again by a coalition of religious parties, Arab parties and feminist MKs. But the television cable companies appealed to the courts against the Playboy ban in 2003, and the courts ceded to Playboy with a number of provisos – including that the channel would be aired only from 10 pm to 5 am; and one requiring instructional adverts telling parents how to block the channel from children. Instead of being part of a package, people (over 18) would be required to purchase it individually. Feminist groups appealed the Supreme

Court in 2004 against the court decision, but lost. Notwithstanding the reversal, the law considerably limited the broadcasting of pornography.

But what was achieved through parliamentary scrutiny would have to stand the scrutiny of the law courts. Religious values would make way in favour of values which underlay the Israeli constitution. The ban opened a public debate about how to define pornography. The 2002 amendment had banned the following types of broadcasts: sexual relations that include violence; abuse, 'degradation', humiliation or exploitation; sexual relations with a minor or person perceived as a minor; the presentation of man – and any of his organs – as an available object of sex. Yet this version deleted a ban on 'acts intended to stimulate sexual arousal' and 'content dealing with sex via the presentation of sexual relations'. This version opened a Pandora's box regarding soft porn like the Playboy channel, as opposed to hard porn like the Blue channel. In the end the Cable and Satellite Council, the public body which overlooks cable television channels in Israel, took a stringent view and also banned Playboy, arguing that showing women fully naked had as its main object the sexual arousal of viewers and the presentation of women as 'sex objects'. In the Supreme Court's decision to accept the Playboy appeal and allow it, the 11-judge Supreme Court panel argued that Playboy broadcasts did not suffer from 'objectification' of sex. Hard porn would be banned. Yet, pornographic expression merited the constitutional protection of the right to freedom of expression. 'An expansive approach should be taken in interpretation of the degree of the constitution's extension of the right to freedom of expression, which would not require examination of content and moral judgement of the specific expression. The erotic and pornographic expression including any description of sexual act, minor or major – is no different in this context', wrote Judge Daliah Dorner in the court's majority opinion. But in a minority opinion, Judge Yaacov Turkel wrote that there is room to say that 'programmes that show naked women, not in the framework of a feature film or series depicting a person, a person's organs become an object for sexual use'. But ultimately, all the judges agree that the decision should be reached 'against the background – of the existing reality, which embodies the perspectives of society as to what is permitted or prohibited in it'.[29] It contrasted with the conglomeration of different views represented by the various parties and groups in the Knesset.

Ideology and the Israeli media – the Temple Mount case

The place of ideology in news reporting in Western societies is a controversial subject. The Israeli media, like the media in Western countries as a whole, are characterised by aspirations towards objectivity with a general standard of a separation between facts and comment. In addition to the fact that ideology is most prominent in editorials, op-eds and analytical commentaries, it can be an underlying factor in news reporting itself. Hall (1982) argued that news values should be explained in terms of structural ideological meanings. A case illustrative of ideology entering even reporting was the diplomatic negotiations in 2002 at Camp David concerning the holy places in the city of Jerusalem – which generated reaction in certain sectors of Israeli public opinion. The Temple Mount in Jerusalem's Old City enjoys an important place in Israeli consciousness. With the destruction of the Second Temple in 70 CE and the subsequent Jewish Diaspora, a return to Zion and the rebuilding of the Temple became key motifs in Jewish liturgy.

After the recapture of the Temple Mount by Israeli troops in 1967 re-established Jewish sovereignty over the site for the first time in 1,900 years, Israel handed over administrative control of the Dome of the Rock and the Al-Aqsa mosque to the *Waqf* (Arab Trust), and most Orthodox rabbis banned Jews from visiting the site on grounds of ritual uncleanliness. The only visible remnant of the Temple structure at the time, its western retaining wall (traditionally known as the Wailing Wall), known as the *Kotel*, became the worldwide focus of Jewish spiritual life.

The Jewish public's fixation with the Western Wall as opposed to the Temple Mount proper became the focus of talks at Camp David between US President Bill Clinton, Prime Minister Ehud Barak and Palestinian Chairman Yasser Arafat. The Clinton proposals linked solution of the Palestinian refugee problem to the Temple Mount issue: In return for millions of Palestinian refugees giving up a 'right of return' to family homes in Israel, Israel would surrender the Temple Mount to Palestinian sovereignty. Besides taking over East Jerusalem, the Palestinians would gain control of the Muslim and Christian quarters of the Old City, while the Israelis would retain the Western Wall and the Jewish and Armenian quarters. While his foreign minister supported the Clinton proposal, Barak himself offered a compromise in the form of 'handing over sovereignty of the site to God' – a proposal the media dubbed 'Divine sovereignty'.

The Israeli media defined and gave expression to Israeli Jewish concerns over the future status of the Mount (Cohen, 2001), not only in the editorial columns but even in the news reporting itself – suggesting that Hall's thesis that news values should be explained in terms of structural ideological meanings was valid. Besides daily coverage of the latest developments in the negotiations, there was an unending stream of features on different facets of the Temple Mount question, ranging from interviews with the Chief Rabbis to stories on the Jewish presence in the Old City's Muslim Quarter to accounts of Jerusalem Mayor Ehud Olmert's decision to move his office across from the Western Wall. In the biggest demonstration in the city's history, an estimated 400,000 Jewish Israelis protested against the Clinton proposals at a rally at the walls of Jerusalem's Old City. The Chief Rabbinate Council, a state body, met in emergency session, and Chief Rabbi Israel Meir Lau marshalled his finely honed PR talents throughout the broadcast and print media to attack any removal of the site from sole Jewish sovereignty.

Ideology came to expression in commentary pieces and editorials. *Ha'aretz*, which for years had favoured territorial compromise on the West Bank (and separation of 'synagogue and state'), took the predictable step of supporting a compromise on the Temple Mount. On 26 December it editorialised that 'at the end of the day, the Arab-Israeli dispute over Jerusalem revolves around a hub of symbols, not around elements fundamental to existence'.

In their respective institutional perspectives, expressed in commentaries by senior staff writers, the centrist *Yediot Aharonot* and right-of-centre *Maariv* were distinctly less enthusiastic about giving up the Temple Mount than *Haaretz*. On 28 December *Yediot Aharonot* senior editor Sever Plotzker dismissed the Clinton proposal 'as having been devised by two rival real estate agents, on the principle of population size: What is populated by the Jewish people will belong to the Jewish people [the Western Wall], and what is populated by the Muslims as belonging to the Palestinians [the Temple Mount]. The plan,' Plotzker claimed, 'doesn't manage to deal with historical rights or religious connection. These are stronger than anything political or anything demographic.' On 26 January *Yediot Aharonot*'s senior political columnist, Nahum Barnea, perhaps the country's foremost political writer, characterised the Temple Mount as 'a difficult matter: For religious and political reasons it [a peace settlement] is impossible with it. For religious and political reasons it is impossible without it'.

The religious press was divided between the modern Orthodox and Haredi presses, whose divergent reactions reflect fundamentally opposed views of the legitimacy of the modern state of Israel. The national-religious community perceives the creation of Israel and the reunification of Jerusalem in 1967 as part of the messianic redemption. No Israeli community was more critical of the Clinton proposals than the national-religious. On 29 December, reporter Haggai Huberman of *Hatzofe* bemoaned the equation of Israeli sovereignty over the Western Wall with Palestinian sovereignty over the Temple Mount: 'The holiest site for the Jews is not the Western Wall – which is a mere supporting wall erected by Herod to allow for the building of the Temple.'

One related issue addressed by *Hatzofe* was whether to revise the rabbinical ban on entry for Jews to the Temple Mount, instituted lest 'ritually impure' Jews intrude on the site of the Temple. The ban only undermined Jewish connection to the site, critics claimed. In a 29 December column *Hatzofe* editor Gonen Ginat agreed, criticising the Chief Rabbinate for 'witnessing what is transpiring but failing to take the steps which beg to be taken – to allow Jews to ascend the mount'.

The Haredi media likewise devoted attention to the Temple Mount issues like the rest of the Israeli media. *Yated Neeman* and *Hamodia*, the two politically affiliated Haredi newspapers, devoted news and feature articles to the subject, as did newer, non-party-affiliated commercial Haredi magazines like *Bakehilla* and *Mishpacha*. But for all the coverage, the Haredi press was distinctly relaxed about the Temple Mount issue. Its ideological outlook is that the creation of the Jewish political entity is premature and that the building of the third Jewish Temple is a step that only the Messiah himself can undertake. Any discussion about the contemporary political fate of the site is therefore premature and irrelevant. In an editorial entitled 'The Temple Mount – a Little Sanctuary' on 8 January, *Yated Neeman* appeared to belittle concern for the fate of the site (given that it will be rebuilt by the Messiah at the appointed time): 'True Jews recognise that even more important is the "holy sanctuary" that should characterise the atmosphere of every Jewish Home – which bases itself on the Torah.'

It was another mount, the Mount of Olives, that was of immediate concern to Haredi Jewry. Located in East Jerusalem, the Mount of Olives would, under the Clinton proposals, have been turned over to Palestinian sovereignty. Venerable Haredi sages are buried in the cemetery there, and thousands flock each year to pray at their gravesides. On 10 January *Hamodia*, the biggest selling Haredi daily, opined that 'the Israeli-Palestinian talks notwithstanding, it is forbidden to tamper or damage the graves of the righteous'.

Ideology, therefore, clearly entered all levels of coverage. There was virtually no attention in the news pages or commentary to views and reactions of the Muslim world, including Israeli Arabs and Palestinians. Ideology could also be seen as a factor in the structural division of the news-gathering operation. What the Israelis might do with the site in the long run (assuming they retained sovereignty) received scant attention. This can be attributed in part to the fact that the story had been covered exclusively by political correspondents and reporters on Arab and Jerusalem affairs. Had religion reporters been involved in the coverage, the theological differences and debates among the different Jewish religious streams would have focused more on the contemporary significance in Judaism of the Temple and its site.

Conclusion

Even if ideology has a place in Western media, the major determining factors in news production are the psychological factors. It needs to be asked whether the focus on conflict-ridden religion news distorts the public image of religion which Israelis receive from the media. In Chapter 7 it will be argued that the media has an impact on secular–religious relations. In order to widen the coverage of religion, editors need to reassess whether religion-related news on the news pages should comprise mostly conflict-related developments – like so much else in the news – or whether longer term and positive developments and trends could receive more coverage in order that a more positive picture be painted. To be true, the inside pages of newspapers, and talk shows on television and radio, do relate to developments and trends, albeit solely of the Jewish religion. In one sense, the Internet offers a solution because it is less limited by space considerations. Major news websites like Y-Net and NRG have the greater availability of space and run Judaism sites, with their own staff writers focusing on the subject. But while this has led to more religion-related information available to the Israeli public, and while the headlines on the stories appear on the home page, in practice only those with real interest in religion turn to the Judaism sites.

References

Buddenbaum, J. (1986) 'An Analysis of Religion News Coverage in Three Major Newspapers', *Journalism Quarterly*, Autumn.

——(1990) 'Network News Coverage of Religion', in J. Ferre (ed) *Channels of Belief: Religion and American Commercial Television*. Ames, IA: Iowa State University Press.

Cohen, Y. (2001), 'Palestinians and Israelis: Oh, Jerusalem', *Religion in the News*. Hartford, CT: The Leonard E. Greenberg Center for the Study of Religion in Public Life, Trinity College, 4:1.

Dayan, D. and Katz, E. (1992) *Media Events: The Live Broadcasting of History*. Boston: Harvard.

Ferre, J. (1980) 'Denominational Biases in the American Press', *Review of Religious Research*, 21.

Galtung, J. and Ruge, M. (1965) 'The Structure of Foreign News', *International Journal of Peace Research*, 1.

Garrett-Medill Center for Religion and the News Media (1999) *Media Coverage of Religion, Spirituality, and Values*. Evanston, IL: Northwestern University.

Hall, S. (1982) 'The Rediscovery of Ideology: Return of the Repressed in Media Studies', in M. Gurevitch, T. Bennett, J. Curran and J. Woollacott (eds), *Culture, Society and the Media*. London: Methuen.

Hart, R., Turner, K. and Knupp, R. (1980) 'Religion and the Rhetoric of the Mass Media', *Review of Religious Research*, 21, 3.

Hoover, S. (1998) *Religion in the News*. Thousand Oaks, CA: Sage.

Janaway, M. (1993) 'The Press and Privacy: Rights and Rules: the Morality of the Mass Media', in W. L. Taitte (ed) *The Morality of the Mass Media*. Dallas: University of Texas Press.

Jemayel, A. (2006) *The Culture of Media Consumption Among National Minorities: The Arabs in Israel*. Nazareth: I'lam Media Center for Arab Palestinians in Israel.

Mowery, R. (1995) 'God in the New York Times', *Journal of Communication and Religion*, 18(2), September.

Olen, J. (1988) *Ethics in Journalism*. Englewood Cliffs, NJ: Prentice-Hall.

Shepherd, A. (1995) 'The Media get Religion', *American Journalism Review*, December.

Underwood, D. (2001) 'Secularists or Modern Day Prophets? Journalist Ethics and the Judaeo-Christian Tradition', *Journal of Mass Media Ethics*, 16(1).

Zecharya, Z. (1989) *Ha-itonut ha-Haredi ha-Hadasha* [The New Haredi Media]. Master's thesis. Jerusalem: The Hebrew University.

5 Mikva* news

On 9/11 Rabbi Israel Feinhandler boarded the fated United Airlines Flight 175 from Boston which crashed into the World Trade Center. Feinhandler took his seat on the plane, but then realised that he had forgotten his 'tephillin' (phylacteries used by Jewish males in their daily morning prayers). But the door of the plane had already closed. Seeing that his tephillin were at stake he screamed 'I am going to lose my tephillin.' When the crew asked him to be quiet, he declined. The head steward came over to him, 'Listen we have decided that you are a nuisance and we are allowing you off the plane to get your bag, but we are not waiting for you and you will lose your flight.'

(Excerpt from a feature article, 'Even in the Darkest Moments: True Stories From Those Who Survived 9/11', published in the Haredi newspaper, *Hamodia*, on the anniversary of the 9/11 attack)[1]

The religious media may be divided according to sector and according to whether the media is institutionalised or commercial in structure. The religious media may be divided between the Haredi media and the modern Orthodox Jewish media. Both reflect Jewish values. There are no large scale media published by the Conservative or Reform communities in Israel. According to the Central Bureau of Statistics (2009), 8 per cent of Israel's Jewish population in 2009 defined themselves as Haredim. Of all sectoral communities, the Haredim have been most active in creating their own community media. Reflecting its philosophy of withdrawal from modernity, and seeking to maintain religious values in a cultural ghetto framework, the Haredi (Hebrew for fearful ones) community or ultra-Orthodox Jews have felt most threatened by changing mass media.

As advanced by Theodore Adorno (1991), of the Frankfurt School of critical Marxist thought, the media are a powerful agent for legitimising political structures, providing consumers with illusory choices and unimportant choices turning their attention from participating fully and creatively in mainstream societal structures. If news is the outcome of structure then in a religious society the news will be different than in a secular Israeli religious society.

---

* ritual bath

While ideology cannot be ignored even with the general media, its major impact on coverage is in the religious media.

The exposure of Haredi Jews has been heavily influenced by their spiritual leaders. Their rabbis have over the years issued religious decrees (*pesuk din*) against exposure to mass media regarded as a threat to Torah family values. From the appearance of newspapers in the nineteenth century, through to the development of radio and television, and latterly video, computers and Internet and cellcom phones, Haredi rabbis have enacted such decrees. When Israel Television was established in 1968, Haredi rabbis banned their followers from watching television because its content was considered morally inappropriate; while entertainment per se is not invalidated, the Haredi perspective is nevertheless critical of it regarding it as more than a relief from such higher values as religious study. The bans on television and secular newspapers were the most successful of the bans against media with the overwhelming number of Haredim respecting it. The earlier ban on radio – based on the prohibition against hearing gossip (*loshon hara*) as well as the importance of modesty because radio programming prior to television had a much wider gamut of subjects including drama – is nevertheless less respected than the television ban because Israel's ongoing political-defence problems of the country make it difficult for people to adhere to the ban. When videos cameras were produced – with many Haredi families using them to record family celebrations – no rabbinical ban was introduced initially because its usage could be controlled. However, after it was discovered that television programmes could be seen if videos were plugged into computers, Haredi rabbis in 1993 banned videos.

The structure of the Haredi press

The daily Haredi newspapers were initiatives of rabbinical sages belonging to different branches of Haredism. Going back to prior to the Second World War, there was a recognition of the need to balance the secular press. The Haredi press has been a party- or institution-affiliated press. Their influence was particularly wide given that Haredim are not exposed to television or to secular newspapers, making the Haredi press important agents for political recruitment. *Hamodia* is the organ of the Agudat Israel political party, and is the older of the two papers, and *Yated Neeman* the organ of the Degel HaTorah Party. The existence of the two newspapers reflects an ongoing dispute between the Hassidic and the *Mitnagdim* Lithuanian (Litvak) branches of Haredi Judaism which originated in the eighteenth century between hassidism which reflects a more emotional approach to Jewish belief, combined with a high level of adulation for the rabbi or 'rebbe', in contrast to the Lithuanian school which laid greater stress on study of the Talmud and opposed the excesses of rabbinical authoritarianism. The Hassidim and the Lithuanian Haredim read only their respective newspaper. The Gerar will not read the paper of the Mitnagdim, and vice versa. Given both the great political clout the papers enjoy, politicians of all stripes – religious and secular – go to great lengths to be publicised in these papers, for this is the surest way to bring their activities to the attention of the Rebbes (Hassidic leaders) or rabbis, who will ultimately decree how voters should vote.

The newspaper is also a public message board, the fastest way to make a decision public. Rabbinic decisions regarding the kashrut of various products and other such proclamations sometimes appears on front pages, And the decisions, which include boycotts of specific companies, have immediate impact.

The media are important channels for the political parties – *Hamodia* in the case of the Agudot Yisroel party, *Yetad Neeman* in the case of Degal HaTorah, and the weekly *Yom leYom* in the case of the Shas party – to engage in political recruitment, in particular prior to general elections. In addition to party journalism, *Hamodia* and *Yated Neeman* act as an educational instrument in both an active and passive or filtering sense. The separate supplement also enables these religious readers who prefer not to read 'secular' subjects on the Sabbath holyday to read only the holy, or '*kadosh*', supplements. Heavily influenced by Jewish theological principles, the content of Haredi media in particular reflects less what reality is and more what it should be. Drawing on the biblical precept that 'the camp shall be holy' (Deuteronomy 23:15), Haredi editors seek to ensure that the newspaper that enters the Haredi home does not 'impure' the family atmosphere. When *Hamodia*'s English daily edition was launched in 2003, its first editorial, entitled, 'In the name of Hashem [God] we will do and succeed', opined:

> It is possible to be up on the news, to be informed about what is going on in the world, from an acceptable framework, one that is free from anything not befitting the Torah home. We want to offer you a newspaper that filters inappropriate news from your home, and which helps us all grow in Torah and *yiras shamayim* [fear of God].[2]

Each newspaper has a rabbinical censor whose job is daily before edition time to check the next day's edition. Above him is a board of rabbis who determine editorial policy.

In one sense, the Haredi sectoral media may be compared to the purified atmosphere of the *mikva*, or ritual bath. The mikva is the ritual bath used by religious women to immerse themselves following their monthly menstrual cycle. It comprises rain water and ensures a heightened spirituality. Purity is the standard by which everything is measured in Jewish life. The Haredi home centres around the yeshiva hall and synagogue, and whatever is intrusive and threatens the purity of the Jewish home – including the media's language – is rejected. The media is controlled and sanitised through a type of filter or 'mikva' which ensures that only media content which does not challenge and threaten the Haredi home 'seeps' in. To be true, many Haredi men, notably of the Hassidic branches, go to the mikva daily, and even litvaks increasingly attend the mikva if only on the Sabbath eve. Not dissimilar from the atmosphere in a sauna, men sit in a communal ritual *mikva*, or before or afterwards in the changing rooms, and chat about the news. With an estimated 50 per cent of

Haredim who do not even follow the Haredi press or Haredi radio stations, the mikva, in addition to its religious ritual function, provides, as a byproduct, 'mikva news' or has become a Haredi town square for updating on the news.

The Haredi media is also characterised by an overwhelming attitude towards modesty in sex-related matters. The standards regarding sexual modesty are interpreted by Haredim in the strictest manner. There are no pictures in the Haredi media of women. Nor is reporting done about women. Women reporters themselves sign their articles with their initials only. There is no editorial content about entertainment, sport, singers, or women, or sexual abuse. AIDS, for example, is referred to as 'a contagious disease'. Even when then Prime Minister Ehud Olmert had a medical examination for suspected cancer of the prostate, the Haredi media reported only 'suspected cancer'.

Haredi media avoid stories with sexual content, but sometimes the matter is so central to the country's news agenda that they cannot avoid discussing it. They will use different means to report the case without relating to it. When a government minister Chaim Ramon was found guilty of forcibly kissing a female soldier, *Yated Neeman* began its report on page 1: 'After former Justice Minister Chaim Ramon was found guilty on criminal charges, it had an unnerving effect on the political system' – without informing its readers the nature of 'the criminal charges'.[3] This was even when then President Moshe Katzav was charged in 2007 with rape and resigned the presidency. It presented a challenge to Haredi editors. On the one hand, they do not discuss matters like rape. On the other hand, the indictment of a president cannot be ignored. Ways and means were found – which sometimes create more confusion than less. Thus, *Yated Neeman* reported: 'Yesterday, the attorney general decided to indict Katzav for a series of criminal offences, such as using state funds and obstructing legal procedures.'[4] And, the *Bakehilla* weekly, under the headline 'Presidents and the Atmosphere', reported that 'a flood of criminal suspicions and new revelations are likely to bring about the resignation of the president'.[5] One of *Yated Neeman*'s columnists Hayim Walder said that 'the Haredi media will never report on serious crime, whether bribery or murder and certainly not matters regarding modesty. The very deed of mentioning the sin makes the reader more tolerant of it. But not even mentioning the deed by name sends an important moral warning to the reader that it is forbidden. The less you know about evil, the better'.[6] Similarly, broadcasters at the Haredi radio station, Radio *Kol Chai*, were instructed in reporting the Katzav story not to mention or use words like 'sexual harassment', 'rape' or 'abuse'. A news conference by Katzav, at which he announced his resignation and which was broadcast live in its entirety in special broadcasts on television and radio, was not broadcast on Radio *Kol Chai*, but only after offensive phrases had been deleted. Earlier, *Kol Chai* news anchor Mordechai Lavie told listeners 'there was a report that one of his workers approached the president saying "If you will not pay me, I will reveal"'. 'When a father sits in his car with his children listening my job is to protect the children and not use terms alien to the children's pure world' Lavie told one reporter later.[7] When in 2010 Katzav was found guilty of rape, not a word was published in the Haredi press. Katzav had left the presidency, and therefore there were no political implications from the court's verdict.

Illustrative of the religious supervision in the Haredi press is the case of *Yated Neeman*. When *Yated Neeman* was established by Degel HaTorah its spiritual mentor, Rabbi Eliezer Shach established the paper under a board of seven members: heads of *yeshivot* (talmudical academies of higher learning), rabbinical judges (*dayanim*) and experts in Jewish law (*halakhah*). While they do not frequent the offices of the paper their representatives, or 'censors', do. Their representatives have been known to eliminate offending words of an advert or even the whole advert that does not accord with the policies, politics, ideology or lifestyle of the movement's leadership. The role of the censor is to make sure that concepts or ideas that the newspaper's board of rabbis do not accept are not printed in the paper. 'The censor is not himself a rabbi but rather very learned who, while understanding the secular world, also understands the principles including about education on which the paper stands for,' an editor of a Haredi newspaper remarked.

Sometimes, the censor's system falters and something regarded as inappropriate slips into the paper. For example, in early August 1990 *Yated Neeman* received numerous phone calls from embarrassed mothers and enraged rabbis after it published a syndicated article detailing an attack on a female soldier at an Israeli military base: the perpetrator, the report said, was in custody on charges of assault and 'rape'. The term 'rape' is never used by a Haredi person. The news got past the paper's censor because, it was explained, the previous day was the Tisha B' Av fast and the exhausted censor overlooked this 'small word'. In another case, in 2007, *Hamodia*'s education supplement showed a picture of a child painting an Easter egg. No Haredi paper refers to non-Jewish religions. The following day an announcement printed on the front page, under the headline 'errors which the wise understand', apologised to readers for the error – without explaining what the error was about.[8] Similarly, when in 1999 the weekly magazine *Mishpacha* published a picture of Kate Winslet, star of a film on the Titanic, 10,000 copies of the magazine were destroyed, and the magazine subsequently moved to another printing press. Weeks later the magazine suffered another blow when an advert accidentally slipped into the magazine at the printers which had been intended for another print job of a nude woman being carried by two men.[9] The price may even be greater: when one desk editor at *Hamodia* failed to stop an agency report about neo-Nazi demonstrators in Europe which included the phrase demonstrators 'attacked supporters of homosexual rights', the sub-editor responsible was fired; many subscribers cancelled their subscription.

Crime is another item subject to circumspection. In 2008 a child, Rose Pisum, was kidnapped by an estranged father and her body was found in the Yarkon River, in Tel Aviv. The affair, including the search for the dumped body, captivated the Israeli public for weeks, but the Haredi media ignored the story in its entirety. Even when the story climaxed after divers discovered the body in a suitcase in the river, the Haredi op-eds did not cover it and Radio *Kol Chai* reported it briefly in its news bulletin. 'Our newspaper is a book of education. Every parent who brings the newspaper into the house knows that its contents are fit for the Haredi world,' said Itzhak Tennenbaum, *Hamodia* editor.[10] 'In addition to the terrifying murder we are talking about family incest. Children are curious; we don't want them to ask questions,' he added.

To get around the limitations when important information needs to be published, *Hamodia* and *Yated Neeman* carry columns entitled 'From Day to Day' and 'On the Agenda' respectively which through attacking a subject as unJewish – for example, an Israeli success in an international sporting event – are thereby informing their readers that it occurred. The party media see the censor's role in inclusion terms. For example, the way a newspaper describes a religious leader as *gaon* (most learned) or simply rabbi is an allusion to that rabbi's standing in the eyes of the paper and its sponsors (Baumel, 2002).

While Jewish theology in mass media behaviour prohibits the divulging of previously unknown information, regarded in Jewish law as talebearing, party political media, even if religious, necessarily publish information which is critical of the party's opponents (Chwat, 1995).

The daily edition of the three Haredi newspapers comprises some eight pages including national political and economic news, world news, news about the Haredi sector – the Hassidic branches in the *Hamodia* case and Lithuanian in *Yated Neeman's* case – and news about their Knesset representatives. Haredi newspapers have few reporters, relying mostly upon the news agencies. 'The level of accuracy in reporting is lower than in the secular media,' according to a political reporter. 'The level of credibility is lower than it is in the secular media, and the principle of getting reactions of the other side is notably absent,' he added. This may be due to the fact that suing for libel occurs less in the Haredi media than the secular media. Most of the material produced in *Hamodia* and *Yated Neeman* comprise analyses, op-eds and interpretations of news developments, according to the Haredi viewpoint. One scoop, for example, was that of *Hamodia*'s Israel Katzover, a reporter then for *Shearim*, the organ of the extinct Poale Agudat Yisroel party, who in 1977 reported that an official ceremony for Israel's first F-15 aeroplanes from the US had run into the Sabbath. The story triggered a government coalition crisis that eventually brought down the Rabin government.

The absence of sports coverage is illustrative of the Haredi perspective on life. Discussing why it did not cover sport, *Hamodia* stated:

> We don't wish to castigate any individual whose personal interest in sports coverage serves as his own individual lightening rods – if you will – to deflect other detrimental influences. We hope that he has a mentor in his life, who is helping him to navigate the turbulence of our times. But for the Torah-true public to be encouraged to celebrate the achievements and antics of the decadent and often criminal icons of the body is a desecration of no small proportions.[11]

By contrast, world news is a regular ingredient of Haredi daily newspaper coverage – providing in many cases the Haredi reader's only source not only of foreign news information but even knowledge of the outside world. An analysis of 18 days of coverage in 2007 in *Yated Neeman* and *Hamodia* found that foreign news appeared in almost every issue of *Hamodia* (94 per cent) and *Yated Neeman* (89 per cent). Moreover, 56 per cent of foreign news appeared on the front page of *Yated Neeman* and 39 per cent of *Hamodia*'s front page. There was a heavy interest in foreign news relating to Jews and Jewish communities abroad: 33 per cent of *Yated*'s foreign news and 50 per cent of *Hamodia*'s foreign news had a Jewish connection, which confirms that cultural proximity is a factor in editors' criteria of selecting news stories.[12] Yet, even world news has its own special dimension in Haredi media eyes, drawing upon the educational role the media play. News reporting is no less objective than in the secular media, but editorial commentary and op-ed columns provide fertile territory for drawing Jewish moral teaching from news events. Noting that world events have moral messages, *Hamodia* editorialised in its post-Yom Kippur (Day of Atonement) issue in 2004 that 'What we call the news' is in fact nothing more (and nothing less!) than the hand of God carrying out his New Year decree for humankind. From time to time people ask us: 'Who needs to know so much about what's going on in the world? The best answer, we believe, is that a Torah Jew should indeed care about God's masterplan. The headlines you see in the paper may be written by various reporters and editors – but they are composed in the Jewish New Year by the Editor-in-Chief whose every key stroke carries an important lesson for us.'[13] And, in its post-Yom Kippur issue a year later, the paper's editorial, taking as its cue a massive earthquake in Pakistan a week earlier and hurricanes in central America, said 'It is not for us to divine God's purpose in all this devastation. But harsh decrees befall the nations only because of the Jewish people.' Quoting the French Bible commentator, Rashi, the paper added:

> God visits devastation upon the nations as a wake-up call to us to inspire fear and awe among the Jewish people to do repentance. When we see pictures of hurricanes and the earthquakes and the landslides, when we hear about all those who were killed. injured or left homeless, we should be moved not just in some general humanitarian sense by the tragic plight of so many people – though that is surely an appropriate reaction – but also in the specific Jewish sense of repairing our own relationship with God ... Nothing transpires anywhere in this world simply as a random occurrence, but is instead God's way of speaking to us and calling his Chosen People to do repentance.[14]

The Haredi outlook sees the role of the Jew, and therefore the role of media in Jewish society, as possessing a responsibility to build the model society. Drawing upon Jewish social responsibility as an ideal, Israelis or Jewish heretics need to be rescued. The *Haredi* media report the secular world from a perspective of superiority, hostility and self-correction. There are Jews – Haredi – and there are Israelis – secular Jews. Secular Jewish education is coined progressive education in a derogatory sense, decried as a factor in rising crime patterns. The Left are associated with the universities and academics. The modern religious are criticised as misled religious Jews. Non-Jewish religions are not referred to. Most criticism is reserved for Zionism. Israeli institutions such as the Army are often the butt of criticism. Particular angst is reserved for the Supreme Court in its court decisions which are against the spirit of Orthodox Jewish legal rulings. The Israeli Army is not called by its formal name, the Israel Defence Forces, since the true defender of Israel is God. Israel's Supreme Court is criticised for not basing its decision on Jewish religious law (*halakhah*); court decisions are therefore not described as rulings, instead 'the court decided' is written. The secular media is pictured as being permissive, anti-establishment, and atheistic (Levi, 1990).

Discussing a spate of car accidents in the country in 1997 *Hamodia* columnist Menahem Klugman wrote that 'secular drivers are not well-educated about the value and sanctity of life. This will be strengthened if the fear of God exists among the population'.[15] Discussing the danger of terrorism, *Yated Neeman*'s Nathan Zeev Grossman attributed it to secularism and secular education. Terrorists are 'for our good and for our self-correction, in order that it should be understood that we have diverted from the path of the Torah'.[16]

The anniversary of the 9/11 attack on the World Trade Center, New York, is an opportunity for moral education. A feature article in *Hamodia*'s weekly magazine entitled 'Even in the Darkest Moments: True Stories From Those Who Survived 9/11' related the story of Rabbi Abraham Yisroel, who headed the Hazon Yeshaya Soup Kitchens, which gives free meals to the hungry. Yisroel had an appointment in the Twin Towers, but when he heard the crash of the two planes he decided not to enter the building. 'I came to the conclusion that my work in the soup kitchen for the poor and sick saved me,' he said.[17] But sometimes the Haredi media are forced to explain when the good die. For example, in Israel's worst train crash in 2005 in which seven died and 180 were injured, a rabbi, Yosef Dermer, died. A cover story entitled 'Who Will Live, Who Will Die?' (a play on the Yom Kippur prayer '*Unesana Tokef*' about the day of judgement) had to discuss his death as no less than the miracle which saved another rabbi who 'missed' his regular journey on the fated train that day.[18]

Hamodia

Established in 1950 by Yitzhak Meir Levin, son-in-law of the Gerrar Rebbe, and edited by his son Yehuda Leib Levin, *Hamodia* ('The Announcer') enjoyed a circulation in 2005 estimated to be 28,000 daily. Twenty-five per cent of Haredim saw *Hamodia* daily and 26 per cent at weekends.

Historically, the paper played a role in raising morale and providing empathy in the aftermath of the Second World War when Haredi Jews had been killed in many numbers. The origins of a Haredi daily were already felt years earlier in Europe. Following earlier examples of religious journalism in Europe in the nineteenth century, the Gerar Rebbe, or Imrei Emes of Ger, the leader of Haredi Jewry in Poland, together with two other key rabbinical Haredi figures, Rav Chaim Ozer Grodzinski, a leader of Lithuanian Jewry, and Rav Chaim mi-Brisk founded *Hamodia* in 1910 in Koltova, Poland, to create a new paper with content suitable for their Haredi community. Publication was interrupted by the First World War in 1915. It began again in 1918 under the name *Das Yiddishe Vort*, and continued in different forms until the outbreak of the Second World War in 1939. It opposed the Zionist movement – both in establishing the State of Israel prior to the arrival of Messiah – as well as opposing the irreligious character of the new state.

Going back to when it was the only existing Haredi daily newspaper, *Hamodia* gave expression also to the non-Hassidic branches of Haredim Jewry. In addition to the Gerrar Rebbe's own Hassidic or 'central' stream – the dominant stream reflected in the newspaper – there is the so-called 'young' Agudat Yisroel identified with the Lithuanian (or 'Litvak') stream, and the 'Shomrei Emunim' ('Guardians of the Faith') or Jerusalem stream. The paper was strapped for cash in its earlier years, its reporters poorly paid, but in the early-1960s, the paper's economic situation improved with new printing equipment. When Yehuda Leib Levin died in 1981 he was replaced by a troika of three editors, Hayyim Knopf, Moshe Akiva Druck and Yisroel Spiegel, who were on the paper from its early years as reporters, or in Knopf's case had been on the business side of the paper. The three men were identified respectively with the Hassidic stream, the Shomrei Emunim stream and the Lithuanian stream. In practice, while Knopf formally had the title of editor he handled the newspaper's business side, the editing being done by Druck and Spiegel on a rotation basis.

During the Levin editorship, content comprised mostly political news, including the full texts of speeches by its party Knesset representatives, as well as news about the Haredi community. Supplements occasionally appeared such as marking the death of a famous sage. Under the 'troika', news coverage expanded to include national Israeli news, economics news and foreign news.

The Lithuanian stream withdrew to form its own paper, *Yated Neeman,* in 1985 after Rabbi Eliezer Shach resigned from the Council of Torah Sages, an umbrella group of leading Haredi rabbis, over the question of the construction of a hotel in Tiberias on the site of Jewish graves. Shach was affronted by the newspaper's preference in 1982 for the Gerrar Rebbe's lenient ruling over Shach's more stringent one in the matter. *Hamodia* subsequently became more identified publicly with the Hassidic stream of Haredim. Today few from the Lithuanian Haredim read *Hamodia*; a 1995 survey found that 65 per cent of *Hamodia* readers were hassidim, 31 per cent were Haredim 'uncommitted' (only 9 per cent of Lithuanian Haredim saw the paper). (Israel Advertisers Association: Haredim, 1995)

With Druck's death in 1992, he was replaced by Itzhak Tennenbaum. By 2000, Yisroel Schneider (of the Hassidic or 'central' stream) had become

Knopf's right-hand man as acting editor. News coverage was expanded with specialist correspondents covering politics in addition to the Knesset, the military, economics, Jerusalem and the religious city of Bnei Beraq. A weekly economics supplement was introduced. In the face of competition from the rise of a commercial Haredi weekly press in the 1980s and 1990s the newspaper expanded. On Friday, the Sabbath eve, the newspaper has two supplements: on general news features, and a *'kadosh'* section containing articles penned by rabbis discussing the week's Bible reading (*parshat shavua*), *halachic* issues and Jewish history. It added a 16-page children's supplement. (A children's supplement existed, albeit for a short period, already in the 1950s.) An economics section was added in the 1990s – to compete with the non-party Haredi weeklies. There was a women's section, edited by Mrs Shaindel Weinstein. *Hamodia*'s layout was Conservative with small print and headlines. It added colour. In the 1990s and the beginning of the 2000s *Hamodia* introduced English and French language weekly editions, inside Israel, in the USA and Britain and France, as well as a daily English edition for the USA. The US operation, managed by the daughter of Yehuda Leib Levin, *Hamodia*'s founding editor, Mrs Ruth Lichtenstein, while producing much editorial content within the US and the local Haredi community, also translated a large amount from the Hebrew paper in Israel.

In 2010 *Hamodia* faced a serious crisis. Reflecting the internecine fighting within hassidism, the paper which is controlled by Gur failed to back the candidature of Menachem Porush, who belonged to the Shlomei Emunim faction of Agudat Yisroel, in the elections for the Jerusalem majority, backing instead the secular candidate of Nir Barakat. Porush broke away to found his own paper, *Hamevaser*. The crisis was not dissimilar to that which occurred with the break with the Lithuanians, or Litvaks, and the creation of *Yated Neeman*.

Yated Neeman

Established in 1985, *Yated Neeman* is the acronym for 'Yoman Da'at Torah' ('The Torah Opinion Daily'). After the Degel Ha-Torah political party was founded following the resignation of Rabbi Shach from the Council of Torah Sages, the supporters of Rabbi Shach – (1894 (?)–2001), who headed the Ponevezh Yeshivah, in Bnei Beraq, and was regarded as the spiritual head of Lithuanian (or 'Litvak') Haredim – launched *Yetad Neeman* as the party newspaper. Its founding editor was Moshe Grylick. In 1988 he was succeeded by Natan Grossman. The newspaper gave expression to the party's politically moderate viewpoint when it declined to publish advertisements for housing in the Haredi town of Emanuel because it was situated in the occupied territories, captured in the 1967 war. Shach argued that the Jewish law edict of *pikuach nefesh* (the saving of life) was superior to any obligation not to relinquish Jewish biblical territories. With an estimated daily circulation of 22,000, 19 per cent of Haredim read *Yated Neeman* daily in 2005. A 1995 survey found that 64 per cent of the newspaper's readers defined themselves as Lithuanian

Haredim, and 22 per cent undefined Haredim (only 7 per cent replied that they were hassidim). (Israel Advertisers Association: Haredim, 1995)

Like *Hamodia, Yated Neeman*'s weekend Sabbath eve issue has two supplements: a magazine, and a *kadosh* section containing inspiring essays by rabbis on the weekly bible reading (*parshat shavua*), Jewish law issues and Jewish history. On Thursdays there is a family supplement geared for women, 'Bait Neeman' ('A faithful house') with articles about family issues, health education and recipes, etc., and on Tuesdays a children's supplement 'Yated Shelanu' ('Our Yated'). It established a weekly English language newspaper with the same name but this broke away from the Hebrew paper and was published in the USA.

Shach's death in 2001 left a void in the newspaper's management. The dispute over whether Rabbi Elyashiv or Rabbi Steinemann would become Shach's recognised successor was also played out in *Yated Neeman*. The editorship became divided between the daily and Sabbath eve issues, with the daily issue, edited by Grossman, identifying with Rabbi Elyashiv, and the Sabbath eve issue identifying with Rabbi Steinemann.

Other institutional Haredi media included *Yom LeYom*. The Sephardi Shas political party which evolved in the 1980s against the Ashkenazi or European dominated Haredi world, seeking funding for institutions headed by their spiritual mentor, Rabbi Ovadiah Yosef, a former state chief rabbi, founded its own daily newspaper, *Yom LeYom* ('From Day to Day') in 1993 but it became a weekly shortly afterwards. Its estimated circulation is 3,000. *Yom LeYom* allots more space to covering the activities of the party and its spiritual mentor Rabbi Ovadiah Yosef than do *Hamodia* and *Yated Neeman* to their respective party sponsors.

Hamahaneh HaHaredi, the weekly of the Belze Hassidic court; *Haedah* of the Council of Torah Sages; and *Hahomah* of the Neturei Kartya, part of the Satmar Hassidic court, characterised by its trenchant opposition to Zionism and the modern Israeli state, have limited circulations.

Although the Haredi newspapers are strapped financially, the demographic trend for large families in the Haredi community, combined with the educational functions they fill within their communities, suggests that *Hamodia*'s and *Yated Neeman*'s long-term chances for survival and growth were good.

In recent years the monopoly enjoyed by the party papers has been successfully challenged since the 1980s by a commercially-orientated independent Haredi media. These are commercial attempts by journalists from a Haredi background to deploy such techniques as modern graphics, fetching headlines, covering a broader range of subjects than those in the party 'establishment' Haredi media. The openness of the new press was characterised by the fact that unlike the daily institutionalised Haredi papers, each of which covered only their own political party, it reported the activities of all religious MKs. Some of them also consult rabbinical authorities over content. But as Haredi journalist Itzhak Nachshoni, formerly editor of *Yom Shishi*, said, 'in principle I am opposed that a newspaper has a religious board. As a journalist who knows how to keep "kosher" at home, I can also do so here in the paper. I believe that no newspaper is fully "kosher" in Israel. No paper, including the institutionalised Haredi daily papers, abides by the standards of *halakhah* in terms of no gossip. Whoever is able to cut themselves off entirely from the media is invited to do so'.[19]

The first papers, today obsolete, were *Erev Shabbat* and *Yom Shishi*, which in turn became *Erev Shabbat*. To be true, Yom Shishi was not geared solely for the Haredi community but sought to interest the entire religious world in its coverage, within the confines of not hurting Haredi tastes such as with pictures of women. The main Haredi weeklies today are *Mishpacha* ('Family'), and *Bakehilla* ('In the Community'), both of which were established in 1997. Another is *Sha'a Tova*, originally *Ha-Shavua*, edited by Asher Zuckerman. Whereas *Mishpacha* and *Bakehilla* are non-political, *Sha'a Tova* has a right-wing orientation – and even incited against Rabin in the heady atmosphere which followed the Oslo accords and preceded Rabin's assassination. More recently, *Shavua*, published by the Kav Ha-itonut Ha-Datit group, is a national chain of free newspapers drawing entirely upon advertising comprising local editions in key Haredi populated areas like Jerusalem, Bnei Beraq, Betar, Kiryat Sofer and Elad. Another Haredi 'freebie' is *Mercaz Inyanim*. In 2007 the TGI survey found that 29 per cent read *Mishpacha*, 21 per cent *Bakehilla*, and 7 per cent *Sha'a Tova*, 6 per cent *HaMachana Haredi*, and 6 per cent *Yom LeYom*. A clue to their success was that *Hamodia* and *Yated Neeman* were read by 26 per cent and 25 per cent respectively.[20] By 2011 *Mishpacha*'s dominant position rose to 32 per cent. There are also upmarket Haredi magazines like '*Fine*', edited by Shalhevet Hasdiel, which discusses design, fashion, lifestyle and tourism for the Haredi sector. There is even a Haredi Hebrew edition of *National Geographic*.

The commercial Haredi media, while respecting the code of not publishing immoral matter which will upset Haredi Jewish sensitivities, have introduced a new level of press freedom in an otherwise highly hierarchical media environment. As Dudi Zilbershlag, formerly proprietor of *Bakehilla*, remarked, 'The representatives of the ultra-Orthodox public, as we all now, are the emissaries of the rabbis, and only the Council of Torah Sages decides who they will be. But, as our sages said, representatives of the public should not be appointed without first consulting with the public.'[21] According to Israel Katzover, who was editor of *Yom Shishi*, jointly with Nachshoni:

> Previously, a broad interpretation of the halakhic edict against gossip and scandal, and a deep-rooted aversion to washing dirty linen in public, had limited coverage of the Orthodox world. The new independent Orthodox press has been comfortable discussing the misuse of public funds by Knesset members and Orthodox leaders, or the distortion or corruption of the kashrut system.[22]

It reports and discusses behind the scenes wheeling and dealing of the Council of Torah Sages (the umbrella board of Haredi rabbis in Israel), the politics inside the Haredi political parties and instances of corruption in Haredi institutions. It has also opened a Pandora's box of issues previously denied in Haredi circles such as the problem of Haredi drop-outs from the yeshivot, discrimination in the Ashkenazi Haredi school system against Sephardi children, and Down syndrome children. Their success may be attributed to a desire within sections of Haredi society to be better informed and in particular to be less estranged from the modern Israeli state. Haredi rabbis failed to stop the phenomenon of the commercial media. In 1977 the Council of Torah Sages – worried that they would lose the authority they enjoyed over their community – launched a campaign against the commercial weeklies because whereas the institutionalised daily papers were created by rabbis, the commercial weeklies were the result of economic initiatives. This extended in 2001 when a body entitled 'The Committee for Purity and Sanctity of the Camp', which was identified with a Haredi politician Yaacov Litzman of the United Torah Judaism political faction, fought to close the weeklies. An attempt in 2003 to launch a commercial daily Haredi newspaper failed to bear fruition (Micolson, 1990).

Ha-Mishpacha

Established in 1987 first as a monthly, it became a weekly magazine in 1991. It covered a broad range of subjects of interest to Haredi readers. Reflecting its name Mishpacha or family it included a 'twilight zone of social issues' not covered by the daily Haredi newspapers, among them youth dropouts from the yeshiva world, discrimination against oriental Sephardi students in European or Ashkenazi Haredi schools, Haredim serving in the Israeli Army, returnees to Judaism, special education and psychology, as well as non-Jewish subjects – not usually covered then in the Haredi media – like Martin Luther King and Rembrandt. Established by Yehuda Paley, and owned today by his son Eliahu, its editor is Moshe Grylack, whose background reflects a more open outlook than other Haredi journalists. An immigrant from Belgium in 1945, he studied at the elite Lithuanian Haredi yeshiva of Ponovezh in Bnei Beraq. After years in education – including a stint as an emissary for the Zionist Jewish Agency in Brazil – he was appointed by Shach to edit the *Yated Neeman*, which he led until appointed *Mishpacha* editor in 1991. Grylack's outlook was not dissimilar from Paley himself who came from an atypical Haredi background; his father once ran for an independent Haredi list for the Jerusalem municipality. The magazine was centrist in editorial policy, catering for both the Haredi Hassidic and Haredi Lithuanian streams. It even sought to interest – albeit with limited extent – those in the modern religious sector, like the *hardal* (*haredi leumi*) stricter community. Its high position in the Haredi circulation war was despite its relatively high cover price of 15 shekels (or four dollars) particularly in that many of its readers rather than work studied in yeshivot full-time and had large families. Readers came from a relatively high socio-economic status; 49 per cent of *Mishpacha* readers possessed a car according to a 2002 reader survey, in contrast to 34 per cent and 33 per cent of *Yated Neeman* and *Hamodia* readers respectively. Also, 53 per cent of *Mishpacha* readers had spent their last holidays in a hotel, in contrast to 41 per cent and 37 per cent of *Hamodia* and *Yated Neeman* readers respectively.

Originally only a glossy magazine, a separate news section was added in 1994. Its separate place from the magazine itself enabled readers not wishing to read political gossip not to. Since then, other sections have been added including in 1999 a women's magazine ('Inside the Family') on such topics as fashion and food. Twenty-eight per cent of Haredi women saw the magazine, in contrast to 24 per cent of women who saw *Hamodia*, 17 per cent *Yated Neeman*, and 14 per cent *Bakehilla*.[23] A scholarly supplement on Jewish law and religious culture, *Kolmus*, which began in 2002, raised the magazine's respectability to the level of the 'kadosh' section of the daily Haredi newspapers. A financial section, *Mamonot* ('Property'), was added in 2006, a feature which also began to appear elsewhere in Haredi dailies and weeklies – a recognition of a trend for some Haredim also to work. It had a rabbinical censor, whose name, Rabbi Menaham Cohen, was published – in contrast to the anonymous rabbinical censors elsewhere in the Haredi media – with the task of ensuring that 'unclean language' was left out, together with gossip, immodesty and 'insults to Torah scholars'. Given that the rabbi's appointment was an inhouse appointment, the Haredi rabbinical leadership were inclined to accord the magazine a sense of legitimacy – as a letter by the leading Haredi sage, Rabbi Shlomo Aeurbach, was intended to do, which was published in the magazine. But after Grylach penned an essay, 'The Direction of the Newspaper', a week after the letter appeared, in which he said that the newspaper 'was a stage for a range of views in our community', Auerbach in a subsequent letter withdrew his religious sanction, writing that 'it's clear that all the weeklies come out for economic reasons, and were not founded by the sages'.[24]

Religious broadcasting

The objections of the Haredi community to the general press and television extend to a slightly lesser extent to secular radio given it is more an informational than entertainment tool and given the changing political and defence situation. Thus, according to the above 1995 survey by the Israel Advertisers Association,[25] 20 per cent listened to secular stations like Israel Radio (14 per cent) and Galei Zahal (6 per cent), 26 per cent listened to religious radio then at the time of the survey in the nationalist guise of Arutz 7. The pirate nationalist-modern religious station, *Arutz 7*, broadcast from 1988 until it was closed in 2003, and the contents of which were not regarded as morally problematic. Fifty-six per cent did not listen to any radio. (The survey was carried out prior to the rise of the Radio *Kol Chai* religious station.)

In 1996, the Israel Government, recognising the need to provide the religious communities with their own station, approved the establishment of

Radio *Kol Chai* ('The Voice of Life').Though geared to both the Haredi and modern Orthodox communities, Haredim managed to take control of the station and such features as women announcers and women singers which are anathema to Haredi male ears were limited to certain hours when most men are not listening such as the morning hours. There are a large number of pirate radio stations. Most pirate radio stations in Israel belonged to the religious sector. It reflects the fact that religious populations, in particular the Haredim, feel estranged from mainstream Israeli life. Mainstream radio stations (Israel Radio and Galei Zahal) failed to give expression to their belief system. Some of the private radio stations were affiliated with supporters of the Shas religious party, *Radio Emet* ('The Radio of Truth'), Radio 2000, Radio 10 mostly broadcasting inspirational content comprise religious lessons (*shiurim*), and religious songs. The Shas Party unsuccessfully lobbied in the 1990s to legalise the stations.

Radio Kol Chai

Radio Kol Chai ('the Voice of Life') was established by the Knesset approval together with nine other regional radio stations, but whereas the others were geographically intended to cover different areas, Radio *Kol Chai* was the only one geared to a specific sociological sector. In addition to programmes with Jewish music like *chazanut* (cantorial music) and Hassidic songs, and Jewish study programmes like *shiurim* on the air, programmes included those on property, transport, as well as a 'helpline' programme. Originally intended for the entire religious community, modern Orthodox and traditional non-strictly Orthodox as well as Haredi, the station, facing economic difficulties with small audiences, altered direction to be an all-Haredi station after the station's directorate – which only numbered one Haredi member – argued that the non-Haredi listeners were inclined to listen to general stations like Israel Radio. In order to attract more Haredi audiences, the station had to take steps to remove things which upset some Haredim, like women singers. In a dramatic moment two broadcasters, who were identified with the modern Orthodox, resigned after the station manager stopped on air the broadcasting of a woman singer.[26] In the years since the station started broadcasting, the station's ratings soared, becoming the most popular radio station within the Haredi population. In 2003 the station, which previously broadcast only in certain areas like Benei Beraq upon a franchise for broadcasting to religious audiences, today also broadcasts in the Jerusalem area, giving the station a nationwide audience. There were more programmes of Jewish study. Years later the station, which had earlier taken its news from another station, created its own news divisions comprising editors, reporters and anchormen. There are hourly news bulletins and a two-hour-long news diary in the evening at 7–9 pm – a time when many Haredim have returned home from yeshivot, and radio is, in the absence of television, a key attraction. Notwithstanding that news content was controlled, it was not dissimilar to the commercial

Haredi weeklies, incrementally more open than the institution dailies. For example, it scooped with a report about discriminating against Sephardi-born girls in a Haredi girl's school. Another scoop disclosing that a 'kosher cell phone', promoted as disabling any Internet access to pornographic sites, was incorrect. The station received threats after it disclosed the power struggles in the Ponovezh Yeshiva.[27]

Haredi Internet news websites

By 2009 a handful of Haredi news websites operated independently from rabbinic supervision. These include *Kikar Shabbat* (also the name of the main intersection of the Jerusalem Haredi neighbourhood of Geula-Mea Shearim) *BéHadrei Haredim*, and *LaDaat* ('To know'). Economically successful, the sites were targeted by outside interests, in the case of *Kikar Shabbat* by the *Globus* business news daily. While there were no pictures of women, and aware of the acceptable social limits within the Haredi religio-culturo ghetto, the sites did not subject themselves to the rabbinical censors which, for example, nightly inspect the copy of the Haredi daily newspapers. The news sites print uncensored information about the political infighting within different sections of the Haredi world such as between rival hassidic courts. At times the information transgressed the prohibitions of *loshon hara* (the Jewish law prohibition against political and social gossip). But they are all for expressing criticism – sometimes vehemently – regarding the positions and behaviour of Haredi leaders. The websites, most of which sprang up since 2008, drew upon the prototype model of www.BeHadrei Haredim (a play on the word Haredim, and meaning the inner sanctums (in Hebrew 'hadrei') of the Haredi world, established towards the end of the 1990s by journalist David Rottenberg. Originally a forum on a website, appropriately called 'Hyde Park' – expressing the democratic, populist challenge to rabbinical authority – *BéHadrei Haredim* evolved into an independent news site. By 2008 it had an estimated 6,000 entries an hour. *LaDaat* was established in 2004 – in the wake of the No. 2 bombing in which many Haredim died, as they returned from prayer at the Western Wall – by journalist Noam Zigman and his brother after they identified a large potential Haredi interest from the mass outpouring of Haredim following the bus bombing.

In light of the Haredi ban on the Internet, some Haredi leaders refuse to be interviewed by the sites, and the names of those sponsoring the sites, and editing them, have been hidden from public light.

Whereas in the Haredi newspapers each community newspaper covers their own goings-on – Askenazi Haredi or Sephardi Haredi; European Lithuanian or Hassidic; or a specific Hassidic stream – the websites are intra-Haredi in content. The new media contributed to generating competition within the Haredi media and contributed, within the confines of the limited resources of the Haredi media, to in-built competition, and ultimately to greater professionalism.

Constructing reality in the religious media

Given the Haredi's lack of secular education, or exposure generally to foreign travel, the image constructed by the Haredi media has a very impactful role on the Haredi's perception of the world.

The author's content analysis of newsprint, radio and television in Israel, which also included Haredi media like *Hamodia* and Radio Kol Chai, examined for such quantitative questions as the amount of space religion receives in the media, and for such qualitative questions as media attitudes towards different religious streams and religious themes.

There was much greater coverage of religion in the Haredi press than in the general press: It comprised 27 per cent in *Hamodia*, and 44 per cent on Radio *Kol Chai*'s midday news programme. (It contrasted with 5 per cent both for *Yediot Aharonot* and *Haaretz* and 8 per cent on Israel Radio's early morning newsreel.) The contrast between the secular and religious press was also found by Zecharya (1989) who examined the front pages of *Hamodia*, *Yated Neeman* and *Haaretz* in September 1985 and September 1988: 27 per cent of *Hamodia*'s front page in 1985 and 7 per cent in 1988 dealt with religion issues, and 30 per cent and 3 per cent respectively of *Yated Neeman*'s front page dealt with religion as compared to the secular *Haaretz* in which there was 15 per cent and 4 per cent on religion respectively. (The decline in the Zecharya study from 1985 and 1988 was due to the debate over the Jewish religious status of Ethiopian immigrants to Israel in the first period.)

It was only natural that the Haredi media should focus on their own community, according to the author's content analysis of religion coverage in the Israeli media. In terms of its own community *Hamodia* gave a similar amount (55 per cent) of its religion coverage to Haredim as the secular papers (54 per cent), notwithstanding the overall greater coverage which the religion press gives to religion. Noteworthy is that Haredi newspapers give little coverage to other Jewish religious streams: thus *Hamodia* gave only 2 per cent of its religion coverage to dati leumi or the modern Orthodox despite the shared political agenda of the ultra-Orthodox and modern Orthodox political parties, and despite certain theological proximity of the two Orthodox communities. It reflects also the in-built rivalry between the two religious communities.

Non-Orthodox streams fared even worse. The Reform and Conservative communities accounted for only 0.2 per cent and 0.1 per cent respectively.[28] The Reform stream received more treatment than the Conservative movement in the Haredi media (*Hatzofe, Hamodia*, Radio Kol Chai) – all of which belong to the Orthodox stream of Judaism – since the Orthodox feel theologically more threatened by the Reform movement than the Conservative movement on how Jewish Law should define who is a Jew.

The religious media had a far broader range of religious subjects. Haredi media were found to be more inclined to cover religious news; that the range of themes defined as religious news was wider than in the general media which was limited to religious political parties, religious public personalities, and rabbis; and that the coverage of religion and sub-categories was more balanced and favourable, and that stereotyping was less in the religious media than in the general media. As a hierarchy, the Jewish religion fulfils criteria of involving elites, important people and institutions. There are elite individuals, such as community rabbis, Chief Rabbis and heads of Hassidic courts ('*admorim*'), the last of whose winces and comments are reverently followed in the Haredi media. Coverage of religious holidays, religious youth movements and religious institutions was relatively greater in religious media.

If the secular media was taken up with government-related religion subjects and had little space for internal religious communities, this was not the case with Haredi papers. The general press (*Haaretz* and *Yediot Aharonot*) had 23 per cent of its religion coverage on religious political parties in contrast to 4 per cent in *Hamodia*, even though the religious paper was a party newspaper which might have given far more coverage to government-related matters. Rabbis took up a slightly larger percentage of religion coverage in *Hamodia* (12 per cent) and Radio Kol Chai (10 per cent), which is not surprising given the manifold roles which rabbis fulfil in community life as, amongst others, mentor, Jewish law instructor, spiritual leader, family adviser and marriage guidance counsellor – in contrast to 7 per cent and 5 per cent in *Yediot Aharonot* and *Haaretz*. Festivals (examined was coverage of the holiday of Shavuot, commemorating the receiving of the Torah at Mount Sinai) scored 14 per cent in *Hamodia*'s religion coverage and 3 per cent in the general papers; it was noteworthy that *Hamodia*'s coverage of festivals was far higher than the modern Orthodox *Hatzofe* (9 per cent), reflecting the elevated value which religious holidays have particularly for the ultra-Orthodox. Religious institutions scored 5 per cent and 2 per cent respectively; and youth groups 3 per cent and 0 per cent.

Unsurprisingly, there was a positive image of Haredim. Only 1.6 per cent of *Hamodia*'s religion coverage was stereotyped. And, measured on scale of 1–5 (1 = most negative, 5 = most positive), the image of sub-categories about religion in the religious media were also positive. Thus, rabbis were 3.3 and 4.4 on Radio Ko Chai and *Hamodia* respectively. God was 3.8 in *Hamodia*. Even religious political parties which have a generally poor image in Israel were 3.2 and 2.9 in Radio Kol Chai and *Hamodia* respectively.

Deeper theological issues draw the wide attention of the Haredi media. The religious papers have fat supplements at the weekend dealing with the Torah weekly reading, the religious holydays, theological issues concerning religious observance, and Jewish history – past and present. A telling example of the detailed look at Jewish law was a two-part series in *Hamodia*'s magazine entitled 'The Complex Story of Pareve Orange Juice: Kashering Dairy Equipment for Pareve Production'[29] in *Hamodia* magazine, which discussed whether equipment previously used for the manufacture of milk products could by Jewish religious law be used for the manufacture of pareve products (neither containing milk or meat products).Yet, the end of the age of prophecy in

Jewish belief meant that the deeper theological significance of events could not be extrapolated by the religious communities and therefore minimised the potential for theological depth on the news pages of the religious media.

Conclusion

The religious media help to strengthen religious values and religious structures within the Haredi community, as well as, to a lesser degree, within the modern Orthodox community. It is true that the new Haredi independent commercial weekly press, radio and Haredi internet sites have challenged the institutionalised Haredi press, but the former respect no less the religious values. The only existing challenge in the Haredi case is from the internet, but this is truer outside Israel where the internet ban by Haredi rabbis has been less widely accepted by their followers.

As discussed in the forthcoming chapter, the modern Orthodox, with one foot inside the general community, are exposed to the wider media such as television and internet and could be seen as religiously endangered were it not for the 'balancing effects' of the religious education inside this community.

References

Adorno, T. (1991) *The Culture Industry: Selected Essays on Mass Culture*. London: Routledge.

Baumel, S. (2002) 'Communication and Change: Newspapers, Periodicals and Acculturation among Israeli Haredim', *Jewish History*, 16, 2.

Central Bureau of Statistics. (2009) *Jerusalem*. Social Survey.

Chwat, A. I. (1995) *'Itonim V'Hadashot Mitzva O Isur'* [Hebrew: Newspapers and News: Religious Obligation or Prohibition]. Elkana: T'Lalei Orot.

Israel Advertisers Association: Haredim (1995) *Survey of Exposure to Mass Media: Haredim*. Tel Aviv: Israel Advertisers Association.

Levi, A (1990) 'The Haredi Press and Secular Society', in C. Liebman (ed) *Conflict and Accommodation between Jews in Israel*. Jerusalem: Keter.

Micolson, M. (1990) 'Itonut Haredit B'Yisroel' [Hebrew: The Haredi Press in Israel], *Kesher*, 8.

Tabory, E. (1998) *Reform Judaism in Israel: Progress and Prospects*. New York: The Institute on American Jewish-Israeli Relations of the American Jewish Committee.

Zecharya, Z. (1989) *Ha-itonut ha-Haredi ha-Hadasha* [Hebrew: The New Haredi Media]. Master's thesis. Jerusalem: The Hebrew University.

6   Dual loyalties: the modern Orthodox dilemma

> I see in my work a sense of journalistic mission. My religious beliefs accept that the media with all its deficiencies is a vital element in democratic society. It's impossible to correct society without journalism.
> (Israel Vollman, Journalist *Yediot Aharonot*)[1]

The modern Orthodox or *dati leumi* (lit. national religious) are characterised by a search to synthesise between the Torah and the modern worlds, or between modernity and Orthodoxy. By contrast to the Haredi separatist approach, the modern Orthodox seeks to reach a synthesis, or compromise, between the two worlds. According to the Central Bureau of Statistics (2009), 12 per cent of Israel's Jewish population defined themselves in 2009 as 'modern religious' (as distinct from another 8 per cent who defined themselves as Haredi). Among the questions facing the community are Judaism's view on freedom of expression in mass media and art, and the right to know. For example, some rabbis within the *dati leumi* community have not issued legal rulings limiting the Jew's exposure to modern media – reflecting an intellectual commitment to the search for a synthesis. A stricter sub-stream of the community, the '*hardal*' or '*Haredi leumi*', is a combination of a Haredi separatist view towards modern culture but a nationalist or 'leumi' view towards nationalism and the Zionist state. The hardal contrasts with the Haredi view which does not embrace the nationalist Zionist verve but shares a common view of the need to control the exposure of the community or wider world, including to the media and arts.

In one sense, the modern religious–*hardal* divide raises the question of whether Judaism is a code of moral teachings on a limited number of subjects (known as the 613 positive or negative commands), beyond which Judaism has nothing to say and the individual is freed to act according to his wisdom and moral conscience or whether Judaism is an all-embracing rule of life. If the latter, it is incumbent upon the modern Orthodox Jew to reconcile the two worlds. There is a seemingly endless Hegelian-type struggle between loyalty to Judaism and to the modern world of science with the mid-point thesis moving in one or other direction.

The evolution of a modern Orthodox media

The press in the modern Orthodox sector has enjoyed a far less proliferative existence both in numbers and circulation than the Haredi media owing to the exposure of most members of this sector to the general media. The wider philosophical debate between tradition and modernity was played out by the National Religious Party and its organ, *Hatzofe,* established in 1937 ('The Spectator') (12,000 circ. daily, 18,000 Sabbath and holyday eve) which until its demise in 2005 played an important role in articulating the goals of the *dati leumi* or modern Orthodoxy community during the first 50 years of Israeli statehood. The newspaper expressed and moulded the general outlook of this sector and in particular the view of the community that modern Orthodoxy should become an integral part both of the state's institutions such as the armed forces, and of the general population.

Up to 1967 the newspaper's op-ed and editorial columns dealt at length with the relationship between religion and state, with particular attention to the budgetary needs of the state religious education sector, and to strengthening the chief rabbinate institution – which itself is a creation of the modern Orthodox sector. In campaigning for the new state of Israel to take on a more religious character, the paper clashed with the Prime Minister David Ben Gurion after the latter attacked the modern Orthodox community. It saw the establishment of the Jewish state as the beginning of the messianic redemption. The change in agenda of the party's 'Young Guard' after the 1967 war and the capture of vast tracts of the West Bank, Gaza and the Golan – which had also been part of the Israelite state in ancient times – gained expression editorially inside *Hatzofe* with the newspaper's demands for the right of Jewish settlement in a greater Israel. In later years, as the Arab–Israeli peace process gained momentum, statements by leading Zionist rabbis castigating withdrawal from biblical territory were given prominence – raising afresh the question of the relationship between the modern Orthodox and contemporary state institutions like the Army. With the modern Orthodox from the 1980s onwards dividing into three strata – the moderate veterans, *hardal* and the nationalist right – the newspaper needed to attempt to appeal to all. But editorially, Moshe Ishon, who was editor from 1980 to 1997, wrote skilled polemics against territorial withdrawal from the biblical lands of Judea and Samaria – the West Bank – captured in the 1967 war.

In terms of quantitative content, the religious Orthodox press was found in the author's content analysis of religion in the Israeli media to have had the widest range of non-party political religious content, reflecting also the role they perform in providing information about their own community. This contrasted with the secular press which was mostly interested only in the religious political parties and their impact upon the country's coalition system of government. Religion content comprising the religious political parties in *Hatzofe* was only 10 per cent of all religion content in contrast to the non-religious press: *Yediot Aharonot* 21 per cent and *Haaretz* 25 per cent. Twenty-nine per cent of

Hatzofe's overall editorial content concerned religion in contrast to 8 per cent and 10 per cent of *Yediot Aharonot*'s and *Haaretz*'s content. The dominance of the religious parties in the general media contrasted with the religious papers like *Hatzofe*. This was despite the fact that the religious papers were publications of the religious political parties.

It was only natural that the religious media should focus on their own community: 42 per cent of religion in *Hatzofe* concerned the modern Orthodox community, in contrast to 8 per cent in *Yediot Aharonot* and 10 per cent *Haaretz*. (*Hatzofe* had only 14 per cent of its religious content on Haredim.) The Haredim received a particularly low figure in *Hatzofe* (14 per cent) despite the proximity and in some cases shared political-religious agenda between the modern religious and ultra-Orthodox. It reflects also the in-built rivalry between the two religious communities. The Haredi–modern Orthodox rivalry was also experienced in the opposite direction.

When Ishon retired in 1997 at the behest of the paper's directors, facing ever dwindling circulation, *Hatzofe* took a sea change of direction with the appointment as editor of Gonen Ginat, a *Maariv* journalist, who turned the paper into a brash tabloid with racy headlines. In revamping the news coverage, recruiting younger journalists, it investigated the relationship of the Shin Bet agent Avishai Raviv with Yigal Amir, Prime Minister Itzhak Rabin's assassin. At times the paper became so scurrilous – such as accusing a Haredi girl's seminary students of engaging in prostitution – that Ginat on several occasions was forced to apologise on the paper's pages. The paper played an important role in generating opposition among the modern Orthodox camp against the Sharon Government's withdrawal from Gush Katif in 2005. Though many rabbis and religious educators were among its readers it failed to widen its readership with a circulation of 12,000 to the broad modern Orthodox public.

Shlomo Ben Zvi and **Mekor Rishon**

Since the 1990s the *Mekor Rishon* ('First Source') newspaper carved for itself an important place in the community. Nationalist in tone, it became the voice of the Israeli Jewish population living in Judea and Samara or the West Bank. To be true, *Mekor Rishon* is not a religious newspaper but walks a thin line between this and being the voice of the nationalist camp, including secular right-wing Israelis. The paper's readers include many modern religious Israelis, not only identified with the Right. The weekend issue of the paper – comprising nine supplements, including a political weekly, a weekend magazine, a Sabbath and literature supplement, an economics supplement, sports supplement, fortnightly women's magazine and entertainment billboard – has earned for itself wide regard. Noted for its quality of writing, and intellectual liveliness, the newspaper was less regarded as a major scooper, despite journalists' close ties with Likud circles. The daily paper, by contrast, lacking journalistic resources or drive, covers the news of the day in a superficial manner at best.

While the weekend issue had a readership of 30,000, or was seen by 3.8 per cent of Israeli households according to the 2011 TGI survey, the daily had a minuscule circulation.

Established in 1997 by Gidi Listenberg and Rabbi Shmuel Tal with Meir Uziel, a former *Maariv* journalist, as editor, the paper, which then appeared only in a weekend edition, comprised three sections – a weekly magazine, a political section and a culture section. Facing economic difficulties, the paper closed for a short period in 1999, when it was sold to an American Jewish immigrant Michael Krish. The paper attracted a number of right-wing orientated journalists from a modern Orthodox background including Kalman Lipskind, Uri Elitzur, a former Netanyahu aide, and Haggai Segel. A lack of stability in its first years was reflected in the paper having a succession of five different editors. Uziel was replaced by Yehuda Levi, who had been the *Jerusalem Post* publisher, who was, in turn, replaced by *Kol Hair* journalist Ofer Shapiro, who was replaced by Emmanuel Shiloh, and later by Amnon Shomron.[2] When Shlomo Ben Zvi acquired the paper in 2004 he appointed a secular journalist Amnon Lord, who had moved from Israel's Left to the Right. Its 30,000 readership in 2011 was, according to the TGI survey, nearly 4 per cent of the Israeli population – a long way from its target 50,000 readership. In 2003 Ben Zvi bought out the *Hatzofe* newspaper from the National Religious party and in 2007 absorbed it into *Mekor Rishon* – leaving *Mekor Rishon* as the daily identified with this community.

By the turn of the century, Shlomo Ben Zvi had become modern Orthodoxy's pre-eminent media mogul. In addition to *Mekor Rishon*, he owned *Segula*, a monthly magazine about Jewish culture and history (an offshoot of the former West Bank monthly *Nekuda*), and *Otiot*, a children's magazine. A Hebrew University graduate in physics and maths, he also studied at the Merkaz Harav Kook Yeshiva in Jerusalem. He was identified with the Likud right wing of Moshe Feiglin which sought to emboss Israeli public life with traditional Jewish characteristic features of old. His media reflects both the economic need to draw as wide a readership as possible including beyond the narrow modern religious sector as well as an intellectual open atmosphere which is represented, for example, by his paper's Sabbath supplement having both editorial content and cultural listings beyond Orthodox circles such as the Conservative Masorati movement. Economically successful from real estate, Ben Zvi married into one of the wealthy Jewish families in London. However, he has faced a series of media setbacks. After failing to establish Israel's first free give-away newspaper, *Ha-Yisroeli* ('The Israeli'), he failed to create a Jewish television channel *Techelet*, or win a public franchise for a Jewish radio station. Some questioned whether it was healthy for so much of the modern Orthodox media to be owned by one person.

The media map in modern Orthodoxy moved yet further with the establishment in 2002 of *Basheva*, which reflected the stricter *hardal* perspective. Founded and edited by former *Mekor Rishon* editor Emanuel Shiloh, a trained rabbi and educator, himself the son of one of the community's leading rabbis, it followed a line which, in Shiloh's words, was 'more closely tied to Torah and Jewish religious law (*halakhah*), more single tracked on matters dealing with the State of Israel, and covering what's happening inside the dati leumi or modern Orthodox community'.[3] In his column, 'Table of the Editor' ('Shulkhan Arukh', a play on the halakhic code, the *Shulkhan Arukh*), Shiloh wrote in the paper's first issue, 'Up to now the religious population were exposed to matter from a secular and left-wing press.'[4] Its stance was stricter than that reflected in the *Hatzofe* paper. In addition to its hardline stance of not giving up the biblical territories like the West Bank, the *Hardal* – identified with rabbis like Rabbi Shlomo Aviner and Rabbi Yehoshua Shapiro – is mostly characterised by a cultural isolationist outlook. These range from with fewer secular studies in their schools or exposure at home to television and the Internet. Travel outside the Holyland is frowned upon. The newspaper's strict view is illustrated by its advertising policy. It declined, for example, to publish advertising for foreign travel, or certain events which they regarded as heretical. A freely distributed weekly – with a circulation of 110,000 copies in six localised editions – it was the widest publication of the community, reaching over 85 per cent of modern Orthodox homes, according to the TGI survey, and gave the paper considerable influence in reflecting and articulating the *hardal* substream.[5] Economically, the paper has either profited or balanced its books.

While the modern Orthodox listen to mainstream public radio stations like Israel Radio and Galei Zahal, many also watch public television. These radio stations failed to reflect the views of those living beyond 'the Green line' in the Judea and Samaria territories, or West Bank. To be true, given that no Israeli government since formally annexed the territories to the state, with the exception of the city of Jerusalem, Israeli public broadcasting – reflecting the political uncertainty over the future of the territories – referred to these simply as the West Bank, failing to give expression to the aspirations of the settlements there that the territories were part of the Jewish state.

Partly reflecting their frustration at the coverage, residents of the area decided to establish their own radio station. Established in 1988 by Shulamit Melamed, Arutz 7 filled the vacuum as a pirate station. Given its illegal status, it was forced to broadcast from outside Israel in international waters, but in practice broadcasts were fed to the ship from studios in the territories including its main studio in the Bet-El settlement. The station played an important role in generating a social identity among the residents of Judea and Samaria, including at times of tension such as periods of terrorism directed by Palestinian groups at Jewish residents of the territories.

That Melamed's husband, Zalman Melamad, headed a leading yeshiva in Bet-El alludes to the proximity of the station to the modern religious population not only in the Judea and Samaria areas but also within the state of Israel. Its broadcasts were stridently Zionist in flavour, including much Jewish religious culture as well as Jewish (and no foreign) music. But the station also avoided some of the secular extremities of Israeli radio. According to the 1997

Rokeach Survey, 48 per cent of modern religious or 'dati leumi' Israeli Jews were 'generally inclined to listen to' the station. Moreover, prior to Radio Kol Chai's becoming an all-Haredi station, Arutz 7's clean content drew a sizable Haredi following; 51 per cent of Haredim said they 'were generally inclined to listen to Arutz 7'. In one sense the underground nature of the pirate station and its struggle to become legal echoed the broader struggle of the settlement movement as a whole. The station, therefore, not only succeeded in stamping a sense of solidarity and identity among Jewish residents of the territories but this extended beyond their target audience to the broader Israeli religious population, both modern and Haredi. It also contributed to deepening Jewish traditional values among the residents of the settlements who were not religious, many of whom were drawn to live there by the opportunity of cheap and spacious living.

Despite the fact that right-wing nationalist governments ruled, there were not a few attempts of the authorities to close down the Arutz 7 station, as there were against all pirate radio stations. Attempts to legalise the station to become a legal regional radio station failed in part because the station insisted on producing its own news operation rather than accept a news feed from Israel Radio like other legalised regional stations. In 2003 Arutz 7 closed following a court order, which included arrest warrants for some of its staff but it continued as a radio internet operation. In one sense, the Haredi station, Radio Kol Chai, which had started as an all-religious station geared also for the modern religious, failed to take an opportunity to fill the vacuum after Arutz 7's closure. But in 2010 the Israel Government, reflecting the changed political atmosphere in Israel in a rightward nationalist direction, allowed the establishment of a legal radio station 'Galei Yisroel', for the Judea and Samaria areas, including its right to produce its own news operation.

Is Jewish television feasible?

This question arose in the first decade of the millennium in two contrasting formats and each with different goals. Shlomo Ben Zvi sought unsuccessfully to create a Jewish television channel with broadcasting matter suitable for an audience comprising religious and traditional audiences. Reflecting dissatisfaction among some of the religious segments of the modern Orthodox community with television programming, there was a felt need for a station with traditional content and one free of material unsuitable for family watching. By contrast, Motta Sklar, the head of Israel television, and who was religious, sought successfully to incorporate Jewish cultural content within mainstream broadcasting.

A 2002 poll found considerable interest for a television channel comprising Jewish values and traditions: 21 per cent and 22 per cent of 830 Israeli Jewish respondents surveyed were 'very interested' or 'somewhat interested', and a further 23 per cent 'interested to a certain extent' in a channel comprising Jewish values and traditions, in contrast to 18 per cent who were 'not at all interested', and 13 per cent who were 'not very interested'. And, asked whether they would watch such a channel, 22 per cent replied definitely, 45 per cent thought they would, 13 per cent thought they would not, and 14 per cent definitely not. Of those who said that they would not watch it, 20 per cent were not interested in Judaism, 6 per cent had no time, 4 per cent said there were other channels which they preferred to watch, and 3 per cent were concerned about religious coercion.

The poll found that different sub-categories rated up to 35 per cent 'to a great interest' and up to 27 per cent 'to some extent'. Programmes about Jewish travel around the world generated 35 per cent of respondents who said they would be 'very interested' and a further 27 per cent who said that they were 'interested to some extent'. Jewish historical documentaries found 32 per cent and 26 per cent respectively; Jewish traditional cooking 31 per cent and 22 per cent respectively; basic Judaism 25 per cent and 26 per cent respectively; programmes about Jewish philosophy 25 per cent and 26 per cent respectively; programmes for children on Jewish tradition 24 per cent and 21 per cent respectively; Jewish mysticism 21 per cent and 17 per cent respectively; current affairs 18 per cent and 23 per cent respectively; Jewish music 18 per cent and 19 per cent respectively; personal advice shows 16 per cent and 21 per cent respectively; and programmes comprising Torah *shiurim* (religious lessons) or featuring rabbis 14 per cent and 12 per cent respectively.[6]

In 2003 Ben Zvi established the 'Techelet' channel (a Hebrew reference to the blue colour in holy fringes which observant Jewish men wear). Its programme line included 'the wandering Jew' in which a stand-up artist Jackie Levy tracks Jewish communities around the world; 'The Pashkevil' hosted by a Haredi journalist (the name for poster announcements hung on walls in Haredi areas); a daily soap opera set in a hassidic court in Tel Aviv; a Jewish satire programme; a programme dispensing advice on marital life and education; a 60-second-long programme on different Jewish concepts, 'The Techelet House of Study' presented alternately by former Chief Rabbi Israel Meir Lau and educator Rabbi Motti Elon; and 'The Modest and the Charming', a chat show hosted by different religious women discussing women-related issues, male–female relations, and Jewish current affairs. In addition to its original programme content, the station's schedule also included American television classics for children.

But if audience polls showed considerable interest in a channel like Techelet, in practice it was doomed. When broadcasting began in May 2003 with the first two months free, the station reached a peak of 100,000 audience. But this dropped to 70,000 when audiences had to pay – and this included 40,000 viewers who automatically received the station as part of a package of satellite broadcasts provided by the Israeli *Yes* satellite broadcast company. Six months after the station began, most of its viewers were secular (42 per cent) or traditional (42 per cent) and the modern Orthodox were only 16 per cent. Partly in order to widen its base to the broader population, Ben Zvi took the strategic step of appointing Iris Hod, a secular television producer from Israel

Educational Television, as Techelet's director-general. Hod's appointment produced conflict with the station's head of programmes, Uri Orbach, who was identified with the modern religious community. A year later, by April 2004, revenues had dropped to 500,000 shekels a month (or 120,000 dollars) – a marginal amount considering that 60 per cent of its programming was originally produced. The low audience which the station achieved from the modern religious reflects that they vote with their feet, many fulfilling their programme needs from the mainstream national television broadcasting, which enjoy far greater assets. Nor could a religious television project like Techelet count on the ultra-Orthodox Haredi population which could not free themselves from the community's stigma against television – even if its contents were theoretically acceptable to them. One alternative was to turn the station into carrying advertisements so that its revenue would be generated externally, which audiences were required to pay.

By contrast, the Israel Broadcasting Authority, which includes Israel radio and the first television channel, took a revolutionary stand under Sklar's direction of widening Jewish cultural content in existing programming at times of Jewish holidays. Holidays should be more than their gastronomical side and should penetrate deeper existential questions of God. It included a Sabbath-eve-night programme centring around a sophisticated discussion with a secular figure about the weekly Bible reading. Broadcast on Friday night after the commencement of the Sabbath – when religiously observant Jews are prohibited from viewing television – the programme was clearly targeted towards the mainstream, secular Israeli Jewish audience. In the week between the Jewish New Year and the Yom Kippur Fast of Atonement the television channel ran an hour-long programme each day entitled 'Heshbon Nefesh'. At Hanukah (the Festival of Lights), the television channel's news department was instructed to include an angle on the holiday in the daily nightly news during the eighth day-long holiday. On the eight day festival of Tabernacles or Sukkot the radio music channel, the Third Channel, comprised more songs with a Jewish content. The fast of Tisha B'Av, commemorating the destruction of the two Jewish Temples in Jerusalem, generated day-long programming commemorating the event – whether of an archaeological nature or about secular–religious understanding, in accord with the motif that the Second Temple was destroyed because of Jewish self-hatred.

This approach broke away from the authority's existing organisational model in which television and radio each had a Jewish tradition department. It reflected Sklar's raison d'être of reducing secular–religious tensions through generating understanding of Jewish culture via the mainstream media.

Sklar's long career centred around the potential of mass media as a bridge builder between different segments in the Israeli Jewish population. He began his career in running an educational institution at Hisbin, on the Golan Heights, providing courses for Israeli Army soldiers on Jewish culture. After completing a degree in mass communications at Bar-Ilan University he established the Maale School of Film. In 1999 Sklar was appointed, as the nominee of the National Religious Party, to the coveted role of chairing the Second Television and Radio Authority, and later he was appointed by the government to be the Israel broadcasting authority's director-general.

Sklar also worked to recruit more religious journalists to radio and television. If initially veteran editors and producers were suspicious of his motives, Sklar skilfully used his position to widen religion-related content. Yet if Sklar managed to win greater understanding about Jewish-related matter among the secular audience, this was not true in the opposite direction of the Haredim, given they were exposed exclusively to the Haredi press. They did not see television and learnt little about the secular Israel from the Haredi press or from the Radio Kol Chai.

'Capturing' the national media

The modern religious community were characterised by two contradictory trends. While there is an unquestionable trend for sections of the modern religious to withdraw from mainstream Israeli society and create their own community newspapers, television and Internet websites, there is also a counter-trend of continuing the synthesis, in which the modern religious are fully integrated into modern society. In the past, when the Israeli establishment was characterised by the Mapai and a broadly secular outlook, there was a perceived prejudice against people from a religious background. For some editors there was a practical question of employing people who would not work on the Sabbath. In the latter trend – comprising a synthesis between religious people and Israeli society – religious people are succeeding to make their mark in the Israeli media, as they have in other strata of Israeli life like the military and politics. But the entry of religious people into mainstream Israeli media also reflected a frustration of how religious people were painted and presented by the media – which increased yet further after the 1967 war with the modern Orthodox at the helm of the controversial settlers' movement. In an essay, penned for the settlers' journal, *Nekuda,* journalist Uri Orbach, under the title 'The Media is Good for Me', called for religious people to look to the media profession as a sense of mission not dissimilar to the Israeli army in which many modern religious soldiers have reached senior officer rank.

But what is clear is the number of skull caps and hat-wearing women in Israeli television news programmes, for example, Amit Segel, Amnon Meir and Sarah Beck. More seriously, whereas in the past journalists who happened to be religious were inclined to draw attention away from it, and almost apologetically take on the wares and norms of the liberal and secular media, some religious journalists today present unabashed right-wing agenda, like reporters Hanoch Daum and Uri Orbach. In one case, the Galei Zahal radio station, which is staffed by military conscriptions and civilians, decided in the first decade of this millennium to incorporate more soldiers from peripheral social sectors including religious people – not a simple managerial decision for a station which broadcasts on the Sabbath.

Regarding cinema and television film production, there was an assumption inside the modern Orthodox community that the film world was anathema to Jewish values. But an assumption that the visual arts were an antithesis to Judaism raises fundamental questions about Judaism's reaction to the modern world. Indeed, not a few in the community, in particular the hardal stream, questioned whether a synthesis between cinema and Judaism was feasible practically, such as visual screen expression of romance and love. For some though the corrective lay partly in training religious people in film-making to be absorbed into the Israeli film workplace. In the mid-1980s members of the National Religious Party encouraged the creation of a religious school of film to train the religious. The doubts notwithstanding, the Maale school was created in 1989 by Motta Sklar. The four-year curriculum is divided into theoretical and practical sections with a clear focus on the latter, notably training in film production. Among its students were the crème de la crème of the children and leading lights in the community. Within the confines of Jewish law writings, mainly regarding sexual modesty, Maale mostly succeeded in creating a cadre of religious film producers. Their graduates found their places in television where previously few were seen. Not a few taught film and communications studies notably in the modern religious education sector.

The Avital Livne-Levi affair

The limits of how far the modern religious community could go in training its members for the film world were tested when a Maale student, Avital Livne-Levi, prepared a film in the workshop on experimental film-making, which included a nude woman wearing religious phylacteries (*tephillin*) normally worn by men in daily morning prayers. Livne-Levi screened her film, before students and the teacher, and after word of the showing reached the college management – and later the Israeli media – the student was suspended. The affair would not only bring the school to its knees but raised again doubts of whether the modern religious could find a *modus vivendi* with the Israeli film world or not. Rabbis in the community called for 'clearing out the stables'. The college director, Itzhak Recanati proposed the preparation of a charter to determine what is permissible and what is not. But one teacher, Rami Levi – who, like most other Maale teachers was secular – resigned over the intervention in freedom of expression. But under the title, 'Is Religious Television Possible?'[7] one writer in the modern religious organ, *Hatzofe,* Benjamin Zvielli (a former of head of Israel Television's Jewish Tradition department) argued that freedom of expression is an acceptable argument for a system which necessary justifies boundaries. Moreover, if sexual-related matter motifs were problematic, 'there were', Zvielli argued, 'hundreds of other Jewish themes and subjects in history, building the land, and family life' which may be addressed. Another teacher, Rabbi Shai Piron, a part-time teacher on Jewish aspects of film, resigned at the absence of a full-time rabbi in the college.

Pushing the red lines of *halakhah* to its apparent limits was too much for some in the community. In its attempt to win legitimacy within the framework of religious Zionism, the school was on the edge of acceptability. As Jacobson remarked, the fact that a majority of Maale's students are women is an indicator of its lack of acceptability (Jacobson, 2004). Rabbis called on people not to register for the school. Applications dropped the following year so dramatically that it was decided not to open a first year. The school fell into a deficit and faced closure. When the school finally reopened, its curriculum was altered to include more classes on Judaism. Separate classes between male and female students were introduced. A monthly forum of rabbis and educators was introduced – the so-called Institute of Torah Creative Endeavour – to view movies and debate issues raised from a Jewish perspective.

Livne-Levi was isolated by fellow Maale students. Even her parents and sisters were criticised by friends in their community. 'I was slapped for the school not opening that year, for not betting budgets, for its collapse – and my reaction was – Wow is that really so? Do I have so much power? When I look back on that period, I understand that this collision was a necessary stage in my development.'[8]

Conclusion

As the modern Orthodox media evolved into a separate media sector, it necessarily challenged the ethos of the idea of the modern Orthodox as full partners in the wider modern society. Instead the sector created its own separate identity like Haredist separatism if significantly different in tone. It reflected a fundamentalist trend – whether Jewish, Christian or Muslim – to reconstruct and invent its traditional image, in a withdrawal-of-sorts from the modern world (Gellner, 1992). Their community preferred also to be exposed to their own media rather than the mainstream – or 'secular' – media. The community media played a role in the formation of the modern Orthodox sector's self-identity. The media are a powerful agent for legitimising political structures, turning the attention of their members towards participating fully and creatively in its societal structures (Adorno, 1991). It also reflected a broader trend not only in Israel but the Western world itself at fragmentation in media, characterised by broadcast media deregulation and multiple internet sites. That the community were less exposed to the general media challenged the raison d'être of seeking full integration with modernity, and the resulting long-term implications of their exposure to their own media, of strengthening the nationalist exclusivist character of what was modern Orthodoxy.

A counter trend by the end of the twentieth century was that the modern Orthodox were achieving key positions in Israeli society like the civil service, the armed forces and to some extent academia. Their role in key positions in Israeli society, including in the general media, had a domino effect that purely secularist thinking would be channelled, confidently, into a rewritten formula that modernity now embraced Jewish culture unashamedly – reflecting the very synthesis of religion and modernity, albeit on the former's terms and conditions.

References

Adorno, T. (1991) *The Culture Industry: Selected Essays on Mass Culture.* London: Routledge.
Central Bureau of Statistics. (2009) *Social Survey.* Jerusalem: Central Bureau of Statistics.
Gellner, E. (1992) *Postmodernism, Reason and Religion.* London: Routledge.
Jacobson, D. C. (2004) 'The Maale School: Catalyst for the Entrance of Religious Zionism to the World of Media Production', *Israel Studies,* 9, 1.

7 Identity, unity and discord

> While the media is not hostile to the religious as a general rule, the media is generally hostile towards *Halakhah* (Jewish religious law) and its leaders. *Halakhah* is presented as a dark force which interferes in private life, and above all is cruel. One Haredi politician once said that it's good that that there was no law requiring male circumcision because if there were there would be no chance that most people would have their sons circumcised. It is not coincidental that the Israeli media is much more tolerant of non-Jewish religions than they of the Jewish religion. Rabbis fix the way of life. There would be no better way to improve the image of religion in Israel than were religious groups to cut their ties with politics.
>
> (Shahar Ilon, Haredi affairs reporter, *Haaretz*)[1]

The effects of media content of religion and of religious media may be measured at a number of levels: in terms of exposure to media, and the effects of the exposure both upon Israeli's religious identity, and upon the social perception of other Jews. These are, first, the exposure of Israelis to religious content in the media. One byproduct of media content of religion is that it circumvents traditional forms of religious authority providing people with alternative sources of information. Secondly, there is the impact upon religious identity. A byproduct is the exposure to media of rabbis in terms of their being 'religious decisionmakers', as influential leaders of communities, educators and religious court judges. Thirdly, there is the impact of media coverage on the mutual perceptions of secular–religious relations.

Exposure to media

To be examined first is the public's exposure to the media. Seventy-two per cent of Israelis read Israeli newspapers daily, and 84 per cent read a newspaper at weekends, according to a 2000 TGI survey. Notwithstanding this, there is a declining trend of exposure to newspapers, reflecting an incremental trend towards Internet websites. By 2009 one survey found that while 67 per cent read newspapers from time to time, only about 50 per cent did so daily (Pnim, 2009). A 2007 survey found a decline in newspaper reading: 42 per cent of Israelis canvassed read a newspaper daily, 12 per cent do so a couple of times

Identity, unity and discord 109

a week. 12 per cent do so once a week. Television remained the most used source of news out of all media (including newspapers, radio and Internet news websites): 51 per cent view television news daily, 25 per cent several times a week, 8 per cent once a week, and only 15 per cent not at all. Radio was in second place as most popular news source: 45 per cent daily, 20 per cent several times a week, 8 per cent once a week, 27 per cent not at all. More surprising, and perhaps indicative of future trends, was the low position which Internet websites received among Israeli surfers. Only 32 per cent surfed a news website daily, 10 per cent several times a week, 8 per cent once a week; 50 per cent did not surf news websites at all. This suggests that more traditional news sources, like television, radio and newspapers, may be expected to remain key news sources for the foreseeable future (Haim Herzog Institute, 2007).

This chapter will discuss differences in patterns of exposure among audiences according to religiosity. Forty-four per cent of strictly observant Israeli Jews (comprising the Haredi and modern Orthodox communities) read a religious newspaper regularly, 9 per cent frequently, 10 per cent sometimes, 9 per cent seldom, and 28 per cent never. By contrast, 7 per cent of Israeli Jews who describe themselves as 'observant to a great extent' always read a religious newspaper, 6 per cent frequently do, 12 per cent sometimes, 10 per cent seldom, and 65 per cent never. Ninety per cent of 'somewhat observant' and 98 per cent of 'totally non-observant' never do (Rokeach,1997).

Broken down between different sectors of religious identity there was considerable difference of media exposure. First, the ultra-Orthodox or *Haredi* community – numbering 8 per cent of the Israel's Jewish population which in 2009 reached 5,700,000 – is characterised by a tendency of withdrawal from modernity. Second, the modern Orthodox community (or *dati leumi*), numbering some 834,000 Jews, while strictly observant, seek to reconcile Jewish life with modernity and believe that the messianic Third Jewish Commonwealth, promised in Biblical texts, has arrived. The third trend, the secular community, encourages the separate of religion and state: 42 per cent of Israeli Jews in 2009 defined themselves as secular, according to the Central Bureau of Statistics (2009). A fourth bloc, an estimated 42 per cent of the Jewish population, between the secular community and the religious community, comprises a middle group of traditional Jews, who identify with Judaism and observe Jewish laws and customs selectively. This bloc comprises an estimated 38 per cent of the Jewish population. This was broken down, according to the survey, between 13 per cent who defined themselves as 'traditional-religious' and 25 per cent as 'traditional but not very religious'.

Sixty-six per cent of secular Israelis read daily newspapers in contrast to 77 per cent of traditional Israeli Jews, and 59 per cent Haredi and modern religious combined (Pnim, 2009). There was considerable difference in most preferred media from sector to sector. Forty-two per cent of the secular population said that the Internet was the first source, television in second place (33 per cent), radio third place (13 per cent) and newspapers fourth place (8 per cent). For the religious sector (Haredi and modern Orthodox combined) radio was in first place (34 per cent), Internet second place (26 per cent), newspapers third place (19 per cent), and television in fourth place (13 per cent). Twenty-eight per cent of religious people (Haredi and modern Orthodox) defining themselves as religious do not see a daily newspaper in contrast to 17 per cent of secular Israelis (Israel Advertisers' Association, 1997). The traditional sector were found to be between the religious and secular sectors, but the first and second place were reversed with television in first place (45 per cent) and Internet (22 per cent) in second place. Newspapers were in third place with 16 per cent, and radio fourth place with 12 per cent (Pnim, 2009). It is true that a clear distinction needs to be drawn in the religious between Haredi and the modern Orthodox or *dati leumi*.

Exposure of Haredim to the press

Religious communities are not as exposed to the mainstream media as the general Israeli Jewish population. This is particularly true of the Haredi community. A considerable section of the Haredi community are not exposed to any modern mass media. Thirty-two per cent of the Haredi community do not read any newspaper. Only 14 per cent of Haredim read general newspapers (Israel Advertisers Association, 1995). In an earlier survey, Lieberman in 1992 came to a not dissimilar conclusion: 50 per cent of Haredim did not read any paper, 50 per cent read Haredi papers, 10 per cent read secular papers.[2] Haredim have banned television both because its content is considered to endanger religious values and because television viewing takes up time which could be better spent in Jewish educational study. Only 33 per cent of residents of the predominantly Haredi city of Benei Beraq possessed a television set in contrast to most other Israeli cities where the number of households with a television set ranged from a low of 82 per cent of Ashdod to 100 per cent in the Rishon LeZion survey (Central Bureau of Statistics, 2008). There was little change over the years. According to a Millward Brown survey in 2010, 75 per cent of Haredim were nevertheless exposed to either newspapers, radio or Internet. The most exposed medium among Haredim was daily newspapers (45 per cent), and contrasted with radio 14 per cent and Internet 12 per cent. But Haredim broken down between Lithuanian Haredim, hassidic Haredim and Sephardi Haredim showed considerable difference with Lithuanians generally more restrictive, and with Sephardi Hassidim more open to non-print media. Twenty-six per cent of Sephardi Haredim listened to radio daily in contrast to 11 per cent of Lithuanians and 7 per cent Hassidic Haredim. Fifty-eight per cent of Hassidic Haredim saw a daily newspaper, 53 per cent Lithuanians, and 29 per cent Sephardi Haredim. And, according to one of the first surveys of Haredi usage of the Internet, 13 per cent of Sephardic Haredim surfed the Internet daily, and 12 per cent Hassidic Haredim in contrast to 6 per cent of Lithuanian Haredim alone.[3]

These findings contrast with one in the US which found the more religious the person, the more he was inclined to read papers; 64 per cent of Americans who attend at least once a week read a daily newspaper in contrast to 49 per cent who attend church less than once a week, and 49 per cent once a year or less (Hoover, 1988, Table 7:19).

There are clearly delineated patterns of the most read Haredi newspapers among the ultra Orthodox Haredi population. *Hamodia*, the Hassidic daily, had an exposure to its weekend Friday edition of 27 per cent, and *Yated Neeman,* the Lithuanian Haredi paper, to 26 per cent, according to a 2007 TGI survey. The daily editions were seen by slightly smaller figures. As a factor of the broader Israeli population, *Hamodia* was seen by 2.3 per cent of the Israeli population, *Yated Neeman* by 3 per cent.[4] Exposure to *Hamodia* changed by 2009 with the establishment of the rival hassidic Haredi newspaper, *Hamevaser.* But the biggest Haredi print medium was the *Mishpacha* weekly magazine. In 2006 *Mishpacha* had 110,000 readers in contrast to *Hamodia*'s 93,000 readers (which preceded the establishment of the breakaway *Hamevaser* paper) and *Yated Neeman*'s 90,000 readers. Despite that *Hamodia* then had a lead over *Yated Neeman* it is noteworthy that *Yated Neeman* was stronger in the cities with the largest Haredi populations, Jerusalem and Bnei Beraq; 40 per cent of Haredim in Bnei Beraq saw *Yated,* and 32 per cent *Hamodia,* and 21 per cent of Haredim in Jerusalem saw *Yated Neeman* and 15 per cent *Hamodia.*[5]

Patterns of radio exposure according to religiosity

The Rokeach study (Rokeach, 1997), established by the Israeli government to examine radio as a tool for strengthening of traditional values, carried out an unpublished wide-ranging survey of radio listening among four sectors: Haredim, modern Orthodox, traditional (i.e. non-strictly observant) and secular. Various surveys over the years have produced different statistics, but there has been an undoubted Haredi trend of withdrawal; 46 per cent said they did not listen to any radio (Israel Advertisers' Association: Haredim, 1995). The 2010 Millward Brown survey found that 14 per cent of Haredim were exposed to radio.[6] Twenty-four per cent of Haredim are estimated to listen to the *Kol Chai* Haredi station. Before Kol Chai's establishment, many Haredim listened to Arutz 7, which is identified with the settlers and controlled by modern religious interests, which was surprising given the station's ultra-Zionist agenda. The inspirational Haredi-orientated pirate radio stations have a following: 2 per cent and 1 per cent of Haredim listen to *Kol Neshama* ('The Voice of the Soul') and Radio Emes (Israel Advertisers' Association: Haredim, 1995). Only 14 per cent listen to Israeli radio, and 6 per cent to the *Galei Zahal* military radio station. The low figures for radio are surprising given the rapidly changing security situation in the country. Thirty per cent of Haredim who do not listen to radio said they do not do so for reasons of religiosity. According to the Millward Brown survey, only 14 per cent of Haredim said that radio was the medium they were most exposed to.[7]

Given Haredi qualifications with identifying with the Zionist state, and Galei Zahal's broadcasting of pop music including female singers – which is anathema to the Haredi population – Galei Zahal is a useful case for analysing Haredi listening patterns. The Rokeach survey found that 16 per cent of Haredim said they listened to Galei Zahal in contrast to 38 per cent of the modern religious, 50 per cent of the traditional, and 50 per cent secular (Rokeach, 1997). But there was little difference among Haredim and the other streams in listening to the main news channel (Channel 2) of Israel Radio: 36 per cent of Haredim listened to it, in contrast to 43 per cent modern religious, 36 per cent traditional, and 38 per cent secular. Arutz Sheva, having content more acceptable to this sector than Israel Radio and Galei Zahal, which are secular in character, was preferred over Galei Zahal. Fifty-one per cent of Haredim listened to Arutz 7, notwithstanding that its news operation and general infrastructure is considerably weaker than the other two stations. Given the station's fervent Zionism and Haredim's anti-Zionism, it suggested that the Haredi – choosing between secular content, including female singing regarded as immodest – prefers Zionism. A further 24 per cent listened to Radio Kol Chai, which at the time of the survey was in its infancy (which since the 1997 survey was taken had blossomed into becoming the major Haredi radio station).

When asked why they do not listen to radio at all, 30 per cent of Haredim in the Rokeach survey said they do not do so for religious reasons, in contrast to 0 per cent of each of the other three streams – modern Orthodox, traditional and secular – who said they do not listen to radio who cited the religious factor. Asked whether the Galei Zahal station clashed with religious values, 51 per cent of Haredim said so in contrast to 29 per cent of modern Orthodox, 14 per cent traditional and 18 per cent secular. Thirty per cent and 25 per cent of Haredi were 'very dissatisfied' or 'dissatisfied' with public broadcasting, in contrast to an average of 5 per cent and 16 per cent of the other three streams. Only 25 per cent of Haredim said they were satisfied (an average of 58 per cent of the other three streams they were satisfied).

Haredi daily listening patterns contrasted with the other religious streams. While the cases of the other three streams listened, mostly in the morning, moving to television as the primary medium in the evening, most Haredim listened in the evening leisure hours, due both to the Haredi ban on television and to Haredim being occupied in the morning in daily prayers in the synagogue. While 46 per cent, 47 per cent and 44 per cent of secular, traditional and modern Orthodox listened to radio in the 06.00–09.00 period in the morning, only 20 per cent of Haredim do so. And, while 10 per cent, 9 per cent and 13 per cent of secular, traditional and modern Orthodox listened in the 18.00–21.00 period, 24 per cent of Haredim did (Israel Advertisers Association: Haredim, 1995).

The modern Orthodox community are less restrictive in their exposure to media and in the main watch television as well. For example, in the report of the Rokeach Committee 12 per cent and 25 per cent of modern Orthodox Jews listen to radio or watch television all the time or frequently respectively.

Exposure of the modern Orthodox to the press

There are patterns of the most read print media among the modern religious sectors. Until its closure the newspaper of the then National Religious Party, *Hatzofe*, was seen daily by 7 per cent and 12 per cent saw the weekend Friday edition, according to a 2000 survey. Reflecting their outlook to synthesise religion with modernity, the modern Orthodox were more inclined to follow mainstream patterns with the secular and traditional streams. *Mekor Rishon*, the independently-owned nationalist quality paper was, according to the survey, seen at weekends by 20 per cent of the modern Orthodox population. The free weekly nationalist-religious weekly *Basheva* had a print-run of 120,000 copies resulting in a very wide exposure among the modern religious sector. As a factor of the broader Israeli population, *Mekor Rishon* was seen by 4 per cent of the Israeli population, and *Basheva* in 2010 by 6.4 per cent of the Israeli population.[8] Thirty-eight per cent of modern Orthodox listened to Galei Zahal (in contrast to 16 per cent of Haredim), like 50 per cent of the secular and 40 per cent traditional. Given both the modern Orthodox's acceptance of secular life as well as their identification with Zionism including the Israeli Army, this was not so surprising. Yet, asked whether Galei Zahal damaged religious values, 29 per cent of modern Orthodox said so, in contrast to 14 per cent of traditional respondents and 18 per cent secular respondents. The modern Orthodox also responded far higher than Haredim to whether they listened to radio 'throughout the day' (as did 37 per cent of traditional respondents and 30 per cent of secular respondents) in contrast to 23 per cent of Haredim.

While 56 per cent of modern Orthodox were more satisfied than Haredim with public broadcasting regarding whether it damaged religious values (like 58 per cent secular and 60 per cent traditional by contrast to 25 per cent of Haredim), the modern Orthodox were less inclined than the traditional and secular to be very satisfied, and were more inclined to express dissatisfaction or great dissatisfaction: 20 per cent of modern Orthodox expressed dissatisfaction with public broadcasting in contrast to 7 per cent of traditional and 6 per cent secular respondents.

Overall public satisfaction among the broad Israeli public in media coverage of religion is limited. Public confidence in the media is low, and public confidence in coverage is even worse, if not quantitatively at least qualitatively. A 2008 poll by the Israel Democracy Institute found that only 37 per cent of respondents expressed confidence in the Israeli media. It was much lower, for example, than public confidence in the Israeli Army (71 per cent) or the Supreme Court (49 per cent).[9] And 53 per cent of Israelis polled in 2000 thought that media institutions were corrupt (in contrast to the Israeli Army

(30 per cent) or the Supreme Court (28 per cent)).[10] The Israeli media enjoyed a public confidence rating in 2003 (1 – no confidence, 5 – full confidence) of 2.9 – but, broken down according to religiosity, the more religious the respondent the lower the level of confidence he had. Thus, while secular Israelis gave the Israeli media a confidence rating of 3.07, traditional Israelis gave it only 2.98, modern religious or *dati leumi* Israelis 2.65, and Haredim 2.32 (Haim Herzog Institute, 2007). (Not dissimilar, a 2004 poll found that 61 per cent of Haredim said that the general media were antagonistic, and a further 19 per cent of Haredim said this was true in the case of some of the media.[11]

Media effects and rabbis

Rabbis are the key 'decision-makers' in the world of religion. Given that the rabbi has a leadership and guidance function in his community, it needs to be questioned whether, and if so to what extent, the rabbi is in touch with the wider environment and to what extent rabbis are exposed to the same media as their community.

In the poll of rabbis carried out by the author, exposure of rabbis themselves to the media was stronger in the case of the printed media than the television media. Yet, even newspapers were less widely seen than might otherwise be postulated for persons who hold key posts in their communities: 58 per cent, 50 per cent and 28 per cent of modern Orthodox rabbis, Haredi rabbis and non-Orthodox rabbis do not see a daily newspaper. Breaking down the 58 per cent figure for modern Orthodox, 70 per cent of hardal rabbis and 50 per cent of modern Orthodox rabbis do not read a daily newspaper.

There was a greater inclination for Western-born rabbis (67 per cent) to read a daily newspaper, and a lesser inclination of rabbis born in the Arab world (39 per cent) to.

An age difference could be drawn in reading daily newspapers, with younger rabbis inclined not to: 74 per cent of rabbis born 1967–1980 did not read a daily newspaper in contrast to 44 per cent of those born 1941–1960, and 28 per cent born 1921–1940. Of those who do not read a daily newspaper, 39 per cent, 27 per cent and 12 per cent of Haredi rabbis, hardal rabbis, and modern Orthodox rabbis cited religious reasons for not doing so. Of those who do not read newspapers, the most given factor was time; 93 per cent, 78 per cent and 48 per cent of non-Orthodox, modern Orthodox and Haredi said time was the factor.

In the case of television, 81 per cent of Haredim and 63 per cent of hardal rabbis said they do not view television for religious reasons as opposed to 47 per cent of modern Orthodox. Fifteen per cent of Haredim cited time; 46 per cent of modern Orthodox and 65 per cent of non-Orthodox also did so. Of those rabbis who do not have television, 58 per cent of those who have children at home gave religious reasons as opposed to 31 per cent of rabbis who do not have children at home. Similar figures were given for those who replied they do not listen to radio. Fifty per cent and 20 per cent of Haredi and modern Orthodox rabbis cited religious reasons.

The impact on rabbis of their exposure to the media should be differentiated between religion-related information and news or background features about developments in the wider environment not related to religion. In the former, media had little impact on the rabbis' knowledge of religious matters: 53 per cent of all rabbis said that the media had no impact at all, 29 per cent a little impact, 14 per cent at times. Haredi rabbis were less inclined than non-Orthodox rabbis to be influenced. The influence of the media on the rabbis' understanding of the religious environment was low: 37 per cent replied that the influence of the media upon their understanding of the religious environment was 'not at all', 38 per cent 'a little' and 20 per cent 'at times'. Rabbis had other, non-mass media, channels for learning about changes on the religious scene. And the extent to which the media altered the rabbis' outlook towards the religious world was even less given that the rabbi, by virtue of identifying with and belonging to a religious stream, had a definite view on the subject: 49 per cent not at all and 34 per cent a little.

The influence on rabbis of the media's coverage of the secular environment, by contrast, was considerable – 26 per cent of rabbis said so to 'a very great extent', 31 per cent 'a lot', 22 per cent 'at times'. This was particularly true with non-Orthodox rabbis: 44 per cent of non-Orthodox rabbis replied 'to a great extent'. And a further 31 per cent of non-Orthodox rabbis replied 'from time to time' in contrast to only 24 per cent of Haredi rabbis (modern Orthodox: 32 per cent). The exposure to the media changed the outlook about the general secular environment 'a lot' for 8 per cent of all rabbis, and 'at times' for 27 per cent of rabbis; however, 35 per cent of rabbis said it changed only a little and 28 per cent not at all.

Religious identity

In addition to acting as a source of information, mass media fulfil a number of such functions as strengthening religious identity, an important ingredient of Israeli society. There is considerable variance among the Israeli Jewish public in interest in religion. The 2009 Central Bureau of Statistics social survey found that 43 per cent of Israelis wanted more information about religion while 56 per cent did not (Central Bureau of Statistics, 2009). This was an increase from 1982 when Shye (1983) found that 70 per cent of Israelis polled were either not at all interested (40 per cent) or not so interested (30 per cent) in the topic of religions in the media. Only 5 per cent were 'very interested'; 24 per cent were interested to some extent. The demand for more information about religion varied according to the religiosity of the respondent. The 2009 survey found that, broken down, 91 per cent of Haredi respondents wanted more information, 78 per cent of modern religious and 42 per cent of traditional-religious in contrast to 38 per cent of 'traditional-not so religious' and 24 per cent of secular respondents (Central Bureau of Statistics, 2009).

Audience interest in religion: The Rokeach survey

The Rokeach governmental inquiry (Rokeach, 1997) sheds light on patterns of exposure to the media among different religious streams. It was not surprising that two extreme patterns were found – in the Haredim and the secular, the former seemingly singlemindedly interested in religious instruction (*shiurim*) on the air and the latter only interested in Jewish music from the various Judaism-related options. More surprising was an overlap between the traditional and modern Orthodox patterns in religion content tastes, and by corollary a considerable gap between the traditional and secular streams. The Rokeach's unpublished survey found that 80 per cent of secular Israelis do not listen at all to religion-related radio programmes, 15 per cent listen but only at long intervals (and 2 per cent from time to time, and 1 per cent each day) in contrast to 51 per cent of traditional Jews who do not listen, 29 per cent at long intervals, 11 per cent from time to time (1 per cent each day). Similar ratings were found for modern religious and Haredi Israelis: 29 per cent and 24 per cent of modern religious and Haredi Israelis respectively do not listen at all to religious programming, 30 per cent and 22 per cent at long intervals; 25 per cent and 32 per cent from time to time, and 12 per cent and 19 per cent each day.

In order to produce a picture of their preferences in religion-related content, respondents were shown a list of radio programmes including on religion and tradition, and religious lessons on radio (*shiurim*). Two of ten types of programming were on 'religion and tradition' and 'lessons in religious study and ethics (*shiurim*)'. In addition to these two, the other types of programming were news bulletins; the news diary of current affairs; Israeli music; current affairs documentaries; classical music; soap opera; radio quiz; radio educational programmes.

A considerable difference in interest in religion among different publics was found – posing a challenge to the broadcasting authority to satisfy public taste. Among the secular, 'religion and tradition' and 'radio lessons in religious study and ethics (*shiurim*)' were in tenth or lowest place; 3 per cent and 2 per cent of secular respondents respectively listened 'from time to time' to religion and tradition programmes, and to religious lessons ('*shiurim*') on the air. The survey found that 44 per cent and 37 per cent of modern Orthodox Jews, and 55 per cent and 51 per cent of Haredi Jews listened frequently to *shiurim*, and programmes on religion and tradition (Rokeach, 1997). By contrast, only 2 per cent and 3 per cent of secular Israelis listened frequently to *shiurim*, and programmes on religion and tradition. Between the two extremes, 21 per cent and 17 per cent of 'traditional Israelis' listened frequently to *shiurim*, and programmes on religion and tradition. Among the traditional respondents, 21 per cent (albeit in bottom place) listened to (*shiurim*) from time to time of which 5 per cent sought to listen daily. Seventeen per cent (in ninth place) listened to religious tradition programmes from time to time (of which 6 per cent sought to listen daily) This rose very considerably by the modern religious in the case of *shiurim* (to fifth place), or 44 per cent 'from time to time', including 15 per cent who sought to each day. In the case of programmes on religious tradition (sixth place) 37 per cent of modern religious respondents listened 'from time to time' of which 12 per cent sought to daily. The figures went up even further for the Haredim. *Shiurim* (in second place) were listened to by 55 per cent 'from time to time' of which 26 per cent did so daily. Programmes on religious tradition (third place) were listened to by 51 per cent of Haredi respondents who did so 'from time to time', and 19 per cent who sought to daily.

The Rokeach survey surveyed respondents regarding four types of religious content programming: programmes on family or religious tradition; Jewish music; Jewish ethics; religious lessons. Among the secular, the most wanted category was Jewish music (29 per cent of secular respondents were interested and 6 per cent very interested) and programmes on Jewish family and tradition were wanted by 24 per cent and 'much wanted' by a further 9 per cent. In less demand among secular respondents were programmes on Jewish ethics, and even less on religious instruction: 22 per cent and 4 per cent 'wanted' or 'much wanted' programmes on Jewish ethics, and 10 per cent and 3 per cent 'wanted' or 'much wanted' programmes on religious instruction.

There was a considerable gap between the demands of traditional Jews over secular Israelis, with traditional Jews close both to the modern religious and the Haredim. For the traditional sector, the programmes in most demand were for Jewish family and tradition (51 per cent and 20 per cent of traditional respondents 'wanted' or 'much wanted' them). Forty-three per cent and 20 per cent of traditional respondents 'wanted' or 'much wanted' programmes on Jewish ethics. Forty-three per cent and 15 per cent 'wanted' or 'much wanted' Jewish music. Noteworthy was that 43 per cent and 11 per cent of traditional respondents 'wanted' or 'much wanted' more programmes with religious instruction.

Among the modern religious, all categories were in demand. Jewish music was 'wanted' or 'much wanted' by 48 per cent and 33 per cent respectively. Programmes with religious instruction was 'wanted' or 'much wanted' by 48 per cent and 32 per cent respectively; programmes on Jewish family and tradition were wanted or much wanted by 48 per cent and 35 per cent respectively; and programmes on Jewish ethics by 43 per cent and 21 per cent respectively.

Among the Haredi respondents, 45 per cent and 39 per cent 'much wanted' or 'wanted' *shiurim* respectively. This was the most popular of the four categories for Haredi respondents, and confirms how much the Haredi's life centres around the synagogue and talmudical study hall. In second place among Haredi respondents was Jewish music (45 per cent and 31 per cent 'wanted' or 'much wanted'). In third place was Jewish ethics: 43 per cent and 31 per cent of Haredi respondents 'wanted' or 'much wanted'. Forty-two per cent and 31 per cent of Jewish family and tradition was 'wanted' or 'much wanted'.

Overall, the modern religious and Haredi were inclined to complain that there was a felt absence of religious programming; 51 per cent of modern religious and 32 per cent of Haredim felt 'an absence', and a further 25 per cent of Haredim and 11 per cent of modern religious respondents felt 'a great absence'. By contrast, 36 per cent of traditional respondents felt an absence of religious programming (4 per cent felt 'a great absence'). Only 6 per cent of secular respondents felt 'any absence' (1 per cent felt 'a great absence' of religious programming. Fifty-eight per cent and 29 per cent of secular respondents did not feel, or did not feel at all, any absence on religious programming. Forty-seven per cent and 36 per cent of traditional respondents felt 'no absence' or 'no absence at all'. Only 33 per cent and 12 per cent of modern religious 'did not feel any absence', or 'any absence at all'. Thirty-one per cent and 7 per cent did not feel 'any absence', or 'any absence at all'.

In complex industrial societies, individuals construct religious meaning from a variety of sources. Religious and spiritual issues are increasingly mediated through print and electronic technologies. Mass media have become sub-agents of contemporary religious identity. Increased emphasis upon personal choice in moral and religious matters is reflected in the development of religion outlets, including religious broadcasting, religious press and the Internet. The choice orientation in modern societies strengthens the potential religious and theological significance of media for construction of personal belief systems. News media play opposite roles for religious communities and for the secular Israeli population.

For Haredim, synagogue communities are frameworks for strengthening religious values. While the new Haredi independent commercial weekly press poses a challenge to the institutionalised Haredi press, the former also respect no less the religious values. The only existing challenge in the Haredi case is from the Internet – which is truer outside Israel where the Internet ban by Haredi rabbis has been less widely accepted by their followers.

The modern Orthodox, with one foot inside the general community, are exposed to the wider media such as television and Internet and could be seen as religiously endangered were it not for the 'balancing effects' of the religious education inside this community.

For the traditional, the media are important agents of religious identity. Hoover has argued that the media have become today important framers of religious faith (Hoover, 2006). Traditional Jews span a wide spectrum from those almost secular to those almost religious. The more affiliated of traditional Jewish Israelis at least frequent the synagogue occasionally or have their children educated in traditional 'Tali' schools (affiliated with the Conservative 'Masorati' community) or modern Orthodox schools.

Rabbis received greater attention in the religious media suggesting that the role of the media within the religious community was greater inside the religious community than the secular community, notwithstanding that religious communities are characterised by the existence of other more dominant agents of religious identity like the synagogue and religious instruction.

Rabbis – protectors of the faith – received great attention in the religious media. In the author's study of religion content, rabbis took up 12 per cent of all religion coverage in the religious Haredi daily *Hamodia* and 10 per cent in the religious radio station Radio *Kol Chai,* in contrast to 7 per cent and 5 per cent in *Yediot Aharonot,* the country's biggest mass circulation popular daily newspaper, and *Haaretz,* the quality daily newspaper. Religious media – both the Haredi media, daily and weekly, and modern-Orthodox media like *BaSheva* and *Mekor Rishon* – have far greater religious content than the secular media. Religious holidays, religious youth movements, and religious institutions, for example, are covered by the religious media much more than in the secular media. Yet, the influence of such agents of religious identity like the synagogue and religious instruction were even greater than the religious media within the ultra-Orthodox and modern Orthodox communities.

Quantitatively, there was little coverage of strictly theology related matter in the general, non-religious media. Rabbis themselves comprised a total of only 8 per cent of the sum total of religion content in the Israeli press, radio and television examined. Deeper theological issues draw the attention of the media rarely or, at best, infrequently, with the exception of the religious media. God – the ultimate, elite symbol of religion – accounted for only 0.3 per cent of religion coverage. Alternatively, only 10 of the 3,618 items examined in the content analysis on religion concerned God. The deeper theological issues rarely draw the attention of the general media beyond the weekly column on the Torah reading in the weekend issues of *Yediot Aharonot, Maariv* and *Haaretz.* The weekly religious broadcast programmes on the Sabbath eve and after the end of the Sabbath on radio and television include interviews with rabbis on a range of theological issues.

In the case of the traditional though not strictly religious population, much information about religion is provided by the media, given that the frequency of contact with synagogue and religious institutions is less. It supports the idea that religious structures have today been replaced by media structures. Mass media help to popularise religion at the grassroots level where institutionalised religious forms have become weak. There are certain similarities between Judaism and mass media with both fostering certain shared social values.

Quantitatively there is considerable coverage of the Jewish religion. While this was only natural for the religious media, it was true also for the general media, including even the popular media. Ten per cent of content in the general Israeli media comprised religion. It is much higher than the Buddenbaum (1990) study spanning ten years (1976–1986) of US religion coverage of network television, which found that an average of only 4 per cent of television news content mentioned or discussed religion.

The general daily media – press, radio, television and Internet, both serious and popular – are also key sources of information for secular audiences. But the media impact on them is largely negative – generating criticism such as for attempts by religious groups to impose their standards on Israeli public life. A survey of Israel journalists, conducted by the author, found that 24 per cent of respondents, asked to rate the newsworthiness of religion, said it was either 'high' or 'very high', and a further 35 per cent gave it an average rating.

And, asked to rate the newsworthiness of Judaism, 53 per cent of journalists rated it 'high' or 'very high', and a further 32 per cent as average.

Yet a closer examination suggests that the media's role as a framer of religious identity and agent of spirituality in Israel is only partly true, and does not replace the synagogue. It is questionable, both in quantitative terms and even more so in qualitative terms, as to the extent to which mass media are an alternative instrument for generating Jewish religious identity and spirituality. Much of the religion coverage comprised such non-strictly religion subjects as political parties, synagogue-state tensions – like state budgeting for religious educational institutions like *yeshivot* (or institutions of higher Jewish learning) and army exemptions for Haredi *yeshiva* students. True, the media's potential as an agent of religious identity has become acute with the Internet, by enabling the Jewish surfer – including Jews who are uncommitted or are unaffiliated to a community structure – to gather information relating to his own beliefs, thereby strengthening his belief system. The Internet fulfils roles in strengthening religious identity. Participation in forum and chat questions of religious belief, and participation in religious lessons (*shiurim*) conducted on the web, contribute to creating virtual communities. The Internet's impact upon Jewish identity is in making religious information much more accessible to those accessing it. But the Internet also enables him to surf to get information beyond his religious stream or indeed his Jewish faith. Two popular subjects on the web are Jewish genealogy and Jewish dating. The Internet also has the potential of reaching Jewish communities in closed countries. But the extent to which the Internet will act as an agent of religious identity in practice is unclear. A clue may be had by comparing it to radio; the Rokeach study found that only 2 per cent and 3 per cent of secular Israelis listened 'all the time' or 'frequently' to *shiurim* on the radio, and programmes on religion and tradition.

Rabbis perceive the media marketplace less in positive terms of being an alternative pulpit but mainly in terms of being a threat to religious identity. Orthodox (Haredi and modern Orthodox) rabbis showed wide dissatisfaction with the religion coverage in the general Israeli media: 95 per cent of Orthodox rabbis said that the press damage religious values to some extent, to a large extent or to a very great extent. Within the Orthodox, Haredi rabbis were more inclined (64 per cent) than modern Orthodox (32 per cent) to say that the press damage religion to a very great extent. Yet, even 39 per cent of modern Orthodox rabbis agreed that the press damage religious values to a large extent. In the case of television there was a significant increase in modern Orthodox rabbis (56 per cent) saying that television damages religious values to a very great extent. Similar findings were found for radio, the theatre, cinema and Internet.

Moreover, there is much mass media content which is anathema to Jewish belief. Mass media draws upon populism, whether in the entertainment media such as sexual freedom, sensationalism, glorification in crime, and challenges to traditional authority, or in news values which by nature appeal to commercial taste.

The media and secular–religious relations

Religious coverage has implications for the uneasy relationship between secular and religious communities in Israel. In constructing images of the three main communities of the Israeli Jewish population – secular, modern Orthodox, ultra-Orthodox – the mass media has a powerful impact on the way the communities perceive one another.

Television was the primary source of acquaintance about the Haredim for 35 per cent of the general Israeli population, 28 per cent personal acquaintance, 15 per cent newspapers, 10 per cent literature and 7 per cent radio, according to a 1995 poll. On the question of whether television presents Haredim in a fair manner, 34 per cent of the Israeli public said it does so 'as a general rule', 28 per cent from time to time, 17 per cent said television was inclined not to do so in a fair way more than an acceptable manner, 10 per cent said it almost never presents them in a fair manner.[12] The Israeli case was comparable to other social conflict situations. Examining content on religious conflict in the Nigerian media, Hackett found that the media had a negative role in exacerbating tension between the Muslim and Christian populations (Hackett, 2003).

In the first decades of the state, Israeli society was characterised by mutual recognition of different groups making up Israeli Jewish society and by a high sense of solidarity. By contrast, in the last two decades there was a widening gap between groups, and social solidarity among the Israeli Jewish population has faded. Yet, Israeli society has moved from a society fostering a single Israeli identity to a multicultural one in which different religious and ideological groups win legitimacy and recognition.

Much of the tension between the religious and secular center around the question of whether the state of Israel should be a state based upon Jewish religious law (*halakhah*) or be a secular democracy. Rather than just a theoretical question, it reflects both deep ideological differences between secular and Jewish religious groups, and differences within Jewish religious communities, notably Haredim (or ultra-Orthodox Jews) and religious Zionists. Sharansky delineates six key areas about the place of religion in statehood between non-Orthodox and the official Orthodox religious establishment: Conversion, Marriage, Divorce, Burial, Non-Orthodox at Western Wall, Non-Orthodox members in local religious councils (Sharansky, 2000).

The disagreement over conversion was the extent of study and commitment demanded of a convert, with the Orthodox rabbis charging that non-Orthodox rabbis perform superficial conversions. Conversion has only become an issue in Israel in recent years, with the migration of close to one million people from the former Soviet Union and Ethiopia since the late 1980s. Part of the problem is associated with Jewish religious law (*halakhah*) which divides Jewish into three groupings: the priestly tribe, the Levitical tribe and the Israelites. According to Jewish tradition, the priestly tribe served in the ancient Jewish temple in Jerusalem, and were required to achieve an elevated holiness – which entailed amongst others certain limitations on personal status such as a prohibition on marrying a convert to Judaism or a divorcee. Issues associated with marriage are perhaps the most complicated of those setting Orthodox Israelis against the non-Orthodox. Indeed, a child born from such a forbidden marriage is regarded by Jewish religious law as a bastard.

A separate source of religious–secular relations is the *aguna*, or a husband of a couple who have separated and refuses to give his wife a divorce, or a husband who disappeared as a result of armed conflict. The spouse is unable to remarry until there is clear proof that the husband either is dead or is willing to give a divorce.

Another source of tension concerns the aesthetics of the Orthodox marriage ceremony, and the requirement in order for the marriage to be officially recognised by the state rabbinate and be registered at the Interior Ministry for the bride prior to the marriage ceremony to immerse in a ritual bath, the *mikva*. Another objection concerns the requirement by Jewish religious law that the two witnesses who witness the marriage document to be Sabbath-observant Jews. One way out of the problems was to marry abroad. Yet another way is to make arrangements with one of the numerous Orthodox rabbis with a reputation for accommodating the style desired by a couple for not insisting on seeing a certificate testifying to the bride's immersion in a *mikva* prior to the ceremony, and not examining the Sabbath behaviour of the individuals who come forward as witnesses.

Another point of friction is in the case of the laws of divorce – also monopolised by the Orthodox – and that Orthodox rules of procedure provide substantial advantages to the man in a case of dispute.

Orthodox burial rituals also disturb some Jews. Jewish law prohibits cremation. The burial in a Jewish cemetery of non-Jewish relatives is not done. As a result, a non-Jew and a Jew who had lived together as man and wife cannot be buried alongside one another in a Jewish cemetery. Some of these cases have provoked widespread dismay and anger, such as recent immigrants killed as Israeli soldiers, who thought themselves Jewish, but who could not be buried in the Jewish section of an Israeli military cemetery where burials are also controlled by the Orthodox-dominated military rabbinate.

An issue of religious freedom which arguably has generated most media spin concerns feminist groups and non-Orthodox Jewish movements that want to perform their own prayer services at the '*Kotel*' or Western Wall, on the Temple Mount, Jerusalem. According to Orthodox Jewish religious law, only ten males may comprise a *minyan* or an organised prayer service. The Western Wall is viewed as a remnant of the Temple, destroyed by the Romans in 70 CE. Responding to an appeal for women who wish to organise their own prayer services, the Israeli Supreme Court ruled that women should receive police protection for their prayers at the Western Wall on condition that they refrain from reading from the Torah and wearing prayer shawls. Against their petition were Orthodox Jews who did not want their own prayers disturbed by the presence of women doing what they viewed as unacceptable. Reform and

Conservative rabbis remain insulted at the need to segregate their followers from the area of the Wall. Arrangements were made to for non-Orthodox prayer services at what is called the 'little wall,' a separate section of the Wailing Wall a half kilometre from the main site or '*Kotel*'.

Another source of tension is public funding for religious institutions, distributed by state-sponsored local religious councils. Membership by non-Orthodox representatives like the Reform and Conservative religious is necessarily required in order to win financial allocations for non-Orthodox synagogues, schools and social services. Orthodox members of religious councils boycott the participation of non-Orthodox representatives, and attempt to stop non-Orthodox communities receiving budgeting and religious facilities. Non-Orthodox groups have won judgements in Israel's Supreme Court that one's identity among the competing streams of Judaism should not disqualify an appointment to a local religious council.

Another area of secular–religious tension is the question of exemptions for Haredi yeshiva students from army national service, which is mandatory in Israel. If these arrangements generated anger among some sections of the Israeli population, like the non-religious, these were no less also compromises for the Haredi population which would have wanted the state to take upon more the trappings of a theocracy rather than democracy.

The media of one sector – whether secular, traditional, modern religious or Haredi – is a prism through which to see the other community. In the case of the Haredi media, for example, the media image shows secular Israelis as not observing religious laws – deemed so important by the Haredim. Carmi argues that there has been a quantitative increase in the content of the Haredi press criticism of secular Israeli society. Examining Haredi press content at five year intervals from 1950 onwards, Carmi found that from 1977 to 1990 there was an increase in coverage: among subjects covered were the question of religious conversion, the State of Israel as a sovereign Jewish entity, and how the secular media relate to Haredim. It peaked in 1989 with 99 articles in *Hamodia* and *Yated Neeman*. But Carmi argues that involvement by Haredim in the political system is inadequate to explain the increased coverage because there is no consistent pattern – some years showing an increase in media coverage and others no increase. Haredi political involvement began to increase in 1970 but media increase only jumped in 1990. The Haredi media freely quote from the secular press (they do not view secular television) to show how secular society perceive – or misperceive – Haredi society (Carmi, 2002).

The secular media's pre-occupation in coverage with the religious political parties, and with the wheeling and dealing over state–religion matters, including funding for Haredi institutions, distorts the perception of Haredim in the eyes of the secular population. State–religious relations and the religious political parties are featured in the electronic media in particular – enabling different sides to give vent to their feelings – and discussion inevitably focuses on the conflictual aspects.

But changes in the style of writing in recent years have muddied the separation between facts and opinions, with greater expression of prejudice. If newspapers have been characterised over many years by a clear distinction between facts and opinion, this is less true with reporting on radio and television by correspondents comprising more a combination of facts and commentary-cum-interpretation together with impressions. The place which religion content has in discussive formats in press, radio and television has important implications for the overall image produced of religion because discussive frames in the media focus more on the conflictual aspects bringing or providing views than does news reporting The discussive section of newspapers (editorials, op-ed, letters to the editor) accounted in the author's content analysis for only about a fifth of the overall output on religion: 14 per cent comprised op-ed, 2 per cent editorials, 4 per cent letters to the editor and 0.7 per cent cartoons. About 33 per cent of religion content was in television discussion programmes and a further 7 per cent of discussive content was in television religion programming. And, as newspapers themselves define their function when news consumers receive the news from the electronic media, and move away from breaking the news to greater analysis, in depth background, even the traditional boundaries between facts and comments in newspapers are getting greyed at times – even if the discussive nature of radio and broadcasting – where positions and prejudices win greater expression – are not by and large for this. And, while news reporting on the Internet is not dissimilar from the standards of objectivity of newspaper writing, the blogs and reactions have widened debate even beyond the norms and terms of reference of radio and television because the Internet is open to all, not only journalists, having become a truly democratic public space. As a result of media diversification, both in licensed radio and television, and in pirate radio, public discussion has become more populist, with each audience listening and viewing its 'own' station – resulting in media discourse which is less balanced, expressing 'my side', and less the other side's.

The less religious were more inclined to see tension than the more religious, according to Ben Rafael (2008). He examined religiosity as a factor in secular–religious relations through surveying the attitudes of ultra-Orthodox, traditional and non-religious. Most tension was between the non-religious and the ultra-Orthodox rather than between the modern religious and traditional Jews. Respondents were asked to describe the level of tension with the other communities, and given three options – sharp tension, some tension and no tension – reached the following conclusion. In the case of non-religious respondents vis-à-vis the ultra-Orthodox, Ben Rafael found that 69 per cent and 19 per cent of the non-religious described 'sharp tension' and 'some tension' with the ultra-Orthodox. By contrast, 47 per cent and 22 per cent of ultra-Orthodox described as sharp tensions and some tensions with the non-religious. In the case of perceptions of the tension between traditional Jews and modern Orthodox, 23 per cent and 31 per cent of traditional Jews said that there were sharp tensions and some tensions with the modern religious.

In contrast, 2 per cent and 18 per cent of the modern religious saw sharp tensions and some tensions with the traditional sector.

Stereotypes and bias

The media stereotype religion and religious people. Surveying American clergymen, Dart and Allen (1993) found that between 58 per cent and 91 per cent of clergymen from different Christian streams agreed that US religion coverage was biased against ministers and organised religion. Examining coverage of the Catholic Church, Lichter et al. (1989) found that 39 per cent of press stories in the US media discussing Church policy added in their reporting internal debate including secular reactions. Surveying church leaders' views on the appropriateness of the media as providers of entertainment, Buddenbaum (1997) found that US church leaders rated 1.8 and 2.1 (on a three-point scale) the appropriateness of television and radio as entertainment media respectively. But in the case of Israel the author's study of religion coverage in Israel found that even this should not be exaggerated. The author's study of coverage in the Israeli media, which comprised 3,611 news reports and articles on religion – measured on a scale of 1–5 (1 = most negative, 5 = most positive) – found that the media did not strengthen stereotypes and were inclined to be neutral. Sixty-four per cent of all reporting was neutral, 5 per cent very negative and 7 per cent negative to some extent. Moreover, 14 per cent was rated as very positive and 10 per cent as positive. Four per cent of religion coverage in newspapers, 7 per cent in television and 14 per cent of radio were rated as stereotyped. Stereotyping was said to be highest in the reporting of the secular media (10 per cent) and lowest among the religious media (2 per cent) – which confirms the Ben-Rafael finding. Highest stereotyping was Israel Radio's current affairs radio programme 'Hakol Diburim' (20 per cent).

It would be wrong to blame the lack of religion coverage on the individual journalist. The journalist is neither pro-religious or anti-religious. He works in a competitive media environment characterised by providing interesting and important information. The impression that the media is anti-religious is less due to the individual article or report – which generally fulfil professional standards of journalists – but rather caused by, first, total volume of reporting in religion is so considerable that it clearly has an important influence on the public's image. This was particularly true in the case of Haredim; 43 per cent of all media news reporting in the author's study concerned Haredim; this was even more so with secular newspapers (*Yediot Aharonot* and *Haaretz* 54 per cent each) and television (59 per cent). All this was despite Haredim accounting for only 8 per cent of the Israeli Jewish population. The media preoccupation with Haredim may be explained by the Haredi political influence and by the visual nature of the Haredi style of life.

In measuring whether religion categories were perceived positively or negatively, 94.4 per cent (or 3,408 reports and articles) did not include a stereotype, and 5.6 per cent were stereotyped. Sixty-four per cent of reports were measured as neutral on the 1–5 positive–negative scale, 14 per cent very positive and 10 per cent positive, in contrast to 7 per cent which were negative and 5 per cent very negative. Those not stereotyped were inclined to be 3.29 positively inclined on the 1–5 positive–negative scale. Those stereotyped, however, were inclined to be only 1.88 on the 1–5 positive–negative scale. Types of religious categories broken down – after God at 3.8 – found surprisingly that rabbis were highest on the 1–5 positive-negative scale at 3.7, followed by festivals (3.6) and religious youth movements (3.6). Religious public personalities rated 3, and political parties 2.8.

It was also surprising that only 2.4 per cent of reports of rabbis were stereotyped. It contrasted with 12.6 per cent of reports of religious political parties and religious institutions 9.3 per cent. Least stereotyped were festivals (1), followed by religious public personalities (2.2). It confirmed that the coverage which the religious political parties generated with wheeling and dealing to improve budgetary and other conditions create a relatively negative image among the media.

There is, therefore, no justification for criticism of any lack of coverage of the Haredim. A Smith poll in 1995 had found that 38 per cent of the Israeli public thought that Haredim received enough time to present their opinions in the media, 30 per cent said not enough time and 11 per cent said Haredim received too much. On the question of whether television needs to give more time to Haredim, 16 per cent said so, and 16 per cent said there was a need for a little more. Thirty-eight per cent said they received enough time. (20 per cent said they received too much time.)

Qualitatively, there was considerable criticism, but as for the question of whether the media present the views of Haredim in an objective manner, there was no consensus: 30 per cent of Israelis polled said so generally, 30 per cent from time to time, 32 per cent said 'generally not'.[13]

Journalists acknowledged that the media played a role in secular–religious tensions. In a poll by the author of Israeli journalists (270 filled responses were received) on their role, 50 per cent of journalists questioned agreed to a great extent that tension between the media and Haredim was inevitable, and a further 19 per cent say so 'to a certain extent'. By contrast, 26 per cent of journalists said that tension between the media and modern Orthodox was inevitable to a great degree, and a further 22 per cent to some degree.

Israelis were inclined to view journalists as anti-religious; 22 per cent of Israeli Jews polled in 1995 said journalists were anti-religious, 32 per cent said some of the journalists were anti-religious, but 27 per cent said that just a few were anti-religious.[14] However, to journalists and the broader Israeli public, not defined as narrowly religious, the journalists are merely reflecting popular appeal rather than being intentionally anti-religious. But most journalists questioned do not think that the media damage religious values: 53 per cent do not think so in the case of the Internet, 58 per cent television, 67 per cent newspapers and 73 per cent radio. Asked to rate their religious identity between secular/anti-religious, secular/not anti-religious, traditional, Reform, Conservative, modern Orthodox, 'hardal' (a stricter form of modern Orthodoxy) and Haredi, 45 per cent of journalists replied they were secular/not anti-religious, and a further 8 per cent secular/anti-religious. Thirteen per cent described themselves as traditional.

Examining religions and Jewish religious streams, the Orthodox streams were rated relatively high. On the 1–5 negative–positive spectrum, the author's content analysis study found that reports on Haredim were rated 3.24 and on the modern Orthodox 3.23. These were much higher than the Reform at 2.4 but less than the Conservatives which rated 3. Christianity rated only 3.1 and Islam, not surprisingly given its political implications for the Israeli Jewish public, only 2.6. But if only 6.1 per cent of reports on Haredim were stereotyped, this was still higher than other religious streams. Ferre, examining religion coverage in *The New York Times* and *The Washington Post,* also found that the Baptists, a less mainstream Christian stream, received the highest percentage of stereotyped coverage (Ferre, 1980). And, by contrast to Haredim, in the author's Israeli media study 4.9 per cent of modern Orthodox reports were stereotyped. By contrast, only 2.8 per cent of reports on Islam were stereotyped.

Little difference was found in the author's study between reports concerning religion in Israel and that in the Jewish Diaspora. On the positive–negative scale, religion in Israel amounted to 3.6 and the Jewish Diaspora 3.3. But while 2.5 per cent of Diaspora reports had stereotypes, 5.7 per cent of Israel-related reports had stereotypes, suggesting that the closer to home, the freer the Israeli media felt to discuss freely, if aggressively sometimes, the subject.

Not surprisingly, the secular media (2.74) were less positively inclined to religion than the religious media (3.52). Nevertheless, the study did not find a strongly anti-religious trend in the religion. For example, Haredim and modern Orthodox in the secular papers, *Haaretz* and *Yediot Aharonot,* had an average of 2.73 and 2.67 respectively. Also, reflecting the discussive nature of radio, with spokesmen identified with different trends in Judaism often presenting extreme positions, the study found little difference among different forms of secular media in the extent that stereotypes appeared: stereotypes appeared in 9.5 per cent of newspapers in contrast to 15.9 per cent of radio (7.8 per cent of television had stereotypes). And, in the positive–negative spectrum, television and radio were more inclined to be negative (2.87 and 2.74 respectively) than newspapers in the secular media which were more positively inclined (3.27). Religious political parties on Israel Radio's discussion programme 'Hakol Diburim' rated 2.43, and on the news 2.65. The Garrett-Medill study (Garrett-Medill Center for Religion and the News Media, 1999, pp. 29–30) of religion coverage in the newspapers, television and news magazines confirmed the general trend that religion coverage in the US media was balanced, with little bias, and that coverage was comprehensive as reflected in the contextualising of reports and articles. This US study showed that key words and religious traditions were depicted on the whole neither negatively nor positively. Context was provided with a greater tendency in daily newspapers; 38 per cent of the news stories provided context, in contrast to one third of news magazine stories, and one quarter of television news stories. However, the absence of comprehensive coverage of the non-Christian religions suggests the likelihood of unfair coverage.

The Israel study found that within newspapers, news reporting and feature articles were relatively positive about religion, 3.13 and 3.23. Caricatures were lower (2.58) given their function of expressing a point of view. Surprising was the newspaper editorials; in spite of the function of the newspaper editorial to give a viewpoint, editorials were found to be surprisingly high in their positive–negative view of religion (3.57). A distinction was found between front page news, which draws on controversial headline-breaking news (2.97), in contrast to the inner news pages (3.32). No significant difference was found in terms of positiveness/negativeness between those articles accompanied by photography and those not. Stereotyping in newspapers was broken down by department: not surprisingly, the highest category of stereotyping in newspaper occurred with caricatures (16 per cent), editorials (13 per cent) and feature articles (11 per cent). Front page stories were more inclined to stereotype (6 per cent) than stories on the inside pages (4 per cent). Articles accompanied by photographs were more inclined to stereotype (7 per cent) than those without (5 per cent).

The overall make-up of the presentation of religion varied widely between general media and religious media. The modern Orthodox stream was rated as 2.96 and 3.43 in *Hamodia* and *Hatzofe* as opposed to 2.74 and 2.63 in *Yediot Aharonot* and *Haaretz* respectively. Stereotypes about religion appeared in 9.5 per cent of the secular newspapers in contrast to 1.9 per cent of religious newspapers. Moreover, broken down between a popular paper, *Yediot Aharonot*, and an elite newspaper, *Haaretz*, stereotypes were inclined only marginally to appear more in the popular paper (10.25 per cent) than the quality paper (9 per cent). There was also an inclination for stereotypes to appear less in hard news, where the basics of objectivity exist, in contrast to the features; thus 4.6 per cent of reports on the Mabat news programme had stereotypes in contrast to 12.6 per cent of 'Five with Gadi Zukenik', the early evening current affairs daily programme.

In the general media, not one religion sub-category rated higher than the midpoint 3 whereas in the religious media (with the possible exception of the religious political parties [*Hatzofe* 2.89]), all sub-categories were located above the midpoint of 3. Religious political parties were more positively presented in the religious papers, themselves party political organs (*Hamodia* 3.12; *Hatzofe* 2.89) than in the general papers (*Yediot Aharonot* 2.73; *Haaretz* 2.72). In broadcasting, with the tendency to give a platform to extremist positions, the difference in the news programmes on Israel radio (2.65) as opposed to the news programmes on Radio *Kol Chai* (3.23) was also noted with religious political parties.

A trend of general media to be less positive about religion than the religious media was also found in the presentation of religious public figures. While religious public figures reached 3.15 and 3.20 in *Hamodia* and *Hatzofe*, they only reached 2.79 and 2.85 in *Yediot Aharonot* and *Haaretz*.

Identity, unity and discord 129

The two religious dailies held their own community in higher esteem than did other communities. Thus, Haredim received in *Hamodia* 3.88 compared to 2.7 in *Yediot Aharonot* and *Haaretz*. Similarly, in Radio *Kol Chai* Haredim and modern Orthodox had an average of 3.30 and 3.07 in contrast to 2.90 and 2.67 on Israel Television news 'Mabat' to 2.62 and 2.78 on Israel Radio.

The most telling differences between religious media and general media concerned the image of the rabbi. Whereas the rabbi is glorified within the religious media (rabbis were 4.38 in *Hamodia* and 3.34 in *Hatzofe*), in non-religious newspapers, rabbis were only 2.60 (*Haaretz*) and 2.65 (*Yediot Aharonot*). The particularly high number for the Haredi paper reflects the unquestioning adoration which Haredim possess for their spiritual leaders. Moreover, rabbis received the highest rating of all sub-categories in the religious press but received the lowest rating of all religion sub-categories in the general press. It illustrates the wide gap in Israel between religious and secular as reflected by coverage of rabbis. While rabbis are ideal role models for the audiences of religious media, they are despised role models for general media audiences.

Secular and Haredi media battlefields

Coverage of religion have wide ramifications for secular–religious relations. According to Israel Katzover, political reporter of *Hamodia,* 'As a general rule the secular media sees itself as permitted, for example, to write about the religious in a manner which it would be forbidden to write about other areas in the country. The commercial media search for ratings, and to be anti-religious, anti Haredi, is convenient to promote.'[15]

The secular perceive Haredim as threatening the democratic and free society by seeking to impose their lifestyle and religious standards on the wider population. Shahar Ilan, formerly the correspondent for Haredi affairs in *Haaretz*, said that:

> the general impression about Haredim which comes out of the secular media is of a community having a disgusting lifestyle, of a people who have chosen to 'sit and learn' (rather than work) and let others sustain them, of a people who have chosen not to serve in the Israeli Army but let others defend them. Is all this true? The answer I think is yes. Is this all the truth – certainly not. There are other aspects: it is a society virtually without criminal violence. It is a society with a very impressionable record of inter-communal help. It is a society which appreciates moral leaders – something which would do little harm in the secular community. There are several reasons but I believe that ultimately it is secular panic of the Haredim and of the future for secular life in Israel.[15]

The entry of Haredim into Israeli politics – particularly big since the 1990s, with the entry of the Shas party to government – generated resentment and hostility from the secular and even traditional populations. The media has shown since the 1970s a declining willingness to show respect to governmental and other institutions and are more questioning today, insisting upon accountability; the same is true regarding all other, non-governmental institutions including religious institutions. Said Moshe Ishon, formerly editor of the *Hatzofe* newspaper, 'The media today are not prepared to limit themselves. it is too open, with the result that there is unnecessary conflict as a result of the writing.'[15]

The Haredi media are ideologically against the secular, seeing them in negative terms, as lesser Jews, failing to fulfil the Torah. Given a sense of collective responsibility, Haredim feel a moral obligation to correct the sinners. Sasson-Levi, examining coverage of the secular community in the Haredi media, found 32 mentions in a two-month period of secular people as unethical and value lacking. Even some Haredi journalists have their quandaries about the attacks in the Haredi media (Sasson-Levi, 1998). Yisroel Shpiegel, formerly of *Hamodia,* thought that Haredim should respect the 'clean language' characteristic of *talmidei hachamim* (learned sages). And, Moshe Gerelick, editor of *Mishpacha,* noted that while it was true that most secular Israelis do not read the Haredi media, secular journalists do, and thus their attacks nevertheless do add oil to the fire of secular–Haredi relations. But, Katzover argued, 'It's a dialogue of the deaf, since most secular journalists are not able to read the Haredi media and understand it. It appears to them another world, another planet. The more that the 'dialogue' disintegrates to the extreme Haredi, it loses direction. The matter is a little better in the opposite direction since religious journalists are more acquainted with the secular world. So there is a lack of symmetry in reading and understanding the writing.'[15]

Despite the mutual criticism, the media also have a positive role in clarifying matters in secular–religious relations where the issues are defined, discussed, and even resolved and closed. Yet, it is inconclusive whether Israelis want greater media coverage of the other communities 'in order to learn about them better'. A survey of secular, modern religious and Haredi students found that only some 40 per cent of secular respondents wanted an expansion of media coverage about Haredim in order to be better acquainted with them (Tsarfaty and Cohen, 2009). A similar amount of secular respondents wanted greater media coverage of the modern Orthodox in order to better acquainted with them. Religious respondents were incrementally more inclined to want greater media coverage in order 'to be better acquainted with the other religious community'. A similar amount of Haredi respondents, wanted more media information in order to be better acquainted with the modern Orthodox, and 10 per cent wanted greater coverage about secular Israel in order to better acquainted with them. Among modern Orthodox respondents, a fifth wanted greater media coverage of Haredim in order to be better acquainted with them, and Facebook offered a framework for social networking for Jews from different religious sectors. 'Haredim – Pleased to meet you' was the application of media to improve secular–religious relations.[16]

Conclusion

Yet, the media also play a separate role in constructing a sense of ambiguity. Ravitzky (2005) writes of the 'constructive ambiguity' which exists in Israel with different and clashing expectations between secular, modern religious, and Haredi communities about how they envisage Jewish statehood. In particular, the 'ambiguity' is a linchpin in the status quo between the secular and religious. The status quo plays a role in creating the ambiguity. At the first sign of public controversy between religious and secular political forces, the aggrieved party (sometimes both parties) appeals to the status quo, maintaining that the other side is violating its provisions. The status quo has an almost sanctified aura to it, and functions in many cases like a constitution that no one fully understands and that leads itself to multiple interpretations. The only way to reconcile different aspirations and ideologies has been to create double or treble meanings. The media play a role in creating and preserving the ambiguity because in fact the media covers the secular–religious conflict, including reporting and commenting upon the issues. As has been argued, the more the media cover – and clarify – the aspirations of the various parties, the more the public perception of these differences becomes accentuated. Nevertheless, to the extent that the media project a belief that there are firm criteria and a fixed process for resolving political disputes – and that maintenance of the process is more important than the advantage to be gained by one side or another in a particular controversy – the media also play a positive role.

References

Ben Rafael, E. (2008) 'The Faces of Religiosity in Israel: Cleavages or Continuum?', *Israel Studies* 13,3, Fall.
Buddenbaum, J. (1990) 'Network News Coverage of Religion', in J. Ferre (ed), *Channels of Belief: Religion and American Commercial Television*. Ames, IA: Iowa State University Press.
——(1997) 'Reflections on Culture Wars: Churches, Communication, Content, and Consequences', in M. Suman (ed), *Religion and Prime Time Television*. Westport, CT: Praeger.
Carmi, L. (2002) 'The Attitude of the Ultra-Orthodox Newspapers towards the Secular Population and Secularity since the Establishment of the State of Israel', MA thesis. Bar-Ilan University.
Central Bureau of Statistics. (2008) *Social Survey*. Jerusalem: Central Bureau of Statistics.
——(2009) *Social Survey*. Jerusalem: Central Bureau of Statistics.
Dart, J. and Allen, J. (1993) *Bridging the Gap: Religion and the News Media*. Nashvilee, TN: The Freedom Forum First Amendment Center, Vanderbilt University.
Ferre, J. (1980) 'Denominational Biases in the American Press', *Review of Religious Research*, 21, 3, Summer.
Garrett-Medill Center for Religion and the News Media (1999) *Media Coverage of Religion, Spirituality, and Values*. Evanston, IL: Northwestern University.

Hackett, R. (2003) 'Managing or Manipulating Religious Conflict in the Nigerian Media', in J. Mitchell and S. Marriage (eds), *Mediating Religion*. London & New York: Clark.

Haim Herzog Institute (2007) *Public Confidence in the Media: Research Report 7*. Tel Aviv: Tel Aviv University, Table 3.

Hoover, S. (1988) *Religion in the News*. Thousand Oaks, CA: Sage, Table 7:19.

——(2006) *Religion in the Modern Age*. London: Routledge.

Israel Advertisers Association: Haredim (1995) *Survey of Exposure to Mass Media: Haredim*. Tel Aviv: Israel Advertisers Association.

Israel Advertisers Association (1997) *Exposure of Israeli Public to News Media* [Hebrew]. Tel Aviv: Israel Advertisers Association.

Lichter, S. R., Amundson, D. and Lichter, L. S. (1989) *Media Coverage of the Catholic Church*. Washington, DC: Center for Media and Public Affairs.

Pnim (2009) *(48)* Winter.

Ravitzky, A. (2005) *Religion and State in Twentieth Century Jewish Thought* [Hebrew]. Jerusalem: Israel Democracy Institute.

Rokeach, E. (1997) 'Israeli Governmental Inquiry into Strengthening Jewish Values Through Radio' [Hebrew]. Unpublished.

Sasson-Levi, O. (1998) *Hishtakfut Ha-Hilonim B'Itonut Ha-Haredit* [Hebrew: Secular Israelis As Reflected in the Haredi Press]. Ramat Gan: Am Hofshi Oifshi.

Sharansky, I. (2000) *The Politics of Religion and the Religion of Politics: Looking at Israel*. Lanham, MD: Lexington.

Shye, S. (1983) *Public Attitudes Towards Religious Literature and Religious Institutions*. Jerusalem: The Israel Institute of Applied Social Research.

Tsarfaty, O. and Cohen, Y. (2009) 'The Influence of Mass Media upon Secular-Religious Relations in Israel', Association of Israel Studies annual conference, Sapir College, Beersheba. June (*Hamevaser*) 30.12.2011.

Part 3
Issues in mediated Judaism

8 www.techno-Judaism

> May it by Your Will to cause us to connect in peace, to web surf in peace and to reach the Web site of our desires in peace. And may you disconnect us in peace and make sure that the connection not have been too costly. And deliver us from the hands of viruses and computer crashes, licentiousness and idol worship that may befall in the virtual world. And may you send a blessing to all the deeds of our mouse, and grant us favour and kindness and mercy in the eyes of every computer screen ...
> (From a Jewish prayer for Jewish web surfers)

The Internet has affected Israel's religious populations no less than religious communities in other countries. The place of the Internet in the Jewish religious experience is undoubted. No less than in other religions, the Internet has created a revolution in accessibility to information about Judaism and Jewish-related matters. In 2007 Technion scientists inscribed the entire Hebrew text of the Old Testament – 300,000 words – onto a tiny silicon surface; the surface measured less than 0.5 square millimetres.[1] A search of Google in 2007 discovered that Judaism had 15,900,000 hits (Patrick, 2007, p. 71, footnote 2). There were an estimated 8,500 Jewish websites in 2005.[2] The plethora of religious websites was testimony to the positive value which the media technological revolution had on religion. Yet, like religions in other faiths, Jewish religious communities had mixed reactions, between the fears that seamier sides to the Internet, including pornographic sites, would weaken religious identity. Yet, whether they disliked it or not, the Internet was so embedded in the twenty-first century that the chances of banning it were next to nil even in the case of tightly embedded religious enclaves. This raised the question of how the Internet should be integrated into their lifestyle to cause as limited damage to religious identity as possible. This chapter analyses the response of religious Jewry in Israel to the Internet.

Religious exposure to the Internet

Haredim have lower exposure to computers and to the Internet than the rest of the Israeli Jewish population. In 2006, 50 per cent of Haredi families possessed a computer at home in contrast to 90 per cent of Israeli Jews who defined themselves as secular.[3] Similarly, in 2007, 55 per cent of Haredi households possessed a computer. Some 57 per cent of these households were linked to the Internet.[4] This was higher than a 2005 official survey, by the Central Bureau of Statistics (2005) which found that only 10 per cent of Haredi families were linked to the Internet in contrast to 61 per cent of the total Israeli Jewish population. By contrast, 51 per cent of *dati leumi* (modern Orthodox) Jews, 54 per cent of Jews defining themselves as traditional-cum-religious, and 62 per cent of traditional Jews possessed the Internet.[5] Yet even by 2008 a notable increase in Haredi usage of the Internet had occurred: 55 per cent of all Haredim with computers (77 per cent of the Haredi 'academic' population and 40 per cent of non-academic Haredim) were using the Internet (Central Bureau of Statistics, 2008). And, by 2009, the Haredi usage of the Internet went up yet further to 65 per cent.[6] And, in a survey of those without computer or the Internet, Haredim were found in 2005 to be the largest grouping: 42 per cent of Haredim had no computer at home in contrast to 29 per cent of the general Israeli population. Of those who possessed computers but were not linked to the Internet, 27 per cent were Haredi Jews. Haredim were also less inclined to be heavy Internet users. Broken down according to 'light users' of the Internet (less than once a day), one to three times a day, and 'heavy users' at least four times a day, 58 per cent of light users were Haredim and other religious Jews.[7] In terms of Israeli neighbourhoods, while in mixed neighbourhoods and cities like Ramat Gan and Ashkelon, 73 per cent and 71 per cent of households in 2007 possessed personal computers, in the Haredi town of Benei Beraq, situated near Tel Aviv, only 53 per cent did. And, while 66 per cent and 61 per cent of households in Ramat Gan and Ashkelon used the Internet, only 29.5 per cent of Benei Beraq households did.[8] Yet, the low Haredi exposure is not static. An incremental increase occurred since 2002. The 53 per cent of Benei Beraq residents who possessed computers in 2007 was an increase from 37 per cent in 2002, and the 29.5 per cent of Benei Beraq residents who possessed the Internet in 2007 was an increase from just 6.4 per cent in 2002 (Central Bureau of Statistics, 2007).

Haredi women are less inclined than Haredi men to use the Internet: 35 per cent of Haredi women in 2004 used the Internet in contrast to 65 per cent of Haredi men. The male–female different was far greater with Haredim than with other groups, reflecting that the Internet was only permitted in the Haredi community at the place of work. Among secular Israelis, 55 per cent of secular men and 45 per cent of secular women used the Internet, and, similarly, 55 per cent of *dati leumi* (modern religious) men and 45 per cent of *dati leumi* women used the Internet. Moreover, the major usage of the Internet among Haredim was for electronic mail (29.5 per cent) and news sites (4 per cent) in contrast to surfing for work (15 per cent), searching for information (15 per cent), financial/bank information (11 per cent) and sales/purchases (10 per cent).

The number of modern religious using the Internet is today no less than the general population. The Central Bureau of Statistics in 2009 found that 95 per cent of modern Orthodox are linked to the Internet. And, in 2008, the Central

Bureau of Statistics found that the modern religious population divided between the academic and non-academic communities had the highest number of computer users: 97 per cent in contrast to 89 per cent of 'academic' secular Israeli Jews, 85 per cent of 'academic' traditional Israeli Jews and 77 per cent of academic Haredim. There was also a higher percentage of *dati leumi* (combined academic and non-academic) Internet users at 95 per cent, which was also the same as secular 98 per cent and 93 per cent traditional, but much higher than Haredim: 55 per cent of Haredim using computers (77 per cent of Haredi academics and 40 per cent non-academics) have the Internet (Central Bureau of Statistics, 2009). There was little difference between the religious (Haredi plus modern Orthodox) on the one hand and traditional on the other in usage of the Internet. The major group is the secular community. According to a 2009 poll, 37 per cent of Haredi-religious did not surf the Internet in contrast to 17 per cent of secular; noteworthy was that 37 per cent of secular also did not surf. Fifty-three per cent of the combined Haredi–religious were inclined to, when surfing the Internet, also surf news websites, in contrast to 66 per cent of secular and 47 per cent of traditional (Pnim, 2009). The Barzilai-Nahon and Barzilai study found that in 2002 while 23 per cent of the population were modern Orthodox, 14 per cent were Internet users (Barzilai-Nahon and Barzilai, 2005). By 2008 this had increased and 95 per cent of homes of students of high school *yeshivot* (talmudic colleges) and *ulpanot* (religious girls secondary schools) were linked to the Internet. While 71 per cent of the Israeli Jewish population were secular, 84 per cent were Internet users. In terms of men and women 55 per cent of Internet users were men and 45 per cent women – the same fraction as the secular population, different to the Haredim where 65 per cent were men. In terms of socio-economic status, surfers among the modern Orthodox were similar to the secular. Only 16 per cent of modern religious surfers had a college education, in contrast to 50 per cent of the ultra Orthodox; 84 per cent had a high school education. The Goodman study (Goodman, 2010) found that 28 per cent of modern Orthodox youth in yeshivot/ulpanot surf up to one hour a day, 42 per cent more than one hour a day. Only 8 per cent of parents limit the amount of time their children spend on the net, and only 4 per cent require parents' permission to surf.

Haredi rabbis and the Internet danger

In 2000, just a few years after the Internet entered Western lifestyles, the Haredi rabbinical leadership imposed a prohibition on the Internet 'as a moral threat to the sanctity of Israel. The Internet threatened the high walls which Haredi rabbis had set up to resist secular cultural influences.' The ban followed upon a special rabbinical *bet din* (or religious law court) established to deal with the spread of computers. In part the ban was directed at children whose religious studies had been distracted by computers, both Internet and data bases. A distinction within the Haredi world could be delineated between the so-called European Lithuanian school and the European Hassidic and

Sephardi or oriental branches of Haredim. The stricter Lithuanian school placed a ban not only upon the Internet but also upon computers as a whole, calling upon its members to get rid of them from their houses. The statement included a cartoon with the snake of the Garden of Eden, which caused Adam to sin, exploding within the computer screen and bringing down the Haredi child. Hassidic and Sephardi Haredi branches, on the other hand, were more flexible. The Sephardim generally are more tolerant, and the European hassidim are more inclined to go to work in contrast to the Lithuanians who study in *yeshivot* (talmudical colleges), surviving economically on stipends. The hassidim were more sensitive of the need for the Internet in businesses, and drew a distinction between the Internet at home, which they banned like the other Haredim, and businesses. One leading Haredi rabbi, in formulating his position on the Internet, counselled a family member who was in charge of computer operations at a Haredi newspaper. He told him that sometimes he succeeded in fixing problems on computers at the office through his computer at home. That relative recommended that he ban all dishes used in a kitchen lest they be used to serve pork. Similarly with computers, it depends what you cook, the rabbi concluded. He refrained from signing the call for an entire ban on the Internet and computers.

The ban was presented in different terms. A typical response by one Hassidic rabbi was the Novaminsker Rebbe, who said 'The Internet, with a flick of a button, invades a Jewish home, a Jewish soul, makes moral disaster. If your business cannot get along without it, you must create the strictest controls around its use. Do not give it free rein! Remember that you are dealing with a force that contains spiritual and moral poison.'[9] A different view by another rabbi, Benjamin Scharansky, focused on the social-pedagogic consequences. 'Our great scientists knowingly utilise the cleverest of machines to inflame their bestial instincts and fan dangerous desires. Through violent computer games, experienced programmes guide players – adults and children alike – to fight with cruelty, take revenge and generally behave like animals. Never have walls so thick separated man from his fellow man as in our generation, where technological culture flourishes.'[10] The variegated bans by Haredi rabbis against new media forms have caused the wider meaning of modesty in Judaism as concerning personal behaviour such as regarding wealth and self-assessment to be somewhat lost in the overwhelming concern about sexual modesty (Cohen, 2001, 2006). In a typical Haredi view emphasising the consequences of the Internet for self-discipline, Hanoch Eidelberg, under the heading 'Where is no fear of God', wrote that 'any child brought up to believe that the world is his and every experience is permissible cannot understand the meaning of self-discipline'.[11]

Printing for the first time in their newspapers the word 'Internet', Haredi newspapers in December 2007 carried announcements from 'the rabbinical committee for communication matters' allowing businesses to use the Internet. An agreement was reached with the Israeli telephone company, Bezek, to provide access for businesses to a small number of websites.[12] The committee had devised three concentric circles of control: the first circle was a safety device – which only a computer technician could remove – stopping a child from going beyond the permitted sites. The second circle was a device on the computer mouse itself which enabled people to go only on to permitted sites. A third device, on the telephone itself, stopped somebody from, say, ordering an ADSL line to his telephone. But the system was not foolproof, as was shown when the Belze Hassidic court became in 2008 the first hassidic branch of Haredim to allow its community a special package of some 150 websites both at home as well as in business. The Belze court reached what would be a short-lived agreement with a religious Internet server, Rimon, to create a special package of 150 sites – both sites of general interest, including some quality Israeli newspapers, as well as business-related websites. There was an immeasurably longer list of forbidden, or 'black', sites. The problem was that seemingly okay sites led to other sites which were problematic, such as through links, or themselves carried problematic advertising, or originally deemed okay but which were subsequently updated with problematic material. The rabbinical committee for communication affairs recommended an alternative system of 'white' sites. Access would be allowed to only sites relevant to a specific profession. The weakness with this system was that there was inbuilt a contradiction in which some Haredi customers would be prohibited access to websites which were allowed to other Haredi customers whose businesses needed those sites.

Parallel to the rabbinical bans upon computers were a number of attempts by Haredi entrepreneurs to create computer filtering programmes. One early attempt, 'Torahnet', undertook to process requests for clearance to websites within 24 hours. Another, 'Nativ', comprised software blocking everything but e-mail or access to a limited number of websites operated by business-related and official institutions.

The Shas bill

Haredi demands for dealing with the Internet took on a parliamentary form in 2007 when Itzhak Cohen, a member of Shas, the Sephardi Haredi political party, placed a private members bill in the Knesset, the Israel Parliament, which required Internet servers not to supply pornographic material to any children, or to adults with the exception of those adults specifically requesting to receive pornographic matter. Lemish, Ribak and Aloni (2009), examining the exposure and usage of the Internet by Israeli schoolchildren, found that 73 per cent of high school students were exposed to pornography on the Internet, but only 29 per cent of elementary schoolchildren and 53 per cent of junior high school students were. Also while 67 per cent of all the boys were exposed to pornography, only 53 per cent of all girls were. The study also found that 78 per cent of parents prohibit their children from giving out personal details, and 45 per cent limit surfing time. Yet, only 18 per cent use computer filtering devices. Cohen enjoyed the backing of the Minister of

Communications, Ariel Attias, who also belonged to the Shas Party. In effect Internet servers would be required to use a screening device that prevents unsolicited pornographic material from reaching its clients. Clients would be sent two letters informing them about the filtering device, followed by a third letter announcing its installation. Only those identified as adults would be able to request that the service not be installed. A server sending out such matter except to those requesting it could be fined the equivalent of 75,000 dollars. Tactically, Shas rightly concluded that it would be difficult to enforce anti-porn Internet legislation by requiring citizens to install filtering devices on their computers; it would be less controversial to place the onus of responsibility on the Internet server companies. The Shas bill was not so much aimed towards their own Haredi communities; but its significance lay in the fact that it was a Haredi attempt to influence the Internet surging of the entire population.

The bill passed its first reading in 2008 with 46 for and 20 against after Shas mustered the votes of other religious political parties, both Haredi and modern Orthodox, as well as feminist MKs and the Arab political parties. Supporters included the National Council for the Child. The bill generated opposition from the Left, but also secular right-wing MKs suggested that censorship of the Internet should be voluntary and not imposed. Arguing that it was an invasion of freedom, the Israel Association for Civil Rights threatened to appeal to the Supreme Court if the law reached a second or third reading in the Knesset. It was also an invasion of privacy because people requesting the pornographic access would have to register. There was the danger that a data base of potential customers for porn-related material would be exploited for commercial purposes. Moreover, the fact that a public committee appointed by a government minister himself determined which sites were pornographic or not added to the criticism.

However, the chances for the bill floundered after the government ministerial committee which examines upcoming parliamentary legislation decided, with the exception of the Shas minister, to oppose the bill, arguing that more democratic and pedagogic means rather than censorship should be used to educate the young about the dangers of the Internet. The ministers' decision was a powerful message from the non-Haredi Israeli majority that the Haredi tool of censorship to deal with problematic matter was anathema in a progressive society. True, similar anti-porn Internet legislation had been proposed in other Western countries, but the fact that the bill was initiated by a Haredi party weakened its long-term chances to reach the statute book.

Haredi leaders faced a new Internet challenge with the creation of Facebook. True, Haredim have always emphasised the importance of interpersonal relations both in terms of family and community. And Facebook did not pose the direct threat from access and exposure to Internet sites with sex content. But social networking did breach the Haredi rules of conduct notably by building relationships between men and women. It also resulted in the free passage of information and gossip in a society in which rabbis had supervised the information flow – such as through the supervised Haredi daily papers. The free passage of information threatened the grave prohibition of evil gossip (*loshon hara*). 'The development of Facebook is a tragedy. It is not possible that the Haredi community – trained from a young age towards the separation between men and women – should have a mixed social network,'[13] said Rabbi Mordechai Blau of the so-called 'Committee for the Purity and Sanctity of the Camp'. Some members of the community got around rabbinical bans on Facebook by using anonymous names lest they be detected – penalty of which could involve such social excommunication tactics as threatening a child's chances of a *shidduch* (lit. arranged marriage) or of being admitted to a school or yeshiva. But like the earlier Internet battles, the chances of rabbinical bans against Facebook being wholly accepted were low. Instead, the matter lay with grassroots Facebook users to themselves develop their own Haredi Facebook code of networking – not dissimilar from the codes which the unofficial Haredi Internet websites like *BeHadrei Haredim* did.

Modern Orthodox and the Internet dilemma

The variegated bans by Haredi rabbis against new media forms have caused the wider meaning of modesty in Judaism as concerning personal behaviour such as regarding wealth and self-assessment to be somewhat lost in the overwhelming concern about sexual modesty (Cohen, 2001, 2006). By contrast to Haredi rabbis, the rabbis of the modern Orthodox (*dati leumi*) stream (which account for 12 per cent of the Israeli Jewish population) have not issued legal rulings regarding media exposure, reflecting their broader philosophy of seeking to create a synthesis between Judaism and modernity. Yet some of their rabbis, particularly those identified with the *'hardal'* (*Haredi leumi*) substream, encourage controlling exposure particularly of children to the general media. There is a surprising similarity between all the rabbis not just Haredim and the *dati leumi* but even between the two and non-Orthodox Jewry – the Conservative and Reform movements – in their criticism that the Internet damages religious values. The difference between some of them is less in outlook and more in the practical measures to be taken. The mainstream *dati leumi*, as well as non-Orthodox, disagreed with the Haredi worldview of cutting oneself off from wider society but Haredim have found in the growing sub-section of *hardal* natural allies in limiting exposure of children to these various websites.

In contrast to the blanket Haredi ban on the Internet, for the modern Orthodox or *dati leumi* the question of the Internet went ideologically even deeper because by nature these seek to reconcile modernity with Jewish values. Rather than living in a cultural ghetto, the modern Orthodox believe in the inherent virtue of full harmony with modern technology. Yet given the pornographic matter on the Internet, they, no less than the Haredim, have been faced with the question of whether to compromise their open culture view in order not to be exposed to the pornographic matter. Three approaches evolved. The most traditional view concerned media literacy, or the believing

Jew having the self-discipline and maturity not to enter forbidden websites. A more cautious view involved external means of self-discipline. In the case of children or youth, parental supervision controlled access through filtering processes. The most extreme position is that identified with a sub-section of the modern Orthodox entitled 'Haredi leumi', under which the Internet is banned in its entirety. The Haredi leumi are characterised by ideological support for the modern Zionist state and they see the Israeli state as a religious deed and contrast with other Haredim who are critical of the state because its establishment should await the messianic era, and should be in turn in accordance to Jewish law. *Hardal* schools are reflected by limited study of secular topics, and their homes do not have television. Travel abroad is discouraged.

A debate on the pages of former daily organ of the modern Orthodox movement, *Hatzofe*, entitled the 'The War on Internet', in 2007 provides an insight into the modern Orthodox thinking. The series began after Dr Toviah Peri, an educationalist, wrote an op-ed article bemoaning excessive terminology in discussing the educational and religious dilemmas of the usage of the Internet. Terminology like 'the War on Internet' or 'the struggle for the souls of our children', Peri said, were counterproductive. 'The usage of extremist language could lead to the opposite results with religious people who surf pornographic sites, rejected, and distant, denying therapy. Moreover, complaints by religious woman that their husbands have fallen to the temptation of surfing pornographic sites, have led to marital breakdown and were grounds for divorce in Jewish law, could be dealt with through counselling, thereby saving the marriage. Furthermore,' Peri argued, 'surfing pornographic sites was less a sin against a fellow man and more against God, which should be dealt with through prayer and repentance on Yom Kippur.'[14] The following week in the newspaper, under the headline 'The War on Internet: Have We Exaggerated?', *Hatzofe* published op-eds in response, which called for a critical stance. A leading rabbi, Yaacov Ariel, was unwilling to rely merely on self-discipline. Quoting the biblical edict, 'do not put a stumbling block before the blind', Ariel favoured computer filtering devices.'[15] According to Rabbi David Stav, head of the Petach Tiqva Yeshiva, 'One does not have to be religious to realise that not everything should be allowed to enter the home unhesitatingly. Jewish education includes the ability to deal with modernity.'[16] A yeshiva student, Itamar Lieberman, labelling the need for a response to the Internet as an obligatory positive war – one of the Jewish law categories on military conflict – called for more efficient ways to 'fight the war'. And, the following week, another rabbi, Elisha Aviner, coining the problem 'a war against the evil inclination', also favoured a computer filtering device. Moreover, he proposed that applications for children to religious schools should be conditioned on the parents using computer filtering devices.[17] The '*hardal*' view of banning was expressed by Rabbi Yehoshua Shapiro, head of a yeshiva, who argued that 'Internet is a dangerous matter seducing good people to the depths of spiritual impurity. I believe that it should be banned in its entirety.'[18]

The first synagogue of cyberspace

One of the first cyberspace synagogues, Temple Beit Israel, founded in 2006, in 'Second Life' has members residing in amongst other places Brazil, The Netherlands, the US and Israel. Lacking any physical structure, its 400 members, or 'residents', and thousands of visitors every week, meet on-line.[19] Another on-line community is OurJewishCommunity.org, whose spiritual leader is Rabbi Laura Baum. In addition to on-line services at its synagogue, Beth Adam, in Cincinnati, this virtual synagogue provides access to rabbis, sermons, educational materials and social networking. Its High Holiday Services are Shreamed on iPhone, Blackberry and Droid.[20] In 2008, JTN Productions broadcast the first online Yom Kippur service.

Of all the branches of Judaism, only the Reform have fully incorporated modern technology into the synagogual service. Off-line Reform synagogues have gone on-line. For example, Temple Emanu-el, a leading New York Reform synagogue, has since 2000 broadcast its High Holyday services. Temple Emanu-el holds a virtual seder on the first night of the Passover holiday, enabling people in different locations to participate in the seder. Temple Beth El, in Charlotte, North Carolina, has since 2006 offered evening holiday services on the Internet. An estimated 2,500 people in 15 countries watch the High Holiday services of Rosh Hashonah and Yom Kippur of Temple Emanuel in Birmingham. Temple Bnai Shalom, in Fairfax Station, Virginia, has podcasted since 2006, enabling the ill, elderly, as well as armed personnel with US forces in Iraq and Afghanistan and foreign service personnel to follow Temple services. According to Temple Bnai Shalom's Rabbi Amy Perlin, 'when a woman tells me that she had listened to a podcast while walking on a beach to sort out her life, when a "new Jew" is able to learn the service by listening to Friday's podcast, when a Jew becomes comfortable reciting the Kaddish that way, or when a man hears the "*Mishebeirach*" (prayer) with the voices of fellow congregants before surgery or during chemotherapy, we are meeting needs beyond our walls and touching hearts and lives'. Rabbi Dan Cohen of Temple Shaarei Tefilo-Israel, South Orange, NJ, remarked:

> I was officiating at a wedding. One grandparent was not able to be present due to health issues. The bride was heartbroken. At the beginning of the service I pulled out by cellphone, called the grandparents and placed the cellphone, on speaker, on the podium in front of me. While being present via telephone is a poor alternative from being physically together, having the grandparent present via this device was itself a cause of celebrating.[21]

A West Coast website, Oy-Bay provides details of young Jews who are interested in setting up independent prayer groups. To be true, prayer services in the Reform movement had benefited from technology even before the Internet age. The microphone is used in the Temple service. For years Temple Emanu-el in

New York has broadcast the reading of the Book of Esther on the *Purim* festival on the community's local radio station.

Yet, fully-fledged prayer services comprising a communal *minyan* have not taken effect among the Orthodox and Conservative streams, given that they are bound by *halakhah*. These reject on-line virtual prayer services. As discussed in Chapter 2, a fundamental criterion for communal prayer for the Orthodox is the physical presence of ten men. This is similarly true with Conservative Judaism, with the exception that some communities recognise that women may also form the *minyan*. So central is the place of the *kaddish* prayer in the Jewish religious psyche as a familial obligation that even some Jews who are not generally observant make a point of attending services to recite the *kaddish* – raising the question of whether a mourner, unable to reach a synagogue, may fulfil his commitment in a virtual type of *minyan*, in which the individual situated at a separate location is connected on-line to a physical *minyan* of ten.

Orthodox rabbis reject the possibility that Jews at another location from a *minyan* – whether for reasons of bad weather, or ill health, or physical danger such as wartime – may fulfil one's prayer obligations by going on-line to an existing *minyan* prayer service. Yet it seems unlikely that even if a solution to the Net *minyan* were found within the limits of Jewish law that most people would prefer to pray at home, rather than come together for a group religious experience in a physical setting, as they have done for centuries.

In Christianity, while on-line churches have appeared such as the First Church of Cyberspace, most appear to prefer off-line communities, including, for example, making confessions off-line. Indeed, the Vatican Pontifical Council for Social Communication issued in 2008 a decree that the Roman Catholic Church would not accept confessions over the Internet. According to a 2004 poll by the Pew Internet and American Life project of Americans of all faiths, the Internet is little used for actual prayer. Only 7 per cent of respondents had made a prayer request on-line – in contrast to 38 per cent who used the Internet to gather religion information, 35 per cent to send a holiday greeting, 32 per cent to gather on-line information about religious events, 21 per cent to gather information about how to celebrate religious holidays, 17 per cent about whether to attend religious services, and 11 per cent to download religious music.[22]

Notwithstanding that the minyan.com is limited to the Reform, all sections of Judaism have nevertheless benefited from certain religion-related matters. Prayer requests are posted on the web. Thus, KEY, a Hebrew acronym for 'Kulani Yehudim Kulani Yachad' (KEY), or 'We're all Jews and united together' coordinates a "tehillim campaign" (prayers from the Book of Psalms) for individual cases, especially of sick people. And, thanks to the Internet, tehillim campaigns have become cross-border, embracing Jewish communities worldwide.[23] In 2006 Israeli Ashkenazi Chief Rabbi Yona Metzger established a day of prayer, on a special Internet website, 'Embracing the World', to pray for missing Israeli soldiers; thousands of Jews worldwide signed on.[24] Going back to before both the age of the Internet and faxes, Jews have been leaving messages in the Western Wall, the last remaining outer wall of the Temple Mount in Jerusalem. But since the Internet they have been sending their prayers virtually. Prayer services at the wall may be seen on the Net. Charity-giving is done on the Internet, making e-charity – or e-*tzedaka* – a growing area of Jewish philanthropy. The obligation of returning lost objects has also taken an internet turn, and www.ebood.co.il has become an informal website or noticeboard for announcing lost and found. The custom prior to the New Year and Yom Kippur holidays of Jews seeking forgiveness – or *'mechilla'* – from fellow Jews whom they have hurt or caused damage in the outgoing year has taken an Internet dimension and some now request 'mechilla' by doing it by e-mail rather than meeting, encountering and apologising in person. Yet this failure to encounter the person has weakened the value of e-mechilla. As one New York Orthodox rabbi put it, 'you have to have the experience right in front of the person, for them to see your face, and you have to see theirs, the face of forgiveness'.[25]

Mourning rituals have also benefited from the Internet era. Burial societies in some Israeli towns, including Tel Aviv (www.kadisha-tlv.co.il) and Kiryat Shemona, have erected devices so that funeral addresses at cemeteries may be seen on the Internet. This enables those who cannot participate in a funeral, particularly given the custom in Jerusalem of burying the same day as death, to follow, including from abroad. The custom of comforting mourners during the seven day *shivah* or mourning period after the funeral has taken on an Internet connection, with some people sending condolences on e-mail. But one rabbi, Shmuel Eliahu, rabbi of the northern town of Safed, has spoken against this, arguing that comforting the mourner is a religious obligation which should be done in person; moreover, honouring the dead ought to be done, Eliahu argued, by going to the house of the deceased soul.[26] The custom among observant and traditional Jews of visiting the graves of the righteous to pray such as, for example, for livelihood, a spouse, health, legal success has taken on an Internet connection in the case of kabbalist rabbi Itzhak Kadduri, where a website erected by his followers (www.kaduri.net) includes a 'Book of Requests'. This has similar connotations to the electronic churches of the 1980s in the US, where pastors like Pat Roberston and Jerry Fallwell offered to pray for followers in lieu of a monetary contribution (Hoover, 1988).

Given the centrality of prayers in Judaism, the other branches of Judaism, bound by limits of halakhah, have not been able to benefit fully from modern information technology. All the other benefits, whether educational websites or other websites like the synagogue, pale into the background given that the synagogue remains on the physical realm.

Jewish religious and educational websites

The discussions within the Haredim and *dati leumi* respective rabbinical leaderships about the threat from the Internet occurred at the same time as a parallel proliferation of Jewish-related websites happened which made it more difficult for rabbis imposing their anti-Internet line. These websites included many which fulfilled seemingly neutral educational and other social matters. The technological information highway is affecting the Israeli religious world no less than other non-Jewish religious communities, particularly given the high priority which religious study has in the religious community, if albeit at a slower pace given the wariness of the Haredi rabbinical leadership to the Internet. Lerner surveyed the manifold types of resources available digitally about Orthodox Judaism, emanating from institutions, organisations and individuals, covering historical, theological, institutional and communal information (Lerner, 2009).

Moreover, it minimised the limitations in access to Jewish education which geographic distance caused in the pre-computer era. This was true in particular with Jewish communities in 'difficult countries' such as Iran, Yemen and Syria, with which Israel has no diplomatic ties.

Typical websites used by Haredim and the modern religious are educational websites. An early site was the Shema Yisrael Torah network.[27] The website www.shemayisrael.co.il is a 'closed and secure' Jewish site, founded in 1992, providing educational material, on a 'restricted' site that prevents users from going into 'forbidden' sites. The site comprises 'Day Yomi', a growing religious learning tradition since the last century involving the study of one page a day of the Talmud (which comprises the major corpus of Jewish law writing) which enables the Talmud to be completed over a seven year cycle of study. The site also comprises *Halakha Yomi* (or Jewish religious laws), the weekly Bible reading, stories of Jewish faith (*hashgacha pratis*) and Jewish content suitable for children. The site was accessed in a 50 day period in 1997 over 100,000 times (16 per cent being users in Israel, and the remainder 50 per cent in the US, and the rest elsewhere in the Jewish Diaspora).[28] Originally free, the site expanded and became fee-paying courses offering a broader spectrum of educational-related materials geared beyond the strictly Haredi population to the newly religious offering courses like a 25-part course entitled 'the making of a kosher kitchen', a course on *Shaatnes* (a biblical prohibition of wearing a fabric comprising both wool and linen), a course on Jewish business ethics and laws such as concerning usury and interest. The Jewish Theological Seminary has a selection of on-line classes on Judaism (courses.jtsa.edu/registration). The Orthodox Union (www.ou.org) offers essays on basics in Judaism, and the Reform movement (www.uahcweb. orgqeducate/parent/) provides Jewish holiday projects and discussion projects. *Otzar Hachochmah* contains over 28,000 searchable books and periodicals in their original format. MyJewishlearning, founded by Edgar Bronfman, is a transdenominational source of Jewish information comprising articles of seven topic areas – History and Community; Holidays; Ideas and Belief; Culture; Texts; Daily Life and Practice; and Lifecycle.[29] Drawing upon Wikipedia, Wikiyeshiva was established in 2008, as an on-line Jewish encyclopaedia drawing on some 800 Jewish terms. Other sites include www.jewfaq.org

which covers Jewish belief, people, places, scripture, holidays, practices and customs.

Rosen (2001), in *The Talmud and the Internet: A Journey between Worlds*, sought to draw lines between the world of Internet and the world of the Talmud. Both worlds are characterised by vastness and the categorisable nature, and both comprise users who function across time and space in engaged dialogue. To be true, the early computerisation of Jewish religious sources had an influence which extended beyond Jewish religious sites. One of the earliest attempts to computerise Jewish sources was the Bar-Ilan *sheiltot* project – which stored in a computerised form 100,000 rabbinical *sheiltot* – or rabbis' answers from the Geonic period in the sixth century to the present day to a range of questions concerning the application of Jewish law to particular situations. There are an estimated half million *sheiltot* contained in 300 books. Their value is mostly concerning law-related matters but they are also valuable historical sources concerning Jewish communities, Jewish figures and events. In a project, which began in 1963, by Professors Aviezer Frankel and Jacob Shoika, the 100,000 sheiltot, comprising 160 million words, were fed into a computer retrieval system at Bar-Ilan University. Its significance was that was it was one of the first computer systems in the world, and the first in the Hebrew language, which was based on full text – enabling the inquirer to determine the key words – rather than the conventional classification system of categories and sub-categories. Indeed, there was scepticism, in the academic world and in the computer science industry, about the alternative to the hierarchical classification system. The Bar-Ilan project also had to teach the computer Hebrew and Aramaic, the language of the Babylonian Talmud, and the Hebrew script used by Rashi, the French-born Jewish Bible commentator. The Haredi world supported the key word system from the beginning. Even though Bar-Ilan University, Israel's religious university, is affiliated with the modern Orthodox community, the Haredi world warmly embraced the project. Additional *sheiltot* have been added over the years. One problem has been that the sensitivity of ancient texts did not enable them to be scanned in, requiring each text to be added manually.[30] In 1994 the entire data base was placed on a CD Rom – 'the Global Jewish data base' – enabling individuals and institutions to purchase it. The project provided access which had beforehand been limited to a few in libraries or private manuscript collections to the entire Jewish learning world.[31]

The 1980s, and even more the 1990s, saw a proliferation of attempts to apply different technologies to Jewish religious study. While these attempts did not replace traditional frameworks for Jewish education, notably the shiur – a frontal lecture by the rabbi to students – they were a new dimension to '*limud Torah*' (or the study of Judaism). In 1982 the Torah Communication Network, created in New York by Rabbi Eli Teitelbaum, enabled people to listen to *shiurim* (religious lessons) about the Talmud on the telephone or on audio cassettes. Originally planned to comprise lessons on the Talmud by radio, the network abandoned this in favour of a dedicated Torah telephone system coined 'Dial-a-*daf*' (a *daf* is a page in Hebrew, a reference to a page of the Talmud) with tape recorders that would restart the *shiur* every hour, enabling a person to telephone on the hour. It was considered a marvel of technology, with hundreds of people simultaneously listening to a *shiur* on audio cassette in English, Yiddish, or Hebrew.[32] Later, the tape recorders were replaced with computers, enabling the user to fast-forward to any place on the page, to rewind to review any point which required clarification, as well as to pause during a *shiur* and return later. Today, the network has expanded beyond the Talmud to include the Five Books of Moses, the Prophets, *Midrash,* Jewish legal codes like Maimonides, and Jewish Thought. By the end of 2008, the entire Talmud was available on an iPod. Once reviled by Haredim, the MP3 enables the Haredi Jew to listen to *shiurim* at every place, including while travelling.

All *hesder* yeshivot (yeshivot of the modern Orthodox sector which combine yeshiva study with army service) have incorporated computers into the study hall. Thus, their websites list the rabbi teachers, the history of the institution and its learning styles, the ideological bent of the yeshiva, as well as up-to-date news and events in the yeshiva. But some have incorporated the computer into yeshiva life more than others, all providing passive information and some more interactive. Otniel yeshiva, for example, was one of the yeshivot to introduce laptops for students into the *bet hamidrash*, or yeshiva hall, enabling them to open additional data base sources as the rabbi refers to additional sources. There is printed access to shiurim but also shiurim recorded on MPs. The breadth of services partly reflects a particular yeshiva's own openness to the wider society. Thus, Yeshivat Har Etzion reflecting its openness is diverse. Students can receive shiurim on their e-mail. The yeshiva's archive numbers over 2,000 shiurim. A website DayByDay (lit. *Yom be Yom*) comprises abbreviated *divrei torah* (Torah lessons). And 'Keshet' are recorded shiurim which can be heard on a MP3 track lasting 40 minutes.[33] The benefits of shiurim transmitted through technological means have been questioned. The traditional one-on-one student–rabbi shiur over the years enabled interactive learning which has been a basic ingredient of study in *yeshivot* (talmudical colleges) over hundreds of years. According to one teacher, Marc Bleiwess, 'the discourse of Jewish study comprises partners breaking their teeth for hours trying to understand sometimes just two lines of ambiguous and deliciously profound text. Each interaction that relates to those lines – with a study partner, another student, a teacher – probes that much deeper. The solitary and usually shallow world of the net surfer rarely offers this kind of rigorous inquiry.' And, quoting the dictum, from the book of *Ethics of the Fathers* (Avot 5:26), 'The reward (of Jewish learning) is in proportion to the effort.' Bleiweiss continued: 'By reducing the effort required for serious study in modern web may be inventing a whole new mode of Jewish discourse – that loses in authenticity, depth and intellectual precision whatever it gains in accessibility.'[34] Some of the reservations were allayed with the establishment in 2007 of the Web Yeshiva, which is identified with the modern Orthodox stream – ironically an outgrowth of Yeshiva Hamivtar in Efrat, where Bleiwess was director. In the Web Yeshiva, students study in a live on-line *shiur* – as well as learning on-line with a *chavruta* (a study partner). Transcending geographical limitations, classes are available from 4 am to midnight in Hebrew, English and Russian.

Beyond the educational-related websites, a vast network of sites have evolved providing a welter of religion-related services on-line, including lists of synagogues, kosher restaurants, institutions like burial societies, cemeteries, and the Jewish calendar. In 2007 there were an estimated 8,500 websites of Jewish interest.[35] The challenge is to locate them. Indeed, there is a longer term challenge for key Israeli and Jewish libraries to archive web content – characterised by its temporality – for future scholars and researchers (Lerner, 2009).

An early website, Jerusalem One, established in 1993, included a Jewish events calendar as well as other services of albeit lesser interest to the Haredi community specifically including JUNK, a Jewish student university network, regarding immigration to Israel, information, and the websites of Israeli government agencies. A site called JewishParentCoaching.com comprises a Jewish parenting coach who provides parents with advice regarding family and children problems.[36] An interactive CD-Rom Hagada produced in 1996 comprises a three-dimensional Seder service, for example, a click on the frog, and an animated video of the ten plagues is depicted.[37]

Online educational and religious websites have regenerated debate about the pros and cons of outreach as a Jewish goal, even to the extent of seeing the conversion of Gentiles to Judaism as a goal (Schulman, 2008). Websites offer a range of other religion-related services from selling religious artifacts like religious books and Jewish gifts. One site offers training in cantorial music (*chazanut*); another, training in singing the weekly *Torah* portion – the trope – to prepare barmitzvah boys who celebrate their coming of age at 13 by reading that week's Bible portion in the synagogue.[38] Yet another site enables a woman to calculate her 'nida' menstrual cycle which includes that part of the month when she is ritually unclean and forbidden to maintain marital relations. The Israel Government's Ministry of Religious Affairs' and the Chief Rabbinate's websites[39] list rabbinical courts for matters of marriage, divorce and religious conversion (all of which in Israel are the responsibility of the rabbinical courts) and circumcisers (*Mohel*). The decision to computerise the Chief Rabbinate came partly after a government poll found that 70 per cent of the secular Israeli public were not interested in contact with the official rabbinate, and that 41 per cent of the public (including 61 per cent of secular Israeli Jews) thought that it no longer has a role.[40] But also there are explanations of Jewish custom. The site even caters for *agunot*, or married women whose husbands have disappeared or refuse to give them a divorce – including under the banner WANTED a gallery of photographs of these men. Jew Tube (www.JewTube.com) comprises Jewish cultural themes.

One of the most prominent sites catering for the modern Jewish community is *Kipa* (the name of a Jewish male's skullcap), began in 1999 by Boaz

Nachtstern, which comprises a set of forums with a range of Jewish questions, as well as forums for dating, for young married, for parents. Kipa also performs well as a site for Talmudic Jewish sources, and running a panel of rabbis. Some 35,000 people are claimed to enter daily, and a quarter of a million a month go in. Among the controversial questions which Kipa has carried is Jewish homosexuality. 'Only as a result of the Internet did rabbis come to realise homosexuality is a widespread phenomenon. Before the Internet, no one came up to their rabbis saying "I am gay. What should I do?". But someone who uses an on-line nickname can ask, and the rabbis had to deal with it,' Nachtstern said.[41]

More Conservative sites include *Moreshet*, set up by Yossi Miller in 1997, comprising a set of websites approved by modern Orthodox rabbis, as well as news of the Jewish and religious worlds, and a panel of rabbis. *Moreshet* comprises a white list of approved sites. Many educational institutions including secular schools use *Moreshet,* ensuring that children surf only controlled sites. An estimated 39–40,000 enter a day, and 8 million visit sites a month. Yet religious critics of *Moreshet*, including Rabbi Yehoshua Shapiro, saw a loophole in *Moreshet* providing a code button which enabled the surfer to create his own 'white list', with lesser or more sites. This led to the setting up of a more restrictive site called Rimon (after the Hebrew words 'Reshet Miogenet Ve-nekiya', or the Safeguard and Clean network), which does not a have a code button for free surfing. Rimon has been adopted not only by the modern Orthodox, including its hardal stricter sub-stream, but also mainstream Haredim.

Yet even Kipa lacks the resources to develop into a website comparable to major websites, drawing one religious journalist, Hadar Ravid, to bemoan the lack of quality in the modern rigorous orientated sites, and calling for 'shocking, controversial, challenging sites which reflect the changes in religious sites. Instead of a lively, liberating atmosphere, the religion sites enclose themselves in dry old frameworks,' said Ravid.[42] While the Judaism section of the major Israeli portals YNET, owned by the mass circulation *Yediot Aharonot* newspaper, and NRG, owned by *Maariv,* another newspaper, have generally been able to draw upon the resources of the main site itself, even the quality of the Judaism pages have varied depending upon the journalist who heads the Judaism section at any particular time.

But what irked the Haredi rabbis was the development of Haredi Internet news sites which operated independently from rabbinic supervision, like *BeHadrei Haredim, Kikar Shabbat*, and *LaDaat*. In light of the Haredi ban on Internet, some Haredi leaders refuse to be interviewed by the sites, and the names of those sponsoring the sites, and editing them, have been hidden from public light. To be true, the rabbinical leadership had already been challenged with the establishment since the 1980s of a range of commercial Haredi weeklies – including *Yom Shishi, Erev Shabbat, Mishpacha, BeKehilla, Sha'ah Tova* – and in the nineties by the Haredi radio stations, which were not subject to rabbinical control. But the Haredi websites went a stage further and challenged the ban on the Internet itself. If the independent news weeklies looked over their shoulders not to offend rabbis, this was passé for the Haredi news sites. Moreover, forums like *Hadrei Haredim* became a platform for the Haredim to speak out against rabbis and institutions.

The campaign by Haredi rabbis which began at the end of 2009 against the Haredi websites developed in the ensuing weeks and months into an all-out onslaught against the Internet. By February 2010 the top Haredi rabbis had got together the heads of most of the Haredi schools in the country. In an extraordinary meeting in Benei Beraq one top rabbi after another assailed the moral decadence of the Internet, and reiterated that only businesses would be allowed to use the Internet and then under the supervision of Haredi-approved filtering devices. Moreover, school heads canvassed all parents regarding whether they possessed the Internet; if so, school managers were instructed to refuse to let the children stay in the school.

Jewish dating has been altered by the Internet with the setting up of Jewish dating sites. They are an important channel for Jews wishing to marry within the Jewish faith. The first dating site began in 1995; within five years there were 120 dating sites. The biggest site is www.cupid.co.il geared for the broadstream Israelis. Established in 1997, some 700,000 Israelis had hooked up to its first six years.[43] Another large site is JDate, geared towards the English-speaking population. Yet not only does it socially network people, but also is a community itself, embracing single life from the pressures focused on families, liberating the single person to make his or her own choices. Other sites include JQS (Jewish Quality Singles) and YID. Dating sites have since become diversified with social networking, providing free of charge, for which the earlier sites charged. Inquirers are asked to state their stream of Judaism, whether or not they keep kosher, and whether or not they observe the Sabbath, the types of information which the other side clearly wishes to know.

While most dating sites serve the Reform community abroad, as well as Conservative community, a number of sites serve the orthodox community. These include datidate established in 2001, *ShneihemShehemEhud* (lit. Two make One) and Glatt Kosher. These sites require more detailed information of a religious nature including such specifics as whether the person is *dati leumi, hardal,* Haredi Hassidic, Haredi-Lithuanian, Haredi Sephardi, and other questions like the Jewish education of the person, whether he or she has studied in yeshiva or ulpana, whether the person prays, whether he participates in Jewish religious study, whether the female plans to cover her hair after marriage, and even whether she wears a skirt or trousers. These sites offer certain challenges to the traditional matchmaker but the Haredi community, where marriages are almost all arranged, overwhelmingly prefer off-line arrangements since the matchmaker knows both sides, and operates with the blessing of the rabbi. In a poll of surfers of the modern Orthodox Kipa site in 2006, 72 per cent of surfers said they use the Internet as an alternative to the traditional shadchan.

Yet the Net is also a framework for Jewish blogosphere providing alternative, sometimes anti-Jewish establishment escapes. Solomon Schimmel of Hebrew College, Boston, identified four types of things which bloggers criticise: 1) Doctrines and dogmas that they consider to be false, foolish, or unethical; 2) obsessive preoccupation with the minutiae of ritual behaviour; 3) perceived hypocrisy of their communities and leadership; and 4) violations of ethical and moral behaviour that are 'covered up' or whitewashed by leaders of the community. Schimmel (2008) identified seven reasons why bloggers blog: 1) to articulate thoughts and feelings that would otherwise be repressed (as one Orthodox lady remarked, 'blogging affords people who live in communities where conformity is part and parcel of their lives to express their frustration and anger of communal life in an anonymous forum');[44] 2) to converse with likeminded individuals because they cannot do so in their real lives; 3) to criticise their communities in the hope of rectifying communal deficiencies; 4) to entertain through parody and satire of its leaders; 5) to take revenge against the communities by those perceived to be hurt by it; 6) to destroy the community by exposing the faults and evils and deficiencies of the community; 7) to help doubters feel comfortable with their doubts.

The socio-religious impact of the Internet

The impact of the Internet upon Haredim may be measured in a number of directions. The Internet was part and parcel of modern day transactions. A 2006 survey of 1,000 religious surfers of the Kipa religious website, which includes Haredim, found that the Internet was used by 26 per cent for friends and pleasure, 25 per cent for electronic mail. Its value as a source of Jewish religious information is undeniable even if Jewish religious study remitted only 6.6 per cent.[45] Another 2006 survey found that 38 per cent of Haredim purchase on the Internet and trusted on-line bank transactions, but this was less than the secular population; 53 per cent of secular used the Internet for purchases and 50 per cent trusted bank transactions on the Internet.[46] And a 2007 survey found that 17 per cent of Haredim order foreign holidays on the Internet.[47]

Mamo, drawing upon a survey of 257 respondents, broken down between Orthodox, semi-Orthodox and not religious regarding relationships they developed on Internet, found that Orthodox respondents were less inclined to enter deep relationships on the Net in contrast to 'not religious' and even more so to 'semi-Orthodox'. Just 17.9 per cent of Orthodox reported 'only deep relationships' in contrast to 40 per cent of 'semi-Orthodox' and 28.1 'not religious'. Some 44.7 per cent of Orthodox reported having 'only shallow' relationships on the Net in contrast to 33.3 per cent of semi-Orthodox and 32.6 per cent of 'not religious'.[48] Yet, the Internet was rated by Haredim as a bad influence on their religious identity. The more religious the surfer, the greater inclination to acknowledge this. In the 2006 Kipa survey, 43 per cent of Haredi respondents said that the Internet damaged their religious level in contrast to 14 per cent of modern Orthodox surfers. And, 56 per cent of Haredi respondents said that they would not recommend to acquaintances to connect to the Internet in contrast to 12 per cent of modern Orthodox respondents.

Hierarchical rabbinical structures have been challenged by the egalitarian nature of the Internet. 'Authority does not work on the Web. A rabbi needs to speak of issues deeply and profound essence to be able to reach people', the modern Orthodox rabbi, Yuval Sherlo said.[49] The challenge to authority appears to be less pronounced in the Haredi world since both the Internet had been less intrusive and rabbinical authority is stronger there. Indeed, there is evidence suggesting that rabbis have succeeded to a considerable extent in maintaining the legitimacy of rabbinical decrees in the eyes of the Haredi population. Some 91 per cent of Haredim were aware of the instructions concerning computers and the Internet of Haredi rabbinical committees for communications, and 81 per cent agreed with them, according to a survey by Bezek, the Israeli telephone company. Given that a criterion in Jewish law-making is that law pronouncements must be acceptable to the community, otherwise this will bring into question the very legitimacy of the law-making body itself, this was no mean achievement. It does not mean that rabbis did not need to employ various means to impose their will, notwithstanding the limits of their powers in the modern democratic state of Israel. Thus, Gerar Hassidim received housecalls from the sect's representatives seeking them to get rid of the '*treifah*' (literally, ritually unclean) device. Gatherings and conferences were held in different Haredi communities in Israel, and abroad, to generate consciousness over the Internet 'danger'. In the Haredi city of Betar, south of Jerusalem, the local rabbinate in 2009 declared that Betar would become the first Internet-free city. 'Internet is like a tsunami that threatens to envelop and endanger the entire Haredi community.'[50] Residents who required the Internet for business purposes would need to install an Internet-restricted connection with a filtering device. Schools in Betar were instructed not to accept children who had unlimited access to the Internet. Elsewhere, there have been instances of so-called 'modesty squads' demonstrating outside netcafes used by Haredim to surf.

A telling example that rabbinical decrees have been respected was the case of cellphones which had had Internet access and the ability to receive and send SMSs. No less than computers, mobile phones have also occupied the attention of the Haredi rabbinical leadership. For example, in 2002 Haredi rabbis forbade talmudical college students from using mobile phones, seeing them as threatening the appropriate atmosphere for the yeshiva study hall. As the mobile phone's capabilities widened, Haredi rabbis instructed the rabbinical committee for communication affairs to negotiate with mobile phone companies to provide mobile phones with telephone facilities alone. An estimated 30,000–100,000 Haredim changed their phones to kosher Internet-less and SMS-less mobile phones in 2008. Indeed, four major Israeli mobile phone companies competing for the Haredi market offered 'kosher Internet-free' phones.

Conclusion

The increasing number of communication delivery systems, together with the greater diversification of programmes enabling individuals to choose messages that reinforce already held attitudes, thereby strengthen religious identity. On the other hand, the plethora of messages challenge the religious hierarchical authority of organised religion, as people find alternative, perhaps more deeply spiritually meaningful, means to give religious expression.

In the case of the Haredim, it would be wrong to exaggerate the effects on Internet. True, the cultural ghetto failed to withstand the pressures of the computer in contrast to, for example, television and cinema. Yet, Haredim have sought to create their own on-line cultural ghettos by isolating Internet access except to 'kosher sites', in a not dissimilar way to their separate Haredi newspapers and Haredi radio stations. Haredim came latterly to recognise that the Internet has a positive role both in modern life and in Jewish education.

Notwithstanding the wide, on-going and, at times, challenging discussions which have occurred in some religious communities in Israel over the last 15 years regarding the Internet danger, the extent to which the Internet has changed religious life should not be exaggerated. As before the Internet era, the synagogue remains the centre of Jewish spiritual life. So is the Jewish home. The Jewish home functions in accordance with a Jewish code of life as expressed in the 613 positive and negative commandments in the Bible-regulating man's relationship with God and with his fellow man. These include kosher food, Sabbath observance and marital life, to name a few. If Jewish study has been enhanced through the application of technology like Torah educational websites, the traditional frameworks of Jewish study such as the rabbi's shiur, and off-line yeshiva study, remain paramount.

References

Barzilai-Nahon, K. and Barzilai, G. (2005) 'Cultured Technology: The Internet and Religious Fundamentalism', *The Information Society,* 21.

Central Bureau of Statistics (2005) *Jerusalem*. Jerusalem: Central Bureau of Statistics.

——(2007) *Jerusalem*. Jerusalem: Central Bureau of Statistics.

——(2008) *Jerusalem*. Jerusalem: Central Bureau of Statistics.

——(2009) *Jerusalem*. Jerusalem: Central Bureau of Statistics.

Cohen, Y. (2001) 'Mass Media in the Jewish Tradition', in D. Stout and J. Buddenbaum (eds), *Religion and Popular Culture: Studies on the Interaction of Worldviews*. Ames, IA: Iowa State University Press.

——(2006) 'Judaism', in D. Stout (ed), *Encyclopaedia of Religion, Communication and Media*. London: Routledge.

Goodman, Y. (2010) 'The Modern Religious Youth and the Internet', *Tzohar,* Tamuz, 5770.

Hoover, S. (1988) *Mass Media Religion: the Social Sources of the Electronic Church*. London: Sage.

Lemish, D., Ribak, R. and Aloni, R. (2009) 'Israeli Children Online: From Moral Panic to Responsible Parenting', *Megamot,* 46, 1–2, February [Hebrew].

Lerner, H. G. (2009) 'Internet Resources for Researching Orthodox Judaism', *Journal of Religious and Theological Information,* 7.
Patrick, G. (2007) 'Hinduism in Cyberspace', *Religion and Social Communication,* 5, 1–2.
Pnim (2009) Winter, 48 [Hebrew].
Rosen, J. (2001) *The Talmud and the Internet: A Journey Between Worlds.* New York: Farrar, Straus and Giroux.
Schimmel, S. (2008) 'Anonymous Blogging as a Safe Haven for Challenging Religious Authority and Creating Disident Communities'. Paper, Conference on 'Media, Spiritualities and Social Change'. Boulder, CO: University of Colorado at Boulder.
Schulman, J. (2008) *The Evolving Role of the Internet as a Support for Conversion to Judaism.* MA Thesis. Boston: Boston Hebrew College.

9 Kosher advertising

'You publish a picture of a man or woman wearing only underwear. Don't you think that this is offensive?' Yigal Bibi, a National Religious Party Knesset member.

'How can somebody persuade you to buy a product if he is unable to see the usage of what the product is put to?' countered Yair Feldman, head of the Israel Advertisers Association.

Session of the Knesset's Interior Committee (initiated by the United Torah Judaism Party) debating in 1994 whether the authorities were doing enough to enforce laws prohibiting the publication of nude photos.[1]

Like the other monotheistic religions, Judaism views positively the role of advertising in providing the consumer with information. Advertising also plays a multiplier effect and contributes to economic growth through creating jobs – all towards raising living standards. Pava (1998) and Tamari (1997) extrapolate from biblical and Talmudic sources Jewish perspectives on business ethics. As a society espousing ethical values, Jewish Israel ought to provide witness to the impact of ethics in the field of advertising. No less important in the question of the impact of ethics on the media is the question of its impact on advertising. Accuracy is just as important to advertising and public relations as it is to journalism because it would lead to consumer dissatisfaction (Bivins, 2004). Friedman (1984) argues that, as far back as the age of the Talmud, Jewish values impacted upon marketing and business ethics. Green (1997) argues that Jewish business ethics have had an impact beyond the religious community. Dorff (1997) contrasts between Conservative Jewish views on business ethics and other Jewish religious streams.

Clearly the information has to be accurate and complete. It also has to avoid techniques which lapse into immorality such as degradation of the image of the women. The problem of deception is acute in advertising, where a customer is persuaded to buy a product which he or she would not otherwise do if they knew all the facts. Kosher advertising raises the question of whether advertising itself can be kosher if it is intended to persuade someone to purchase something he would not otherwise do. Reflecting that truth is regarded as a foundation of the world, the Book of Proverbs (12:19) states, 'Truthful lips shall be established forever, but a lying tongue is only for a moment.' So important is truth that lying is a fundamental breach of the monotheistic code and is equated in Judaism to be idol worship.

The advertising–religion nexus in Israel has variegated dimensions. The question of whether Judaism relates positively or not to the advertisement and the act of advertising was discussed in Chapter 2. The most obvious is whether Judaism ought to promote itself through modern advertising – to be discussed in Chapter 10 – and if so how it does so. One question is whether religion symbols should be deployed in the service of marketing, and, if so, to what extent it is done. Another is whether advertising in Israel generates criticism, in particular from religious populations such as the Haredim. Yet another question is how commercial companies are projected towards the growing Haredi audience. The single-minded focus of the Haredi community in terms of advertising and Jewish law has been the issue of modesty in advertising. The term 'kosher advertising' refers to advertising in religious sectors. This chapter will discuss how the religious community perceives the usage of sexually related themes in advertising. The chapter will then turn its attention to the challenges facing Israeli companies in marketing in the Haredi sector in light of these strictures. In recent years, Israeli companies have identified the Haredim in particular as a target market. The Haredi cultural ghetto, which is not exposed to the general media, has raised questions about how companies and advertisers can reach this growing consumer base.

Sex shalt not sell

Sexual attraction is an integral element in advertising. Limburg argues that the real appeal of advertising is that sexual inducements are embedded in human nature (Limburg, 1994). Fromm argues that far from recognising a universal need for love in a society which has little love, advertisements suggest that love may be gained through purchasing an object.[2] Moreover, there had been an increase in the application of sexual inducement in advertising. In the mid-1980s, examining patterns in the US, Reichert et al. found that sexually orientated appeal in American advertising had become increasingly explicit through the media and women were three times more likely than men to be portrayed explicitly. But images of men had also become more sexually explicit (Reichert et al., 1999).

Over the years Israel's Knesset and public authorities like the broadcasting bodies have formulated guidelines of what is acceptable and what is not in sexual-related context. One Israeli law forbids pictures of nudity or photos of intimate parts of the body. Another law forbids newspapers from carrying adverts of prostitute services. But the lines are not clearly cut – perhaps deliberately – resulting in the subject becoming a political soccer field of clashing interests. For example, the Knesset's Interior Committee in 1994 held a discussion initiated by the Haredi party United Torah Judaism of why the judiciary and the police were not doing enough to ensure that the laws prohibiting the publication of nudity of photos of intimate body parts were implemented. A representative of the police said that while it received complaints, it sometimes concluded that a crime had not been committed. Aryeh Rottenberg, a representative of the Israel Advertisers Association, charged that

> the law was imprecise about what was permissible to publish and what was not. Are lips regarded as sexual parts? At times an expression of eyes is more tantamount to arousement than a naked breast. Even the paragraph in the law forbidding documenting the sexual act is unclear: Is kissing considered sexual relations? If the Knesset wants to, let them pass a law which clearly delineates what is permitted and what is forbidden to publish.[3]

The debate between advertisers and its critics was conducted in the Second Television and Radio Authority when, against the background of a ratings war to draw more viewers, the various television companies which broadcast on the second channel were allowing a very liberal attitude in sexual and violence-related content in advertising. About two thousand adverts are produced for television yearly in Israel, 5 per cent of which require emendation. One per cent alone are invalidated, half of which for reasons of sexual or violent content.[4] The then authority head, Motta Sklar, argued that the authority had a supervisory role to play in developing a code for advertising. The authority had commissioned a poll which found that 41 per cent of viewers said that sexual innuendos were the key issue which bothered viewers; 83 per cent of viewers favoured censoring adverts. And 69 per cent backed the authority's plans for an advertising code.[5] According to Sklar, there was a need for stricter control over advertising than over programme content because, whereas viewers were forewarned about provocative content of programmes, there was no advance warning for viewers regarding advertising matter. Under the code, partial nudity such as a topless woman was forbidden, as was the portrayal of sex even if one of the actors was dressed. However, it allowed hints of nudity when it concerned advertising underwear, or sexual attraction. Sklar sought to woo advertisers by saying that those who signed the code would not have to submit advertising copy for prior approval, whereas those who declined would have to submit.

The proposal generated a debate within the Advertisers Association. The head of the Telad television company, Zvi Peled, accused the second television and radio authority of 'seeing itself as the modesty squad'. 'Sex sells, is the prime mover in the advertising sector, and nothing can change this,' he said.[6] Some advertisers appealed to the Supreme Court against the decision of the authority to scrutinise advertising copy. But 26 company members of the Advertisers Association agreed to sign the code, against 16 who refused to. Some relented and signed the code after two Knesset members tabled bills in which infringement of the code would be a crime. The 'voluntary' nature of the code was a not untypical Israeli solution for the establishment to woo the cooperation; the application of military censorship, for example, is based on a voluntary editors' agreement in which editors agree to a code, a framework for appeal, and the authorities give up placing on trial journalists from Israeli newspapers who breach censorship.

Even the Israeli government is not innocent in playing the sexual motif. In an effort to improve the country's image, which was tarnished by international perceptions during the intifada and the resultant military situation, the Israeli Foreign Ministry invited a team of photographers from the American male magazine, *Maxim*, to shoot scantily dressed Israeli models on Tel Aviv's beaches. 'We want to show that we are a normal society like others,' said the country's press consul in New York.[7] Even more controversial was a Tourism Ministry campaign in 2007 to draw the international homosexual and lesbian community to visit the country. An advert featuring two men with religious skullcaps in a close embrace against the background of the walls of the ancient city of Jerusalem aroused the anger of the religious political parties. Said Zevulun Orlev of the Jewish Home political party, 'If a government agency attempts to market the capital of Israel as Amsterdam, this is a serious eclipse of light.'[8]

Haredim have taken to the streets literally in protesting what they regard as immodest advertising. Not satisfied with ensuring that their own media keep their rules, some Haredim have argued that given that they get around everywhere, advertising has to be clean in all public places. Haredim lobbied public bus companies not to carry immodest advertising. Their campaign was been characterised by a combination of political lobbying with (illegal) violence. In 1992 Haredim torched 40 bus shelters in Jerusalem which had a picture of a model promoting female swimwear. When promoters of the film *Sex and the City* sought to promote the local screening in 2008, the municipalities of Jerusalem and Petach Tiqva said that the word 'sex' would have to be removed from advertising, because it would hurt religious sensitivities. In 2001 Haredim achieved a victory when they managed to negotiate with Egged, the public bus transportation company, that all advertising on Jerusalem buses would require approval of a Haredi body called the 'Committee for Purity and Sanctity of the Camp'. This reached excessive proportions during Jerusalem municipal elections when one of the parties, 'Wake Up Jerusalem', wanted to advertise a picture of a woman candidate on buses and Egged declined. The party appealed the Supreme Court which instructed Egged to carry it.

Haredi pressures in their modesty advertising campaign have extended even to the advertising agencies themselves. In 1993 Haredim sought to pressure one advertising agency that had used immodest photos by threatening catering establishments that they would lose their kosher certification if they would continue using that particular advertising company. This turned the kashrut certificate – the function of which was to assure the consumer that the ingredients and preparation of the food adhered to religious dietary laws – into a political weapon. Seeking to justify this, one Haredi source remarked that 'it is not possible that a company should seek to be in touch and profit from the Haredi community, and at the same time offend the sensitivities in such a brutal manner'.[9]

Haredi victories encouraged them to lobby in other areas of advertising. In 1998 Egged gave in to Haredi pressure to remove advertisements from the Labour Party, headed 'One people, one army recruitment', favouring that Haredim be recruited for the Israeli Army.

The Haredi campaign against unsuitable images on advertising posters has extended to the skies, with Haredim objecting to the in-flight films shown on El Al, the Israeli national airlines. They threatened to place a ban on the airline, not dissimilar to one placed years earlier on the airline for flying on the Sabbath.

The Haredi victory in the poster war even persuaded a group of women from the modern Orthodox sector to campaign in the late 1990s against the usage of women and children in advertising. They found a common language with Israeli feminist groups and the Prime Minister's adviser for the status of women.

Religious symbols in advertising

A separate question is the use of religious imagery in advertising promotion. The extent to which religion is used in general in advertising is a subject of debate among researchers. Mallia (2009) argues that there is an increasing trend to use religious images in advertising as well as to do so more explicitly. Moreover, Marmor-Lavie et al. (2009) claim that images of spirituality feature more in advertising than religion. But neither provided quantitative data. By contrast, Moore (2005), examining American news magazines (*Time*, *Newsweek* and *US News and World Report*), found that only 1.13 per cent had religion-related adverts. This confirmed Maguire and Weatherby's own study of advertising on American network television comprising 797 ads that only 2.01 per cent of adverts had religious or spiritual content. It begs the question of why religion was not used more (Maguire and Weatherby, 1998).

While a few ads had religious themes relevant to more than one faith, like Adam and Eve, and Mount Sinai, most adverts concerned one religion. Whether the relative absence of religious imagery is as true in non-Western media is doubtful. In traditional societies, for example, the Arab world, religious imagery appears to be more relevant. In a content analysis of pan Arab, Egyptian, Lebanese and Emirati magazines, Al-Olayan and Karande (2000) found that 83 per cent of Arabic adverts showed women wearing long clothing, as compared to 29 per cent of women in US adverts.

Maguire and Weatherby (1998) offer a reason for the low amount of religion in advertising: advertisers think that religion has become largely irrelevant in daily life. The separation of church and state draws advertisers to follow this, and advertisers are reluctant to highlight religious content because religion is not considered dramatic enough to capture or hold viewers' attention. Just as all advertising is intended to draw attention, surprise and shock, religion-related advertising has become more provocative, according to Mallia (2009). But this appears surprising given that according to secularisation theory there has been a decline in the standing of religious institutions in West Europe, reflected in declining church attendances. Advertisers might refrain from using religion because they are worried that the 'commodification' of religion runs the risk of alienating religious people in the audience. It is not surprising that Haredi Jews as well as Catholics and Muslims have each been alienated, and protested the desecration of religious symbols.

The claim that spirituality – a personal expression of faith – is more present than religion in advertising symbols offers researchers wanting a wider base beyond religion per se (Zinnbauer et al., 1997). The Garrett-Medill study of editorial content in the US media (Garrett-Medill Center for Religion and the News Media, 1999) did not limit itself to religion content but also embraced spirituality and faith – a recognition that any assessment of content on religion requires also to be taken into account personal experiences of faith or spirituality.

Spirituality may appear to be the opposite of advertising and consumerism, but they are not so opposite. Marmor-Lavie et al. (2009) argue that advertisers and marketers are not selling products but rather communicating meaning to consumers.

Hag Sameach! Religious holiday advertising

Advertising plays a significant role in religious holidays. This, in turn, contributes to religious identity in the contemporary era particularly in the case of non-religious populations who draw much of their 'religious' identity from the media themselves of which advertising is a major segment.

The Jewish life-cycle – which has a richer number of different religious holidays than some other religions – offers the researcher an opportunity to see quantitative patterns in religious holiday advertising including contrasting goals of holiday advertising. Religious holydays – upon which Jews wish each other the traditional greeting of 'Hag Sameach' or 'Happy Holyday' – fulfil an important place in contemporary Jewish identity in Israel and in the Jewish Diaspora. To generate a picture, religious advertising was examined by the author during the run-up to, on the eve of, and during six key Jewish festivals.[10] These were the Jewish New Year (*Rosh Hashonah*) and the Day of Atonement (*Yom Kippur*), both of which are regarded as the premier Jewish holydays, when, according to Jewish tradition, Humanity is judged by God and their fate for the next year decided upon. Also examined were three festivals of thanksgiving: Passover (*Pesach*), which celebrates the Israelite exodus from Egypt; the Feast of Weeks (*Shavuot*), which celebrates the Decalogue or the Giving of the Ten Commandments at Mount Sinai; and the Tabernacles holiday (*Sukkot*), which remembers the 40-year journey by the Israelites through the Sinai desert to the Promised Land. Later in the first and second Jewish Commonwealth the three festivals became centred around the Temple in Jerusalem. They are celebrated in the first case with eating *matzot* (unleavened bread) for seven days; in the second case, milk products; and third, by living in temporary booths for seven days. A sixth holiday, the minor – but popular – eight-day long festival of *Hanuka*, which marks the rededication of the Second Jewish Temple after it was liberated from the Greeks, is examined.

Seven daily newspapers – the secular quality paper *Haaretz* and three secular popular papers, *Yisrael Hayom*, *Yediot Aharonot* and *Maariv*, and three religious dailies, *Mekor Rishon*, a nationalist paper partly identified with modern orthodox population, and two Haredi or ultra-Orthodox newspapers, *Hamodia* and *Yated Neeman* – were examined, as were key Haredi weekly news magazines.

The research discovered differences in advertising patterns between the different holidays, between the secular and religious media, between different types of festival-related advertising. Differences were also found in the ratio of advertising before the holiday and during the holiday. *Rosh Hashanah* and *Sukkot* are the biggest holidays for advertising, in both the secular and religious newspaper sectors. These are followed by *Pesach* and *Hanuka*. Overall, *Rosh Hashanah* accounts for 35 per cent of festival advertising, and *Sukkot* for 26 per cent. *Pesach* accounted for 20 per cent and *Hanuka* 16 per cent. By contrast, *Shavuot* accounts for 1 per cent, and *Yom Kippur* 3 per cent.

There was no major difference in the overwhelming number of religious holiday advertising between the religious and secular press, with the exception of *Hanuka* where 18 per cent of the total of festival-related advertising in religious media appeared in contrast to 10 per cent of holiday-related advertising in the secular media. In addition, 40 per cent of the secular media's festival-related advertising was on *Rosh Hashanah* in contrast to 32 per cent in the religious media. *Sukkot* was the same 26 per cent in both sectors, and *Pesach* 21 per cent in the secular media and 19 per cent in the religious media.

Religious holyday advertising was broken down according to six categories. First was public service announcements such as companies' operating hours during the holyday period and public transport arrangements to holy sites. Second was events during the period – which was particularly noteworthy with *Sukkot* and *Pesach* due to these festivals having intermediate days used for recreational activities and *Hanuka*. These include both events of a specifically religious nature and events not of a religious character. Third was greetings for the festival; fourth, consumer products and the holyday; fifth, charity appeals and voluntarism; and, sixth, promotion of the newspaper's special holiday issues. The three most advertised categories were consumerism (41 per cent), holiday events (24 per cent) and holiday greetings (13 per cent). Charity appeals and volunteer activity accounted for 9 per cent, public announcements 6 per cent, and promotion by newspapers of their holiday issue 2 per cent.

There was considerable difference from festival to festival. Some 38 per cent of *Pesach* ads were about consumerism. It reflects that the festival is characterised by new utensils and special *Pesach* food. Yet, 52 per cent and 58 per cent of all holiday-related ads at *Rosh Hashonah* and *Hanuka* concern consumerism – surprising since neither *Rosh Hashonah* nor *Hanuka* are especially noted for their consumerism.

Shavuot generated only one thirtieth and one twentieth of the number of advertisements which *Sukkot* and *Pesach* produced respectively. While consumerism – notably milk products – is a feature of the *Shavuot* holiday – indeed, 60 per cent of all *Shavuot* advertising was accounted for by consumerism – the overall number of adverts in consumerism for *Shavuot* were surprisingly small (14).

The study also compared the advertising in the run-up to the festival with that during the festival. The latter comprise advertisements for holiday attractions and events geared for the family – at a time when schools are closed and businesses have restricted hours. Advertisements for events were significantly greater for *Sukkot* than *Pesach*; 53 per cent (373 ads) on *Sukkot* concerned holiday-related events in contrast to 19 per cent (96 ads) on *Pesach*. Ten per cent of *Hanuka* advertisements (42 ads) concerned events. The holidays which were seven or eight days long like *Pesach*, *Sukkot* and *Hanuka* had a considerable amount of advertising during the festival itself; 57 per cent (257 ads) of all *Hanuka* ads were during the holiday itself.

Holiday greetings comprised 21 per cent (205 ads) at *Rosh Hashonah*. But *Pesach* – which is not noted as a time of greetings – also registered a high number of greeting adverts: 23 per cent (119) of *Pesach* festival adverts comprised greetings.

The trend for charity-related advertising at times of holydays was also found in Keenan and Yeni's study of Ramadan advertising in Egyptian television (Keenan and Yeni, 2003). Seventeen per cent of public service ads aired on Egypt's Channel 1 in the Ramadan period had a charity theme in contrast to 2 per cent in the non-Ramadan period. In the Israel case, advertising for charities was monopolised by the religious media – a recognition of the central place which charity has in the community. Eighteen per cent (341 ads) of all advertising for holidays in the religious sector comprised charity or voluntarism in contrast to 0.4 per cent of holiday advertising in the secular media (four adverts). While it was not surprising that 10 per cent (98 adverts) at *Rosh Hashonah* were for charities/volunteerism – given that *Rosh Hashonah* is a traditional time for charity – it is noteworthy that *Hanuka* and *Sukkot* – not generally thought of as times for charity – were even greater. Twenty-seven per cent (120 ads) of *Hanuka* ads and 12 per cent (87 ads) at *Sukkot* concerned charity; 6 per cent (32 ads) at *Pesach* were for charity.

The wide gap between the Jewish holyday annual lifecycle as reflected in advertising patterns contrasted with the traditional status which the respective holydays hold in Jewish religious culture. While *Rosh Hashonah* maintains its dominant position, *Yom Kippur* clearly did not have the central place in advertising trends as it does in Jewish religious culture. Notwithstanding the similar statuses which *Pesach*, *Sukkot* and *Shavuot* enjoy in the traditional culture, there were wide differences both in the overall number of adverts which each of the three festivals generate – notably the very low number of *Shavuot* – as well as the wide differences between *Pesach* and *Sukkot* in the types of religious advertising. Despite it being considered only a minor holiday from a Jewish religious perspective, the high volume of advertising for *Hanuka* was identical with the popular standing the festival also enjoys today in American Jewish life where polls show that *Hanuka* is the most frequently observed holiday together with the *Pesach Seder* meal and *Yom Kippur*. The media fulfil a role in the contemporary world of generating religious identity when formal frameworks like synagogue attendance have been declining. In this sense, media coverage of festivals, including advertising, contributes to the religious festival holiday atmosphere. But inevitably advertising takes on a materialistic consumerist image, particular in the case of the secular media. Overall, consumerism takes a greater percentage of all holiday advertising in the secular media (49 per cent) compared to the religious sector (34 per cent).

The boundaries in marketing among Haredim

Advertising in religious and traditional societies like the Haredi Jewish community in Israel poses a special challenge requiring sensitivity in advertising certain products. Research carried out in other country and religion contexts is also relevant for the Israeli model. Vitell and Paolillo (2003) examined how religion plays a role in consumer practices. Mittelstaedt (2002) analysed various ways religions and religious institutions affect marketing. Wilson and West (1981) propose marketing strategies for products regarded as 'unmentionable' in certain societies. Waller (2000), examining cultural values in advertising in Malaysia, where a number of religions are practised including Islam, Taoism, Buddhism, Hinduism and Christianity, found that major limitations were cultural and sexual in type, affecting the national aspiration of achieving a Malaysian identity and conforming to the values of Islam. Radically extremist groups, guns, gambling, religious denominations and political parties may not be advertised. And condoms, female contraceptives, female underwear and female hygienic products, alcohol and cigarettes, while allowed to be advertised, face limitations.

In an expansion of the research, Waller, Fam and Erdogan (2005) examined the advertising of controversial products in four geographically distant countries – Malaysia, New Zealand, Turkey and the UK – and confirmed that religion and history were far more important factors than geography in determining attitudes to advertising controversial products. Of 17 controversial products presented in the researchers' four-country survey (comprising 954 respondents)[11] 11 resulted in similar answers for New Zealand and the UK (both predominantly Christian countries), and seven were similar for Malaysia and Turkey (both predominantly Muslim countries). And, in a study of advertising agents, Shao (1993) confirmed the differences between Europe and more traditional zones like Africa and the Middle East. He found that 7.6 per cent, 3.5 per cent and 3.4 per cent of advertising agents in Europe surveyed replied that condoms, female underwear and male underwear respectively could not be advertised in contrast to 31.3 per cent, 6.7 per cent and 6.7 per cent of advertising agents in Africa respectively and 31.3 per cent, 20 per cent and 20 per cent of advertising agents in the Middle East respectively.

Yet no less true was Shao (1993) who also confirmed that within Europe, which is regarded as more enlightened than other areas of the world, 11 of 16 European countries indicated limitations in television advertising of eight categories of products, including cigarettes, alcohol, condoms, female hygiene products, female undergarments, male undergarments, sexual diseases and

pharmaceutical products. And, in magazine advertising, 8 out of 16 countries indicated restrictions in all the eight categories.

All this confirms the need for advertisers targeting the Haredi media to show sensitivity. No adverts, for example, for the Internet are accepted, nor, in the case of the *Hamodia* newspaper, for even computers. The only adverts for portable phones allowed are for the 'kosher' phones, which do not have access to the Internet or send text messages. All this results in tens of thousands of shekels of lost advertising. Advertising portraying women is not published. In accord with modesty codes women do not appear addressing 'You' in the singular but only in the plural. A tourist promotion for a hotel would not show a picture of a bedroom but show instead, say, the hotel lobby. Like editorial matter in the Haredi press is censored, as described in Chapter 5, so are advertisements subject to censorship. The rabbinical censor must be knowledgeable enough in order to adjudicate in the advertisements submitted for publication; in one instance, one rabbinical censor on the *Yated Neeman* newspaper passed an advert for Viagra, not aware of its purpose.

There are other examples of religious allusions made in advertisements: in one advert for Time cigarettes, a religious man is lighting up at the termination of the Sabbath, under the heading 'Shavua Tov' ('Have a good week'), the traditional greeting that Jews give each other at the termination of the Sabbath, during which smoking is one of the activities forbidden by Orthodox and Conservative religious law. An advertisement for Golf cigarettes, under the heading 'Sifsei Chachamim' ('the lips of the sages'), was a play on the classical Jewish Bible commentary of the same name, 'Sifsei Chachamim'.

However, the usage of religious motifs can become controversial, at times offending religious sensitivities. For example, McCann Erickson in 2007 produced an advertisement for the Internet in the shape of a computer mouse and its wire wrapped seven times around a man's arm, rather similar to the seven times which *tefillin* (phylacteries) are wound around the arm of the Jewish man at daily prayers. Under the heading 'Believing in Internet', the foot of the advert read, 'So it is that we believe in Internet, our customers believe in Internet, and, God willing, also you will believe in Internet.' Readers reacted critically.[12]

The application of religious verses to promote products has generated discussion within the Haredi community, as well, and some Haredi media decline to carry such adverts, deeming them sacrilegious. According to Abraham Brisk, a Belze chassid belonging to the Haredi advertising company, 'Potential': 'A basic rule that guides me, which is clearly fundamental to the boundaries of what is permitted and what is forbidden, is not to mix holy with the secular or profane. Religious verses and Jewish teachings should appear in holy books and not on news pages intended to draw the eye.'[13]

The growth of the Haredi advertising sector

Since the early 1990s, Israeli commerce has identified the Haredi market as a lucrative one. Until then advertising for the Haredi sector was limited, untargeted, because products were not geared to their specific needs. About 70 per cent of the Israeli population may be tied to a particular sector like the Russians, Arabs, as well as the Haredim, yet only 15 per cent of the advertising budget has been used in specifically targeting all of these sectors.[14] While Haredim comprise 8 per cent of the Israeli population, they only draw 3 per cent of the advertising budget.[15] But this may also be partly explained by the fact that reaching the Haredi audience is relatively cheap, since it excludes television and cinema. Also, the cost of advertising in the Haredi press is much cheaper than the mass-circulation newspapers of the general media, which are not read by the Haredi population. The discovery of the Haredi sector has resulted in an increase in advertising for the sector[16] and naturally has been accompanied by the need to conceptualise how to reach the Haredi consumer. Haredi advertising companies, working within the sector and staffed by Haredim who understand the nuances and motifs of what should be emphasised and what should be avoided, have evolved.

The Haredi population comprises 100,000 households, with some 6.2 children per Haredi family – in contrast to 3.5 children among the secular population. There are 450,000 children under the age of 18. The Haredi sector is estimated to grow by 6 per cent annually. According to the Shilav Research Institute, by 2020 the sector will account for 19 per cent of the population. Of 105,000 births in Israel per year, 30,000 comprise the Haredim.[17] Forty per cent of Haredim are concentrated in Jerusalem and 33 per cent in Bnei Beraq. This has changed as young Haredi couples sought cheaper housing in new Haredi towns, and 15 per cent of Haredim today live in Kiryat Sefer, Betar Illit to the north and west of Jerusalem, Ashdod on the coast, and Petach Tiqva, a suburb town of Tel Aviv.

There are wide differences between the consumer needs of the Haredi and general Israeli markets; 45 per cent of output of the Haredi family budget is on food, in contrast to 30 per cent in the case of the general Israeli population. Toiletries account for 10 per cent of the Haredi family budget in contrast to 2 per cent of the general Israeli budget. By contrast, entertainment accounted in the mid-1990s for 10 per cent of the Haredi family budget in contrast to 15 per cent of the secular family.[18]

An examination of the largest categories, based on the quantity of advertising in the general Israeli sector and the Haredi sector in 2006, illustrates the wide differences in the two advertising sectors. The categories of the Haredi sector which do not appear in the top ten categories of advertising in the general Israeli sector included milk products; books; colleges and *yeshivot*; health and clinic; and travel agencies. And, by contrast, among the key categories of advertising in the general Israeli sector which did not appear in the top ten categories of Haredi advertising are cars, electrical goods, credit companies, furniture, and such media as computers.[19]

But Haredi consumer patterns were changing by the millennium as Haredim became more accustomed and inclined to purchase frozen meats, natural foods, and a broader range of cheese products. Ten per cent of food purchases are, according to the Israel Manufacturers Association,[20] decided upon in the Haredi sector according to the level of kashrut of the food product. The change is reflected in that food companies provide today – more than they once did – more kashrut supervision of a standard that would meet with approval from the Haredi consumer. There are some 100 organisations in Israel granting kashrut, of which seven are leading Haredi ones. The largest, Eidat Haredit ('Righteous Court of Law of the Haredi Community') had in 2010 over 200 food companies it supervised throughout Israel. The second largest is the Belze Bet Din. Another leading supervisory Bet Din is the Sephardi or oriental 'She'erit Yisrael'.

Thirty-six per cent of Haredim in 2007 were car owners and a further 15 per cent intended to purchase a car in the next two years, according to the Shiluv Institute.[21] Haredim are more inclined today to possess housing appliances like air conditioners, washing machines, freezers and microwave ovens. A growing interest in interior design, for example, is partly a means to learn how to deal with overcrowding in large Haredi families, who often live in cramped flats. Haredi newspapers carry columns on interior design, and courses have opened for Haredi interior designers in colleges of design.

Some of the Haredi consumer patterns revolve around the Jewish life cycle. In addition to religious artifacts, the religious holidays are a time to purchase new clothing. Kitchens comprise two sinks, one for milk dishes and other for meat dishes.

Dating too provides an impetus for consumerism. When a decision on an arranged match may often be made after a few meetings or even just one, considerable preparation goes towards these arranged meetings. Fashion is the most challenging area because of religious strictures about dress modesty. The specific needs for women vis-à-vis clothing are long sleeves, skirts at mid-calf, no trousers and stockings – 50 per cent of stockings in Israel are sold in the Haredi sector.[22] Cosmetics also have their boundaries in the Haredi sector. Nail polish and eye make-up is generally frowned upon, but face powder and lipstick are more accepted. The prohibition upon married women of appearing with uncovered hair for reasons of modesty has created a local retail wig industry. With a wig purchased on average once in three years, at an average price of 3,000 dollars, there is a lively industry among Haredi women. Men also have their specific sartorial needs; 25 per cent of all men's suits sold in Israel are in the Haredi sector. Given their specific needs, Haredim shop for fashion in shops located in specific localities, like Haredi areas of Jerusalem and the city of Bnei Beraq. Some shop owners go abroad in their search for suitable, but chic, Haredi fashion.

As the Haredi consumerism and the resultant advertising sector have evolved, so have the creative and copywriting fields of Haredi advertising become more sophisticated and attuned to the Haredi psychology. Group leaders are important in the Haredi sector. A Geographa poll found that credibility was even more important for the Haredi consumer than in the general Israeli market, in light of the paternalistic and hierarchical nature of

Haredi society. Given that the manufacturing is done elsewhere, away from Haredi eyes, the product has to be perceived as 'kosher' in the Haredi consumer's mind. Most products enjoy a 60–65 per cent credibility in contrast to, for example, a 40–50 per cent credibility in the Russian sector.[23]

If there is an absence of models like women and girls, in contrast to the general Israeli sector, a couple of Haredi modelling agencies have opened up, providing training to Haredi men in advertising promotion. But 'models' in the religious sector come in a variety of forms from rabbis to religious motifs. And there have been cases where well-known (but poorly paid) Haredi journalists have muddied the traditional boundaries between objective journalism and public relations to appear in and promote advertisements.

A rabbinical endorsement of a product is highly valuable. This is particularly the case in the Hassidic Haredi sector where the *admor* or hassidic community spiritual leader is far more than a posek, or rabbi providing religious law decisions, but is consulted by his flock on a broad range of issues from whom to marry to which yeshiva to learn in and which occupation to pursue. However, rabbis themselves do not endorse a product by appearances in the adverts themselves. Instead, use of them is made by companies in creative ways: For example, the chocolate company, Elite, and its Haredi imprint, 'Megadim', gave out albums of 64 pictures of well-known rabbis in the Haredi stream – with the approval of Haredi authorities.

By corollary, if the rabbis put a ban on a product, it can be a death sentence, as far as the Haredi consumer is concerned. The rabbis placed such a ban on shopping at the 24-hour-a-day supermarket AM-PM after it opened on the Sabbath. Likewise, when mobile phones were launched, Haredi rabbis banned them, because they were accessible to the Internet and to text messaging. It was only once kosher phones, which lacked these links, were introduced that those became endorsed by the rabbis. One advertising company promoting the mobile phone went further, adding a label to the phone that stated that it should not be left on in the synagogue at the time of prayers, and another label promoting 'speech, in accordance with Jewish law' – a veiled reference to the religious prohibition of gossip.

As Israeli commerce discovered the Haredi market in the 1980s and early-1990s a number of existing advertising companies opened up separate departments or appointed staff with special responsibilities for the Haredi sector. But their approach was to convert existing advertising copy by simply adding religious images such as a religious child, while the underlying strategy remained unchanged. Later, independent companies opened up by religious persons, like the Haredi Ruth Bolton and Reuven Gal, ensured that Haredi marketing considerations entered the decision-making process from the onset.

In practice the impact of the changes within the Haredi advertising sector has been gradual. Zak-Teller, examining advertising in the Haredi media in the period 1997–2001, found that only 56 per cent of advertisements examined were specifically suitable for the Haredi audience, whereas 44 per cent were also suitable for a secular audience. Food-related adverts had a far greater tendency to be suitable for Haredi audiences than those of other categories, like health and baby-related products. Moreover, factors used to persuade the consumer were primarily non-religious. These were the consumer himself as the deciding authority (first place), a reasonable price (second place), newness (third place) and humour (fourth place). Only further down in fifth, sixth, seventh and eighth place were such criteria as whether the item was Torah-approved, tradition, the 'acceptable way' and rabbinical respectively (Zak-Teller, 2003).

A couple of professional programmes have opened for the Haredi and modern religious population to receive training in advertising and public relations. A Rishon Letzion private college, Shofar (appropriately named after the ram's horn blown on the Jewish New Year), runs courses on advertising and public relations, alongside other mass-media-related training such as radio broadcasting and written journalism, geared toward the religious community. An academic college, Touro College's international school of management, established a programme on media and advertising and public relations. Ad hoc one-day workshops have been held; for example, one given by Benny Gal comprised 'the Haredi media; myth versus reality; the world of the Haredi women; the world of the Haredi child; Haredi media – to where? marketing with values; a symposium of manufacturers and sales personnel with the participation of Israeli business executives'.[24]

The modern religious sector

If the Haredi community has been identified as a target market in its own right, Israel's advertising community has overlooked the modern religious community, even though it is double the size of the Haredi population. The purchasing potential of the modern religious consumer is also higher. Surveyed at the end of the 1990s, 85 per cent of the modern religious were car owners, 73 per cent took a holiday in the previous year, and 38 per cent took one abroad in the previous two years.[25] While, by definition, the modern religious has one leg in the modern world and another in the religious community, neither meet the needs of the modern religious consumer. For example, their fashion needs are both different from the general population but also more liberal than the Haredi standards. The women often wear long dresses, sleeves in many cases to the elbow. Some live in housing communities built especially for the community.

Yet advertising either fails to reach them or is unsuited. They are not exposed to the Haredi media. True, many – though not all – in the sector are exposed to the general media. A 2000 survey found that 31 per cent of the modern religious listened daily to the Arutz 7 nationalist radio station, and 28 per cent several times a week; 28 per cent listened to Israel Radio's Moreshet (or 'Tradition') channel, 22 per cent to Israel Radio's second channel (the main news channel) and 18 per cent to Galei Zahal.[26] Yet the audience was offended by some of the advertising, for example, those featuring immodest models or including sexual innuendoes.

Conclusion

Jewish law and the rules of trading have been studied both in high schools and in *yeshivot* in both the Haredi and modern Orthodox sectors for innumerable years. Even though there are well-articulated Jewish principles regarding advertising of what is and what is not permitted in persuasive promotion, these have had little impact, even inside the Haredi media, which aspires to function according to the letter of Jewish religious law. It is difficult to measure the extent, if at all, to which religious qualifications about marketing practices have become in an explicit sense translated into common practice in Western society, through the influence of Western ethical marketing values. There is no reason to think that Jewish law qualifications about marketing practices will become translated into common practice in Israel, unless it's through the influence of Western ethical marketing values. But to the extent that the latter reflect Jewish ethics, the dos and don'ts of what is acceptable persuasion and manipulation in trading would contribute to trading standards in Israel that would be regarded positively in the eyes of Judaism.

References

Al-Olayan, F. S. and Karande, K. (2000) 'A Content Analysis of Magazine Advertisements from the US and the Arab World', *Journal of Advertising*, 29.

Bivins, T.(2004) *Mixed Media: Moral Distinctions in Advertising, Public Relations, and Journalism*. New York and London: Routledge, p. 126.

Dorff, E. (1997) 'Judaism, Business and Privacy', *Business Ethics Quarterly*, 7, 1.

Friedman, H. H. (1984), 'Ancient Marketing Practices: The View from Talmudic Times', *Journal of Public Policy and Marketing*,3, Spring.

Garrett-Medill Center for Religion and the News Media (1999) *Media Coverage of Religion, Spirituality, and Values*. Evanston, IL: Northwestern University.

Green, R. M. (1997) 'Guiding Principles of Jewish Business Ethics', *Business Ethics Quarterly*, 7, 1.

Keenan, K. L. and Yeni, S. (2003) 'Ramadan Advertising in Egypt: A Content Analysis with Elaboration on Select Items', *Journal of Media and Religion*, 2(2).

Limburg, E. (1994), *Electronic Media Ethics*. Boston and London: Focal Press.

Maguire, B. and Weatherby, G. A. (1998), 'The Secularisation of Religion and Television Commercials', *Sociology of Religion*, 59(2).

Mallia, K. L. (2009) 'From the Sacred to the Profane: A Critical Analysis of the Changing Nature of Religious Imagery in Advertising', *Journal of Media and Religion*, 8(3), 172–90.

Marmor-Lavie, G., Stout, P. A. and Lee, W. (2009) 'Spirituality in Advertising: A New Theoretical Approach', *Journal of Media and Religion*, 8(1).

Mittelstaedt, J. D. (2002) 'A Framework for Understanding the Relationships between Religions and Markets', *Journal of Macromarketing*, 22, 1 June.

Moore, R. C. (2005) 'Spirituality that Sells: Religious Imagery in Magazine Advertising', *Advertising and Society Review*, 1.
Pava, M. L. (1998) 'Developing a Religiously Grounded Business Ethics: A Jewish Perspective', *Business Ethics Quarterly*, 8, 1.
Reichert, T., Lambiase, J., Morgan, S., Castarphen, M. and Zavoina, S. (1999) 'Cheesecake and Beefcake: No Matter How You Slice It, Sexual Explicitness in Advertising Continues to Increase', *Journalism Quarterly*, 76(1), 70.
Shao, A. T. (1993) ' Restrictions on Advertising Items That May Not Be Considered "Decent": A European Viewpoint', *Journal of Euromarketing*, 2, 3.
Tamari, M. (1997) 'The Challenge of Wealth: Business Ethics', *Business Ethics Quarterly*, 7, 1.
Vitell, S. J. and Paolillo, J. G. P. (2003) 'Consumer Ethics: the Role of Religiosity', *Journal of Business Ethics*, 46.
Waller, D. (2000) ' Cultural Values and Advertising in Malaysia: Views from the Industry', *Asia Pacific Journal of Marketing and Logistics*, 12(1).
Waller, D., Fam, K.-S. and Erdogan, B. Z. (2005) 'Advertising of Controversial Products: A Cross-Cultural Study', *The Journal of Consumer Marketing*, 22(1).
Wilson, A. and West, C. (1981) 'The Marketing of Unmentionables', *Harvard Business Review*, January–February.
Zak-Teller, D. (2003) *Religious Advertising: Examining the Way to the Heart of the Religious Consumer*. Master's thesis, Bar-Ilan University.
Zinnbauer, B. J., Pargamenty, K. I., Cole, B., Rye, S., Butter, E.M., Belavitch, T. G. et al. (1997) 'Religion and Spirituality: Unfuzzying the Fuzzy', *Journal for the Scientific Study of Religion*, 36, 4.

10 The marketing of the rabbi

> In the marketplace, goods are judged by how well they please us. God is the opposite. Judaism asks us to restrain our consumerism and open up to yearning.
> (Jay Michaelson, marketing executive and returnee to Judaism)[1]

The traditional framework for rabbis over hundreds of years has been the address from the pulpit. But, like many Christian clergy (Biernatzki, 2006; Johnstone, 2009), rabbis are beginning to recognise the value of using mass media channels to communicate their messages, supplementing the synagogue pulpit, even if in practice they have had mixed reviews. The use of mass media channels reflects the changing social contexts in which the rabbi functions in the twenty-first century.

If religion in traditional societies was based upon authority vested in religious bodies, in complex industrial societies there is increased emphasis upon personal choice in moral and religious matters as reflected in the development of niche markets for religion outlets, including religious broadcasting, religious press and the Internet. Indeed, religious and spiritual issues are increasingly mediated through print and electronic technologies, with mass media in effect a sub-agent of contemporary religious identity. Mass media help to popularise religion at the grassroots level where institutionalised religious forms have become weak. The twenty-first century is sometimes called the commodity culture in which consumption appears to be the prime mover of human activity in the Western capitalist world. It is characterised by a multiplication of choices, causing a revolution in decision-making patterns. Judaism is one of a multitude of ideas waiting in the marketplace for purchasers who behave according to the desire for personal enrichment and enjoyment.[2]

Yet Judaism stands not for desire but commitment and obligation to a Higher being and set of values. As one marketing executive put it, 'Judaism cannot use power/sexiness/fun as tools to sell itself; Jews need to recognise that the source of all blessings, sexy and otherwise, is precisely that which cannot be reduced to a logo.'[3] Also, marketing has been regarded by rabbis as crass, as *treifah* (not kosher).

However, Judaism has always been a practical religion. It is inclined to speak in the language and through the issues of the age, such as democracy, feminism, human rights. Yet as Rabbi Hayim Herring, who directs STAR (Synagogues: Transformation and Renewal), a body which trains Jewish organisational leaders with leadership skills, points out, 'The goal is not merely to put people in the synagogue but to build sustaining relationships that enrich synagogue life and the Shabbat experience.'[4]

There is a sense of limbo, with rabbis failing to grasp their changing role in the information age. To be true, the synagogue and the pulpit has for hundreds of years since the Emancipation been losing its monopoly of strengthening moral values.

This is particularly true in the case of the rabbi's social standing and influence in Israel. Reflecting the altered social context of the rabbi and the synagogue in Israel, rabbis do not enjoy a monopoly in being a single focus of Jewish identity, as they do in the Jewish Diaspora. The Jewish state itself, its official organs and other non-official institutions, have replaced the synagogue to a considerable extent as foci of Jewish identity. Moreover, the synagogue in Israel has a limited impact on the lives of Israeli Jews in functional terms and in terms of its relevance beyond the strictly religious. Its functions are narrower, mostly comprising the holding of religious services and educational activities like religious lessons (*shiurim*) and lectures.

Perhaps because of this, rabbis are turning to the media and the Internet to get their message across. Actually, the importance of the media–public dimension varies according to the specific rabbinic professional activity. The rabbinical profession may be broken down into three types: First, community rabbis. Secondly, rabbis teaching in schools or at higher institutes of religious study (*yeshivot*). These rabbis play important roles in the state education system notably the *dati leumi* stream and Haredi stream but also the newer Conservative-affiliated 'Tali' school network. Thirdly, religious court judges (*dayanim*) who are authorised by the state to adjudicate in personal status matters. This includes responsibility by the state rabbinical religious courts (*batei din*) for certain aspects of legislation concerning personal status, such as determining who is a Jew, conversion, marriage and divorce.

Of the three types of rabbis, the media is the most relevant to the community rabbi. While the rabbi's influence has been felt within the religious population, such as through the Sabbath sermon from the pulpit to congregants, rabbis – particularly community rabbis – increasingly recognise the opportunities that mass media channels offer as alternative 'pulpits'.

In the same way that diplomacy, for example, became redefined at the turn of the twentieth century as 'Public Diplomacy' after the inclusion of the dimension of public opinion at home and abroad, and mass media and pressure groups became ingredients to an area which had comprised strictly intergovernmental relations, so rabbis are recognising that in 'Public Judaism' there are such additional players as the media and that there are public dimensions in an area which originally comprised only the rabbi and the synagogue.

Some rabbis have become media personalities because of a political position they held or espoused, irrespective of a synagogue pulpit position. One example was Rabbi Dov Lior, rabbi of the city of Kiryat Arba, considered the heartbeat of the Jewish population of the Judea and Samaria territories (otherwise called the West Bank). His fiery manner, including favouring theocracy above democracy, has won him a strong following well beyond Kiryat Arba, including many in the country's *hardal* community. On the other end of the spectrum was Rabbi Michael Melchior, former chief rabbi of Norway, who led a left-wing religious list in the Knesset, Meimad, which had been created by Rabbi Yehuda Amital, head of the Gush Etzion yeshiva.

All rabbis, according to the author's survey of rabbis in Israel, think it important to appear and be quoted in the media: The author's survey of rabbis found that 24 per cent agree, 28 per cent 'agree to a great extent' and 27 per cent 'to a very great extent' that it was important to appear in the media.

But the actual appearance of rabbis in the media is less. Rabbis are little sought after by the general media in Israel; 61 per cent of Haredi rabbis, 71 per cent of *dati leumi* rabbis, and 47 per cent of non-Orthodox rabbis had not appeared or been quoted once in the general press over the previous 12 months; 28 per cent had 1–2 times. This reflects the view that rabbis are not important sources of information for the media. But in part it also reflects the public's perception – whether true or false – that the authoritarian-type rabbinical personality is unsuitable for the one-on-one dialogue that characterises reporter–source relations in modern mass media. This is exacerbated by the lack of pastoral training for rabbis in Israel – in contrast with rabbinical training institutions abroad – which has failed to provide rabbis with experience in using modern means of communications, like appearing on camera. The relationship between the media and rabbis is complicated further because, in contrast to the hierarchical structure of the rabbi–community relationship, the journalistic community has a tradition of campaigning against those in power – under the banner of the public's right to know – including the obligation of rabbis and religious structures to be accountable to the public.

In order to fill a gap, the Chief Rabbinate initiated in 2011 a series of workshops for rabbis on the state payroll under the heading of communication; amongst the topics were media technology, including responding to Jewish law questions via e-mail and Facebook. 'One of the central problems for the world of the rabbis is the media – not just internet or newspapers but communication with the citizen, to speak to him in the world of his ideas,' said Yaacov Mergi, the Religious Affairs Minister. 'We want to give rabbis the tools to deal with the modern public.'[5]

Chief Rabbi Israel Meir Lau and the media social elite

Israel Meir Lau, today the Chief Rabbi of Tel Aviv and a former Ashkenazi Chief Rabbi of the country, is one rabbi for whom such a workshop is superfluous. He has a warm, engaging manner and a charisma that has made him one of the very few Orthodox rabbis who successfully mingles with the secular Israeli elite. As chief rabbi he received reportedly some 150 invitations a day for public appearances. He officiates at the marriages of Israel's social crème de la crème. He was even mooted after finishing his term as the country's Chief Rabbi to be a candidate for the country's presidency.

Lau contrasted with his predecessor as Ashkenazi chief rabbi, Abraham Shapiro, who was appointed in 1983. Shapiro had spent all his life within study cloisters of the talmudical college as head of the Mercaz HaRav Yeshiva in Jerusalem and, until his appointment as chief rabbi, had no experience of media relations. In an interview following his election, he told the Jerusalem Post: 'I think journalists are a little deaf. They don't distort what I say on purpose, but they hear only what they want to hear.'[6]

Defining the rabbi's role well beyond the pulpit at synagogue Sabbath services for the strictly religious, Lau defined public Judaism goals as comprising three circles:

> The first circle is an inner circle of religiously observant people, and the role of the rabbi is to respond to questions of religious law, disseminate the Torah, and act for all matters concerned with Jewish religious practice – in short a communal leader. Most Israelis are in the second circle, and define themselves as traditional as distinct from strictly observant. It's a community which observes religious law in a selective manner. They light Sabbath candles, have a religious marriage ceremony, respect year-long laws of Jewish mourning, and other matters. The rabbi is not the final arbiter of personal decisions. The third, distant circle is the secular population who attend the synagogue on the High Holidays of the Rosh Hashana and Yom Kippur, are circumcised, have a bar mitzvah and a Jewish funeral. The purpose of the rabbis is to draw people from this circle to the inner second circle and bring those in the second circle into the closest circle.[7]

Lau contrasted with Ovadiah Yosef, who was the Sephardi chief rabbi when Lau was the Ashkenazi chief. Yosef's problematic image outside his own community – resulting from statements that presented him as seemingly primitive, and, taken out of context by the general media, showed the rabbi as even clownish – did a disservice to his high learning.

Yet, as media savvy as Lau is and notwithstanding his popularity, Lau still faces a media and social environment that is broadly secular, not predisposed to the rabbi's message. When, for example, he assumed office as chief rabbi, he proposed that he receive a five-minute spot each week on television, 'in order that I could explain the concepts of Judaism – not to engage in persuasion, but just to explain. The head of religion programming said that he would be in touch to produce a pilot programme. Four and a half years later I am still waiting for a telephone call. I understand that television has spots for sport, for the economy, the Hebrew language; five minutes for religion won't do any harm'.

Non-Orthodox religious streams and public broadcasting

The obstacles to pastoral PR are not just attitudinal but also structural. This is particularly true with peripheral religious streams and groups. For example, the non-Orthodox religious streams, Conservative and Reform, neither of which are recognised by the state rabbinate in Israel, face an uphill battle in projecting their communities through media channels. Their members are miniscule in number in Israel in contrast to the United States where the two combined comprise over eighty percent of the Jewish community. They have, over the years, sought to use broadcasting channels in Israel to win more members, but they have met a wall of bureaucracy. On the eve of the Jewish New Year and Yom Kippur in 1999, the two non-Orthodox streams – in spite of theological differences between them – jointly sponsored 350 adverts on Israel radio, under the heading: 'There is more than one way to Judaism'. The PR message was the egalitarianism of Conservative and Reform religious services. 'Our community', began the advert, 'believes in Judaism in accordance with the spirit of the times and place. In our community men and women sit together. Girls on their *batmitzvah* (confirmation) read from the Torah scrolls, and marriage is not only initiated by the man but also by the women.' The campaign drew on a grant of some $360,000 received from an American Jewish philanthropic organisation.

The radio adverts, in Hebrew and Russian, were targeted towards the native Israeli population and the Russian immigrant community. Having mostly exhausted their attempts to recruit the Anglo-Saxon community, the Reform and Conservative turned to Israelis to offer them an alternative to the Orthodox streams dominant in Israel. Initially, the Israel Broadcasting Corporation declined to run the adverts – as they had also done in earlier years, arguing that, as a public broadcasting body, it was unable to broadcast anything which hurt the religious feelings of one or another of the population. The IBA's governing council comprises members drawn from different political parties, including the religious Orthodox ones, and public figures. The director of the Israeli Movement for Progressive Judaism, Rabbi Uri Regev, remarked that 'it's inconceivable that the freedom of speech could be undermined to the point of denying an organisation that promotes pluralism and democracy the opportunity to reach the public through the airwaves'.[8] But after the two streams appealed to Supreme Court against the IBA's decision, the latter had little alternative but to run the adverts, on condition that they removed the slogan 'There is more than one way to Judaism', which the IBA described as offensive.

A clue to the success of the radio campaign was that, according to the Reform and Conservative movements, attendance that year at High Holiday services held at the 27 Reform synagogues in Israel doubled to 20,000, and increased by 25 per cent at the 46 Conservative synagogues.[9] But this also reflected both an underlying trend for Israelis, secular and traditional, yearning to discover their roots in a setting that conforms to the egalitarian nature of modern Western societies, as well as the failure of the Haredim to generate a positive image in wider Israel.

One Haredi group responded to the non-Orthodox radio campaign with their own campaign: 'Where are you going? Come home.' Initially, the IBA did not agree to the broadcast, but having allowed the non-Orthodox campaign, it could not now refuse the Haredi one.

Perhaps the most impressive application of media technology to recruit members is that of the Hassidic sect of Habad.

The Messiah, the media and Habad

Habad has become one of the most active Jewish movements involved in Torah outreach work. In order to analyse their use of the media in this, it is necessary to understand the role of messianism in the movement for the last 60 years. Habad hassidism is a mystical movement which originally possessed no extraordinary Jewish messianic pretensions. After the Second World War – in the face of the Holocaust and a crisis of faith over where God was at Auschwitz – the Lubavitcher rebbe at the time, Yosef Schneersohn, attempted to inject hope and faith through a messianic theology, namely that the traumatic destruction of European Jewry could only be explained as a preliminary to the messianic redemption (Lior, 1998). This position was further elaborated upon by Schneersohn's son-in-law, Menachem Mendel, when he assumed the mantle of Habad's leadership in 1951. His generation, moreover, was to be the last before the messianic redemption, and the way to bring on the redemption was to rejuvenate Jewry worldwide – given a causal link between the observance of *mitzvot* (religious obligations) and the messianic coming. That required vast educational resources – and with it, the application of advertising techniques to this goal. By the millennium, Habad-Lubavitch had built itself into a billion-dollar Jewish outreach empire with 4,000 emissaries, or *shlichim,* working across ten countries. To be sure, the work of the emissary, *shaliach,* was not to convert gentiles but, through love and caring for the fellow Jew, to bring Jews closer to observance. This could gain expression, for example, for the women through lighting candles on the eve of the Sabbath eve and men by the donning of *tefillin* (the phylacteries).

The mass media were harnessed for the objective. Already in the 1960s the Lubavitcher rebbe had a regular weekly programme about Tanya on a New York radio station, WEVD. With the first international telephone hook up in 1970 and later by satellite, the Lubavitcher rebbe preceded Israeli rabbis in getting his message – through broadcasting his *farbrengen* or gatherings where the rebbe expounded on Torah and hassidism – to audiences in other countries.

Chabad.org was established by a young rabbi, Yosef Kazen, with the appearance of the worldwide web and was itself an outgrowth of an early on-line discussion network 'Fidonet' in 1988, where there were many Chabad documents (Fishkoff, 2003, p. 283). Chabad.org provides a mix of content: about Chabad itself, including the biography of the Lubavitcher rebbe; Tanya, as well as general Torah-orientated matter including the weekly Bible reading; matter about Jewish festivals and about Jewish law codes like Maimonides. In addition, there is also contact information, such as for Chabad houses around the world. The site also hosts Askmoses.com, a panel of some 40 rabbis and women teachers who provide round-the-clock responses to religion-related questions from inquirers – averaging 200 a day. Chabad.org has some 73,000 visitors a day, the number rising at times of religious holidays and reaching a peak on Hanuka, with some 500,000 hits, with a little less on Passover, Rosh Hashanah and Yom Kippur.[10]

In theory, Habad, in contrast to the negativism of other Haredi groups, perceives media technology as neutral, indeed created by God to serve in the work of the dissemination of *Torah*. Information technology is part of the Divine plan. 'In practice, however, the Rebbe was not always favourable toward mass media. He was critical of television in its early days. For example, at the outset of Israel Television in 1968, the Lubavitcher Rebbe told the head of its Jewish Tradition department, Benjamin Zvielli, about his reservations concerning television's influence on the youth. And Zvielli received a negative reply when he sought the cooperation of Habad officials for programming, who simply told him, "The Rebbe does not allow"'.[11]

Inside Israel, Rabbi Menachem Brod, Habad's spokesman, defined his lobbying efforts less towards the Knesset or government departments and more towards the Israeli public. While formally the address for media contacts, his relations with the media have not been an easy ride. Owing to hostile response from different media outlets to Habad's active outreach efforts – regarded by some journalists as missionising – Brod created an alternative channel for the religious public: Habad's own weekly bulletin, a four-page bulletin, distributed in synagogues (a phenomenon discussed later in the chapter). 'The media blocked our access to react – and if our reactions were reported in the Israeli media, they were distorted. We looked for any way to break the barrier and then we came upon the idea of a community bulletin in the synagogue,' said Brod.[12] The format of Habad's synagogue bulletins has remained virtually unchanged since its inception in 1986. The bulletin's first page includes a Torah perspective on the news, written by Brod himself, and reflects Brod's dilemma of whether or not to address current issues: Do readers want a respite on the Sabbath also from current affairs or do they feel a need to have someone address those issues already covered during the week by the media but to do so from a Torah perspective? Page 2 has extracts from the writings of the Lubavitcher rebbe on the weekly Bible reading, with a Hassidic perspective, as well as a popular column 'What's happened', which describes events in contemporary Jewish history.[13] The back page is an interview from a broad range of persons, such as a living Torah personality or a returnee to Judaism. The tone is clearly a popular one, in order to reach the widest audience. Despite Habad having taken a political position in a few of the Israeli elections, it has wisely steered clear in the bulletin from expressly stating a political position. The bulletin has won a popular following, and some 180,000 are printed weekly; apart from a few sold by subscription, all are distributed for free. The bulletin contains almost no advertising. Its popularity has ensured that Hassidic motifs in general and Habad motifs in particular have over the years swept into the general Jewish consciousness, contributing to Habad's popularity today in Israel.

In the 1970s and 1980s, the messianism movements intensified against the background of major international changes such as the 1991 Gulf War and the end of Russian communism. Mendel Schneersohn encouraged Habadniks to declare 'We want Moshiach (the Messiah) now'. In 1991, the Rebbe at the annual gathering of *shlichim* in New York, declared that the world, and in particular the Jews, should prepare for the coming of the Messiah and that the message should be transmitted by posters as well as the synagogue bulletin. The campaign was coined 'Get ready for the Messiah', or, in the US, it was called 'Discover the Messiah'. Habad's advertising advisers, like Ruth Bolton, herself a returnee to Judaism who worked for ten years handling the activities of Young Habad, brainstormed over the visual material to be used to represent the spiritual idea of messianic redemption. They hesitated between a picture of the Third Jewish Temple descending from the heavens onto the Temple Mount and one of an old, white-bearded man riding an ass. But in the end a rising sun was selected – with light and sunrise alluding to redemption. 'How can one give visual expression to the Messiah in a way that the public will catch and relate to seriously? It was difficult to come up with the solution. I tried to imagine what the feeling would be with the coming of the messiah – light, love, warmth, good.' So was born the image of the rising sun, Bolton said.[14] In Israel over 1,000 of these huge wall posters welcoming the Messiah were placed at major road junctions nationwide. In addition, half a million flyers were prepared. The broader Israeli population took the campaign in good spirit; not even in Tel Aviv did anyone seem to find the ubiquitous campaign objectionable.

Media pulpits and media pews

Notwithstanding that rabbis have yet to incorporate the plethora of media techniques, evidence exists that certain use has been made. Haredi rabbis have long used the wall poster ('*pashkevil*') tacked up in religious neighbourhoods to attack or excommunicate those individuals or companies which they regard as behaving inappropriately. The age of the Internet has revolutionised the structure of religious communities of different faith through community websites (Horsfall, 2000). For the modern Orthodox today, the *MyKehilla* website (literally, 'my community') enables synagogue communities to keep in touch with their members and strengthen ties with congregants, including providing an on-line weekly schedule of religious services, Torah lectures and other synagogal events. Whereas in the past, the Sabbath and holiday services were the only opportunity to inform congregants about these, the synagogue website provides an ongoing week-long contact, including urgent information such as notification of the death of a member of the community and related funeral arrangements.

Two phenomena in Israeli synagogues which illustrate how rabbis have gone beyond the traditional pulpit–pew channel are, firstly, rabbis proffering advice through electronic means like e-mail and text messages and, secondly, the weekly production and distribution of printed bulletins containing religious messages and inspiration.

Synagogal bulletins

A phenomenon of the past quarter of a century has been weekly bulletins containing essays by rabbis, mostly on the weekly Bible reading and Jewish law questions. These colourfully produced pamphlets, which are between four and 20 pages long, are distributed free in synagogues on Friday eve, and people take them home afterwards for discussion around the festive Sabbath meal.

Printed bulletins have become popular and successful channels for rabbis to pass on their messages, unfiltered by other mass media channels in the general media. Indeed, since the age of print began with Gutenberg, rabbis have rarely enjoyed as much control over the transmission of their message through the medium. The agenda is unquestionable. They do not aspire to such basic journalistic virtues as separating fact from opinion but instead comprise interpretations of current events from a religious Jewish perspective. Their very influence inside the religious communities raises, therefore, ethical and democratic questions. While the bulletins evolved in part because the mainstream Israeli media failed to give expression to the views of the religious communities – in particular failed from the perspective of their readers to reconcile modern democratic ideas with theocratic Torah ones – they now provide the rabbi free rein, with their uncensored stage for the rabbis' messages (Cohen, 2000).

The bulletins are produced within both the ultra-Orthodox and the modern Orthodox sector, providing their community's view of events. The phenomenon of synagogal bulletins has been felt most among the modern Orthodox, with the rapid growth of the number of bulletins within two decades.

It is difficult to delineate when the phenomenon of the synagogue bulletin began. In 1984 Dr Yitzchak Alfasi, drawing upon a financial subsidy from the National Religious Party, began '*Shabbat V'Shabato*'. However, the renowned female Bible scholar Nehama Leibowitz had already began distributing tightly printed versions of her commentary on the weekly Bible reading. Not a few synagogue bulletins have been local initiatives. Thus, for example, Pinni Isaac began a bulletin in the city of Rishon Le-Zion. And Yaacov Fogelman would deliver his English language bulletin, *Torah Sheets*, each Friday afternoon by bicycle to different synagogues in Jerusalem for distribution that evening.

There is no precise number of copies of the synagogue bulletin today, but one estimate in 1996 said that a million copies, comprising 100 different bulletins, were distributed.[15] A 2004 survey on the modern Orthodox community found that 69 per cent of respondents saw synagogue bulletins each week, and a further 10 per cent almost every week. Only 3 per cent had never seen them, and only 6 per cent did not take them home from the synagogue, so that they are perused by 41 per cent of the spouses and by 26 per cent of the children.[16]

There are synagogue bulletins produced for different target groups by a broad range of institutions, but most are written in a popular vein, intended for the broadest population. Many are produced by religious educational institutions like yeshivot, reflecting a range of theological outlooks, but not a few today are produced by other institutions or interests, often to project their programmes. For example, there are *Kollech* and *Bat Kol*, with a feminist orientation, and while many bulletins express a decidedly right-wing view, one exception is *Shabbat Shalom* (a play on the word *shalom* or peace), put out by Netivot Shalom, a left-wing religious group identified with the Peace Now movement, which draws in its bulletin upon peace motifs in religious literature, like the weekly Bible reading.

By the end of the first decade of the century, it had almost become *de rigueur* for a religious educational institution identified with the modern religious sector to produce a bulletin.[17]

Some of the most popular bulletins are those identified with institutions from the modern Orthodox sector catering to returnees to Judaism ('*hozrei b'teshuvah*'): '*Ma'aynei Hayeshua*' ('The Wellsprings of Salvation') [70,000 copies], which includes columns by leading rabbis identified with the *hardal*, who discuss current events from the perspective of the weekly Bible reading; '*B'Ahavah ub'Yirah*' ('With Love and Fear') (circ. 100,000), published by the Meir Institute in Jerusalem, which is identified with the staunchly Zionist ideology of Rabbi Abraham Kook; '*Me'at Min Ha'or*' ('A Bit of the Light'), providing Biblical religious views with an emphasis on the Land of Israel and using also secular sources.

'*Rosh Yehudi*' ('Jewish Head' or 'Jewish Leadership') (60,000 circ.), which focuses on the family, covers such topics as marriage, socialising, pregnancy, and the education of children. 'Expressing original thinking, the bulletin is written in a style geared for all, not just those within the modern Orthodox, which comes to expression with a request on the front page notice "to pass it on to the rest of the train, and to friends",' one researcher, Leora Ophir, noted.[18]

One of the most celebrated bulletins is *Olam Katan* (A Small World), a folio-sized multi-coloured weekly directed at the youth. 'We felt that the youth had nothing to read that would address those questions that bother them,' said one of its founders, Meir Schwartz. 'Our readers feel comfortable to write to us anonymously to say what bothers them.' Among the many varied subjects it has covered are homosexuality, the existence of God and access to the Temple Mount in Jerusalem. Established in 2005, months prior to the withdrawal from Gush Katif, it quickly filled the media vacuum in dealing with the crisis of faith that the withdrawal caused among many of the modern religious youth. Among its regular features is a column by Rabbi Shlomo Aviner and Rav Shmuel Eliyah, which addresses myriad text-messaged questions. These range from topics such as where was God in the Holocaust to whether it is permitted to invest one's money outside Israel.[19]

Some bulletins are published with the support or sponsorship of a political party. The mushrooming of these bulletins in the 1980s and 1990s occurred at the same time as number of important political developments. All this raised the question of whether these bulletins served as agents of political recruitment among the modern religious. In general, however, the bulletin more gives expression to the party's religious perspective rather than being an active agent of political recruitment.

Many of the bulletins need to generate their own budgets, resulting in bulletins being replete with full-colour glossy advertisements.

Given that the Sabbath should create an elevated spiritual atmosphere free of commercial vulgarism and that the distribution of the bulletins at the Friday night service takes away from the sombre spirituality characteristic of communal prayer, rabbis have pondered the place of the synagogal bulletins. 'It really is disturbing to have the adverts. It really means introducing something alien to the prayers, into the synagogue,' remarked Rabbi Yuval Sherlo of the Tzohar group of rabbis, which publishes the '*Shabbaton*' bulletin.[20]

Fifty-five per cent of readers of the bulletins look at the advertisements on the Sabbath, and 33 per cent do not (no response: 12 per cent). Twenty-one per cent of readers favoured reducing the advertisements or even not carrying any advertisements.[21] Yet one bulletin, '*Alim Terufat*' of the Belze hassidic community, created an imaginative way for generating budget: selling space in memory of deceased relatives to commemorate the Yahrtzeit, or date of the person's death.

Attractively produced bulletins bring a touch of holiness, enriching the educational experience of the Sabbath. Indeed, according to the *Admur* (lit. spiritual head) of the Belzer Hasidim, whereas in the past the Sabbath was characterised by study of the holy books, this generation, which he dubbed 'the instant generation', under the pressures of daily life, lacks the stamina for deep study. The bulletins, with succinct and brief explanations, are suitable.[22] However, Malka Bina, an educationalist who heads a women's study institute, called for 'devising more creative ways to draw the youth to the Torah. The bulletins do not raise spiritual levels, and the way to this is through religious instruction and personal advice'. But Bina admitted that the bulletins do not cause damage. 'It is not these which will lead the youth to pray with less intensity.'[23]

The virtual rabbi

Given that the performance of religious commandments (*mitzvot*) are means of giving expression to a Jew's relationship with God, observant Jews have for hundreds of years sought instruction from rabbis. Instruction includes the interpretation and application of Jewish legal principles of *halakhah* to modern life, in order to answer questions of Jewish law (*sheiltot*). The religious counselling has occurred mostly with the local synagogue rabbi or rabbis in educational institutions, but at times individual Jews have also sought guidance from rabbis beyond their geographical vicinity, who were renowned for their knowledge in particular spheres and enjoyed wide standing among Jewish leaders.

In addition, because Jewish law is all-encompassing, the community rabbi has often been turned to for counselling in matters other than strict *halakhah:* philosophical questions and personal advice with respect to family and career.

One of the developments brought about by the Internet is the phenomenon of on-line rabbinical counselling. Panels of rabbis, composed of some 10–20 rabbis, exist on websites identified with the modern Orthodox, including *Kipa, Moreshet, Moriah, Jewish Answers* and *Project Genesis*. The formal ban by Ashkenaz Haredi sages upon the use of the Internet necessarily limits its impact in Haredi communities. While Sephardi Haredi websites such as *Hidabrut* (or 'dialogue') do exist, most Haredim prefer to consult with their community rabbi, reflecting the strict adherence to rabbinic authority. Yet even many modern Orthodox Jews do not do consult on-line either; 42 per cent of observant Jews had never used the Internet to ask a rabbi a question, and a further 47 per cent fewer than five questions, according to a 2006 Kipa survey based on surfers. Moreover, of those who do ask an Internet rabbi, only 55 per cent see the answer as obligatory and binding. Sherlo, who provides on-line rabbinic counselling and receives between 20 and 40 questions a day, answering approximately 5,000 questions a year, estimated that 30–40 per cent of questions comprise male–female related questions, such as marriage, relationships and sexuality. According to the Kipa survey, asked whom they turn to if they have a religious question, 33 per cent and 8 per cent of women replied an Internet rabbi and an Internet forum respectively, in contrast to 16 per cent and 4 per cent of men respectively. And, while 45 per cent and 35 per cent of men look up the question in religious books or ask the community rabbi respectively, only 29 per cent and 30 per cent of women replied that they go those routes.

On-line rabbinical counselling has generated a debate among modern Orthodox rabbis about the pluses and minuses of the phenomenon. Critics say that, firstly, on-line answers proffered by rabbis are too short. Secondly, personal circumstances cannot be taken into consideration by the rabbi who is unacquainted with the questioner, even though sometimes the personal circumstances can be crucial in a particular instance. Thirdly, quoting the dictum 'Make yourself a Rabbi', of the Mishnaic tome, 'Ethics of the Fathers', Ashkenazi Chief Rabbi Yonah Metzger characterised the rabbi as being not only a functionary but also a role model to emulate and identify with. One would not 'make oneself a rabbi' if one already has a virtual rabbi. Fourth, instead of accepting the decision of the rabbi, people may be inclined to 'shop around' to different on-line rabbis to find the reply most acceptable and comfortable to them. Fifth, the ease of on-line counselling discourages the Jew from studying the original sources in the halakhic literature. Supporters of the new trend argue that non-affiliated Jews now have access to rabbis, which they would not otherwise have. Secondly, on-line counselling offers an anonymity which the local community rabbi does not and enables people to raise questions they would not otherwise feel comfortable discussing.

It is instructive to compare the rabbi's experience with imams. Messick (1996) found, for instance, that answers had to be short and concise. Similar to the preponderance of halakhic questions, half of one radio imam's inquiries concerned ritual inquiries. However, an eighth comprised sexual-related matters and another eighth concerned family law for the imam, compared to Sherlo's experience. Not a few of the Muslim inquirers were women, who would otherwise, in off-line questioning, need to go through their husbands. While the Jewish women do not have this compelling motivation, it is noteworthy that proportionately women were more likely than men to turn to an on-line rabbi – perhaps because of the anonymity.

Conclusion

Participation in forum and chat questions of religious belief, and participation in *shiurim* conducted on the web, contribute to creating virtual communities. The Internet's impact upon Jewish identity is, therefore, in making religious information much more accessible. However, the extent to which media channels have become an 'alternative pulpit' for reaching secular Jews should not be exaggerated. In addition to virtual rabbis, other media channels like synagogal bulletins and *pashkevilim* are more for use inside the community and among the affiliated. Rabbis seeking to reach secular Israelis, amounting to over 40 per cent of the Israeli Jewish populations, are faced by a basic lack of interest in religion-related matter. For example, the Rokeach survey of radio listening and religion, discussed in Chapter 7, found that only 2 per cent and 3 per cent of secular Israelis listened 'daily' or 'frequently' to *shiurim* on the radio, and programmes on religion and tradition respectively (in contrast to 21 per cent and 17 per cent of 'traditional Israelis', 44 per cent and 37 per cent of modern Orthodox Jews, and 55 per cent and 51 per cent of Haredi Jews). Apart from the strictly religious – whether defined in terms of the Haredi and modern Orthodox terms or whether including also the small Conservative and Reform communities in Israel – the rest of the Israeli Jewish population (estimated to be between 70–75 per cent) have no regular daily or weekly interaction with the synagogue in Israel. The traditional Jewish population, as distinct from the Orthodox communities – accounting for 50 per cent of the Israeli Jewish population – have varying degrees of contact with the synagogue, comprising attendance at the Jewish holydays including the New Year and participation in holidays like Passover and Sukkoth and Purim, and life-cycle events, including circumcision, bar mitzvah, or funeral. For the rabbi, the plethora of media technology today presents an unexploited potential, which, if utilised properly, would perhaps enable the rabbi to reach beyond the religious sectors.

References

Biernatzki, W. (2006), 'Some Twenty-first Century Challenges Facing Catholics in Communication Formation', in J. Srampickal, G. Mazza and L. Baugh (eds), *Cross Connections: Interdisciplinary Communication Studies at the Gregorian University*. Rome: Editricia Universita Gregorana.

Cohen, J. (2000) 'Politics, Alienations, and the Consolidation of Group Identity: The Case of Synagogue Pamphlets', *Rhetoric and Public Affairs*, 3, 2.

Fishkoff, S. (2003) *The Rebbe's Army: Inside the World of Chabad-Lubavitch*. New York: Schocken.

Horsfall, S. (2000) 'How Religious Organisations Use the Internet: A Preliminary Inquiry', in J. K. Hadden and D. E. Cowan (eds), *Religion on the Internet: Prospects and Promises*. New York: Elsevier.

Johnstone, C. (2009) 'Marketing, God and Hell: Strategies, Tactics and Textual; Poaching', in C. Deacy and E. Arweck (eds), *Exploring Religion and the Sacred in a Media Age*. Farnham: Ashgate.

Lior, R. (1998) 'The Lubavitch Messianic Resurgence: The Historical and Mystical Background 1939–96', in P. Schafer and M. Cohen (eds), *Toward the Millennium: Messianic Expectations from the Bible to Waco*. Leiden: Brill.

Messick, B. (1996) 'Media Muftis: Radio Fatwas in Yemen', in M. K. Masud, B. Messick and D. S. Powers (eds), *Islamic Legal Interpretation*. Cambridge, MA: Harvard University Press.

11 At bay in the Diaspora

> We try very hard to have at least one Israel story on the front page. Israel is a very important source of pride, feeling and concern for my readers.
> (Jewish newspaper editor)

Religious identity in the Jewish Diaspora – where 8,300,000 Jews live – has over the centuries been determined by such factors as the synagogue, the Jewish school and, ultimately, the Jewish home experience. These 'traditional channels' have been complemented by mass media channels. While Diaspora studies have widened (Cohen, 1997), sparse attention has been given to the communication element in Diaspora–homeland ties.[1] The Israeli case, therefore, provides the basis for wider comparison for studying the role of communication in Diaspora–homeland ties with a religion dimension.

Mass media play a role in Israel and Diaspora Jewry as a sub-agent of contemporary religious identity, or religious social communication, and contribute to the construction of personal (belief) systems. The extent to which Israel is an agent of Jewish religious identity – as opposed to political identity – will itself influence the role of mass media in the process. One school says that religious identity is determined independently of identity with Israel, as was the case in the period prior to the creation of the State of Israel. According to a second school, religious identity is an adjunct of identity with Israel given that the aspiration for the Holyland, or the Promised Land, is an integral element of the Jewish religion. The mass media has a role to play in both. Religion is covered in both the national media abroad and the Jewish Diaspora media. Yet Jewish identity in the Diaspora has often been regarded as an uphill battle against assimilation. The mass media culture has mostly been seen as an agent causing assimilation within the wider culture. Yet the opposite is also true with media coverage of Israel – and coverage in the Jewish community media, in particular – being an agent of Jewish identity.

The exposure of Jews to the media will necessarily determine the extent to which it is a factor in Diaspora Jewish identity. Jewish exposure to the national media has little or no coverage of Judaism – its own coverage of religion comprising mostly the dominant local religion, in most cases Christianity. In its coverage of Israel, it is almost entirely concerning the Arab–Israeli conflict as opposed to internal Israeli matters. The Jewish Diaspora media provides a more complete picture in Israel including of religious life inside the country as well as Jewish life elsewhere in the Jewish Diaspora. But the role of Jewish media in this process is itself undergoing a revolutionary change as a result of the Internet with Jewish identity no longer dependent upon intermediary media sources.

To be examined in this chapter is the state of Jewish media, the role of the local national and Jewish media in covering Israel, and the coverage of religion by the Jewish media. Drawing upon the view that Israel is also a factor for religious identity it is relevant to examine Jewish communal decision-makers and their information sources about Israel. The chapter will examine the case of the Jewish press in the United States, given the political clout of the community. A case study of two leading quality newspapers – the *Forward* of New York and the London *Jewish Chronicle* – will be taken. The revolutionary role of the Internet in Diaspora networking will be discussed, as will the Israeli media's coverage of the Diaspora as an agent of Israeli identity with the Diaspora Jewish world.

The Jewish Diaspora media fulfil a number of functions in strengthening Jewish identity. First, they play an important role in maintaining Jewish identity and solidarity with Jews inside the country. Secondly, solidarity with Jews in countries of distress. Thirdly, solidarity between Jews and the Holyland. Overall, the Jewish media creates a sense of belonging and involvement for things Jewish.

In 2011 there were around 50 weekly Jewish newspapers and a large number of biweekly and monthly publications in the USA, 15 weekly Jewish newspapers in Europe, seven in Canada, three in Latin America and two elsewhere in the world. Today, there are over 40 publications among the ex-Soviet republics associated with the federation of Jewish Communities. The Jewish press provides local Jewish news, national Jewish community news, and news from Israel and overseas Jewish communities. In addition to providing news, there are also articles, essays and reviews on Jewish identity, culture and religion. The New York-based Jewish Telegraphic Agency (JTA) publishes a Jewish daily bulletin in drawing upon reports from correspondents in addition to in Israel from different key Jewish centres inside the USA, and part-time correspondents in other Jewish centres like Moscow, West Europe and central European capitals, South America and other Anglo-Saxon countries.

There are Jewish radio stations in many countries, in most cases broadcasting a few hours weekly; some are sponsored by local Jewish organisations. The most developed Jewish radio stations are those in France, Argentina and New York which broadcast throughout the week. Elsewhere in Europe, much Jewish broadcasting comprises external broadcasting and is mostly geared to foreign audiences.

The medium which failed to make a notable contribution to the Jewish media was television. Attempts to create Jewish television did not generally succeed owing to its high cost. In the US, the Jewish Television Network

(JTN), founded in 1981 as an independent non-profit organisation to provide television programming on the diversity of Jewish life, was carried on some 90 Public Broadcasting Service (PBS) affiliates (which theoretically reaches over 80 million homes). In 2005 the New York-based Jewish Global television was founded as a counter to Al Jazeera. Other initiatives are the Jewish Channel (TJC) and the Shalom Channel. In a few countries (for example, Italy), state television allots time to Jewish religion. The emergence of radio and video on the Internet has cut the costs of television, and offers new hope for Jewish television.

The American Jewish community and Jewish media

As the largest Jewish community in the Diaspora, with 6,000,000 Jews, it is relevant to examine the case of Diaspora Jewry and information in the US context. If quantitatively the US today possesses the largest Jewish press, the quality of the American Jewish press is mediocre at best. After the heyday of quality Yiddish papers at the turn of the twentieth century, the Anglo-Jewish press engages in little of its own reporting. Primarily, the American Jewish press sought to convey information, promote local communal involvement, and if necessary defend Jews against their enemies. Even in the case of the wealthier papers with little investigative journalism there was a small improvement since the 1980s, with newspapers like the *Daily Forward*, *Baltimore Jewish Times*, New York *Jewish Week*, and *Long Island Jewish World* modelling themselves on the American national media. But the investigative journalism does not extend to matters concerning Israel. The lack of investigative journalism elsewhere in the American Jewish press today reflects the still unresolved dichotomy that on the one hand the American Jew is confident and successful, but on the other still looks over his shoulder and thus feels a need to present an image of communality. Against the background of anti-Semitism, Jewish newspapers steered clear of controversy and scandal. As Sarna has argued, 'local Jewish newspapers, especially those outside of major population centres, could not attract the kinds of contributors that a national newspaper could, and their goals became proportionately more modest and consensus-orientated' (Sarna, 2004, p. 326). In the 1970s, Gary Rosenblatt, editor of the New York *Jewish Week*, observed, 'improvements in the Jewish press of recent years have been almost exclusively limited to technology and appearance, and the new visibility of the Jewish press is more a reflection of its potential – and of the political stature of the American Jewish community – than a testament to the quality or clout the Jewish press has achieved'.[2]

The major themes covered in the American Jewish press concern local Jewish community news, national Jewish news, and news from Israel. A content analysis comprising three months of editorial content from four American Jewish weekly newspapers was carried out by the author. Four papers were examined: the New York *Jewish Week,* the *Washington Jewish Week*, the *Northern California Jewish Bulletin* and the *Great Phoenix Jewish News*. It was a period of relative quiet from Israel.

Local community comprised an average of 23 per cent of all editorial content; national Jewish news 14 per cent, Israel news 13 per cent, national Jewish news related to Israel 4 per cent, and US–Israeli news 5 per cent. The Jewish world – news from outside the US or Israel, like Jewish news from East Europe, West Europe, and South America – comprised 5 per cent. 'Others' – personal news, births, barmitzvah, marriages and deaths, as well as obituaries, arts reviews, rabbis' sermons, entertainment and travel – comprised 34 per cent.

When compared with a war situation in Israel there was not a profound change in the quantity of Israel-related coverage. The news from Israel, of which much comprised the war, increased from 13 per cent to 15 per cent, and the national Jewish news related to Israel increased from 4 per cent to 6 per cent.

Economic difficulties facing the Jewish press produced the trend of local Jewish federations buying out the Jewish press. The federation in the US perceives the sponsoring of the community newspaper as a means to ensure the unity and cohesion of the community, and as a channel to the Jewish community. Today, some 70 per cent of the American Jewish press is funded directly or indirectly by the federations or defence organisations. This is an increase from one-third in the 1970s. The Jewish Telegraphic Agency is itself dependent upon federations for half of its income. This has repercussions in the freedom of Jewish press and freedom of editorial comment – even if the actual extent of the impact of federations in practice is debated within the profession. By controlling the paper, there are, it is claimed, many cases with little or no criticism of local Jewish institutions affiliated with the Jewish federation. It is perhaps inevitable that reporting – or 'patronising' – federation personalities and Jewish institutions are given importance in many of the federation-supported papers. Clearly, without federation support some communities could not sustain a paper. As editor of the *Atlanta Jewish Times*, Neil Rubin was 'regularly threatened with withdrawal of federation advertising funds – approximately $50,000 a year – were coverage not favourable' (Rubin, 2004, p. 337). The editor of a successful paper like the Philadelphian *Jewish Exponent*, which often returned the federation subsidy, was pressured by the federation. Years ago, after the New York Jewish federation purchased 70 per cent of the subscriptions of the New York *Jewish Week*, there were occasions, according to Philip Hochstein, its former editor, when the federation encroached on the paper's independence despite earlier contractual obligations guaranteeing full independence.

The independence of the Jewish media in the US has been better in terms of editorial quality with a large range of independent magazines, including *Moment, Sh'ma*, an intellectual review, *Lillith* (Jewish feminism), *Tikkun* (liberal) and *Commentary* (Conservative, despite being published by the American Jewish Committee). Newer magazines like *Presentense*, and alternative magazines like *Heeb* sought to capture the attention of younger audiences. Each in their style has adopted policies of freedom of speech both regarding local Jewish institutions and matters relating to Israel and the Arab–Israeli conflict.

Readership patterns in the US

As the most populated Jewish country outside Israel, as well as politically the most significant in terms of its influence on US foreign policy, it is correct to examine the US case. Jewish newspapers are read widely in the US Jewish community. Nationally, 34 per cent of American Jews in 2007 read a Jewish newspapers or magazines, a decline from 58 per cent in 1984 (Cohen, 1983). There is considerable difference from community to community in their exposure to Jewish newspapers. Broken down, between one third to two-thirds of identifying Jews read a Jewish newspaper, according to Sheshkin (2001). Of 21 Jewish community surveys where the question of reading local Jewish newspapers had been asked the figure moved from 89 per cent in the case of the Tidewater community to 29 per cent in Monmouth. The average found that 9 of the 21 newspapers reported from 60 to 69 per cent, three reported 50–59 per cent, and five from 40–49 per cent (Sheshkin, 2001).

Tobin found that Jewish newspaper reading within the United States was greater in the smaller cities than in the bigger ones.[3] Surveys of the Jewish communities of St. Louis and Pittsburgh showed that in each case 83 per cent of Jews received the local Jewish newspaper whereas a survey of New York Jewry found that 32 per cent said they received a Jewish newspaper (Federation of Jewish Philanthropies of New York: the Jewish Population of Greater New York: A Profile 1984).

Age and religiousity also influence audience patterns. There is a lack of clarity of whether or not older Jews are more in inclined than younger Jews to read a Jewish paper. 34 per cent of Jews of New Jersey aged 13–24 read a Jewish newspaper or magazine, 53 per cent aged between 25–39, 69 per cent aged between 40–54, and 77 per cent aged 55+ (Verbit, 1971, page 47). Similarly, 38 per cent of Jews in Detroit in 2005 aged under 35 read the *Detroit Jewish News* in contrast to 50 per cent aged 35–49, and 63 per cent 50–64 (Shenkin 2005). And, a 1999 study of Palm Beach, Florida – where 40 per cent of residents, always read a Jewish newspaper – found also that the older the reader the more he was likely to read: 43 per cent of readers of The *Palm Beach Jewish Journal* were aged 75 or over, 40 per cent were aged 65–74, only 13 per cent 50–64; and 5 per cent 35–49 (Sheshkin, 1999). Yet, 62 per cent of Greater Seattle Jews under 30 read a Jewish newspaper in 2001 in contrast to 54 per cent and 59 per cent of those aged 30–39 and 40–49 respectively (Herman, 2001). Also, female Jews in Detroit were more inclined (59 per cent) than male Jews 53 per cent to.

In terms of religious identification, more than 60 per cent of Philadelphian Jews who have a religious identity – describing themselves as either Orthodox, Conservative, traditional, Reform, or Reconstructionist – subscribed to the *Jewish Exponent* in contrast to 35 per cent of those who said they were secular or 'just Jewish'. Broken down among the 'religious', slightly more Orthodox (64 per cent) and Conservative (69 per cent) Jews read the *Jewish Exponent* in contrast to 61 per cent, 57 per cent and 59 per cent of traditional, Reform, and Reconstructionist Jews respectively (Chancey & Goldstein, 1984). By contrast,

76 per cent and 64 per cent of Conservative and Reform Jews respectively in Detroit in 2005 were more inclined to read the Jewish paper than the orthodox (36 per cent). Also, 71 per cent of Jewish couples both of whom were Jewish-born were inclined to read in contrast to 57 per cent of couples who included one conversion, or 18 per cent of inter-married couples (Shenkin 2006).

A tale of two papers: **The Forward,** *New York,* **and the London Jewish Chronicle**

The *Forward* and the *Jewish Chronicle* are similar in certain senses. Both are independent, quality weekly newspapers in their respective countries, and they have earned respect well beyond the community. Each has an editorial operation larger and more professional than other Jewish newspapers in the Diaspora. But the similarities are outweighed by the differences. Founded in 1841 the *Jewish Chronicle* is the oldest Jewish newspaper in the world in contrast to the *Forward* which is one of the newest, established in 1990. Notwithstanding its dominant position in the English Jewish community, the *Jewish Chronicle* is facing a rapidly dwindling circulation, and the *Forward* has reached a weekly circulation of 35,000 copies. This section will examine the editorial directions, editorial independence and commercial challenges facing the two newspapers in their respective communities and how these are influenced by the sociological, economic and geographical differences between the two communities in the US and Britain.

Although both papers pride themselves on their editorial independence, the *Jewish Chronicle* is cautious not to place itself beyond the pale. The paper's stand on Israel for many years was to identify with Israel's Labour Party, rejecting Likud's annexationist policy on settlements. But under its current editor, Stephen Pollard (appointed in 2008), the paper moved toward the centre, reflecting in part both the political change in Israel towards the Right and an incremental change of the Anglo-Jewish community facing anti-Semitism. British media coverage of Israel became an important theme of Pollard's editorship.

To be true, the paper's history shows, as its former columnist Chaim Bermant put it, that 'the paper has been different things at different times. The secret of the paper's longevity was its adaptability' (Bermant, 1969).

With regard to theological issues, the paper avoided major crusades, preferring to stay within the community consensus. One exception was during William Frankel's editorship (1958–77), when he alienated the strictly Orthodox sections of the community by backing the appointment of Dr Louis Jacobs for the post of principal of Jews College which, was the community's main rabbinical seminary, against the view of the Chief Rabbi. Jacobs had authored a controversial book *We have Reason to Believe*, arguing that the Torah may not have been dictated absolutely by God and Mount Sinai. It was not surprising that Frankel's successor as editor, Geoffrey Paul (editor 1977–90), sought to close ranks, positioning the paper on the left end of the Orthodox spectrum.

The *Forward*, by contrast, is a far more ideological paper. Seeking to recreate an English version of the legendary Yiddish *Forverts*, Seth Lipsky, its founding editor, was an unlikely candidate for the venture. A right-winger – he backed the Republicans, praising Ronald Reagan as a 'rare politician' – he expressed views diametrically opposed to the board of the *Forward*, which sought to foster social-democratic values, including siding with the workers and the unions. On Israel, his views contrasted with the Forward Association, which stood between the Israeli Government and the Palestinians. Lipsky backed Ariel Sharon. In an essay published in the neo-Conservative *Commentary* magazine in 1997, Lipsky explained: 'My idea of bringing out the *Forward* was not despite its Liberal-Left politics but in large because of them. I sensed opportunities for synthesis.'[4] The *Forward* prided itself that, in contrast to other Jewish community papers which received financial support from the Jewish Federation and which then had to suffer the meddling in the paper's editorial content – this was not the case with Lipsky and the paper's publishers, the Forward Association. Journalistically, Lipsky sought in the *Forward* to address national issues from a Jewish point of view. Lipsky's editorship established the paper's crusading independence with exposés such as a front page report listing the salaries of presidents of leading Jewish organisations. However, Lipsky's right-wing views proved too much for the Forward Association. By 2000, the only way for the *Forward* to part from Lipsky was to threaten to close the paper. So, with no other alternative, Lipsky resigned along with much of the editorial staff. 'Seth Lipsky arrived at a desert and built a beautiful garden,' wrote Jonathan Mahler, who had been the *Forward*'s editorial page editor. 'Now the land's owner's want it back. What they don't realise is that without Lipsky, the garden will die anyway.'[5]

But the garden did not die. Some would say that it blossomed. Jeffrey J. Goldberg was appointed editor. He had an ideological background more akin to the *Forward* publishers.[6] The son of a union lawyer, he identified with Labour Zionism. During the 1970s he was a founding member and secretary of Kibbutz Gezer in Israel. The author of the well-received *Jewish Power: Inside the American Establishment*, he had an intimate knowledge of the American Jewish organisation scene. With the paper moving editorially leftwards, he continued the *Forward*'s investigative crusading spirit with stories like an exposé on the conflict between Hassidic Jews and blacks in Brooklyn.

Jane Eisner, a *Philadelphia Inquirer* veteran, who succeeded Goldberg as editor in 2007, shared similar values. Eisner defined the *Forward*'s role as 'speaking to a community that is less cohesive, wealthier, more politically powerful, but still searching for its place in American society'.[7] With a keen interest in gender matters, she campaigned on the *Forward*'s pages for Jewish women's rights.

In news terms, the paper covered the Bernard Madoff scandal and the losses of major Jewish charities, and the negotiations by the Claims Conference with Swiss banks. Most memorable was the investigation by Nathaniel Popper of scandalous labour conditions and the employment of foreign workers without permits at Agriprocessors, a large kosher meat-packing plant in the town of Iowa. The subsequent 25-year imprisonment of its owner Rubashkin raised the questions of the rights and obligations of Jewish community journalism. But for the *Forward* they typified the progressive Jewish values on which the paper campaigned. 'There were people who thought that it was not wise that we were going after the Rubashkin family,' said Eisner. 'From their perspective the Rubashkins had transformed the kosher meat industry and made it possible for Jews, especially in smaller communities, to have access to a wide array of kosher foods. But it also highlighted the challenge of Jews who want to broaden the ethical scope of *kashrut* or are interested in the fate of undocumented Guatemalan workers,' she said.[8]

The news-gathering structures of the *Forward* and the *Jewish Chronicle* are unusually large when compared with most other Jewish weekly newspapers which comprise one or two editorial personnel and rely mostly for their news gathering on news services like the Jewish Telegraphic Agency and upon news releases. Under their editors, the *Forward* and the *Jewish Chronicle* have a senior editorial staff comprising a managing editor and a news editor who runs a team of full-time local reporters, with reporting beats like religion and inter-ethnic affairs. The *Forward* maintains a full-time Washington reporter, and the *Jewish Chronicle* a reporter covering diplomatic and political affairs in Whitehall. Each has a full-time foreign editor. Israel-related coverage has been an important element of both papers' news pages, and both have a part-time reporter in Israel. The *Jewish Chronicle* has a network of part-time or freelance reporters in key world capitals with Jewish communities. Both papers have a full-time editor for the arts and culture, and in the *Forward*'s case, this has brought distinction to its pages.

The 50-odd years (1958–2006) spanning the *Jewish Chronicle*'s editorship of Frankel, Paul and Ned Temko (a former *Christian Science Monitor* foreign correspondent) produced comprehensive and solid coverage of communal, Israel and Jewish world news. The appointment in 2006 of David Rowan as editor began a period of soul searching. A declining readership from 70,000 in 1970 to 30,000 at the beginning of the twenty-first century reflected two major changes: There was a changing Jewish demography as younger members of the Jewish community were more assimilated and less inclined to buy the paper and, at the same time, there were the challenges with regard to changes in print media and the growth of on-line journalism. The introduction of a free London *Jewish News* paper and a well-produced London edition of the Israeli Haredi weekly, *Hamodia*, for the growing ultra-Orthodox community added to the pressure.

Rowan and Pollard each grappled in different ways with the decline. Rowan focused the news pages almost singly upon local Jewish community news; Israel news was downgraded, and Jewish world news also disappeared. He failed to appreciate how important Israel news was to the Jewish reader. News and articles from Israel and the Middle East were the most read sections and regularly read by 76 per cent of readers of the London *Jewish Chronicle* (21 per cent occasionally).[9] Both Rowan and Pollard expanded the features and opinion pages, a recognition that many obtain the breaking news regarding Israel from the national broadcast media – giving weekly newspapers like the *Jewish Chronicle* more a role of analysing and providing background to the news. Pollard continued with the focus on community, widening an investigative direction, but restored coverage of Israel. The community-news interest peaked with Pollard's introduction of an eight-page pull-out of community news, including pages of photos of readers' celebrations like bar mitzvah and marriages. In 2010 Pollard launched a northern edition of the *Jewish Chronicle*; while the Jewish Chronicle Trust had earlier owned provincial Jewish papers in Manchester and Leeds, the new venture incorporated local coverage with the existing quality of JC's own features and national and foreign coverage. Rowan, a former Internet website editor at *The Guardian*, developed an interactive website. The ultimate in community journalism, JC.com is an on-line community paper in which readers are invited to share their reactions, opinions and photographs of family celebrations and blogs. The newspaper's name on its masthead was abbreviated from the 'Jewish Chronicle' to the 'JC', by which it is popularly known. The legitimate worries of the paper's directors' notwithstanding, a lack of alternative sources for British Jewry of information about local Jewish matters – the community is too small for the national British media, for example, to take even a passing interest – suggests that the JC still has a secure existence, albeit with a shrunken circulation.

Across the Atlantic, the same period found that by 2011, some 20 years after its founding, the *Forward's* circulation had climbed steadily from 26,000 at Lipsky's resignation to 35,000. However, this was far from its projected numbers of 100,000 copies – not to mention a national Jewish daily paper – which Lipsky planned when he established the *Forward*. The paper suffered poor sales promotion, with the overwhelming number of copies being mailed subscriptions. Printing only late Thursday ensures that the paper is up-to-date but results in most mailed copies reaching readers on Saturday or even Monday, missing out the Friday Sabbath eve, a peak time for Jewish newspaper reading. Its circulation is too small to attract many advertisers for a paper defined as a national newspaper. In its first ten years the publishers had invested 10 million dollars in the paper. The paper is kept going by the Forward Association, the assets of which include the WEVD radio station and Manhattan property.

If the *Jewish Chronicle* manages to sell 30,000 papers in a community of nearly 300,000 souls, for the *Forward* to sell only 35,000 in the US community of nearly 6 million Jews signals a failure. It hasn't found the magic formula to break through and become a truly national Jewish paper for a number of reasons. Most Jewish newspaper readers in the US receive for free a Jewish newspaper subsidised by the Jewish Federation and have no need to buy a second Jewish paper. For example, in New York the Federation pays for some 60,000–70,000 copies of the New York *Jewish Week*. For many in New York, their needs are satisfied by the *Jewish Week,* which – in contrast to the *Forward*'s national focus – covers the New York area, a subject of greater interest to most readers. Even the *New York Times* has proven to be a

Forward competitor, given its daily coverage of the large Jewish community in the city. Only highly committed Jews, estimated to be some 40,000 by one *Forward* executive, were prepared to also open a subscription to the paper. The *Forward*'s best chances would be to build upon its proven investigative skills in covering national Jewish affairs, to widen its coverage of the New York Jewish metropolis and compete with the *Jewish Week* – whose own coverage of the city is not comprehensive – making it compulsory reading for New York Jews.

Israel-centredness in Diaspora Jewish identity

The Diaspora relationship is a lopsided one in it being Israel-centred. Jewish connections to the Holyland go back to the Biblical era of the land of Canaan, and subsequently the early Jewish statehood which extended from the thirteenth century BCE to 70 CE including the first and second Temple periods. After the Roman capture in 70 CE dispersed Jewish communities continued to look towards Jerusalem as the focus of prayer, and aspired to a return of Jewish statehood albeit, in part, as a solution to anti-Semitism. In 1948 the Jewish state was established, and in the 1967 war the Old City of Jerusalem including the holy places were captured by Israel.

The Arab–Israeli conflict is an on-going factor in Diaspora Jewish relations with Israel. And the international coverage of the conflict in its various facets like the wars and acts of terrorism has made the flow of media information, and the manner the media cover events, also a factor in Israeli–Diaspora relations. The Arab–Israeli conflict receives considerable coverage in the general media: Israel was the most covered country in the *New York Times* in 1970 (Gerbner and Marvanyi, 1977). In 2007, 49 per cent of American Jews said that newspapers have an important role in shaping their understanding of Israel today, 27 per cent television, and 20 per cent Internet in contrast to the synagogue (13 per cent) and friends (14 per cent).[10] The national media – rather than the Jewish media – are the main source of information for changing developments involving Israel, mostly of a security nature and defence nature. Sixty per cent of Washington Jews surveyed in 1983 gave their local newspaper, the *Washington Post*, as the most important source for news about Israel, 19 per cent television news, and 3 per cent radio news, in contrast to, say, Jewish sources (Tobin, 1984). Similarly, 74 per cent of the Jews of Vineland, New Jersey, surveyed in 1976, used the general press for Israeli news, 68 per cent radio and television, on contrast to 39 per cent Jewish newspapers (Alan Mallach Associates, 1976).

A target audience are community leaders. As decision-makers they must be well-informed about Israeli matters. A survey of 77 American Jewish leaders carried out by the author found that 99 per cent of leaders pay special attention to newspaper and magazine articles about Israel. Forty-one per cent of American Jewish leaders found the American national press was a 'very important source' for learning about Israeli governmental decisions. The *New York*

Times is the preeminent newspaper read by American Jewish decision-makers: 72 per cent of leaders read the *New York Times*, and 32 per cent the *Wall Street Journal* but only 5 per cent each read the *Washington Post* and the *Los Angeles Times*.

The structure of the foreign press corps in Israel confirms that audiences are interested in things which are proximate, whether in terms of geography, politics and economics or in such other terms as religious terms. A survey of foreign correspondents in Israel carried out by the author found that Jewish audience interest was regarded as a higher factor for news interest by the US media correspondents than by the West European media correspondents, reflecting the large Jewish population in the US, in particular in the New York area which was also a centre for US news organisations. Thirty-nine per cent and 28 per cent of US correspondents rated Jewish audience interest very important and somewhat important respectively. By contrast, 11 per cent and 32 per cent of West European correspondents rated Jewish audience interest as very important and somewhat important. Notwithstanding Jewish audience interest, major Israeli news sources, including government sources like the Foreign Ministry and the IDF Spokesman, focus their PR activities towards the general foreign media rather than the Jewish media. One exception is that the activities of the Reform and Conservative Jewish movements, which lack formal official recognition in Israel, are directed to Jewish Diaspora media correspondents among the foreign press corps rather than the mainstream foreign correspondents.

Critical media coverage of controversial Israel-related events like the 2009 Operation Cast Lead in Gaza, 2006 war with Lebanon, the two intifadas, the 1991 Gulf War, and the 1982 Lebanon war raise important questions about the impact of general media coverage in the Israeli–Diaspora Jewish relationship. Acculturated over the centuries to the image of the Jew on the defensive, Diaspora Jews have had to orient themselves over the past 40 years or so to the manifestation of Israeli military power, which drew the admiration of foreign public opinion. Moreover, most recently Diaspora Jewry had to alter its perception of this image, from a respected and admired manifestation of military might – as displayed in the 1948, 1956, 1967, 1973 and 1991 confrontations, following which public opinion surveys supported Israel – to one arousing anathema, embarrassment, even resentment, and incidents of local anti-Semitism.

A few Jewish papers have correspondents, mostly part-time in Israel. But most use the reporting of the Jewish Telegraphic Agency, which maintains a three-person bureau in Israel. Israel arouses much interest among Jews. A couple of Jewish radio stations in France and Belgium receive daily news and current affairs transmissions from the World Zionist Organisation.

News from Israel is an important ingredient of the coverage in the Jewish media today. Although the Israel–Arab conflict is covered already by the daily general media, the Jewish media covers a broader gamut of issues such as internal Israeli politics, the economy, religion, and society which are almost entirely ignored by the general media's coverage of Israel. Examining the distribution of sub-categories of Israel news, the author's content analysis of the four American Jewish newspapers found that the Jewish press provided a wider and more balanced span of subjects in contrast to the general media's focus exclusively upon foreign and defence matters. Of the Israel-related news broken down (during regular periods of non-war), 14 per cent of the Israel news comprised diplomacy, and 17 per cent military, defence and intelligence affairs. Four-fifths of the coverage comprised subjects not normally covered by the general media: internal Israeli politics 12 per cent; the Israeli economy 5 per cent; religion and Israel 12 per cent; local Israeli visitors 10 per cent; local fundraising efforts for Israel 9 per cent; Israeli society 8 per cent; media coverage of Israel 3 per cent; aliya and absorption 2 per cent; Israeli culture 2 per cent; and Israel law and crime 1 per cent.

In terms of how Jewish newspaper editors learn about the news concerning Israel, a separate survey of 25 Jewish newspaper editors in the Diaspora by the author found that the Jewish Telegraphic Agency (JTA) was the primary source of Israeli governmental decisions news about Israel. Fifty-four per cent of Jewish editors said that the JTA was 'very important' and 23 per cent 'somewhat important' for learning about Israeli decisions; 28 per cent replied the national media was 'very important' and 28 per cent 'somewhat important'; and 18 per cent replied that Israeli diplomats were 'very important' and 28 per cent 'somewhat important' sources for learning about government decisions.

Given the impact of the media in framing Jewish public opinion, the manner in which the Jewish newspaper editors decide what is the news is crucial. The Jewish Telegraphic Agency had an important role in determining for editors the news agenda regarding Israel, according to the survey of Jewish newspaper editors: 26 per cent of editors replied that the JTA was the main agenda setter; 21 per cent Israeli governmental statements; 10 per cent other Jewish newspapers; and 8 per cent the American national media.

News from Israel on *Radio Communaute Judaique*, one of Paris's three Jewish radio stations, which carry live broadcasts from Israel, was in the 1980s the second most popular item among listeners (73 per cent). (Most popular were cultural programmes, scoring 74 per cent.)[11] In 2007, 66 per cent of American Jews said that when reading the news they are drawn to reading news about Israel (North American Jewish Data Bank, 2007).

To be true, this is a slight decline from the past. In 1983, 92 per cent of American Jews said they pay special attention to newspaper and magazine articles about Israel (Cohen, 1983). In 1986 the figure was 85 per cent (Cohen, 1989), and in 1988 the figure was 75 per cent (and 4 per cent not sure, 21 per cent no) (Cohen, 1989). Seventy-eight per cent of readers of the *MetroWest Jewish News*, 77 per cent of the *New York Jewish Week* and 72 per cent of readers of the *St Louis Jewish Light* read the news about Israel (United Jewish Federation of Metro West New Jersey, 1986). And, in 1986, it was the most read section in the *MetroWest Jewish News*, and the third most read section in the *St Louis Jewish Light*. The decline may be explained as a certain levelling off in a seemingly endless, on-going and repetitive story. 'The news from Israel is too permeated by local infighting, lacking the big picture. There comes a point when eyes glaze over. People know the stories by heart, are tired of their being repeated, and just want to be told about the major turning points', an American Jewish newspaper editor, remarked.

The Jewish Telegraphic Agency has moved from being a wholesaler of Jewish news to also being a 'retailer' as a result of the Internet. The JTA's website made the agency directly accessible to thousands of Jews in the Diaspora. In addition to providing the hard news, the JTA website provides more background analysis to the news. It also has such other features as Jewish blogs.

Introspective of criticising the Jewish State, the Jewish media generates Diaspora sympathy for Israel. The Jewish media help many Jews to define their own relationships with Israel. The level of 'dialogue' between Israel and Diaspora Jewish communities has been raised in the age of electronically-transmitted information, and in particular the intensive flow of information which portrays Israel and, by extension, the entire Jewish community in a negative light. For, whilst the Jewish news media are unable to compete with the international media as a primary source of up-to-the minute information about Israel during times of crisis, and despite the fact that they do occasionally criticise Israeli policy, they do nevertheless provide a more balanced and comprehensive coverage of the events affecting Israel, and tend more to report the official Israeli line than the international media.

Yet a further channel for following Israeli events has been the Israeli media. Until the development of the Internet, and the websites of the Israeli media, the Hebrew media were seen to a small extent, and almost solely in the United States, where *Yediot Aharonot* and *Maariv* print special local editions, comprising developments in the local American yordim community. The Hebrew media has a significant role in strengthening ties between yordim or Israeli émigrés, as well as networking with other yordim. This is particularly important given the unwelcome feeling which local Jewish communities are perceived by yordim to give them. The *Jerusalem Post* has published a weekly international edition which reaches most English language speaking communities around the world. In addition, the Friday edition has a printing in the US. The fortnightly news magazine *Jerusalem Report* sells most of its copies in the US, but also reaches other mostly Anglo-speaking Jewish communities. The *Report* had become an important source of analysis and interpretation of Israel for Jewish community personnel. Its albeit limited coverage of the Jewish World generates empathy to the Jewish world as a whole.

News from the Jewish Diaspora: blind spot for Israelis

The Israel–Diaspora Jewish relationship ought to be two-directional. For Israelis, religious identity includes identity with the Jewish people and the Jewish experience in the Diaspora. Israeli Hebrew media coverage of the Diaspora has the potential to generate knowledge and awareness of the Diaspora Jewish condition, but in practice the Israeli–Diaspora relationship is one-directional. By contrast to Diaspora Jews' feelings towards Israel, the level of identity between Israelis and Diaspora Jews is limited even though Israelis have a common destiny with the Jewish people as a whole. A major source – and for many the sole source – of knowledge about Diaspora Jewry is the Israeli media. But Diaspora news receives spasmodic attention in Israel's media. This section will examine the channels of news coverage about Diaspora Jewry in the Israeli media, and the factors leading to low level of coverage.

True, the level of interest in the Diaspora has fluctuated over the years. With many recently arrived immigrants from Europe and the Arab world, interest in the subject was considerable in the 1950s, particularly for their former countries of residence. By the late 1960s, interest went down as Israelis became preoccupied with the 1967 war and its after effects: the 1969–70 Israeli–Egyptian War of Attrition, the Yom Kippur war, and Arab terrorism in Israel and abroad. But terrorism abroad directed at Jewish targets did generate some interest in Jewish communities under attack. With the phenomenon of *yerida* (Israelis leaving to settle abroad) and *neshira* (settlement of Soviet émigrés elsewhere than Israel like Germany), interest increased in the 1970s. The mass emigration from the Soviet Union generated interest in the Jewish community there and resettlement of their *olim* (lit. immigrants to Israel) in the 1970s, but interest died off by the 1980s. The departure of Ethiopian Jews in Operation Moses and Operation Solomon for Israel and the problems of their settlement regenerated interest in absorption and the Jews of Ethiopia.

Notwithstanding the impact of American popular culture upon Israeli audiences, there is very limited interest in American Jewry. The positions of major American Jewish organisations – who wield certain influence on US foreign policy – are daily reported at key moments in US–Israeli relations or when the status of non-Orthodox conversions comes up in Israeli politics. For example, less than 10 per cent of the reporting of Israel Radio's Washington correspondent was estimated to comprise American Jewish developments. Even the New York based reporter of the *Jerusalem Post* estimated that only 30 per cent of his reporting comprised American Jewish life – even though all the US political reporting was done by the paper's Washington-based reporter. A number of episodes including the American Jewish spy Jonathan Pollard affair produced some reporting. There was far less interest in trends in American Jewish life. The only Jewish communities in West Europe to generate interest have been German Jewry and Russian Jewry. Israeli interest in the Jewish communities is evident in television programmes on foreign affairs. The scourge of anti-Semitism in Latin America has also been reported.

English and French Israeli language media cover sections of the Diaspora in greater depth. The *Jerusalem Report's* Jewish World section provides information about Diaspora life and developments. So does the *Jerusalem Post*. *Haaretz's* English language edition publishes a weekly condensed version of the New York *Forward*.

Theoretically, there are three structural channels by which information from the Jewish Diaspora is collected. First, there are the foreign correspondents of Israeli news organisations. In practice, all the key Israeli newspapers and broadcasting have correspondents in Washington and most newspapers have in addition a correspondent in New York. They also have mostly part-time reporters in selective European capitals. A clue to the lack of interest is that the local Jewish press is not seen widely even by the Israeli foreign correspondents. Secondly, the reporting of the Jewish World by the Jewish Telegraphic Agency from Jewish communal centres around the world and in particular from inside the US used to reach the Israeli media because their reports reached the Israeli news agency, *Itim,* and were selectively translated and passed on to the Israeli media. But since the closure of Itim this source died down. Instead the JTA is followed on-line by Israeli foreign editors. This necessarily comprises hard copy, with no broadcast material. There are no fixed arrangements for visual material produced by Jewish television abroad – including professional outlets like Jewish programming sponsored by public television channels – to reach the Israeli broadcasters. A third source were the Israel-based specialist correspondents who cover the Jewish Diaspora. Formerly, these were correspondents who covered the aliya beat and reported the goings-on of the Jewish Agency, which has responsibility for assisting aliya. But this decreased following a decline in aliya, a decline of the Jewish Agency as a potential news source, and a greater involvement of Diaspora Jewish organisations within their own communities abroad. For, example, the growth of 'J Street', the liberal Jewish lobby organisation in Washington, and its criticism of Israeli policies, which challenges the activities of AIPAC on Capital Hill. Grassroots Jewish life – in contrast to the communal organisations – receives only sporadic attention. A handicap is that the Israel-based Jewish world correspondents have only limited opportunities to visit Jewish communities abroad – the subject of their news – and in some cases have not even visited these. In certain cases key American Jewish organisations like the ADL and the American Jewish Committee have brought Israeli journalists to the United States to expose them to American Jewish life. All this leaves the role of the media today in generating empathy among Israelis for Diaspora Jewry low – weakening Israeli solidarity with the Diaspora.

Jewish Diaspora networking and the Internet

The Internet has created a revolution in accessibility to information about Judaism, Jewish-related matters and Israel. As a virtual form of communications recognising no boundaries, the Internet has enabled Diaspora networking to an extent never before realised. The Internet may be broken into grassroots groups and individuals, organisational, news, and commercial. Religious content in the grassroots group and individual category includes the Bible, commentaries, the Talmud and Jewish law codes. Sites enable the Jewish surfer in far distant communities to participate in Jewish studies and hear inspirational talks about *divrei Torah*. There are a number of Jewish outreach programmes; among early leaders in identifying the potential of the

Net were Habad and Aish Torah. Jewish organisations with websites include the Conservative, Orthodox and Reform movements, synagogues and community organisations, with listings of synagogues, kosher restaurants, places of Jewish interest and other services. As discussed in Chapter 8, Internet sites strengthen Jewish identity within Diaspora communities and between such communities and Israel through access to innumerable Jewish educational software. Participation in forums and chat contribute to creating virtual communities. The Internet's impact upon Jewish identity is in making religious information much more accessible to those accessing it. Two of the most popular subjects on the web are Jewish genealogy and Jewish dating.

It is early days to fully evaluate the impact of computers and the Internet upon Diaspora relations with Israel, or its impact upon Jewish identity. In the United States 21 per cent of Greater Seattle Jews had in 2000 "purchased an audiotape, CD, or record because it contained Jewish content," and 7 per cent used a CD-Rom or other computer software because it had Jewish content (Herman, 2001). There is a vast age difference in Internet usage. Only 32 per cent of Americans Jews aged 55–64 in 2000 used the Internet for Jewish purposes. Younger Jews were more inclined to: 50 per cent of American Jews aged 35–44 and 44 per cent aged 45–54 used the Internet (Jewish Federations of North America, 2001). As Internet literacy increases in the coming years to cover all ages, these gaps will decline.

Twenty-two per cent of American Jews regularly check out Jewish websites on the Internet (North American Jewish Data Bank, 2007). Fifty-seven per cent of Detroit Jews in 2005 who read the Jewish newspaper used Internet for Jewish related information (Shenkin, 2006). Keysar and Kosmin, examining young adults raised in US Conservative synagogues in 1995–2003, found that 58 per cent had visited Jewish websites in past 12 months, and 5 per cent had participated in Jewish chatrooms in the same period (Keysar and Kosmin, 2003). Nine per cent regularly read Jewish-themed blogs on the Internet, and 23 per cent maintained some sort of web presence such as a website. A Reboot cross-cultural study in 2004 found that 13 per cent of American Jews had participated in an on-line community discussion forum. This was less than some other cultural groups – and contrasted with 35 per cent Muslims, 32 per cent Blacks and 23 per cent Hispanics.[12] News included the website versions of Jewish and Israeli newspapers. Keysar and Kosmin found that 41 per cent of young adult Conservative Jews had visited Jewish periodicals or newspapers on-line in the previous 12 months.

While in the past Jews were limited to Jewish and local or national newspapers, today in the Internet age they are able to plug into Israeli newspapers; 9 per cent of American Jews regularly read Israeli newspapers on the Internet (North American Jewish Data Bank, 2007). When American Jews were asked what factors influenced their understanding of Israel, only 20 per cent listed the Internet in contrast to 49 per cent who said newspapers and 27 per cent television.[13] Israeli Internet sources like the *Jerusalem Post* and *Haaretz* English websites play an important role for Diaspora Jews at times of crisis involving Israel – generating not only solidarity with Israel but also with the Jewish world at large.

Saxe, Sasson and Hecht (2006) examining the behaviour of American Jewish students during the 2006 war in Lebanon found that 59 per cent of students checked out news of the conflict once a day; moreover, 83 per cent of American Jews who had come to Israel in the Birthright programme checked news about the conflict once a day. In the Saxe, Sasson and Hecht study, 57 per cent of American Jewish students who had visited Israel checked out at least one a day from Israeli Internet news websites like the *Jerusalem Post, Haaretz* and *Y-Net*; by contrast 26 per cent of those who had not visited Israel went into Israeli Internet news websites.

Conclusion

Does the identification with Israel strengthen Jewish religious identity itself? And, if so, what is the role of the media in this process? Hoover and Lundby (1997) say that the coverage of religion in the media has supplemented traditional and institutional forms of religion. Accordingly, the Diaspora Jewish media ought to have a major impact on Jewish religiosity in the Diaspora. This should not be exaggerated.

The quantity of strictly religious content in the Diaspora Jewish community media, in particular, is small – reflecting that religion does not meet criteria of newsworthiness. Journalists are not very interested in religion as a news story. Galtung and Ruge's criteria for events to be defined as news events which 'occur between the appearance of two newspapers or between two news bulletins' has limited application to religion news. Judaism has a different time span from the media. Judaism itself today is rarely dramatic as in involving crises today (Galtung and Ruge, 1965).

Israel is sometimes thought of as being a primary ingredient of Jewish identity, raising the question of whether media like the Jewish press plays a role in the process. Yet, for example, only 26 per cent of Jews in Buenos Aires in 2005 said that reading Jewish newspapers was 'quite important' in meaning to be Jewish or feeling part of Judaism, and 39 per cent said that Jewish programmes on Jewish radio and television in Argentina were quite important in this. By contrast, family celebration of Jewish holidays was cited by 76 per cent of Bueos Aires Jews as quite important, eating Jewish food by 66 per cent, listening to Jewish music by 61 per cent, and relatives recalling their Jewish past by 63 per cent (Jmelnizky and Erdei, 2005). According to a study of Nashville and Tennessee Jewry (Jewish Federation of Nashville and Middle Tennessee, 1982), Israel as a factor of Jewish identification was given by less than 2 per cent of respondents in contrast to 44 per cent who said religion was a primary factor of Jewish identification, and 49 per cent who gave culture as a primary function of Jewish identification.

So, though the media have, as has been shown here, an impact on Diaspora identification with Israel, the Diaspora Jewish media may have some ill-defined role in strengthening religious identity. Notwithstanding the information age, globalisation and Internet, the media appears unlikely for the foreseeable future to replace such conventional forms as the synagogue, the Jewish school and *yeshiva*. Rather, they strengthen these forms, acting as a second fiddle.

References

Alan Mallach Associates (1976) *The Vineland, New Jersey, Jewish Community: A Demographic Survey.* Sponsored by Vineland Jewish Community Council in conjunction with Beth Israel Synagogue, p. 489.
Bermant, C. (1969) *Troubled Eden: An Anatomy of British Jewry.* London: Vallentine Mitchell.
Chancey, W. and Goldstein, I. (1984) *The Jewish Federation of the Greater Philadelphian Area.* Philadelphia, PA: Federation of Greater Philadelphia.
Cohen, R. (1997) *Global Diasporas: An Introduction.* Seattle: University of Washington Press.
Cohen, S. M. (1983) *Attitudes of American Jews towards Israel and Israelis: The 1983 National Survey of American Jews and Jewish Communal Leaders.* New York: American Jewish Committee.
——(1989)*Ties and Tensions: An Update. The 1989 Survey of American Jewish Attitudes towards Israel and Israelis.* New York: American Jewish Committee, p. 9.
Federation of Jewish Philanthropies of New York (1984) *Federation of Jewish Philanthropies of New York: The Jewish Population of Greater New York: A Profile 1984.* New York: Federation of Jewish Philanthropies of New York.
Galtung, J. and Ruge, M. H. (1965) 'The Structure of Foreign News', *Journal of International Peace Research*, 1.
Gerbner, G. and Marvanyi, G. (1977) 'The Many Worlds of the World's Press', *Journal of Communication*, Winter.
Herman, P. (2001) *A Demographic Study of the greater Seattle Jewish Population 2000–2001.* Seattle: Jewish Federation of Greater Seattle.
Hoover, S. and Lundby, K. (1997) *Rethinking Media, Religion and Culture.* Thousand Oaks, CA: Sage.
Jewish Federation of Nashville and Middle Tennessee (1982) *A Demographic Study of Nashville and Middle Tennessee.* Nashville, TN: Jewish Federation of Nashville and Middle Tennessee, pp. 17–18.
Jewish Federations of North America (2001) *National Jewish Population Survey 2000–2001.* New York: Jewish Federations of North America.
Jmelnizky, A. and Erdei, E. (2005) *The Jewish Population in Buenos Aires: Sociodemographic Survey.* Buenos Aires: AMIA
Keysar, A. and Kosmin, B. (2003) *Eight Up: The College Years. The Jewish Engagement of Young Adults Raised in Conservative Synagogues, 1995–2003.* New York: Ratner Center for the Study of Conservative Judaism, Jewish Theological Seminary.
North American Jewish Data Bank (2007) *The 2007 National Survey of American Jews.* Storrs, CT: Mandell L. Berman Institute, North American Jewish Data Bank Center for Judaic Studies and Contemporary Jewish Life, University of Connecticut.
Rubin, N. (2004) 'The Economics of Jewish Journalism in the United States', in L. Ford (ed), *Yesterday's News Tomorrow: Inside American Jewish Journalism.* Lincoln, NE: iUniverse, p. 337.

Sarna, J. (2004) 'A History of Jewish Journalism in the United States', in L. Ford (ed), *Yesterday's News Tomorrow: Inside American Jewish Journalism*. Lincoln, NE: iUniverse, p. 326.

Saxe, L., Sasson, T. and Hecht, S. (2006) *Israel at War: The Impact of Peer-Orientated Israel Programs on Responses of American Jewish Young Adults*. Waltham, MA: Maurice and Marilyn Cohen Centre for Modern Jewish Studies, Brandeis University.

Sheshkin, I. M. (1999) *Jewish Community Study Summary Report*. West Palm Beach, FL: Jewish Federation of Palm Beach County.

——(2001) *How Jewish Communities Differ*. Storrs, CT: Mandell L. Berman Institute, North American Jewish Data Bank Center for Judaic Studies and Contemporary Jewish Life, University of Connecticut.

——(2006) *The 2005 Detroit Jewish Population Study*. Detroit: Jewish Federation of Metropolitan Detroit.

Tobin, G. (1984) *Demographic Study of the Jewish Community of Greater Washington*. Washington: UJA-Federation, p. 111.

United Jewish Federation of Metro West New Jersey (1986) *A Population Study of the Jewish Community of Metro-West*. Whippany, NJ: United Jewish Federation of Metro West New Jersey, p. 132.

Verbit, M. (1971) *Characteristics of a Jewish Community: The Demographic and Judaic Profiles of the Jews in the Areas Served by the Jewish Federation of North Jersey*. Paramus, NJ: Federation of North Jersey, p. 47.

12 From out of Zion shall come forth foreign news

> Why are so many people fascinated with Israel? Part of the focus derives from the West's looking in – a fascination fed by the biblical tradition, the role of the Jew in the Christian world, guilt over the Holocaust, and yes, probably also some traditional anti-Semitism. And part of the focus derives from Israel's projecting itself outward – seeking to satisfy a deep longing to be accepted and a need to prove its worthiness to those upon whom it is most dependable.
> (Thomas Friedman, *New York Times*, formerly the paper's Israel bureau chief)[1]

The foreign media play a role in Jewish religious identity by virtue of the fact that there is considerable foreign coverage from Israel. Moreover, the impact of the foreign media is not just in terms of Jewish identity among Diaspora Jews abroad exposed to the foreign media, but also extends to the portal of religion more broadly among all audiences Jewish and non-Jewish. While generally religion is not a major theme of international news, nor is it relatively a major one in the flow from Israel, its potential role cannot be ignored in a study which examines the interplay between media and religion. Moreover, given that as the Holyland, the relative amount on religion will be greater in the case of Israel than it will be from many other countries.

There is little coverage of religion in international foreign news. Much foreign news comprises wars, conflict and diplomacy. Hess (1996), examining US foreign correspondents, found that 24.5 per cent of foreign correspondents replied that armed conflict was the key type of event they covered, 26.6 per cent replied diplomacy, and 17.4 per cent replied economics. Religion was unlisted. While domestic matters inside a state are sometimes the subject of foreign news reporting, including politics, economics and crime, matters which only occasionally make even the domestic media – including religion – are rarely covered by foreign correspondents working there. There is even little research on religion as a subject of international news (Silk, 2000), most research on religion having been carried out in the domestic context (Abelman and Hoover, 1990; Ferre, 1980; Garrett Medill, 1999; Hoover, 1998). To be true, in the age of television, religion news has found a place in international news flows, notably where religion becomes linked to international or domestic conflict such as the al-Qaida attack on the World Trade Center on September 11 2001, the seizure of the US embassy by Muslim students in Tehran 1979–80, the mass suicide of David Koresh and the Davidian sect in Waco, Texas, and the assassination of Israeli Prime Minister Rabin. Yet, most religion news rarely fits headline-breaking international news but instead comprises internal church developments, resulting in religion being covered in foreign news rarely or, at best, infrequently.

The growth of Israel as a foreign media capital

Israel had the tenth largest foreign press corps in the world in the mid-1990s (Cohen, 1995), a position she is estimated to also possess today. The foreign press corps in Israel has shown a gradual growth over the years since 1967 and the dramatic Six Day War in which Israel trebled its territory and captured the West Bank, Gaza and the Sinai Desert. The number of foreign news organisations represented in Israel full-time or part-time increased from 32 journalists in 1957 (the first year when records were kept in the form of the membership list of the Foreign Press Association of Israel, established a year earlier) to over 400 in 2010, which was a slight reduction from the turn of the millennium, both as a result of fewer dramatic newsworthy developments and as foreign publics have tired of the seemingly never-ending Israeli–Arab dispute.

Even before the 1967 war the foreign press corps was not inconsiderable in size. But while many foreign news organisations today are represented with full-time staff posted to Israel for a number of years from abroad, prior to 1967 these organisations were either unrepresented or had part-time local stringers. Only the *New York Times* and Agence France Presse had then full-time staffers from abroad. Even Reuters and AP got by each with a local Israeli representative. The 1947 war of independence and the creation of the state was an important post-Second World War news story, coming so soon after the Holocaust. The interest continued as the infant Jewish state grappled with the economic and social problems and tasks of early statehood. The 1956 Suez war generated wide interest particularly in the US, Britain and France. The Eichmann trial brought many correspondents to cover the trial. But in each case, foreign news organisations which sent correspondents from abroad pulled out afterwards, leaving only local Israelis on a contract, non-full-time basis. After the 1967 war – the fast-changing drama of which fitted so closely to the media clock – a succession of events, mostly related to the Arab–Israeli conflict, provided 'periodic justification' to foreign editors abroad to maintain a staff presence in Israel.

Since the post-1967 war period, Israel has been highly covered in the US media. Examining network coverage of foreign countries on the early weeknight television news on the ABC and CBS networks 1972–81, Larson found that Israel was the second most cited foreign country (Larson, 1984). In

1977–81 the three US television networks (ABC, CBS and NBC) gave the Middle East 32.4 per cent of foreign newstime compared to West Europe (21.1 per cent), East Europe (10.8 per cent), Asia (9.5 per cent) and Latin America (6.2 per cent). It was an increase over 1972–76 when the Middle East received 19.2 per cent, Asia 32.4 per cent and West Europe 28.3 per cent (Weaver, Porter and Evans, 1984). The Middle East and Israel received 9.4 per cent in the US press in 1970 (Gerbner and Marvanyi, 1977). A study of foreign news coverage by the *New York Times* in the first half of 1979 found that Israel was the most covered country (Hopple, 1977).

Factors for foreign media interest in the Holyland

The potential for foreign news from the Holyland originates in the connections which Judaism, Christianity and Islam have with the Holyland. Given the Jewish connections to the Holyland – the Biblical era of the land of Canaan, early Jewish statehood extended from the thirteenth century BCE to 70 CE including the first and second Temple periods – there are filial ties among Jews in the Diaspora for the Holyland. Even after the Roman capture in 70 CE, dispersed Jewish communities continued to look towards Jerusalem as the focus of prayer, and aspired to a return of Jewish statehood albeit, in part, as a solution to anti-Semitism. Both after the Jewish state was established in 1948, and the reunification of Jerusalem in the 1967 war including the holy places like the Temple Mount and the Western Wall, these ties have strengthened yet further today, with the consequential interest of Jews in the Diaspora for news from Israel.

Christianity had its origins in Bethlehem, Nazareth and Jerusalem. According to Christian belief, Jesus was born in Bethlehem, spent most of his life in Nazareth, and was crucified in Jerusalem. Haram al Sharif ('The Noble Shrine', otherwise known as the Temple Mount) is one of the three *kiblehs* in Islam to which Muslims direct their prayer. It was from Haram al Sharif that, according to Muslim tradition, Mohammed ascended to Allah to receive the tenets of Islam.

Given the competition in the Holyland for control over holy sites the conflict element also possesses a religion news dimension. Indeed, a string of events and developments both single religious, like secular–religious tensions within the Jewish population, and mixed religious tensions like Christian–Muslim, Jewish–Muslim, and intra-Christian tensions have drawn foreign media interest. Most notable of the 'mixed religious' conflict spots are the Jewish–Muslim conflict over Temple Mount/Haram al Sharif, and Christian–Muslim tension regarding the status of Christian property in areas controlled by the Palestinian Authority, and Muslim attempts to build a mosque on the site of the Church of the Annunciation in Nazareth. Intra-Christian tensions are reflected in the tension between different Christian communities for control of the Church of the Holy Sepulchre in Jerusalem where Jesus was buried. Within the Jewish state, there is, albeit limited, religion news interest among the foreign media in subjects like the religious political parties which have made up Israel's coalition-style of government since the state's inception 50 years ago, and in secular–religious tensions over Sabbath public observance. Other issues which are covered widely in the Israeli media like the recruitment of ultra-Orthodox students to the Army, and budgeting of *yeshivot* (academies of higher religious learning), draw very little interest among the foreign media.

There is a need to define religion news in foreign affairs. Buddenbaum, examining religion in American television nightly news, defined the entire Arab–Jewish conflict as a Muslim–Jewish religious struggle (Buddenbaum, 1990). The Israeli–Palestinian struggle for control of Judea and Samaria is a subject of foreign news. Yigal Amir said that he murdered Rabin in order to stop the handover of the Biblical Promised Land to non-Jewish control. A narrower definition of religion news is required given that the Buddenbaum definition is too all-embracing, and does not enable a clearer differentiation between religion news on the one hand and political news, economic news, and defence news on the other. Hoover has argued that something is religious if it is essentially religious (Hoover, 1998). Accordingly, if the major element of the particular news story appears religious, it would be defined as a religion news story.

A content analysis was carried out by the author of reporting from 1968 to 1988 by the Israel bureau of the Associated Press, one of the largest international news agencies which provides coverage of international and American news to most of the world's media. Only an average annually of 6 per cent of reporting was taken up with religion; the Arab–Israeli conflict and peace process accounted for 60 per cent of total coverage in an average year.

In order to generate data about religion as a category in foreign news reporting from the Jewish State, foreign correspondents (160 respondents) were surveyed by the author concerning determinants of news interest in the Holyland.

'The Holyland' as a factor was considerably lower than, for example, war and terrorism. Only 21 per cent of foreign correspondents surveyed rated the Holyland as a very important factor to explain news interest in Israel in contrast to 78 per cent and 70 per cent of respondents who said terrorism and war respectively are very important factors, and 39 per cent who said that Arab states' challenges to Israel were 'very important'. A further 40 per cent of correspondents said that the Holyland was a somewhat important variable to explain news interest. The Holyland as a factor to explain news interest was also higher for US media correspondents (67 per cent very important and 17 per cent somewhat important) where religious belief and behaviour is more prominent than West European correspondents (13 per cent very important and 67 per cent as somewhat important) where religious belief and practice has declined in recent years.

News interest in the Holyland may also be measured in terms of religious affiliation of news audiences: 17 per cent and 41 per cent of foreign correspondents said that Christian audience interest was very important and somewhat important respectively; 9 per cent and 42 per cent said that Jewish audience interest was very important and somewhat important respectively; 3 per cent and 27 per cent said that Muslim audience interest is very important or somewhat important respectively. A related question was whether foreign correspondents of Jewish background have a special interest in Israeli news, but only 23 per cent and 33 per cent of correspondents said that this was very important or somewhat important respectively.

The Holyland as a factor to explain the news interest was also higher for US media correspondents (67 per cent very important and 17 per cent somewhat important) than West European media correspondents (13 per cent very important and 67 per cent somewhat important). It reflects the higher level of religious practice among Christian believers in the US today and a declining trend in West Europe. Similarly, Christian audience interest as a factor for news interest was higher among the US media correspondents (39 per cent very important and 33 per cent somewhat important) than the West European media correspondents (20 per cent and 30 per cent very important and somewhat important).

The closer audiences feel to Israel, the greater will be the news interest in the country. Hester (1971) and Zaharopoulos (1990) argued that news interest could be conceptualised in terms of cultural proximity. Audiences are interested in things which are proximate whether in terms of geography, politics and economics or in such other terms as religious terms. Eighty per cent of the foreign press corps comes from the Western Christian world. Broken down by geographical region, Israel is the fifth most important country for the North American media in terms of the most preferred foreign countries to which they post their foreign correspondents, and tenth for West European media (Cohen, 1995). Even though Christianity is a dominant faith in Africa and Latin America, the priority, however, of the media in these two continents, as reflected in the networks of their foreign correspondents, is to cover from within their own region.

Some have seen a connection with the Judeo–Christian tradition as the basis of that interest and a seemingly excessive news interest in Israel in contrast to other countries. Thomas Friedman, a Pulitzer prize-winner and former *New York Times* bureau chief in Israel and Lebanon respectively, has argued that Christian audiences are particularly interested in news from Israel because Christianity originated there. In emphasising Christianity's place in explaining Israel's international newsworthiness, it nevertheless is important to note that while the Friedman thesis may explain the interest which Israel generates in Christian countries in West Europe and North America, it fails to reflect the fact that prior to the dramatic 1967 Six Day War Israel appeared far less on the foreign news pages and had far fewer foreign correspondents – 150, nearly all of whom were local, part-time Israelis who worked in the local Israeli media. Rather, the Judeo–Christian connection as a factor influencing foreign news needs to be redefined in terms of latent and actual news interest. The Judeo–Christian connection contributes to creating the intrinsic or potential news interest in the Israeli–Palestinian conflict but this only became actualised by the blood and drama. For example, foreign coverage of the annual Christmas celebrations from Bethlehem is usually tied to the Israeli–Palestinian conflict.

The early 1990s witnessed a change in the make-up of the foreign press corps with the arrival of correspondents from Arab countries, or the appointment in Israel or the Palestinian territories of journalists representing news organisations there. About 50 news organisations from Arab countries have correspondents. These include today Al Jazeera, MNBC, Abu Dhabi television, Jordan television, Nile Delta television, ART television and Al Arabiya television from Dubai. Prior to the 1990s, the only Arab news organisation represented was *Al Ahram*, the Egyptian daily. It reflects the Islamic religious cultural ties to Palestine. While the growth in Arab media reflects, in part, the Israeli–Palestinian 1993 Oslo Agreement, and the consequential lessening of the Arab embargo upon Israel, it reflects even more the information revolution within the Arab world, and in particular the rise of independent television stations like Al Jazeera, which created demand for coverage from Israel and the Palestinian-controlled areas. The status of the Haram al-Sharif generates acute news interest among Arab audiences. A few of the stations, such as ART from Saudi Arabia, broadcast from there the Friday prayers and each night during the month of Ramadan for the service at nightfall. Interest comes to a climax on the last Friday or the 27th of Ramadan when, according to Muslim tradition, Muhammed ascended to Allah to receive the tenets of Islam.

'Three Holylands'

While the overview picture of the Holyland may suggest a country holy to members of the three monotheistic faiths, a closer examination of audience patterns shows that the Holyland means something different to each audience abroad – Christian, Jewish, Muslim – with each faith group selecting news which is religiously proximate or relevant to its version of the Holyland. This is most noticeable in discussing a sub-set in the foreign press corps of foreign correspondents representing religious media. These include, in the Christian media case, the Catholic News Service, Religious News Service, the KNA or Germany's Catholic News Agency; and, in the Jewish case, the Jewish Telegraphic Agency. Each of these media focus solely upon religion news concerning their own religion or from their viewpoint; given that, although the more religious, the audience are also more interested in religion news, the interest is limited singly and wholly to the religion of the audience. Indeed, those reading their own religion's media are inclined to be religious and are generally closely identified with one's faith.

The term 'Holyland' is more appropriate in media terms to the Christian media than to the Jewish or Islamic media. Christian media follow the activities of the Christian communities in Israel and the Palestinian-controlled areas, the Christian holidays, and the status of the Christian holy places. The Jewish media perceive Israel as the Jewish homeland or 'Eretz Yisroel' with audiences less interested in religion news per se – although this is also covered, and does enrich their Jewish identity – but in the gamut of all news coming out of Israel, including defence, politics and culture. While there are no Islamic media in the foreign press corps, religious news from Moslem audiences concerns less the entire land of Palestine and more Haram al-Sharif. Arab media from religious countries like ART from Saudi Arabia cover both news concerning day by day security problems and the Islamic holy places under Israeli rule, and features about the life and history of the holy places.

Foreign correspondents' knowledge of religion

In spite of the limited news interest in religion news, correspondents said they were well informed about religion. The self-evaluations of knowledge of correspondents about Judaism and Islam was high, particularly in the former: 57 per cent of correspondents described their knowledge of Judaism as good, and 35 per cent as adequate; 10 per cent described their knowledge of Islam as good, 55 per cent as adequate, and 35 per cent as inadequate. The high self-evaluation for Judaism may be explained by the fact that two-thirds of the foreign press corps are, in fact, Israeli nationals or others, mostly Jewish immigrants, who work as foreign correspondents. They have worked as journalists for an average of 22 years, as foreign correspondents for 9.7 years, and lived in Israel for an average of 15 years. Some 57 per cent of locally-based foreign correspondents said that their knowledge of Judaism was good and 35 per cent as adequate. 30 per cent of international correspondents say today that their knowledge of Judaism is good, and 48 per cent as adequate. However, only 10 per cent rated their knowledge of Islam as good; 55 per cent said it was adequate and 35 per cent inadequate. Knowledge competence is much less an assumption among the many visiting reporters at times of crisis, when media interest in Israel is at a peak.

The Pope visits the Holyland

Pope Paul's visit to the Holyland in 2000 was the biggest religion news event in the history of the Israeli state. The visit was the climax of his many pilgrimages to mark the Millennium. The pilgrimage included not only visits to the Church of the Nativity, the Church of the Holy Sepulchre, and sites of Christian interest in Nazareth and the Galilee but also visits to sites of Israeli and Palestinian importance including the Western Wall, the Yad Vashem memorial to the six million Jews killed in the Holocaust, and the Palestinian refugee camp at Dehaishe. The divided news interest discussed above, for example, was one of the characteristics of reporting, with reporters from the Christian media, Jewish media and Arab media each emphasising those aspects of the visit relevant to their faith. Some 1,500 foreign reporters flew in, adding to the foreign correspondents permanently based in the country. The reporters included many from the US, 200 from Italy, 25 from Poland, and many particularly from Catholic countries. But notably absent were correspondents from Latin America.

It was a rare instance where official Israel and other religious organisations engaged in public relations. Israel and the Palestinians each had their own public agenda. Each of the three sides sought to influence the media image. For both the Pope and the Israeli Government the visit was of great importance for the Vatican in terms of its relations with Israel and the Jewish people. It occurred in an era of improved Catholic–Jewish relations, which had in 1994 reached the watershed when the Vatican formally recognised the Jewish state. The Israeli government built a special press centre with 200 work stations and dozens of radio booths. Five large screens broadcast the pilgrimage of the Pope. Live broadcasting enabled viewers to become 'participants' in the media event (Dayan and Katz, 1992). For the Pope it was also the climax of his spiritual pilgrimages. The Pope sought to walk a diplomatic tightrope between Israel and the Palestinians, aware of the 'play' the visit would have for the Catholic Church in the Arab world. The visit was, therefore, also an important opportunity both for the Pope and for the Palestinians in the latter's diplomatic struggle for recognition to the Palestinian refugee problem. Yet, there was a lack of information coordination within the Roman Catholic camp between the Vatican, the local Latin Patriarchate, and the Franciscan Order.

Audience interest and double standards

Has the filial attachment of the Holyland motif to audiences extended beyond being the historical cradle of Judaism and Christianity also to current events involving Israel having a felt meaning in the lives of media audiences today? Some Christian fundamentalist populations, drawing upon a literal interpretation of biblical prophecy, look to events in the Middle East today as part of the salvation which will lead to the second coming of Christ. In this sense, Buddenbaum is right in defining the entire Arab–Jewish conflict as a Muslim–Jewish religious struggle (Buddenbaum, 1990). But few correspondents in the author's survey saw any validity in this as a factor to explain news interest in Israel: Only 3 per cent and 27 per cent said that emotional fear and curiosity in the Supernatural was very important and somewhat important respectively to explain news interest in Israel.

As the ancient Holyland from where so much monotheism began Israel is seen by many as a laboratory for reconciling ethical questions. This is not limited to the Israeli case but is also true with foreign news coverage from other regions involving a democracy also appearing to use double standards. This comes to expression, for example, in questions of conduct by Israeli soldiers in the West Bank. Correspondents surveyed were asked the following two questions. Are events which show failings of the Jewish people (for example, the killing of innocent civilians by official Israeli agencies like the Israeli Army) newsworthy? Only 28 per cent thought it very important, and

38 per cent somewhat important. A separate question is whether news audiences use information about events in the Holyland to reconcile and resolve questions and dilemmas in their own personal lives. Some Christian evangelicals, drawing upon a literal interpretation of biblical prophecy, look to contemporary events in the Middle East as part of the salvation which will lead to the second coming of Christ. This was defined as 'emotional fear and curiosity in the Supernatural'. Only 3 per cent said it was very important and 27 per cent somewhat important.

Foreign news about Israel is to some extent seen by audiences as a biblical prism of right and wrong through which to 'judge' foreign news from Israel: 28 per cent and 39 per cent said that 'moral failings of the Jewish State' were very important and somewhat important respectively to explain the news interest. The Hess study on US foreign correspondents (Hess, 1996) found that 29 per cent of television reporting and 20 per cent of press reporting from Israel comprised 'human rights' reporting. Reflecting the high value accorded to human rights in West European countries, West European media correspondents gave higher ratings for the news interest in Israel to such factors or stories as Rabin's assassination and the Israeli–Palestinian peace process than the US media: 78 per cent and 22 per cent of West European media correspondents said the Rabin assassination was very important and somewhat important respectively as a news factor in contrast to 15 per cent and 35 per cent of US correspondents respectively. The Israeli–Palestinian peace process was also incrementally a little higher as a news factor for the West European media correspondents over the US media correspondents. This was also expressed in perceived moral failings of the Jewish state (for example, the deaths of Arab civilians in Israeli military operations): 29 per cent and 51 per cent of West European media correspondents said this was very important and somewhat important in contrast to 10 per cent and 35 per cent of US media correspondents respectively.

Rather, in a more general sense, the Holyland acts as a latent 'trigger' drawing general interest among Christian, Jewish and Muslim audiences abroad to other categories of foreign news emanating from Israel including Holyland news. Notwithstanding the limited interest in religion and Holyland, some explain the news interest as resulting from the Judeo–Christian tradition. Thomas Friedman, a former *New York Times* Pulitzer prize-winning bureau chief in Israel, claimed that Christian roots in the Holyland is a factor in the intensive news interest.[2] There is evidence to support the cultural-cum-religion proximity thesis: 21 per cent and 40 per cent of foreign correspondents said that the Holyland was a very important variable or somewhat important variable to explain the news interest.

Yet, the Judeo–Christian tradition in explaining Israel's international newsworthiness fails to explain why prior to the dramatic 1967 Six Day War Israel appeared far less on the foreign news pages and had far fewer foreign correspondents – 150, nearly all of whom were local, part-time Israelis who worked in the local Israeli media. And, while the wars and violence confirm

Galtung and Ruge's theory that drama was one of three major criteria determining which foreign events become defined as news and which get dropped, the pre-1967 and post-1967 experience suggests that the Judeo–Christian connection as foreign news should be redefined in terms of latent and actual news interest (Galtung & Ruge, 1965). The Judeo–Christian connection contributes to creating the intrinsic or potential news interest but this only became actualised by the blood and drama.

Holyland public diplomacy

Government and religious communities portray themselves through the foreign media. Given that international media is a primary determinant of Israel's international image, the question of the religion element in foreign media coverage is an important one. In the Jewish State's continuing struggle for international legitimacy in territory which is both the land of the Bible and which is contested by the Arab world, the religious dimension of Israel's international image is of importance.

There is a mutual lack of interest between journalists and officials in religion-related stories. Reflecting the lack of news interest in the Holyland, correspondents do not turn to official religion sources. Correspondents were asked to rate their access to official news sources on a daily, weekly, monthly and less than monthly basis. The Ministry of Religious Affairs was one of the least turned to government departments – 0 per cent daily contact, 2 per cent weekly contact, 18 per cent monthly contact, and 80 per cent less than monthly contact. By contrast, the Army Spokesman and the Foreign Ministry were most turned to: 15 per cent and 22 per cent daily contact; 22 per cent and 31 per cent weekly contact; 30 per cent and 31 per cent monthly contact; and 33 per cent and 26 per cent less than monthly contact, respectively. It not only reflected the dominance of the Arab–Israeli conflict and peace process as the major news story, but also that even in contrast to other domestic Israeli news stories – for example, the Finance Ministry and Justice Ministry – contact with the Religious Affairs Ministry was remarkably low.

The Israeli Government in its international public relations has not articulated a specific religion-related message or information programme beyond a generalised message of Jewish statehood. This is particularly surprising given the competition over religious holy sites. A lack of initiative by the Religious Affairs Ministry to generate contacts with foreign correspondents may be explained as resulting from a number of factors. Over the years there has been an in-built dilemma within Israel's official elite about projecting the Holyland. On the one hand, the Jewish state draws part of its legitimacy – and title to territory – from the fact that it is situated in the ancient Holyland, the land of the Bible. The access which the government guarantees to different faiths ensuring free access to their places of worship also builds support for the country abroad and among other faiths. On the other hand, Israeli officials are divided between building upon the Holyland motif and their desire to project Israel as a modern, democratic state. Moreover, the Holyland motif runs counter to international calls for Israel to withdraw from the biblical territories of Judea and Samaria and to calls for the creation of a Palestinian state there. This was particularly true with the Labour Party which was in power continually up to 1977, which regarded excessive usage of motifs of Holyland as weakening its policy since the 1967 war of relinquishing territory which was captured in the 1967 war for peace. Even the nationalist Likud have not translated its expansionist policy of settling the area with a specifically Holyland message, with the exception of East Jerusalem and the holy places but has rather focused upon the strategic reasons for opposing territorial withdrawal. Also, settler groups in the West Bank, possessing little faith in what they regarded as hostile Western public opinion to their case, saw little purpose in seeking out the media in their search for political legitimacy.

Furthermore, religious political parties – who generally have held the religious affairs portfolio – are hesitant to exploit for PR goals the access given to the holy places of other non-Jewish religions lest this be interpreted as theological legitimacy of other non-Jewish religions. Most of the activities of the Reform and Conservative Jewish movements, which lack formal official recognition in Israel, are directed to Jewish Diaspora media correspondents among the foreign press corps rather than the mainstream foreign correspondents.

With the exception of the Latin Patriarchate, the lack of PR initiative was mirrored among the other faiths. The Palestinian Wakf, which administers the Islamic holy places on Haram al-Sharif, focuses its media PR activities towards the Arab media; its officials believe that the Temple Mount situation is newsworthy enough so that journalists make contact with the Wakf at their own initiative. The Greek Patriarchate focused only on the Greek media. The Latin Patriarchate has a media liaison, and conducts press conferences before Easter and Christmas – which are attended by 20–40 journalists including some foreign correspondents (notably from the Italian, French, Belgian and German media) as well as Israeli and Palestinian media. Yet, given the lack of political certainty which the non-Jewish communities inevitably feel, it was surprising that the media relations were so low key.

While the peace process generated interest among the foreign media at its key junctures – the signing of the Oslo accords in 1993, Rabin's assassination, Arafat's death, and the withdrawal from Gush Katif in the Gaza Strip – foreign editors have tired of reporting about the latest twists and turns of a peace process which appears to be too slow for the media in bearing fruition. But in the unlikelihood of a solution to the Arab–Israeli conflict in the foreseeable future suggests that the foreign media coverage in the conflict will continue to draw audience interest if in the main at newsworthy junctures. Religious tensions in terms of the secular–religious Jewish divide may exacerbate as demographic trends favour an increasing birthrate among religious communities. Moreover, mixed religious tensions – Muslim–Jewish and Muslim–Christian – show no sign of ending.

One problem for Israeli officials is that that foreign audiences are inclined to understand the Jewish religion itself in Israel through the prism of conflict. The richness of the Jewish tradition in its manifold features and multi-layered value system gets narrowed and distorted. Features and values comprising conflict become projected, whereas other features and values lacking a seeming conflict dimension fail to get covered.

If until now Israeli officials have shown scepticism, about whether the Holyland motif may contribute to projecting an advanced modern democratic society, this will be increasingly untrue in the future. There is a religious revival underway abroad. This is particularly true in the case of the monotheistic religions. This includes Christian evangelism in the United States, the spread of Christian Pentecostalism in the Third World, a revival of Christian Orthodoxy in the former Communist countries of east Europe, the spread of Islam, even the growth of Islam and Christianity in China. In such a post-modern world, Israeli officialdom should recognise the potential role of religion in nation-state image building. Yet, no less important than such a recognition is the question of how the application of religion in public diplomacy should be achieved. If Islamic Jihad and Osama Bin Laden are perceived in the West – the target audiences for Israel's public diplomatic efforts – as the antipathy of enlightened religion, Israeli officials should focus, amongst others, upon biblical themes concerning the biblical land of Israel, archaeology, religious tolerance and interfaith dialogue.

Conclusion

Despite the hypothesis that the Holyland is newsworthy, a mutual consensus between journalists and officials exists about the low news value of religion. Yet even though the Holyland figures low in journalists' news priorities, there have been a string of events and developments both single religious, like secular–religious tensions within the Jewish population, and mixed religious tensions like Christian–Muslim and Jewish–Muslim. Moreover, the Holyland acts as a latent 'trigger' drawing general interest among Christian, Jewish and Muslim audiences abroad to other categories of foreign news emanating from Israel. The unlikelihood of a solution to the Arab–Israeli conflict in the foreseeable future suggests that the foreign media coverage in the conflict will continue to draw audience interest. Religious tensions in terms of the secular–religious Jewish divide may exacerbate as demographic trends favour an increasing birthrate among religious communities. Moreover, mixed religious tensions – Muslim–Jewish and Muslim–Christian – show no sign of ending. Furthermore, in the event of future Israeli governments becoming more proactive in integrating the Holyland motif into the country's public diplomacy, this will be expressed in foreign media coverage from the Holyland.

Bibliography

Abelman, R. and Hoover, S. (1990) 'Religious Television: Controversies and Conclusions', Norwood, NJ: Ablex.

Buddenbaum, J. (1990) 'Network News Coverage of Religion', in J. Ferre (ed), *Channels of Belief: Religion and American Commercial Television*. Ames, IA: Iowa State University Press.

Cohen, Y. (1995) 'Foreign Press Corps as an Indicators of International News Interest', *Gazette,* 56, 2.

Dayan, D. and Katz, E. (1992) 'Media Events: The Live Broadcasting of History', Cambridge, MA: Harvard University Press.

Ferre, J. (1980) (ed) 'Channels of Belief: Religion and American Commercial Television', Ames, IA: Iowa State University Press.

Galtung, J. and Ruge, M. (1965) 'The Structure of Foreign News', in *International Journal of Peace Research*, 1.

Garrett-Medill Center for Religion and the News Media (1999) *Media Coverage of Religion, Spirituality, and Values.* Evanston, IL: Northwestern University.

Gerbner, G. and Marvanyi, G. (1977) 'The Many Worlds of the World's Press', *Journal of Communication,* 27.

Hess, S. (1996) *International News and Foreign Correspondents.* Washington, DC: Brookings.

Hoover, S. (1998) *Religion in the News.* Thousand Oaks, CA: Sage.

Hester, A. (1971) 'An Analysis of News Flow from Developed and Developing Nations', *Gazette,* 7.

Hopple, G. W. (1977) 'International News Coverage in Two Elite Newspapers', *Journal of Communication,* 32, 61–74.

Larson, J. (1984) *Television's Window on the World.* Norwood, NJ: Ablex.

Silk, M. (2000) *Religion on the International News Agenda.* Hartford, C. T.: Leonard E. Greenberg Center for the Study of Religion, Trinity College.

Weaver, J. W., Porter, J. and Evans, E. (1984) 'Patterns in Foreign News Coverage on US Network TV: A Ten Year Analysis', *Journalism Quarterly,* 61.

Zaharopoulos, T. (1990) 'Cultural Proximity in International News Coverage: 1988 US Presidential Election in the Greek Press', *Journalism Quarterly,* 67.

Part 4
Conclusion

13 Judaism in the information age

> The voice of the Lord reverberates with power. The voice of the Lord reverberates with majesty ... The voice of the Lord strips forests bare. But in his Temple, All proclaim 'Glory'.
>
> (Book of Psalms 29)

If religion in traditional societies was based upon authority vested in religious bodies, in complex industrial societies there is increased emphasis upon personal choice in moral and religious matters with religious and spiritual issues increasingly mediated through print and electronic technologies. Mass media has, in effect, become a secondary causal agent of contemporary religious identity. While some people unaffiliated with a religious community might use these means, the extent to which traditional media like the press, radio and television, in practice impacted upon religious identity remains unclear. Internet, by providing the surfer with both religion information and enabling him to explore beyond his current religious beliefs elsewhere has a potentially greater role to play.

Rabbis and Jewish educators are beginning to come to terms with the implications of the information age, and with their own changing role.

To be true, the synagogue has for hundreds of years since the Emancipation been losing its monopoly of strengthening moral values. The clash of cultures depicted here is not surprising given that the rabbi emerges from a conservative culture representing established traditions and religious structures, and is confronted with accelerated cultural change exemplified by the media. But this in no way diminishes the challenge and task for rabbis.

Yet, the changed media-religion landscape is not as dramatic as it appears for two reasons. First, much of the media does not comprise religious content or affect, positively or negatively, religious identity. Judaism is infrequently at the forefront of the media's attention span. Second, the Torah and Jewish religious law offer ethical values for media conduct. Common ground between the journalistic and rabbinical roles is evident. After all the Torah not only praised its heroes but also criticised them, reflecting the long tradition of freedom of expression by the prophets speaking out against wrongdoings of the leadership and the people, suggesting that the media today – in their watchdog role, including struggling for the public right to know – are latter day rabbis.

Future trends in media and religion in Israel

Predicting the future may be the stuff of prophets, horoscopes and fools, but trends in media and religion in Israel offer certain clues for the media–religion nexus in the coming years and decades. These may be examined in terms of, firstly, trends in religious belief among the Israeli Jewish population; secondly, trends in media structures; thirdly, the impact of Jewish ethics on reporting and advertising; and, fourthly, the impact of media upon religious identity within the secular–traditional Israeli public; the Haredim; the modern Orthodox; and Diaspora Jewry. Notwithstanding the special characteristics of the Israeli and Jewish cases, the sub-discipline of Media, Judaism and Culture offers clues for understanding media and religion. And these trends suggest questions for academic researchers of the sub-discipline.

Religious trends

There is a growing religiosity in Israel which is parallel to worldwide trends regarding religious belief. They challenge the secularisation thesis of the nineteenth century advanced by Durkheim, Marx, Weber and Freud, according to which religion has been dying with the emergence of industrial society. Norris and Inglehart argue that if there is a decline in religious behaviour in Western society – notably Europe – there is also a counter trend overall in the world towards religious observance (Norris and Inglehart, 2004).

The 2009 social survey of Israel's Central Bureau of Statistics (7,500 respondents) on religious belief among the Israeli population confirmed the trend towards religious observance (Central Bureau of Statistics, 2009). Forty-two per cent of Israeli Jews defined themselves as secular, and the remaining 58 per cent of Israeli Jews in varying terms of religiosity: 8 per cent defined themselves as Haredi, 12 per cent *dati leumi* or modern Orthodox, 13 per cent as religious–traditional, 25 per cent traditional–not so religiously observant. In terms of adherence to religious tradition, there is an undisputed pattern towards observance. Twenty-five per cent of Israeli Jews said that they adhered to tradition 'to a very great extent', 38 per cent 'to a great extent', and 31 per cent 'to a little extent'. Only 6 per cent replied not at all. Eighty-six per cent of those who said they were secular observed some level of tradition; only 14 per cent of secular observed no tradition at all.

Twenty-one per cent of the Israeli Jewish population said that they were more observant today than in the past, in contrast to 14 per cent who said that they were less observant today than in the past. The number of Israeli Jews describing themselves as Haredi was greater among the younger population: 14 per cent of those aged 20–29 defined themselves as Haredi in contrast to only 2 per cent of those aged 65 and above. A future decline in the number of secular Israelis was suggested: 38 per cent of those aged 20–29 defined themselves as secular in contrast to 43 per cent aged above 65. No change in the modern Orthodox or traditional sectors was found.

Despite attempts by the Ben Gurion governments of the 1950s and 1960s to create a new secular Israel, the opposite occurred. Gellner argues that fundamentalism in the world, including Jewish fundamentalism, portraying itself as a return to past tradition, is, in fact, a reconstruction of its traditional image (Gellner, 1992). Norris and Inglehart (2004) argue that rather than sounding the death knell on secularisation theory, religious trends should be redefined: the Israeli Jewish case is similar to other societies which are threatened externally.

The general public, as well as the modern Orthodox public, are not static populations. While Israel has witnessed the growing bloc of traditional non-strictly religious, so also has there been movement from the traditional bloc to the modern Orthodox. And, in one sense, these replace those in the modern Orthodox who have moved to the stricter *hardal* sub-sector.

But the Haredim also may be expected to show movement in the other direction, as some move to the edge of the cultural ghetto, maintaining one foot outside, enjoying a higher economic standard, and the other foot entrenched in the Haredi-like style of life, involving, for example, the yeshiva remaining a focus of their life.

Media structures

Against the background of a return to religion is a thirst for religion-related information. But information about religion will be influenced by the media outlets used by the Israeli public, the level of news interest in religion, and future styles of newsgathering and editing. Media technological change – whether affecting traditional media forms like newspapers, radio and television or the new media – will impact upon the way religion is reported.

A related factor is the level of public credibility in media structures. The low level of public credibility in the media shows little sign of change. This is particularly true among religious communities. Rabbis from the Haredi and modern Orthodox contribute to delegitimising the media – resulting, in turn, in a reduction of the public's faith in democracy as a model for Israeli society. Estranged, the modern Orthodox and the Haredim have each formed their own separate media.

While in the past the modern Orthodox found their needs satisfied by the mainstream general media, this became less true, with events like the Gush Katif withdrawal alienating them from mainstream Israeli institutions. They are now mostly exposed to the new media within the modern Orthodox stream and have a low level of confidence in the mainstream media. And this distancing will only strengthen their sense of separate group identity.

Demographic patterns in both the modern Orthodox and Haredi communities suggest a healthy future for the sectoral media. The modern Orthodox is more of a 'drifting' population towards, on the one hand, the less rigidly observant stream and, on the other hand, the stricter *hardal* substream. In the case of the latter, they have their own sectoral media needs. More generally, professional journalism training for journalists in both the Haredi and modern Orthodox sectors will contribute to raising the quality of the media – creating a domino-type momentum of competitiveness for the eye and ear of the religious media consumer.

The trends towards religiosity suggest an increase in religion news interest among Israelis. A growing number of traditional Jews – either secular or non-strictly religious – produce greater audience interest in religion among the secular media. This contrasts, for example, with the decline of religion interest in Western Europe. Moreover, unresolved tensions between the secular and ultra-Orthodox suggest that religion will remain on the news agenda. Furthermore, the Jewish religion's focus upon religious ceremony – as distinct from religious doctrine – is, by nature, more newsworthy than abstract, theological discussions. It should be noted that religion news remains singly Jewish, given the Arab–Jewish gap, with no news interest in Islam, apart from its potential threat.

Secular–religious relations in Israel are likely to continue to be defined, in part, by how the respective media – secular media and religious media – each define the issues: the secular media from a secular viewpoint of the separation of synagogue and state, and the religious media, particularly the Haredi media, seeing the Torah as the prime mover or criterion whether in private or public life. Moreover, the media of each side continue to be a prism through which each community looks at the other.

Yet, diplomatic and military issues concerning the as-yet-unresolved Arab–Israeli conflict are likely to dominate the media's attention, turning attention away from other subjects, including religion. To be true, unlimited space – which characterises the Internet, as distinct from traditional media like press, radio and television – means that the space religion receives will no longer be determined by the Arab–Israeli conflict in the case of new media.

Ethical constraints

The traditional distinction in the media profession between reporting fact and expressing opinion has become less clearly delineated in the age of the electronic media. Blogging makes this even truer. Background and context enter reporting more than when fact and opinion were distinctly separate, and stereotyping and opinions are likely to characterise reporting even more than in the past. Ethical standards in the general media concerning privacy are in accord with the contemporary standards of reporting in democratic countries. The proactive social agenda of Reform Judaism offers hope that it will continue to speak out on media ethical issues, providing an important role for Judaism in contemporary media ethics.

The extent to which Judaism is a source of inspiration for ethical media conduct remains limited. For the Orthodox, Judaism shows a rigidity of the

613 positive and negative commands with seemingly little relevance to the modern conduct of mass media. To be true, Jewish teachings against gossip, the right to privacy and standards in accuracy and advertising appear to have influenced Western standards on the subject. However, in a sense, it is only in the religious media that Jewish ethics can be seen as such in newspaper reporting and in advertising. Inside the religious media, notably the Haredi media, rabbis are unquestionable moral leaders, and the rabbis remain as icons of perfection and a not-to-be-challenged spirituality. Issues like the broadcasting of pornography on cable or broadcasting on the Sabbath remain subjects of controversy.

The media and religious identity

Religious identity will be influenced by both technology and by rabbis being PR savvy. Regarding information technology, it is too early to evaluate the full implications upon religious identity. This is particularly true in the case of the modern Orthodox, who willingly embrace information technology – notwithstanding the application of pedagogic filtering of their children's exposure to it (Green, 1997).

The Haredi encounter with improved economic standards of living has itself created an identity crisis. Even if the Haredi leadership today recognises that the cultural ghetto of old requires certain modification – incorporating new economic styles, and Haredim going to work – the changes challenge the essence of cultural isolationism that characterises Haredim. It is no wonder that Haredi rabbis have warred with independent commercial Haredi news media – Haredi print, radio and Internet.

For the Haredim, the invention of the Internet poses myriad dilemmas. Rabbinical attempts to place a wall between it and the Haredim have not achieved their rabbis' goal. The Internet not only exposes some Haredim to undesirable matter but threatens the very essence of the Haredi lifestyle as a cultural ghetto. It widens the marketplace of religious ideas, weakens rabbinical hierarchies, and threatens religious loyalties. So, on the one hand, religious leaders raise concerns that the Internet provides access to undesirable sites such as pornography, not dissimilar from the dire concern in the fifteenth century of the Catholic Church to the danger which the development of printing posed (Eisenstein, 1983). However, on the other hand, they are well aware that the Internet also has the potential for providing access to Torah and other Jewish educational software. Beyond narrow religious sites, the Internet also has other sites of a broader Jewish affiliation, including community news, Israel news, Jewish dating and genealogy (Romm, 1998). This is particularly the case for those non-strictly religious, who do not frequent the synagogue or yeshiva regularly. Modern graphical design is more fetching and attractive than the conservative style of religious literature.

The role of the media as a primary agent of identity for traditional Jews who are non-strictly religious may be expected to continue. The implications are that this form of religious identity is a 'diluted' or 'mediated' form – a Judaism-of-sorts, defined as newsworthy by the medium – which is far from the original theology. Further, while Judaism – notwithstanding benefiting from the joys of the physical world – seeks to elevate individual human behaviour to a higher moral level to serve God, Western society including the media draws upon the market values of personal desire and fulfillment.

The media agenda setting also reflects the discourse – indeed, the 'agenda' of rabbis – within religious fora like the synagogue, *shiur*, synagogue bulletin, as well as the religious media, which is used by the religious affairs reporters of the general media as a source and barometer in covering the beat. Rabbis, in formulating their own messages to the media, need to take into consideration that media coverage of religion is influenced by media values.

In terms of rabbis and marketing, synagogues are recognising the value of technology, and many modern Orthodox synagogues see a website as part and parcel of the synagogue organisation. In light of the Haredi ban on the Internet, this has obviously not extended to the Haredi communities.

But rabbis have faced a deeper problem, which has existed for decades if not hundreds of years: the need to be PR savvy – such as when appearing on camera. The rabbi is trained through knowledge of the Talmud in the ability to make decisions for his flock based on Jewish law. However, with regard to homiletics, while it is part and parcel of the pulpit rabbi, little formal training in it is given to candidates for the rabbinate in Israel, and even that little has not been extended to include media relations.

The Internet also will have a continuing role to play in the Diaspora. General press and television coverage of Israel and, more precisely, the Arab–Israeli conflict generates empathy for Israel and for the Jewish people. But interest in the news from Israel, which reached a climax in the years after the 1967 Six Day War, eased off as Jewish communities became more focused inwardly but also as Israel's external image became tarnished and, for some Jews, embarrassing. Jewish identity as a factor of affinity towards Israel therefore became more important. The Jewish community press have created electronic versions and will therefore continue to provide community news and Israel-related information on a broad span of matters, not just Israel–Arab conflict news, which is provided already by the general media. More precisely, through columns about religious topics, the Jewish community media – as distinct from the national media which carry no Jewish-related content – also become agents for religious affinity. Whether Israel-related information generates religious affinity, as distinct from broad Jewish identification, is unclear, and the plethora of educational websites and Jewish community information strengthen religious affinities.

The role of media in Israeli–Diaspora relations remains one-directional, with little or no interest among Israelis regarding the Diaspora, notwithstanding that the Internet – and, in particular, Jewish Diaspora media websites – is a potentially useful source of information.

The virtual synagogue

Information technology has failed to impact upon the synagogue service in Israel. The rejection of the Orthodox and Conservative traditions to allow synagogue worship services – a primary element in contemporary Judaism – to be on-line limits the contribution of the Internet to the educational software level. An inspection of sources suggests, however, that the requirement that the quorum or *minyan* – ten men praying together in the same place, as is stated in one of the law codes, the *Shulkhan Arukh* (55) – has to be physical in nature, and not virtual, is perhaps not so clear cut. For example, one early rabbi Yehoshua Ben Levi is quoted in a minority opinion, in the Babylonian Talmud Tractate Pesachim (85b), that the relationship between God and His people is indivisible and can traverse any physical barrier – which might suggest a virtual *minyan*. Today, while a *minyan* formed on the Internet is ruled out by the Orthodox and Conservative Jewish streams, the possibilities of linking up to an existing physical *minyan* for one who cannot reach the synagogue has been raised by Conservative and a few Orthodox rabbis. But this is limited to 'passive' participation of reciting the prayers with the cantor. The possibilities for 'active' participation, notably the recitation of the mourner's *kaddish* prayer by a Jew not at the service itself, have been ruled out by those Orthodox rabbis and been conditioned by the Conservative movement on that at the very least another mourner is reciting the *kaddish* at the *minyan*.

The synagogue service is in most demand on the Sabbath and festivals. Even the prohibition on the Sabbath of turning on electricity of a computer-*minyan* live hook-up could theoretically be overcome by a time clock, used over hundreds of years by the religious for heat and light. Perhaps it is the very threat to the community structure which holds not a few rabbis back.

By contrast, the Reform and virtual communities like 'Second Life' show the potential that the Jewish information superhighway offers. Many Reform communities and a few non-affiliated ones like Beth Adam in Loveland, Ohio, offer an on-line connection. But the advantage of the virtual community in drawing in those who for whatever reason – including physical distance from the synagogue, or sickness or infirmity – cannot reach a synagogue may in the future convince some Conservative rabbis – and even perhaps a few individual Orthodox ones – to break rank.

One of the developments on the Internet is the phenomenon of on-line rabbinical counselling. The 'virtual rabbi' replies to questions of Jewish law and offers counselling. Observant Jews have for hundreds of years sought instruction from rabbis. Instruction includes the interpretation and application of Jewish legal principles of *halakhah* to modern life, and comprises questions of Jewish law (*sheiltot*). In the past the religious counselling occurred mostly with the local synagogue rabbi or rabbis in educational institutions, but at times individual Jews also sought counselling beyond their geographical vicinity from rabbis who were renowned for their knowledge in particular spheres and enjoyed wide standing among the Jewish people.

On-line rabbinic counselling, however, is a growing trend in the modern Orthodox community. Panels of rabbis – each composed of some 10–20 rabbis – exist on websites identified with the modern Orthodox. On-line counselling exists to a much lesser extent within Haredi communities, most Haredim preferring to consult with their community rabbi, reflecting a strict adherence to rabbinic authority. But long-distance counselling may also increase as e-mailing – as distinct from the Internet – is accepted by a considerable section of the Haredi population.

On-line rabbinical counselling has generated a debate among modern Orthodox rabbis about the pluses and minuses of the phenomenon. Critics say, firstly, that on-line answers proffered by rabbis are too short. Secondly, they note that when the rabbi is unacquainted with the questioner, personal circumstances cannot be taken into consideration, even though sometimes the personal circumstances of the questioner can be crucial in particular instances. Thirdly, quoting the dictum 'Make for yourself a Rabbi', of the mishnaic tome 'Ethics of the Fathers', Ashkenazi Chief Rabbi Yonah Metzger characterised the rabbi not only as being a functionary but also being a role model to emulate and identify with. One would not 'make oneself a rabbi' if one already has a virtual rabbi. Fourthly, instead of accepting the decision of the rabbi, people might be inclined to 'shop around' to different on-line rabbis to find the reply most acceptable and comfortable to them. Fifthly, the ease of on-line counselling discourages the Jew from studying the original sources in the halakhic literature. Despite the scepticism, on-line counselling is likely to increase since it offers non-affiliated Jews access to rabbis, which they would not otherwise have. On-line counselling also offers an anonymity, which the local community rabbi does not, and enables people to raise questions they perhaps would not otherwise feel comfortable doing.

MJC and the media religion discipline

The media, Judaism and culture sub-discipline (MJC) requires to be evaluated in the wider setting of contemporary research about media and religion. Whereas much research on media and religion was inclined to exclude theology as a valid object of study, the media, religion and culture school insists on the inclusion of theological perspectives in analysing media and religion (de Vries & Weber, 2001; White, 2007). The media, religion and culture school of research began in the 1970s in the US against the background of the revolution in religion broadcasting and the rise of televangelism, or televised churches. The revolution included the creation of multi-television channels including those for religious consumers. Mass media not only provided religion information but contribute to individuals' search for meaning in their personal and spiritual life. This became even truer in the Internet era as people surfed on-line religion, pulling away from institutionalised religion to create their own personal religious identity and self-construction (Roof, 1999), producing a unique synthesis of virtual religious messages and experiences.

Soukup schematised categories of the interface of communications and theology. Most of his categories also appear in research about Judaism and media. Among Soukup's categories are pastoral theology which concerns how religion is best communicated, and how communication tools are best used for this end. Another category is the study of motifs of communication in biblical texts and the analysis of biblical texts according to communication models in an attempt to develop a theological model of communication (Soukup, 2006). Each of these have parallels in Judaism suggesting that researchers of religion and media could benefit from absorbing the products of research carried out on these questions from an Israeli–Jewish perspective into the broader discipline, as well as that researchers of media, Judaism and culture could benefit from a lively inter-disciplinary approach. To the extent that the media, religion and culture school is occupied with theological images and the manner in which religion news is covered, the Jewish sub-discipline has much to offer the mother discipline – whether it is the impact of Jewish values on media functioning in Israel, or news coverage of religion, ethical dilemmas in news reporting, the rise of the religious media sector in Israel, and the absorption by religious communities of advanced media technology. To be true, there are also areas in Soukup's schema less relevant to the media, Judaism, and culture sub-discipline like self-communication, or how religions are themselves affected by the communications approach and content. But in attributing to the mass media patterns of religious behaviour, questions are raised about the circumference of the media-religion discipline. As Linderman rightly asks, "If all kinds of human activity can take on religious dimensions, then how meaningful is the concept of 'religion'?" (Linderman 2004). For this study, at least, the Israeli media's impact on religion has concerned its impact on Judaism. While history also influenced Judaism – such as the growth of prayer and the synagogue in the aftermath of the destruction of the First and Second Temple which brought an end to the sacrificial order – it is difficult to identify changes in Judaism as a result of media or communication related developments.

There are areas in media and Judaism which are not included in Soukup's schema – Diaspora ties among religious communities, foreign news concerning religion, and religious aspects of advertising and marketing. That Israel has been undergoing a religious revival makes the Israeli Jewish case study in media and religion more relevant to other researchers of media and religion.

Common characteristics between Judaism, Christianity and Islam – each monotheistic faith being based upon texts, and interpreted by their religious leaders, to name but two – cannot be ignored. Each also recognises an interdependence of responsibility and freedom, with media possessing a role to contribute towards the social good. For example, MJC and scholars of Islam and the media are a case in point. Muhammed was influenced by Judaism – partly in the vain hope of creating a religion which would attract potential Jewish converts in the area of the Arabian desert – and researchers of Islamic teaching on the media should look to Jewish sources regarding the origins of

Islamic teachings on, amongst others, the right of privacy, honour, prohibition about social gossip, and the search for truth. Indeed, Islam expanded on Jewish teaching on some teachings, including honour, and the search for truth such as in reporting or in advertising (Ayish & Sadig, 1997). By corollary, researchers of the Israeli and Jewish tradition should become acquainted with Islamic teachings on the subject.

One example of how MJC has potential benefits is the assumption among media and religion researchers that people draw their religious identity from the media in general and the Internet in particular. According to the Gutman Survey, only 17 per cent of Israeli Jews (2571 respondents) polled in 2009 surfed the Internet for material on the Bible, the Talmud and other Jewish sources. There is no evidence in the Israeli–Jewish case to support the theory that non-religious Jews look for their religious identity via the Internet. Only 5 per cent of 'non-religious but not anti-religious' surf the net 'a lot' or 'considerably' for Jewish religious information like the Talmud and Bible. Moreover, 0 per cent of 'non-religious anti-religious' said so. Just 12 per cent of 'traditional' (ie. non-strictly religious but observe varying degrees of religious ritual) said so. Rather, the religious Israeli–Jew did so. But this does not replace the traditional and superior frameworks for religious Jews like the synagogue; the media was supplementary to it. 26 per cent of modern religious or *dati leumi* Jews surfed the Internet for Jewish religious content 'a lot' or 'considerably'. The biggest group was the more intense form of modern orthodoxy Hardal; 41 per cent of Hardal did so a great deal or considerably. It is also noteworthy given the general reservations which Hardal's rabbis have about Internet. The same was true with the Haredim, where despite their rabbis' general ban on Internet, it was surfed for Jewish religious content by 20 per cent of Haredim 'a lot' or 'considerably'.

Other noteworthy features of the data are that it confirms the age gap which characterises worldwide patterns of exposure to the Internet: Surfing for Jewish religious information was done most by the 20–30 age group. Overall, there was a considerable difference between the under-fifties and over-fifties. No difference was found between male and female surfing. Noteworthy is that there was no difference in socio-economic terms between surfers from high-income, average-income, and low-income backgrounds. Another noteworthy difference was between the Sephardi or oriental Jews and the Ashkenazi or European Jews: 14 per cent of Sephardim surfed the Net for Jewish related content in contrast to less than 10 per cent of Ashkenazim.[1]

In incorporating the theology dimension, media and religion research is occupied with questions regarding the exposure to religion-related information, the effects on religious identity and the construction of religion images. But some researchers do not deal with divine communication. Some scholars argue that communication is an integral part of some religions, including Christianity (Eilers, 2006; Soukup, 2006). This challenges other scholars who, like Durkheim, are at pains not to incorporate the 'godly element' in communication research. Researchers of Haredim have had to incorporate the seemingly non-scientific variable of Haredi belief systems into their analysis. Judaism is not characterised today by direct god-like communication. Instead, since the end of the age of prophecy in the fourth century BCE, Judaism has been based on belief (*emunah*). But this in no way weakens the relevance to incorporate the 'belief' variable. The study of divine communication in media and religion studies enables analysis, for example, of media events, or collective religious experiences.

Media, Judaism and Culture: a research agenda

Aspects regarding media and religion in Israel and Judaism have received researchers' attention. These include anthropological-type inquiries about how the Haredi population relate to the media age; and audience surveys. Certain questions that have been touched on in an albeit limited way include content analysis as to how religion is reported; the production of mutual images of different religious communities, both intra-Jewish and Jewish–Arab; and religious advertising. Unresearched questions include how the modern Orthodox sector are covered; Jewish public relations; and the coverage of Islam and Christianity in the Israeli Hebrew media.

As a sub-discipline, media, Judaism and culture has much to gain by incorporating into research the fruits of other research conducted in the broader discipline of media, religion and culture. Discussing the broader question of media and religion, Mitchell (2003) suggests directions for future researchers. First, there is the need to adopt a comparative perspective. Rather than examine media and religion in a broadly American and Christian perspective, there was a need for comparison with other religions and societies, including the Jewish Israeli ones, in order to identify similarities and differences. The Israeli Jewish experience actually contrasts with the American Christian focus because in contrast to the United States, religion and the Jewish state are by nature interwoven (Don-Yihya, 1999). Little of the existing research on media and religion in Israel and Judaism takes on a comparative perspective; one exception is Campbell's study of the experiences of Jews, Christians and Muslims towards new media (Campbell, 2010).

Secondly, Mitchell emphasises the value of a historical approach in studying media and religion. In order to fully understand theological debates over the media, it is essential to ask why the church has historically held an iconoclastic approach to specific media. The growing body of research on media and religion in Israel fails to incorporate a historical perspective, and Jewish historians have mostly ignored the subject of mass media. The long history of Judaism from the early years of the Israelites and media spectacles like the Crossing of the Red Sea and the Giving of the Torah, or Decalogue, at Mount Sinai to the creation of the first and second Jewish Commonwealth in the Promised Land had important media elements – as did events in later periods in Jewish history.

The research agenda has advanced beyond such sociological questions as content analysis to the culturalist approach. True, the former remains valid – particularly in the Israeli Jewish case, given the overall paucity of research in media and religion. Indeed, Jewish ethics and news reporting has received more attention among Jewish law scholars than by mass communications researchers. Jewish media ethics include the prohibition of gossip and the importance of sexual modesty. There is a need to extrapolate Jewish media ethics theory on violence in the media. As well, Jewish ethical conduct – both theory and practice – regarding advertising and public relations requires researchers' attention. Responsa on media ethics from the Reform and Conservative branches of Judaism are sorely lacking – particularly given the Reform movement's goals of producing a morally progressive society.

The key question of the impact of exposure to the media on religious identity – whether in Israel or in the Diaspora – has received negligible quantitative attention. The question relates to the ethics of media, concerning not only the ethics of journalistic conduct but also the ethics of audience exposure – namely what the religious person may be exposed to. The question of the ethics of audience exposure has risen in the age of the Internet with the creation of virtual communities, with, however, a greater onus of responsibility on the participant.

A question related to identity concerns the application of media and public relations for theological tasks of strengthening religious identity, such as Habad's pro-activism, synagogue bulletins, and Haredi wall posters, as well as professional training for rabbis, which – in contrast to Christian training in public relations – has received only spasmodic research attention.

The media play different roles in strengthening the Jewish identity of the religious, as distinct from the traditional, i.e., non-strictly religious. In the case of the former, while the synagogue, religious education and the rabbinical hierarchy play an important role of providing the 'envelope' of identity, media patterns both provide information and, in the case of religious programming on television and radio, strengthen identity in a meaningful manner. In the age of new media, there are educational and Torah websites. For rabbis, all this serves to correct the 'collateral' from their community's exposure to the general media.

For the traditional, who lack regular contact with the synagogue or rabbis, it is postulated that the general media today have become important sources of religion and agents of religious identity. This is especially true in the American context. The general media's criteria in coverage – an emphasis on appeal, drives, social acceptance – differ from religious criteria like spirituality and self-improvement. Moreover, in the Diaspora, where Judaism is a minority faith which fails to get reflected in the American media culture, the media there does not reflect particularly Jewish motifs. The media's contribution, therefore, to strengthening the religious identity of traditional Jews is even less. To be true, Jewish community newspapers and Jewish websites on the Internet do have expressly Jewish motifs. Moreover, the broad religion-related values, even if communicated in Christian terms, have certain similarity to values also found in Judaism. Researchers need to examine the implications for religious identity of those non-strictly religious Jews exposed to media stimuli rather than traditional religious stimuli.

This is because the gap between media criteria and traditional religious criteria is less than a first impression suggests. The religion coverage in the general media in Israel is an echo of the dynamic debates among rabbis, educators and others within the religious communities. These debates get reported and discussed in the Haredi and modern Orthodox media – which are read by the religion reporters of the general media. The debate also continues in the synagogue bulletins, sponsored by different religious bodies like *yeshivot*. Judaism, with only seven million Jews in Israel and a not dissimilar amount in the Diaspora, is a small and interconnected entity so that while it is true that secular media contribute to the traditional and even secular Jew's religious identity, the weighting of religion in the media–religion nexus is low.

The challenge in Media, Judaism and Culture becoming an established research sub-discipline is to weave the manifold conclusions from research about media content, media effects, and advertising and public relations into a single coherent Jewish approach. This will embrace both the latitudes of Jewish law teaching about mass media – seeking a synthesis between how different streams in Judaism look at questions relating to religion and media. It will also take notice of media-related questions over the centuries, starting from the period of the patriarchs to the current day.

If the differences between Jewish religious streams, as discussed in this book, appear wide, a focus on the principles in Judaism suggests that there is greater consensus than might otherwise appear. For example, while sexual modesty and the media is the subject of wide interpretation and gets expression in different ways, in practice in media and advertising, there is broad consensus of its importance among religious streams. A unified media–Judaism theory – extrapolated from the sub-discipline of media, Judaism and culture – will also bring out points of similarity and difference with other faiths. In doing so, individual human behaviour will be elevated to a higher moral level to serve God, by communicating that Man was made in his image, with the purpose on earth of communicating his *Torah* message from a heavenly Jerusalem.

References

Ayish, M. I. & Sadig, H. B. (1997) "The Arab-Islamic Heritage in Communication Ethics" in C Christians & M Traber (eds) *Communication Ethics & Universal Values*, Thousand Oaks: Sage.

Campbell, H. (2010) *When Religion Meets New Media*. New York and London: Routledge.

Central Bureau of Statistics. (2009) Social Survey. Jerusalem: Central Bureau of Statistics.

de Vries, H. & Weber, S. (2001) *Religion & the Media*, Stanford: Stanford University Press.

Don-Yihya, E. (1999) *Religion and Political Accommodation in Israel*. Jerusalem: Floersheimer Institute for Policy Studies.

Eilers, F-J. (2006) 'Social Communication in Christian Perspective: Some Points for Reflection', in F-J Eilers (ed) *Social Communication in Religious Traditions of Asia*, Manila: Logos (Divine Word) Publications (2006)

Eisenstein, E. (1983) *The Printing Revolution in Early Modern Europe.* Cambridge: Cambridge University Press.

Gellner, E. (1992) *Postmodernism, Reason and Religion.* London: Routledge.

Green, I. (1997) *Judaism on the Web.* New York: MIS Press.

Linderman, A. G. (2004) 'Approaches to the Study of Religion in the Media', in P. Antes, A. W. Geertz and R. R. Warne (eds), *New Approaches to the Study of Religion, Volume 2: Textual, Comparative, Sociological and Cognitive Approaches.* Berlin and New York: Walter de Gruyter.

Mitchell, J. (2003) 'Emerging Conversations in the Study of Media, Religion and Culture', in J. Mitchell and S. Marriage (eds), *Mediating Religion.* London and New York: T. and T. Clark.

Norris, P. and Inglehart, R. (2004) *Sacred and Secular: Religion and Politics Worldwide.* Cambridge: Cambridge University Press.

Romm, D. (1998) *The Jewish Guide to the Internet.* Northvale, NJ: Jason Aronson.

Roof, W. C. (1999) *Spiritual marketplace: Baby boomers and the remaking of American religion*, Princeton: Princeton University Press.

Soukup, P. (2006) "Recent work in communication and theology", *Cross Connections*, Rome: Editrice Pontificia Universita Gregoriana.

White, R. A. (2007) The Media, Culture, and Religion Perspective, *Communication Research Trends*, 26: 1.

Notes

1 Media, Judaism and Culture

1 Marshall McLuhan, *The Medium and the Light: Reflections on Religion*. Toronto: Stoddart, 1999, p. 208.
2 *Maariv*, 23.9.1999.

2 The Jewish Theory of Communication

1 *Yediot Aharonot*, 4.7.2005.
2 Correspondence between Rabbi Sherlo and the author.
3 Correspondence between Rabbis Arusi and Yosef and the author.

3 Constructing religion news: the religion reporter decides

1 *Kol Ha'ir*, 5.9.1993.
2 Walla website: http://b.walla.co.il/?w=//178168 [18.1.2011].
3 *Kol Hair*, 5.9.1993.
4 Yiram Netanyahu, Profile: Uri Revach, *Hatzofe*, 7.3.2008.
5 Judith Baumel-Tydor, 'Larger Than Life', *Haaretz* [English edition], 10.1.2005.
6 *Haaretz*, 11.7.1997.
7 Yigal Mosuko 'Get Out', Seven Days *Yediot Aharonot Aharanot*, 2.4.1999
8 Anat Baliant, 'The Deri Way in the Media', *Ayin Sheviit*, 18, May 1999.
9 Ibid.
10 Judy Siegal-Itzkovich, 'Spying Out the Land', The *Jerusalem Post*, Jubilee Supplement, 1.12. 1982.
11 *Bamachane*, 22.12.2000.
12 *Kol Hair*, 10.7.1992.
13 Siegal-Itzkovich, op. cit.
14 *Haaretz*, 17.9.1997.
15 *Koteret Rashit*, 22.9.1987.
16 Itzhak Segev, 'Broadcasting Authority Representative to Beit Horon', *Nekuda*, August 2000.
17 Mosuko, op. cit.
18 Aviezer Golan, 'Noach Mozes: Editor, Achiever and Man', *Yediot Aharonot*, 8.10.1985.
19 Raheli Edelman, 'Childhood by Schocken', *Hadashot*, 22.9.1991.

4 News values, ideology and the religion story

1 *Haaretz*, 27.2.2002.
2 *Haaretz*, 3.8.2006.
3 *Maariv*, 1.11.2002.
4 *Yisrael Hayom*, 6.10.2010.
5 *Yediot Aharonot*, 16.2.2010.

6 *Mekor Rishon*, 19.2.2010.
7 Ibid.
8 Yifat Ehrlich "Best to disclosure straightaway" *Mekor Rishon*, 19.2.2010.
9 *Maariv*, 25.7.2008.
10 The author acknowledges the assistance he received from the Research Unit of The Lifshitz Religious College of Education, Jerusalem, in carrying out the survey of rabbis.
11 *Haaretz*, 21.11.1991.
12 *Kol Hair*, 5.3.1999.
13 *Kol Hair*, 22.1.1990.
14 *Kol Hair*, 28.11.1997.
15 *Hamodia* [English edition], 10.2.2006.
16 *Jerusalem Post*, 8.11.1996.
17 *Yerushalayim*, 12.12.1997.
18 *Yediot Aharonot*, 8.11.1996.
19 2009 Gutman Survey, by courtesy of the Israel Democracy Institute, Jerusalem.
20 *Jerusalem Post*, 19.6.2001.
21 *Haaretz*, 9.11.1969.
22 *Haaretz*, 5.11.1969.
23 *Haaretz* editorial, 5.11.1969.
24 *Hatzofe*, 3.11.1969.
25 *Hatzofe*, 10.11.1969.
26 2009 Gutman Survey, by courtesy of the Israel Democracy Institute, Jerusalem.
27 *Jerusalem Post*, 7.8.2001.
28 *Haaretz*, 10.7.2002.
29 *Haaretz*, 5.3.2004.

5 Mikva news

1 *Hamodia* (English edition), 13.9.2006.
2 *Hamodia* (English edition), 15.12.2003.
3 *Yated Neeman*, 1.2.2007.
4 *Yated Neeman*, 1.2.2007.
5 *Bakehilla*, 6.7.2006.
6 *Maariv*, 14.7.2006.
7 *Haaretz*, 25.1.2007.
8 *Hamodia*, 5.6.2007.
9 *Yediot Aharonot*, 10.1.1999.
10 *Yisrael Hayom*, 28.8.2008.
11 'Dear Editor, Why Doesn't Hamodia Cover Sports?', *Hamodia* (English edition], 6.12.2007.
12 Moran Cohen, 'The Attitude of the Haredi Press to Foreign News', seminar paper, School of Communication, Netanya Academic College, 2007.
13 *Hamodia* (English edition) editorial, 26.9.2004, 'Composing the Headlines'.
14 *Hamodia* (English edition), 'Ve'al Hamedinos Bo'Ye'ameir', 14.10.2005.
15 *Kol Hair*, 23.8.1991.
16 *Yated Neeman*, 7.11.1996.
17 *Hamodia* (English edition), 13.9.2006.
18 *Mishpacha*, 23.6.2005.
19 *Globus* 'Firma' supplement, March 2010.
20 *Mercaz Ha-Inyanim*, 31.7.2007.
21 *Bakehilla*, 14.11.2002.
22 Israel Katzover, 'The Kosher Press', The *Jerusalem Report*, 22.11.1990.
23 *Mishpacha*, 24.2.2011.
24 *Ayin Sheviit*, May 2001.

25 Israel Advertisers Association (1995) *Survey of Exposure to Mass Media: Haredim*, Tel Aviv.
26 *Yediot Aharonot*, 7.7.1997.
27 *Maariv*, 6.10.2006.
28 The Conservative and Reform communities in Israel number 10,000 and 5,000 paid-up members respectively (Tabory, 1998) (28 per cent did not verify which religious stream; 12 per cent comprised more than one stream).
29 *Hamodia* (English) edition, 18 and 25 October 2007.

6 Dual loyalties: the modern Orthodox dilemma

1 Yaron London, 'Religious People on the Network', *Meimad*, 16, May 1999.
2 Hanah Kleinman, 'Mekor Rishon (Second Source)', *Tzomet HaSharon*, 5.2.2004.
3 Emanuel Shiloh, 'Pen to All Matter', *Maayanei Hayeshua*, 373, 15.11.2008.
4 *BaSheva*, 4.7.2002.
5 Ibid.
6 'Insight' survey, commissioned by Techelet (potential market interest for the Techelet Channel, April 2002); Jessica Steinberg, 'Channel with a God', *Jerusalem Post*, 30.5.2003.
7 *Hatzofe*, 19.2.1999.
8 Aviva Lori, 'The Nonconformist', *Haaretz* (English edition) weekly magazine, 8.7.2005.

7 Identity, unity and discord

1 'Symposium of Religious and Secular Images in the Media', Bar-Ilan University 22.4.1999.
2 *Haaretz*, 11.12.1992.
3 Firma No. 122, March 2010, *Globus*.
4 TGI Survey, reported in *Globus*, 26.7.2005.
5 *Hamevaser*, 30.12.2012.
6 Firma, op. cit.
7 Ibid.
8 Ibid.
9 *Haaretz*, 11.6.2008.
10 *Yediot Aharonot*, 28.1.2000.
11 *Mishpacha*, 28 September 2004.
12 Smith Poll, 'Haredi Image in the Media', April 1995.
13 Ibid.
14 Ibid.
15 'Symposium of Religious and Secular Images in the Media', Bar-Ilan University, 22.4.1999.
16 It had 4,000 'virtual friends' in the first six months of its existence in 2011.

8 www.techno-Judaism

1 *Hamodia* (English edition) quoting the Associated Press news agency, 27.12.2007.
2 Dr Eli Birnbaum of the Jewish Agency, Jerusalem, in communication to the author.
3 Geotopographia survey. *Mercaz Inyanim*, 23.5.2006.
4 Shiluv marketing survey. *Mercaz Inyanim*, 10.7.2007.
5 Center for Research and Information, The Knesset, 29.4.2007.
6 Central Bureau of Statistics, *Jerusalem*, 2009.
7 Survey by Netvision Institute, Tel Aviv University, September 2005.
8 Central Bureau of Statistics, *Jerusalem*, 2007.
9 *Jewish Observer*, November 2003.
10 Benjamin Scharansky, 'The Computer as a Threat to Humanity', *Hamodia*, 24.12.1999.

11 *Hamodia*, 28.2.2007.
12 *Haaretz*, 18.12.2007.
13 *Kikar Shabbat* website, 1.2.2011.
14 *Hatzofe*, 14.12.2007.
15 *Hatzofe*, 21.12.2007.
16 *Mekor Rishon*, 1.1.2008.
17 *Hatzofe*, 28.12.2007.
18 *Hatzofe*, 14.12.2007.
19 Julian Voloj, 'Virtual Judaism: Finding a Second Life in Online Community', *Presentense Magazine*, 3, 2007.
20 *Reform Judaism*, special issue on 'Cyber-Judaism', Summer 2009.
21 Ibid.
22 'Faith Online': Pew Internet and American Life project (www.pewinternet.org), 2004.
23 Jonathan Marks, 'God, You've Got Mail', *Jewish Week*, 28.1.2000.
24 www.HadareiHaredim, 27.7.2006.
25 Debra Nussbaum Cohen, 'You Got Mechila', *Jewish Week*, 29.9.2000.
26 *Yediot Aharonot*, 12.6.2006.
27 www.shemayisroel.co.il.
28 *Jerusalem Post*, 23.3.1997.
29 *Contact*, 3(1).
30 Aviezer Frankel, 'To Turn the Rabbinical Sheiltot into a Ball: A Few Reflections on the Sheiltot Project, on the Occasion of the Israel Prize', *Hatzofe*, 30.3.2007.
31 Batsheva Pomerantz, 'Technology in the Service of Judaism', *Etrog*, 35, April 2007; 'All the Torah on One Disc', *Yediot Aharonot*, 12.10.2007.
32 Yitzhak Cohen, 'Clear Connection: Dial a Daf – Torah Phone', *Hamodia* (English edition), 13.12.2007.
33 Talya Gnetz, Religion and Media pro-seminar paper, School of Communication, Ariel University Center, 2010.
34 Mark Bleiweiss, 'In Defence of the Inaccessible', *Sh'ma*. November 1999.
35 Estimate by Dr Eli Birnbaum, Jewish Agency, to author.
36 *Contact*, 8(3).
37 *Jerusalem Post*, 17.3.1996.
38 www.kolkoren.
39 www.religions.gov.il.
40 *Yediot Aharonot*, 14.4.2008.
41 Oftra Ilani, 'This Blog Keeps the Sabbath', *Haaretz* (English edition) weekly magazine, 19.9.2008.
42 'Internet and the Religious Media', *Mekor Rishon*, 5.2.2008.
43 *Jerusalem Post* magazine, 12.9.2003.
44 Esther Kustanowitz, 'Jewish Blogging 101', in *Contact*, 8(3), Spring 2006.
45 A 2006 survey of 1,000 religious surfers of the Kipa religious website.
46 Geotopographia survey, *Haaretz*, 23.5.2006.
47 *Hadrei Haredim*, 22.1.2007.
48 Yael Mamo, 'Jewish Religious Behaviour on the Virtual Internet world'. Paper, course, 'Issues in the Psychology of Internet Surfers', Open University, 2006.
49 Yuval Sherlo, 'Questions and Answers', *Moreshet*, 23.6.2002.
50 *Yerushalayim*, 25.9.2009. *Bakehilla*, 24.9.2009.

9 Kosher advertising

1 *Haaretz*, 9.2.1994.
2 Erich Fromm, 'You and the Commercials,' transcript of broadcast on CBS Reports, 26.4.1973.

3 *Haaretz*, 9.9.2003.
4 Ibid.
5 Ibid.
6 Ibid.
7 *Jerusalem Post*, 22.3.2007.
8 *Yediot Aharonot*, 30.5.2007.
9 *Haaretz*, 13.6.1993.
10 The author is grateful to Amit Melnik and Hila Mograbi for assistance in collecting the data.
11 Waller, D., Fam., K.S. and Erdogan, B.Z. (2005) Advertising of controversial products: a cross-cultural study. *The Journal of Consumer Marketing*, 22: 1.
12 www.Be-HadreiHaredim, 26.7.2007. Eli Fisher, 'Provocation and *Tephillin* in Shape of "Mouse"'.
13 *Bakehilla*, No. 200.
14 *Yediot Aharonot*, 25.9.2000.
15 *Mercaz Ha-Inyonim*, 27.8.2000.
16 *The Marker*, 7.2.2011.
17 *Mercaz Ha-Inyonim*, 16.7.2007.
18 *Globus*, 12.11.1996.
19 *Mercaz Ha-Inyonim*, 28.1.2007.
20 *Maariv*, 6.7.1998.
21 *Mercaz Ha-Inyonim*, 19.7.2007.
22 *Globus*, 12.1.1996.
23 Yoel Zafrir, 'Not What You Expect', *Nihul*, November 2001.
24 *Bakehilla*, 3.3.2005.
25 Yehudit Gurfein, 'They Forgot Me At Home: The Community Which Disappeared in Israeli Advertising', *Otot*, January 2000 [Hebrew].
26 Ibid.

10 The marketing of the rabbi

1 Jay Michaelson, 'Marketing Undermines Judaism', *Sh'ma*, January 2004.
2 Chava Weissler, 'The Jewish Marketplace', *Sh'ma*, January 2004.
3 Jay Michaelson, 'Marketing Undermines Judaism', *Shema*, January 2004.
4 *Contact*, 6(2), Winter 2004.
5 *Yisrael Hayom*, 24.4.2011.
6 *Jerusalem Post*, 28.3.1983.
7 *Enoshim*, 30.9.1997–6.10.1997.
8 *Jerusalem Post*, 31.8.1999.
9 *Jerusalem Post*, 1.10.1999.
10 Interview by author with Rabbi Zalman Schmotkin.
11 *Hatzofe*, 28.11.1999.
12 *Shearim*, 11, Nissan 2006.
13 For a discussion of Habad and the larger Israel, see O. Tsarfaty, *Mi-Oslo Ad HaHitnutkut* [Hebrew: From Oslo to Disengagement: The Struggle for Greater Israel in the Habad Press], Tel Aviv: Tel Aviv University, 2010.
14 Yael Gavrieli, 'The Messiah – In the Professional Cadre of Advertising Project Manners of Kfar Habad', *Otot*, April 1993; *Haaretz*, 16.4.1993.
15 *Hatzofe*, 13.9.1996.
16 *Shabat V'Shabato*, 1,000, 14.2.2004.
17 For an overview of the structure of synagogue bulletins see: K. Kaplan, 'Weekly Bible Bulletins in Orthodox Jewish society in Israel', in M. Salochovsky and Y. Kaplan (eds), *Libraries & Book Collections*, Jerusalem: Zalman Shazar Center for Israel History, 2006.

18 Leora Ophir, *The Special Qualities of Weekly Synagogal Bulletins from the Communication Perspective*, Jerusalem: Emunah Academic College for Education and the Arts (seminar paper), June 2010.
19 Yotvat Weill (2008) 'The Experience Creates the Recognition' (Hebrew), *Eretz Acheret*, May–June.
20 *Haaretz* (English edition), 2.4.2007.
21 *Shabbat Shabato*, 1,000, 14.2.2004.
22 Benjamin Stern, 'Taasiyut Ha-Alonim' [Hebrew: The World of the Bulletins], *Shaa Tova*, 8.10.2010.
23 *Ba-Sheva*, 31.5.2006.

11 At bay in the Diaspora

1 See, for example, *The Public-Javnost*, journal of the European Institute for Communication and Culture, the issues of 1999 (1) and 2002 (1) devoted to Diasporic Communication.
2 Gary Rosenblatt, 'The Jewish De-Press', *Moment*, November 1977.
3 Gary Tobin, 'American Jewry and the Jewish Press', 1986.
4 Seth Lipsky, 'Abraham Cahan, the "Forward", and "Me"', *Commentary*, June 1997.
5 Jonathan Mahler, 'The End of a Newspaper: Forward Halt!', *New Republic*, 1 May 2000.
6 Gal Beckerman, 'Forward Thinking: So What If the Goyim are Looking? A Jewish Newspaper Lets It All Hang Out', *Columbia Journalism Review*, 42(5), Jan–Feb 2004, 33(4).
7 Interview with Jane Eisner, 'Voices That Must Be Heard', *The New York Media Alliance* (n. 465). 10.3.2011.
8 'In Their Own Words', *The Philadelphia Jewish Voice*, February 2009.
9 Letter to author from Geoffrey Paul, former editor of the *Jewish Chronicle*.
10 The Israel Project Survey, Luntz, Maslansky Strategic Research.
11 Sylvia Strudel, Survey of Communaute Judaique FM, Paris, July 1986.
12 Reboot, 'OMG! How Generation Y is Redefining Faith in the iPod Era', 2006.
13 The Israel Project Survey, Luntz, Maslansky Strategic Research.

12 From out of Zion shall come forth foreign news

1 Thomas Friedman, 'The Focus on Israel', *The New York Times Magazine*, 1.2.1987.
2 Ibid.

13 Judaism in the information age

1 The Gutman Survey, 2009 (2012), Courtesy of the Israel Democracy Institute, Jerusalem.

Selected bibliography

Advertising and public relations

*Jewish religious law (*halakhah*)*

Dorff, E. (1997) 'Judaism, Business and Privacy', *Business Ethics Quarterly*, 7(1).
Friedman, H. H. (1984) 'Ancient Marketing Practices: The View from Talmudic Times', *Journal of Public Policy and Marketing*, 3, Spring.
Green, R. M. (1997) 'Guiding Principles of Jewish Business Ethics', *Business Ethics Quarterly*, 7(1).
Levine, A. (1981) 'Advertising and Promotional Activities as Regulated in Jewish Law', *Journal of Halakha and Contemporary Society*, Spring), 2(5).
Pava, M. L. (1998), 'Developing a Religiously Grounded Business Ethics: A Jewish Perspective', *Business Ethics Quarterly*, 8(1).
Tamari, M. (1997), 'The Challenge of Wealth: *Business Ethics*', *Business Ethics Quarterly*, 7(1).

Religious advertising

Bakehilla. (2007), 'Ha-Pirsum HaYehudi' [Hebrew: Haredi Advertising]. Special supplement, *Bakehilla*, 200.
Gurfein, Y. (2000), 'They Forgot Me At Home: The Community Which Disappeared in Israeli Advertising', *Otot*, January.

Marketing and rabbis, synagogues

Cohen, Y. (2011) 'Rabanim V'HaTikshoret: Maarekhet Yahasim Mesukhsakhot' [Hebrew: Rabbis and the Media: A Conflictual Relationship] in M. Rachimi (ed), *Amadot* (3): *Etgarim V'Yaadim* [Hebrew: Positions (3): The Media: Challenges and Goals], Elkana and Rehovot (Israel): Orot Academic College of Education.
Hershkowitz, Z. (2008) 'Iyun Hilhakhti B-Maamud ha-Rav b'Eydan shel Media Mitkademet' [Hebrew: Jewish Law Discussion of the Social Standing of the Rabbi in the Age of Advanced Mass Communications', in T. Rashi and M. Zaft (eds), *Tikshoret V'Yahadut* [Hebrew: Media and Judaism]. Petach Tiqva: Keter HaZahav.
Shema, January 2004, theme of issue: Synagogues and Marketing.

Synagogue bulletins

Cohen, J. (2000) 'Politics, Alienations, and the Consolidation of Group Identity: The Case of Synagogue Pamphlets', *Rhetoric and Public Affairs*, 3(2).

Kaplan, K. (2006) 'Weekly Bible Bulletins in Orthodox Jewish Society in Israel', in M. Salochovsky and Y. Kaplan (eds), *Libraries and Book Collections*. Jerusalem: Zalman Shazar Center for Israel History.

Audiences and religion

Exposure of religious communities to media

Amran, M. (2006) *The Media in the Service of Ultra-Orthodox Community: The Use of Audiotapes as Indicators of Continuity and Change in the Ultra-Orthodox Community* [Hebrew], Ph.D thesis. Jerusalem: The Hebrew University.

Gabel, I. (2006) *Ha-Tzibur ha-dati leumi v'hu-Tikshoret: Yahasei ahava-sinaa* [Hebrew: The Modern Religious Community and the Media: A Love–Hate Relationship]. Tel Aviv: Herzog Institute, Tel Aviv University.

Katz, E. and Gurevitch, M. (1976) *The Secularisation of Leisure: Culture and Communication in Israel*. London, Faber.

Neriah Ben-Shahar, R. (2008) *Haredi Women and Mass Media in Israel – Exposure Patterns and Reading Strategies* [Hebrew], Ph.D thesis. Jerusalem: The Hebrew University.

Sklar, M. (1992) 'HeOrot Ukhadot Le-Yahso shel ha-Tzibbur ha-Dati le-Media' [Hebrew: Selected Comments Regarding How the Religious Sector Relates to the Media], in D. Lamish (ed), *Tikshoret V'Hinukh*. Kiryat Tiv'on: Oranim.

Religious identity

Baumel-Schwartz, J. (2009) 'Frum Surfing: Orthodox Jewish Women's Internet Forums as a Historical and Cultural Phenomenon', *Journal of Jewish Identities*, 2(1).

Goodman, Y. (2010) 'The Modern Religious Youth and the Internet', *Tzohar*, Tamuz 5770.

Israel–Diaspora relations

Ford, L. (2004) *Yesterday's News Tomorrow: Inside American Jewish Journalism*. Lincoln, NE: iUniverse.

Secular–religious relations

Centre for Jewish Information. (2000) 'Peilut Neged Haredim' [Hebrew: The Manoff Report : Violence Against Haredim]. Jerusalem: Manoff.

Heilman, S. C. (1990) 'Religion Jewry in the Secular Press: Aftermath of the 1988 Elections', in C. Liebman (ed), *Conflict and Accommodation Between Jews in Israel*. New York: Avi Foundation.

Sasson-Levi, O. (1998) *Hishtakfut Ha-Hilonim B'Itonut Ha-Haredit* [Hebrew: Secular Israelis as Reflected in the Harerdi Press]. Ramat Gan: Am Hofshi.

Ethics and Jewish law (*halakhah*)

General

Barkai, Y. and Priman, M. (2003) 'Ero'im Tikshoratiyim B'Mikra' [Hebrew: Media Events in the Bible], *Mayim Medalyo*, Research Annual of the Lifshiftz Religious Education College, Jerusalem, 15.

Cohen, Y. (2001) 'Mass Media in the Jewish Tradition', in D. Stout and J. Buddenbaum (eds), *Religion and Popular Culture: Studies on the Interaction of Worldviews*. Ames, IA: Iowa State University Press.

——(2002) 'Yahadut V'Hitnagshut' [Hebrew: Judaism and Mass Media: Convergence and Conflict], *Mayim Medalyo*, Research Annual of the Lifshitz Religious Education College, Jerusalem, 13.

——(2006) 'Judaism' entry, in D. Stout (ed), *Encyclopaedia of Religion, Communication and Media*. London: Routledge.

'Tikshoret, Hashkaghafa, V'Halakha' [Hebrew: The Media, Worldview, and Halakha (Jewish Religious Law)] (1997) Conference of Rabbis and Journalists (Proceedings). Jerusalem: Ministry of Education, November.

Advertising

Cohen, Y. (2012) 'God, Religion of Advertising: A Hard Sell' in A. Hetsroni (ed) *Advertising and Reality*, New York: Continuum.

Dorff, E. (1997) 'Judaism, Business and Privacy', *Business Ethics Quarterly*, 7, 1.

Friedman, H. H. (1984) 'Ancient Marketing Practices: The View from Talmudic Times', *Journal of Public Policy and Marketing*, 3, Spring.

Green, R. M. (1997) 'Guiding Principles of Jewish Business Ethics', *Business Ethics Quarterly*, 7, 1.

Levine, A. (1981) 'Advertising and Promotional Activities as Regulated in Jewish Law', *Journal of Halakha and Contemporary Society*, Spring, 1, 1.

Pava, M. L. (1998), 'Developing a Religiously Grounded Business Ethics: A Jewish Perspective', *Business Ethics Quarterly*, 8, 1.

Tamari, M. (1997) 'The Challenge of Wealth: *Business Ethics*', *Business Ethics Quarterly*, 7, 1.

Copyright

Bar-Ilan, N. (1987) 'Haatikut Seforim O Kasetot' [Hebrew: Copying Books and Tapes]. Alon Shevut: *Tehumin*, 7.

Batzri, E. (1986) 'Ze'chot Ha-Yotzrim'. Alon Shevut: *Tehumin*, 6.

Goldberg, Z. N. (1986) 'Haaitku Mi-Kassete Le'lo Reshut Ha-Baalim' [Hebrew: Copying from a Cassette Without Permission]. Alon Shevut: *Tehumin*, 6.

Katz, E. (1988) 'Ze 'khut Ha-Yotztim' [Hebrew: Copyright]. Alon Shevut: *Tehumin*, 8.

Internet, technology

Bauron, A. (2001) *Sefer Birkhat Aharon: Dinei Kiyum Mitzvot Ul Yedei Emtzai Dibur, U-Shemuya Electroni*, Part 1 [Hebrew: The Fulfillment of Commandments through Electronic Speech and Hearing Apparatus (including Radio, Satellite, Tape, and Speaker)]. Jerusalem: A. Ben T. Biron.

Brueckheimer, A. (2003) 'Halakha and Technology: Erasing G-d's Name from a Computer', *Journal of Halacha and Contemporary Society*, XLV, 49.
Cohen, A. (2005) 'Internet Commerce on Shabbat', *Journal of Halacha and Contemporary Society*, L, 38.
Cohen, Y. (2012) 'Jewish Cybertheology', *Communication Research Trends* 31(1).
Dickovsky, S. (2000) 'Internet B'Halakha' [Hebrew: Internet and Jewish Law]. Alon Shevut: *Tehumin*, 23.
EretzHemdah, K. (2003) 'Mishar B'Internet Ushmirat Shabbas' [Hebrew: Trade on the Internet and Sabbath Observance]. *Shut B'Bmarei Habazak*. Jerusalem: Eretz Hemdah Institute (5), p. 89.
Goodman, Y. (2010) 'The Modern Religious Youth and the Internet', *Tzohar*, Tamuz 5770.
Lerner, Y. (2005) 'Kesher Romanti B'Internet' [Hebrew: A Romantic Relationship on the Internet]. Alon Shevut: *Tehumin*, 25.
Lifshitz, A. (2010) 'Tefila Mitoch Siddur Electroni' [Hebrew: Praying from an Electronic Prayer Book]. Alon Shevut: *Tehumin*, 30.
Reisner, A. I. (2001) *Wired to the Kaddosh Barukh Hu: Minyan via Internet*. New York, Rabbinical Assembly [OH 55:15 2001].
Schwartz, Y. (2005) *Idan Hamakhshev Velekhav* [Hebrew: The Computer Era and What We Can Learn From It]. Jerusalem: Yeshivat: Dvar Yerushalayim Zichron Tvi. See also: No author stated (2005) *Hamakshev le'or hahalakha* (The Computer in the Light of Halakha). Jerusalem: Talmud Vehalakha Institute.
Teitz, M. M. (1984) 'Limud Torah Ma-Ul Galei radio B-Sfat Ha-Nakhar' [Hebrew: Teaching Torah through Radio in a Foreign Language]. *Moriah*, Kislev.

Right to know, privacy, social gossip

Ariel, A. (2001) 'Loshon Hara B'Maarekhet Tzibnori Democrati' [Hebrew: The Place of Social Gossip in the Public Democratic System], *Tzohar*, 5–6.
Ha-Cohen, I. M. (1873) *Chofez Hayim*, Vilna. [For an English edition: Z. Pliskin (1975) *Guard Your Tongue: A Practical Guide to the Laws of Loshon Hara Based on the Chofez Hayim*. Jerusalem: Aish HaTorah.]
Chwat, A. (1995) 'Itonim V'Hadashot Mitzva O Isur' [Hebrew: Newspapers and News: Religious Obligation or Prohibition], Elkana: *T'lalei Orot*.
Falk, E. (1999) 'Jewish Laws of Speech: Toward Multicultural Rhetoric', *The Howard Journal of Communications*, 10.
Korngott, E. M. H. (1993) 'Tafkido shel Itonei', 'Ha-Iton "Bimah Le-Vikukhim" Ziburiim', 'Pirsum Khashud B'Iton', 'Tviot Nezikin ul Hotzaat Dibah B-Iton' [Hebrew: 'The Role of the Journalist', 'The Newspaper: A Platform for Public Disputes', 'The Publication of Rumours in a Newspaper,', 'Legal Action for Slander in a Newspaper'], in E. M. H. Korngott, *Or Yehezkel* [Hebrew: The Light of Ezekiel: Contemporary Issues in Jewish Law]. Petach Tiqva: Or Yehezkel Institute, pp. 329–66.
Liebes, T. (1994) 'Crimes of Reporting: The Unhappy End of a Fact-finding Mission in the Bible', *Journal of Narrative and Life History*, 4.
Oppenheimer, S. (2001) 'Journalism, Controversy, and Responsibility: A Halakhic Analysis', *The Journal of Halacha and Contemporary Society*, XLI, 99.
Rakover, N. (2006) *Protection of Privacy in Jewish Law*. Jerusalem: The Jewish Legal Heritage Society.
Rashi, T. (2008) '"Zekhut Ha-Tzibbur" Ladaat b'Takanenei ha-Etika ha-Itonaut leumat "Khovat haTzibur laDaat", b'Mishpat ha-Ivri' [Hebrew: 'The Right to

Know' in Journalism Ethics Contrasted with 'the Obligation to Know' in Hebrew Law], in T. Rashi and M. Zaft (eds), *Tikshoret V'Yahadut* [Hebrew: Media and Judaism]. Petach Tiqva: Keter HaZahav.

Stav, D. (1997) 'Pirsum Averot shel Talmidei Hachamim' [Hebrew: 'Publicising the Sins of the Rabbis']. Shut Ha-Shaddurim, *Nekuda*, October), 204.

——(1997) 'Papratzi – Tzilum U-Pirsum shel Enoshim Lelo Haskantoim' [Hebrew: Publicising Sins of Rabbis]. Shut Ha-Shaddurim, *Nekuda*, November, 209.

Warhaftig, I. (2009) *Tzin'at Adam: Hazhut l'prutiut l'or halakhah* [Hebrew: The Right to Privacy in Jewish Law]. Ofra: Mishpetei Eretz.

Zoldin, Y. (1999) *Pgia B'Munhig Tzibbur* [Hebrew: Criticism of Public Figures]. Alun Shevut: *Tehumin*, 19.

Sabbath

Apfel, H. D. (2007) 'Reading Options on Shabbat', *Journal of Halakha and Contemporary Society*, 44, Fall.

Auerbach, S. Z. (1996) 'Shidurei Radio B'Shabbat' [Hebrew: Radio Broadcasts on the Sabbath]. Alon Shevut: *Tehumin*, 16.

——(1997) 'Shidurei Radio Khozer B'Shabbat' [Hebrew: Re-Run Radio Broadcasts on the Sabbath]. Alon Shevut: *Tehumin*, 17.

Cohen, A. (2005) 'Internet Commerce on Shabbat', *Journal of Halacha and Contemporary Society*, L, 38.

EretzHemdah, K. (2003) *Miskhar B'Internet U-Shmirat Shabbas* [Hebrew: Trade on the Internet and Sabbath Observance]. Jerusalem: Shut B'Bmarei Habazak, Eretz Hemdah Institute, 5, p. 89.

Sexual modesty

Lamm, N. (1997) 'Tzeniut: A Universal Concept', in M. D. Angel (ed), *Haham Gaon Memorial Volume*. New York: Sepher-Hermon Press.

Other

Shtipansky, I. (1980) 'Kedushat Seforim V'Kitvei Va-Kodesh Biktav U-Dfus' [Hebrew: Sanctification of Printed Holy Books and Texts]. *Or Ha-Mizrach*, 100.

Internet

Haredim

Barzilai-Nahon, K. and Barzilai, G. (2005) 'Cultured Technology: The Internet and Religious Fundamentalism', *The Information Society*, 21, 25–40.

Baumel-Schwartz, J. T. (2009) 'Frum Surfing: Orthodox Jewish Women's Internet Forums as a Historical and Cultural Phenomenon', *Journal of Jewish Identities*, 2(1), 1–30.

Cohen, Y. (2011) 'Haredim and the Internet: A Hate–Love Affair,' in M. Bailey and G. Reddy (eds) *Mediating Faiths: Religion and Socio-Cultural Change in the twenty-first century*, Farnham: Ashgate.

——'Haredim V'ha-Eden Hameda [Hebrew: Haredim and Information Age] *Kesher*, 43.
Horowitz, N. (2000) 'Haredim, Vha-Internet' [Hebrew: Haredim and the Internet]. *Kivunim Hadashim*, 3.

Modern religious (dati leumi)

Goodman, Y. (2010) 'The Modern Religious Youth and the Internet', *Tzohar*, Tamuz 5770.

Jewish religious law (halakhah)

Brueckheimer, A. (2003) 'Halakha and Technology: Erasing G-d's Name from a Computer', *Journal of Halacha and Contemporary Society*, XLV, 49.
Cohen, A. (2005) 'Internet Commerce on Shabbat', *Journal of Halacha and Contemporary Society*, L, 38.
Cohen, Y. (2012) 'Jewish Cybertheology', *Communication Research Trends*, 31(1).
Dickovsky, S. (2000) 'Internet B'Halakha' [Hebrew: Internet and Jewish Law]. Alon Shevut: *Tehumin*, 23.
Eretz Hemdah, K. (2003) 'Miskhar B'Internet Ushmirat Shabbas' [Hebrew: Trade on the Internet and Sabbath Observance]. *Shut B'Bmarei Habazak*, 5. Jerusalem: Eretz Hemdah Institute, p. 89.
Lerner, Y. (2005) 'Kesher Romantic B'Internet' [Hebrew: A Romantic Relationship on the Internet]. Alon Shevut: *Tehumin*, 25.
Lifshitz, A. (2010) 'Tefila Mitoch Siddur Electroni' [Hebrew: Praying from an Electronic Prayer Book]. Alon Shvut: *Tehumin*, 30.
Reisner, A. I. (2001) *Wired to the Kaddosh Barukh Hu: Minyan via Internet*. New York: Rabbinical Assembly [OH 55:15 2001].
Schwartz, Y. (2005) *Idan Hamakhshev Velekhav* [Hebrew: The Computer Era and What We Can Learn From It]. Jerusalem: Yeshivat: Dvar Yerushalayim Zichron Tvi.
(See also: No author stated (2005) *Hamakshev le'or hahalakha* [Hebrew: The Computer in the Light of Halakha]. Jerusalem: Talmud Vehalakha Institute.

Torah educational websites

Bleiweiss, M. (1999) 'In Defence of the Inaccessible', *Sh'ma*, November.
Lau, B. (2001) 'Hora'ah Torah BiKhlei Va-Tikshoret' [Hebrew: Teaching Torah through Mass Media], *Mabseret*, Volume 1. Jerusalem: Maale School of Film.
Lerner, H. G. (2009) 'Internet Resources for Researching Orthodox Judaism', *Journal of Religious and Theological Information*, 7.
Rosen, J. (2001) *The Talmud and the Internet: A Journey Between Worlds*. New York: Farrar, Strauss and Giroux.
Green, I. (1997) *Judaism on the Web*. New York: MIS Press (see Chapters 2, 20, 21).
Romm, D. (1998) *The Jewish Guide to the Internet*. Northvale, NJ: Jason Aronson.

Other

Kustanowitz, E. (2006) 'Jewish Blogging 101', *Contact*, 8(3), Spring.
Reform Judaism, special issue on Cyber-Judaism, Summer 2009.
Voloj, J. (2007) 'Virtual Judaism: Finding a Second Life in Online Community', *Presentense Magazine*, 3.

Language, semiotics

Baumel, S. (2002) 'Communication and Change: Newspapers, Periodicals and Acculturation among Israeli Haredim', *Jewish History*, 16(2).

——(2005) *Sacred Speakers: Language and Culture among the Haredim in Israel.* Oxford and New York: Berghahn.

Blum Kulka, S., Blondheim, M. and Hacohen, G. (2002) 'Traditions of Dispute: From Negotiations of Talmudic Texts to the Arena of Political Discourse in the Media', *Journal of Pragmatics*, 34.

Gruber, M. (1999) 'Language(s) in Judaism', in J. Neusner and A. J. Avery Peck (eds), *The Encyclopaedia of Judaism.* New York: Continuum.

Sela, P. (2004) *Socio-linguistic Factors in Ultra-Orthodox Newspapers.* Department of Hebrew and Semitics Languages, Ph.D. thesis [Hebrew]. Ramat Gan: Bar-Ilan University.

Zulick, M. (1992) 'The Active Force of Hearing: The Ancient Hebrew Language of Persuasion', *Rhetorica*, X, 4.

Media structure

General

Cohen, Y. (2001) 'Mass Media in the Jewish Tradition', in D. Stout and J. Buddenbaum (eds), *Religion and Popular Culture: Studies on the Interaction of Worldviews.* Ames, IA: Iowa State University Press.

——(2006) 'Israel' entry, in D. Stout (ed), *Encyclopaedia of Religion, Communication and Media.* New York and London: Routledge.

Haredi media

Amior, H. (2002) 'Gedaliah Itzik' [Hebrew: Gedaliah Itzik], *Ha'ayin HaShiviit*, November.

Baumel, S. (2002) 'Communication and Change: Newspapers, Periodicals and Acculturation among Israeli Haredim', *Jewish History*, 16(2).

——(2005) *Sacred Speakers: Language and Culture among the Haredim in Israel.* Oxford and New York: Berghahn.

Blondheim, M. and Kaplan, K. (1993) '"Rishaat Ha-Shidur": Tikshoret U-Keletot B'Hevra Ha-Haredit' [Hebrew: Media and Cassettes in Haredi Society], *Kesher*, November.

Cohen Y. (2012) 'Haredim Vha-Edan Ha-Meda' [Hebrew: Haredim and the Information Age], *Kesher*, 43.

Hamodia (2000) 'Khamishim Shanim le-Iton Hamodia' [Hebrew: Fifty Years to Hamodia], *Hamodia*, 15.9.2000; 19.9.2000.

Ilan, S. (1993) 'Ha-Otzma, Ha-Taharut, Milkhemet Ha-Yehudim' [Hebrew: Power, Competition, the War of the Jews]. *Yearbook of The Israel Journalists Association.* Tel Aviv: Israel Journalists Association.

Katzover, I. (1990) 'The Kosher Press', *The Jerusalem Report*, 22.11.1990.

Levi, A. (1990) 'The Haredi Press and Secular Society', in C. Liebman (ed) *Conflict and Accommodation between Jews in Israel.* Jerusalem: Keter – Avi Chai.

Micolson, M. (1990) 'Itonut Haredit B'Yisroel' [Hebrew: The Haredi Press in Israel]. Tel Aviv: *Kesher*, 8.
Pfeffer, A. (2001) 'Milhemet Atzamaut' [Hebrew: The War of Independence], May.
Sela, P. (2004) *Sociolinguistic Factors in Ultra-Orthodox Newspapers*. Department of Hebrew and Semitics Languages, Ph.D thesis [Hebrew]. Ramat Gan: Bar-Ilan University.
Tsarfaty, O. (2009) 'Alternative Identity and Memory in Ultra-Orthodox Newspapers', *Journal for Semitics*,19(1).
Yated Neeman (1995) 'Eser Shanim L'Iton Yated Neeman' [Hebrew: Ten Years to the Yated Neeman newspaper], *Yated Neeman*, 23.7.1995.
Ha-Yerushalami, L. I. (1998) 'Meda Be-Hekhsher B'Datzim' [Hebrew: Fatigue in Kosher Information]. *Yearbook of The Israel Journalists Association*. Tel Aviv: Israel Journalists Association.

Modern religious (dati leumi) media

Gabel, I. (2006) *'Ha-tzibur ha-dati leumi v'hu-Tikshoret: Yahasei ahava-sinaa'* [Hebrew: The Modern Religious Community and the Media: A Love–Hate Relationship]. Tel Aviv: Herzog Institute, Tel Aviv University.
Jacobson, D.C. (2004) 'The Maale School: Catalyst for the Entrance of Religious Zionism to the World of Media Production', *Israel Studies*, 9, 1.
Tzarfaty, O. (2005) 'Mi Mashpia ul Emdot ha-Zionut Ha-Datit' (Hebrew: Who Influences the Positions of the Modern Religious Community?], *Kivunim*, 12.

Jewish Diaspora media

Cohen, Y. (2008) 'Tafkid haTikshoret Tefutzot Be-Itzuv Hazhut Hayehudit' [Hebrew: The Role of the Diaspora Media in the Construction of Jewish Identity], in T. Rashi and M. Zaft (eds), *Tikshoret V'Yahadut* [Hebrew: Media and Judaism]. Petach Tiqva: Keter HaZahav.
Ford, L. (2004) *Yesterday's News Tomorrow: Inside American Jewish Journalism*. Lincoln NE: iUniverse.
Rosenblatt, G. (1977) 'The Jewish De-Press', *Moment*, November.
Silverman, D. W. (1963) 'The Jewish Press: A Quadrilingual Phenomenon', in M. E. Marty (ed), *The Religious Press in America*. New York: Holt, Rinehart and Winston.
Whitfield, S. J. (2000) 'The Jewish Contribution to American Journalism', in W. D. Sloan (ed), *Media and Religion in American History*. Northport, AL: Vision Press.

Religious journalists

Burg, H. (2008) 'Maaminim BeMedia: Hitpatchut Magamot Tikshoret V'kolnoa B-Hinukh Ha-Mamlakhti Hadati' [Hebrew: Believing in the Media: The Development of Media and Cinema Studies in the Modern Religious Education Sector], in T. Rashi and M. Zaft (eds), *Tikshoret V'Yahadut* [Hebrew: Media and Judaism]. Petach Tiqva: Keter HaZahav.
Ishon, M. (2008) 'Ha-Itoniut – Bein Shlihut l'Miktzoa' [Hebrew: Journalism between Mission and Occupation], in T. Rashi and M. Zaft (eds), *Tikshoret V'Yahadut* [Hebrew: Media and Judaism]. Petach Tiqva: Keter HaZahav.

Jacobson, D.C. (2004) 'The Maale School: Catalyst for the Entrance of Religious Zionism to the World of Media Production', *Israel Studies*, 9, 1.
London, Y. (1999) 'Religious People on the Network', *Meimad*, 16, May.
Marot (1997) 'Yeud U'Miktzoa – Tikshoret' [Hebrew: The Media: A Mission and Occupation], *Marot*, special supplement 4, January/February.
Sheleg, Y. (1998) 'Yaad Haba: Kibush Ha-Tikshoret' [Hebrew: The Next Target: Capturing the Media], *Yearbook of The Israel Journalists Association*. Tel Aviv: Israel Journalists Association.

Religion news coverage

Coverage of religion

Cohen, Y. (2001) 'Palestinians and Israelis: Oh Jerusalem!' *Religion in the News*. Hartford: Trinity College, Spring.
——(2004) 'Ha-Sikur shel Dat B'Radio B'Yisroel' [Hebrew: Religion Coverage of Israel Radio], *Mayim Medalyo*, Research Annual of the Lifshitz Religious Education College, Jerusalem, No. 15.
——(2005) 'Religion News in Israel', *Journal of Media and Religion*, 4, 3.
——(2006) *The Religion News Media Nexus in Israel*, Sociological Institute for Community Studies, Ramat Gan: Bar-Ilan University.
——(2006) 'Israel' entry, in D. Stout (ed) *Encyclopedia of Religion, Communication and Media*, New York and London: Routledge
Heilman, S. C. (1990) 'Religion Jewry in the Secular Press: Aftermath of the 1988 Elections', in C. Liebman (ed), *Conflict and Accommodation Between Jews in Israel*. New York: Avi Foundation.
Hobstein, A. (1999) 'Hod Maalato: Hebrew: His Excellency', *Ayin Sheviit*, May.
Recanati, I. (2002) 'Im Ha-Masakh lo Mashekef et ha-Shinuim Shehallim be'Hevra ha-Yisroelit – hu Yipol. Sikha im Yo'Re Ha-Reshut Ha-Shniya, Motti Sklar' [Hebrew: If the Screen Will Not Reflect Changes in Israeli Society – It Will Collapse. A Conversation with the Chairman of the Second Television and Radio Authority, Motti Sklar], *Mabseret*, Volume 2. Jerusalem: Maale School of Film.

Haredi media content and linguistics

Amior, H. (2002) 'Gedaliah Itzik' [Hebrew: Gedaliah Itzik], *Ha'ayin HaShiviit*, November.
Baumel, S. (2002) 'Communication and Change: Newspapers, Periodicals and Acculturation among Israeli Haredim', *Jewish History*, 16(2).
——(2005) *Sacred Speakers: Language and Culture among the Haredim in Israel*. Oxford and New York: Berghahn.
Hamodia (2000) 'Khamishim Shanim le-Iton Hamodia' [Hebrew: Fifty Years to Hamodia], *Hamodia*, 15.9.2000; 19.9.2000.
Micolson, M. (1990) 'Itonut Haredit B'Yisroel' [Hebrew: The Haredi Press in Israel]. Tel Aviv: *Kesher*, 8.
Sela, P. (2004) *Sociolinguistic Factors in Ultra-Orthodox Newspapers*. Department of Hebrew and Semitics Languages, Ph.D thesis [Hebrew]. Ramat Gan: Bar-Ilan University.
Sasson-Levi, O. (1998) *Hishtakfut Ha-Hilonim B'Itonut Ha-Haredit* [Hebrew: Secular Israelis as Reflected in the Haredi Press]. Ramat Gan: Am Hofshi.

250 *Selected bibliography*

Tsarfaty, O. (2010) *Mi-Oslo ad Hahitnutkut – Hamavak ul Eretz Yisroel HaShlama b'itoinei Habad* [Hebrew: From Oslo to Disengagement: the Struggle for Greater Israel on the Habad Press]. Tel Aviv: Tel Aviv University.

Yated Neeman (1995) 'Eser Shanim L'Iton Yated Neeman' [Hebrew: Ten Years to the Yated Neeman Newspaper], *Yated Neeman*, 23.7.1995.

Jewish Diaspora media content

Cohen, Y. (1991) 'The Jewish Diaspora News Media and the 1982 Lebanon War', in E. Don-Yihye (ed) *Israel and Diaspora Jewry*. Ramat Gan: Bar-Ilan University Press.

——(2008) 'Tafkid haTikshoret Tefutzot Be-Itzuv Hazhut Hayehudit'[Hebrew: The Role of the Diaspora Media in the Construction of Jewish Identity], in T. Rashi and M. Zaft (eds), *Tikshoret V'Yahadut* [Hebrew: Media and Judaism]. Petach Tiqva: Keter HaZahav.

Ford, L. (2004) *Yesterday's News Tomorrow: Inside American Jewish Journalism*. Lincoln, NE: iUniverse.

Neustein, A. and Lesher, M. (2002) 'The Silence of the Jewish Media on Sexual Abuse in the Orthodox Jewish Community', in D. S. Claussen (ed), *Sex, Religion, Media*. Lanham, MD: Rowman and Littlefield.

Foreign media and the Holyland

Cohen, Y. (1994) 'Focus on Israel: Twenty-Five Years of Foreign Media Reporting from Israel', *The Encyclopaedia Judaica*, 1983–92 Decennial Volume. Jerusalem: Keter.

——(2008) 'Eretz Hakodesh B'einei KleiTikshoret Ha-Zarah' [Hebrew: The Holyland Through the Eyes of Foreign Correspondents], *Mayim Medalyo*. Research Annual of the Lifshitz Religious Education College, Jerusalem, No. 19–20.

——(2011) 'War, Religion and the Foreign Press Corps in Israel', in Y. Levin and A. Shapiro (ed), *War, Peace in the Jewish Tradition: From the Biblical World to the Present*. New York and London: Routledge.

Ethics in news reporting

Jacobson, D. C. (2004) 'The Maale School: Catalyst for the Entry of Religious Zionism to the World of Media Production', *Israel Studies*, 9, 1.

Oppenheimer, S. (2001) 'Journalism, Controversy, and Responsibility: A Halakhic Analysis', *The Journal of Halacha and Contemporary Society*, XLI, 99.

Stav, D. (1997) 'Pirsum Averot shel Talmidei Hachamim' [Hebrew: Publicising the Sins of the Rabbis]. Shut Ha-Shaddurim: *Nekuda*, October, 204.

——(1997) 'Papapratzi – Tzilum U-Pirsum shel Enoshim Lelo Haskantum' [Hebrew: Publicising the Sins of the Rabbis]. Shut Ha-Shaddurim: *Nekuda*, November, 209.

Rabbis' attitudes to mass media

Brandes, Y. (2003) 'Livhor V'Lo-Livroach'. [Hebrew: To Be Selective Rather Than Separate From Television], *Nekuda*, November.

Cohen, Y. (2011) 'Rabanim V'HaTikshoret: Maarekhet Yahasim Mesuchsachot' [Hebrew: Rabbis and the Media: A Conflictual Relationship], in M. Rachimi (ed), *Amadot (3): Etgarim V'Yaadim* [Hebrew: Positions (3): The Media: Challenges and Goals]. Elkana and Rehovot (Israel): Orot College of Education.

Eliahu, S. (2003) 'Le-Hitnatek mi-HaTelevisia'[Hebrew: To Separate from the Television], *Nekuda*, November.

Hershkowitz, Z. (2008) 'IYun Halachti B-Maamud Harav B'eydan shel Media Mitkademet' [Hebrew: Jewish Law Discussion of the Social Standing of the Rabbi in the Age of Advanced Mass Communications] in T. Rashi and M. Zaft (eds), *Tikshoret V'Yahadut* [Hebrew: Media and Judaism]. Petach Tiqva: Keter HaZahav.

Korngott, E. M. H. (1993) 'Pirsum Divrei Torah B'Iton' [Hebrew: Publishing Torah Texts in Newspapers], *Or Yehezkel* [Hebrew: The Light of Ezekiel: Contemporary Issues in Jewish Law]. Petach Tiqva: Or Yehezkel Institute.

Lau, B. (2001) 'Hora'ah Torah BiKhlei Va-Tikshoret' [Hebrew: Teaching Torah through Mass Media], *Mabseret*, Volume 1. Jerusalem: Maale School of Film.

'Tikshoret, Hashkaghafa, V'Halakha' [Hebrew: The Media, Worldview, and Halakha (Jewish Religious Law)] (1997) Conference of Rabbis and Journalists (Proceedings). Jerusalem: Ministry of Education, November.

Index

ABC 206–7
Abuse and Vilification Order 64
accuracy 23–4, 30
Adorno, T. 77, 106
advertising 9, 24, 100, 156–71, 230–1
Afghanistan 71
Agriprocessors 192
Agudat Israel 44, 53, 79
aguna 122
Aish Torah 201
Al Jazeera 210
Alim Terufat 182
Allen, J.: and Dart, J. 40–1
Aloni, S. 46
American Jewish Community 188–9, 199; Israelis ('yordim') in the US 198
American news magazines: and religious advertising 160
anti-Semitism 65, 188, 191, 196
Arab media 215
Arab-Israeli conflict *ix*, 186, 189, 195, 196, 206, 208, 212, 216, 224; Palestinians 208, 210, 213; peace process 97; War 56
Aramaic 147
Ariel, A. 9, 21
Ariel, Y. 60, 142
army national service: exemptions from 123
Arutz 7 Station 100–1, 112
Atlanta Jewish Times 189
Aviner, E. 142
Aviner, S. 57, 58–9

Babbakamma (website) 26
B'Ahavah ub'Yirah (With Love and Fear) 181

Bakehilla (magazine) 74, 80, 88, 90
Baptists 127
Bar-Ilan *sheiltot* project 147
Barak, E. 72
Barnea, N. 73
Barzilai, G.: and Barzilai-Nahon, K. 137
Barzilai-Nahon, K.: and Barzilai, G. 137
BaSheva (magazine) 61, 99–100, 113, 119
Bat Kol 181
Be'Hadrei Haredim (Internet forum) 151
Belze Hassidic Court 139
Ben Rafael, E. 124–5
Ben Zvi, S. 98–101
Bermant, C. 191
Betar 153
Bezek 138
bias 125–9
Bibi, Y. 156
Bible 6, 15–17
Bin Laden, O. 216
Bina, M. 182
Blau, M. 141
Bleiwess, M. 148
blogging 152, 222
Bolton, R. 179
Brod, M. 178
Buddenbaum, J. 39–40, 50, 54, 119, 125, 208, 212
Buddhism 54–5
burial rituals 122

Carmi, L. 123
Catholic Church 7, 125, 223
Catholic-Jewish relations 212
CBS 206–7

cell phones 96–107, 153–4, 168
censorship 64–6, 81–2
Central Bureau of Statistics 115, 136
Chabad.org 177–8
Chen, N. 39, 42, 46
Chief Rabbis *ix*, *xi*, *xii*, 41, 52, 58
Christian media 211
Christianity 12, 39, 53–5, 127, 186, 207, 227–9
church and state 160
cinema 45, 105
Clinton, B. 72
Cohen, A. 18
Cohen, D. 143
Cohen, M. 42
Committee for the Purity and Sanctity of the Camp 141, 159
Committee of Torah Sages 19
commodity culture 172
computer filtering programmes 139, 142
Conservative Jews 28–9, 39, 63
conversion 48, 121
copyright ownership 23
Council of Torah Sages 87, 89
crime 81–2
cultural proximity 195–6, 209
cyberspace synagogues 143, 227–8; minyan.com 144; internet mourning rituals 145

Daf Yomi 45
Dart, J.: and Allen, J. 40–1
dati leumi Jews *x*, *xii*, 96–7, 109
dating 151, 167
Davidian sect 206
Degal HaTorah 79
Dehaishe refugee camp 212
Diaspora Jewish identity: and Israel-centredness 195–8
Diaspora Jewish organisations 200
Dickovsky, S. 24
disclosure 20, 21–2, 22, 61–2, 63
divorce 122
Dorner, D. 71
Durkheim, E. 3

e-commerce 24, 26
Eda Haredit 19
Edelman, R. 46
Egyptian television: and Ramadan advertising 163
Eidelberg, H. 138
Eisner, J. 192

El Al 160
Elon, M. 57, 59–60
emunah (belief) *ix*, 16
Erdogan, B.Z.: Waller, D. and Fam, K.-S. 164
Erlich, Y. 61
ethical constraints 56–63, 222–3
ethics 64
European Jewry: destruction of 177
Eurovision Song Contest 67

Facebook 140–1, 174
Fam, K.-S.: Erdogan, B.Z. and Waller, D. 164
Feldman, Y. 156
female reporters 44
foreign correspondents 195–6, 210, 211
Foreign Ministry 214
foreign news 205–17
Foreign Press Association of Israel 206
Forward Association 191–2, 194
Forward (newspaper) 187, 190–4, 199; *Forverts* 191
Frankel, W. 191
freedom of expression 57, 96
Friedman, T. 205, 209, 213
Fromm, E. 172
fundamentalism 221

Galei Yisroel 101
Galei Zahal 36–7, 38, 67, 100, 104, 111–12, 113
Galtung, J.: and Ruge, M. 52, 195, 202
Garrett-Medill study 50–1, 55
Ginat, G. 74
Global Jewish data base 147
Globes (newspaper) 36
God 15–17, 22–3, 50–1
Goldberg, J.J. 192
gossip (*loshon hara*) 21, 141
gossip 19–22, 30, 92
Great Phoenix Jewish News 188–9
Grossman, N.Z. 84
Gruber, M. 15
Gulf War 27, 68, 69, 178, 196
Gutman Survey 228

Ha-Kol Dibburim 49
Ha-Mishpacha (magazine) 89–90
Haaretz (newspaper) 35, 45, 51, 57, 68, 73, 119, 127
Habad 177–9, 201, 230
halakhah (Jewish religious law) *xii*, 17–30, 108, 121, 182

254 Index

Hamevaser (newspaper) 36, 41, 111
Hammer, Z. 69
Hamodia (newspaper) 49, 65, 74, 78–86, 111, 123, 165, 193
Hardal 62–3; 142
Haredi advertising sector 165–9
Haredi community 39, 109–10
Haredi Internet news sites 92–3, 150–1
Haredi media 41, 74, 77, 83–4, 93–4, 129–30, 223
Haredi political involvement 123
Haredi population 166; consumer needs 166–9
Haredi press, newspapers 8, 11, 78–84, 87–9, 111, 166
Haredi rabbis 4–5, 9, 41, 78, 114, 137–41
Haredi radio 3, 49, 150
Haredim (internet news site) *xii*, *xiii*, 92; and press exposure 110–11
Hassidim 78, 177
Hatzofe (newspaper) 49, 53, 74, 97, 98, 113, 128, 142
Hebrew *x*, 147, 149
Hebrew media 198, 229
Hect, S.: Saxe, L. and Sasson, T. 202
Hemdah, E. 26
Herring, H. 172–3
Heshin, M. 48
Hess, S. 213
Hinduism 54–5
Hofetz Hayim (Ha-Cohen) 9, 20, 22
Holocaust 177, 181, 206, 212
Holyland: and foreign media interest 207–14
Holyland *xiii*, 9, 11, 195, 205; public diplomacy 214–16
homosexuality 150
Huberman, H. 73

ideology 72–4, 77
Ilan, S. 39, 43, 108, 129
Index of Forbidden Books 7
Institute of Torah Creative Endeavour 106
intermarriage *ix*, 48
Internet *xii*, *xiii*, 4–5, 8, 11–12, 78, 109, 124, 219; and advertising 165; banning of 92, 137–9, 142, 224; community websites 179–82; extramarital relationships 19; Haredim 118; Jewish Diaspora 187, 200–2, 224; Judaism 18, 135–55; modern Orthodox Jews 141–2; on-line rabbinical counselling 183–4, 225–6;

prayer 28–30, 144–5; relationships 48–9; religious exposure to 135–7; religious identity 120; religious information 228; and the Sabbath 25–8; and sexual content 18–19; socio-religious impact of 152–4
Iran 71, 146
Ishon, M. 130
Islam 30, 54–5, 127, 207, 210, 227–9; and the Arab-Israeli conflict 208, 212
Islamic Jihad 216
Islamic media 211
Israel: as foreign media capital 206–7; and Jewish identity 202
Israel Advertisers Association 90, 158
Israel Association for Civil Rights 140
Israel Broadcasting Authority (IBA) 64, 103, 176
Israel Democracy Institute 113
Israel Education Television 67
Israel Journalists Association 10
Israel Manufacturers Association 167
Israel Press Council 56
Israel Radio *xi*, 36–7, 38, 40, 49, 53, 56, 100, 103
Israel Television *xi*, 29, 36, 38, 68–9, 78, 178
Israeli Arab population: and broadcasting 69–70; readership patterns 55
Israeli Army 27, 84, 160, 213
Israeli identity 121, 187
Israeli Jewish population 220
Israeli media 113–14, 198; Israeli journalists 44, 119–20
Israeli military censorship 56
Israeli Movement for Progressive Judaism 176
Israeli socio-cultural code 5
Israeli-Egyptian War of attrition 199
Itim (Israeli news agency) 200

Jacobs, L. 191
JC.com 194
Jemayel, A. 55
Jerusalem One (website) 149
Jerusalem Post 36, 43, 44, 198, 199, 201
Jerusalem Report 198, 199
Jew Tube 149
Jewish Agency 200
Jewish business ethics 156
The Jewish Channel (TJC) 188
Jewish Chronicle 187, 190–4

Jewish civil law 5
Jewish Diaspora *xiii*, 11, 127, 146, 161, 173, 186–205, 200–2, 230
Jewish education 148, 154, 201; websites *xiii*, 145–52
Jewish ethics 10, 220, 230
Jewish Global TV 188
Jewish identity *xii*, 46, 161, 184, 187, 201, 230
Jewish Law 5, 9, 17, 28, 94–5, 182
Jewish media 198, 211; in USA 187, 189
Jewish newspapers 187
Jewish radio 187
Jewish State 97, 131, 173, 198, 214, 215
Jewish Telegraphic Agency 189, 193, 196, 197–8, 200
Jewish television 101–4, 187–8
Jewish Television Network (JTN) 187–8
Jewish Week (weekly newspaper) 188–9, 194
Jewish women's rights 192
JewishParentCoaching.com 149
journalists 45–6, 56, 222; source-reporter relations 41–5
Judaism 3, 6, 17, 172–3, 181, 207, 227–8; in the information age 219–32; marketing of *xiii*; *mitzvot* (religious obligations) 177, 182; Ten Commandments 17

Kaddish (prayer) 28, 29
Kadosh (holy supplement) 49, 79, 86, 87, 90
Katzav, M. 80
Katzover, I. 88, 129
kedusha (blessing) 29
Keenan, K.L.: and Yeni, S. 163
Keysar, A.: and Kosmin, B. 201
Kikar Shabbat (website) 92
Kippa (skullcap) 46, 149–50, 152
Kirchenbaum, M. 46
Klugman, M. 84
Kol Ha'ir (weekly newspaper) 43, 44
Kopatch, G. 65–6
Koran 66
Kosmin, B.: and Keysar, A. 201

LaDaat (Internet website) 92
Landau, D. 42
Lau, D. 27
Lau, I.M. 174–5
Lavie, M. 80
Lebanon War 202
Levi, A. 35, 39, 43

Lichtenstein, A. 60
Likud 53
Linderman, A.G. 227
Lior, D. 173–4
Lipsky, S. 191–2
Lis, B. 39
Lithuanian Haredim 78, 85
Livne-Levi, A. 105–6
loshon hara (law against gossip) 92

Maale School of Film 11, 105–6
Maariv (newspaper) 35–8, 42, 57–9, 61, 73, 98, 119, 198
Ma'aynei Hayeshua (synagogue bulletin) 181
Mabat (TV news programme) 49
Mahler, J. 192
Maimonides 17, 30
marketing 157, 164–5
mass media 120, 186, 219, 226
Maxim (US magazine) 159
media 77; accountability 19–20; audience interest 212–14; media effects and rabbis 114–15; exposure to 108–10; journalists 44, 119–20, 113–14, 198
and religion 4–9, 7, 9–11, 108, 229; and the Sabbath 25–8; and secular-religious relations 121–5
media, Judaism and culture (MJC) 3–14, 226–31
media structures 220, 221–2
media-Judaism theory 231
Meir, G. 68
Mekor Rishon (newspaper) 36, 61, 98–101, 119
Melchior, M. 174
Mendel, M. 177
Mergi, Y. 174
messianic redemption 177, 179
Metzger, Y. 58
Michaelson, J. 172
military censorship 158–9
Millward Brown survey 110–12
Ministry of Religious Affairs 41, 214
Mishnah 8, 17
Mishpacha (magazine) 74, 81, 111
Mitchell, J. 229
mobile phones 96–107, 153–4, 168
modern Orthodox Jews: and community 5, 109; and rabbis 63, 114
modern Orthodox media 77, 97–101
modesty squads 153

256 Index

monotheism 16, 30, 216
Moreshet (website) 150
mourning rituals: Internet 145
Mozes, Y. 46
Arab-Israeli conflict 208, 212
MyKehilla (website) 179

Nachshoni, I. 87–8
Nakdi Guide 56
National Religious Party 67–9, 97, 104–5, 113, 180
Nativ 139
New York Times 50, 52, 127, 194, 195, 206–7
news 6, 37–8, 45–6, 48–76, 118; source-reporter relations 41–5
newspapers 49–51, 54, 79, 108; and the Sabbath 26–7
Northern California Jewish Bulletin 188–9
NRG (Internet news website) 37, 38, 75, 150

Obama, B. 61–2
Ohana, A. 40
Olam Katan (synagogue bulletin) 181
Old Testament 17
Orlev, Z. 70
non-Orthodox Judaism 10
Orthodox Judaism: and Internet 146
non-Orthodox religious streams: and public broadcasting 175–7
Oslo accords 210, 215
Otot (journal) 10

Palestinians: Arab Israeli conflict 208, 212; refugees 72; State 215
Palestinian Wakf 215
Palm Beach Jewish Journal 190
Peled, Z. 158
Peri, T. 142
Perlin, A. 143
Pinhasi, R. 69
Playboy 71
Plotzker, S. 73
Pollard, S. 191, 193
Pope 42, 211–12
pornography 66, 70–2, 139–42
poverty ix–x
Prayer x, 16–7, 40, 1, 61, 92, 105, 112, 122, 142–5, 168, 182, 195, 207, 210, 227, 229; *baruchu* (blessing) 29; marriage ceremony 122; *mechilla* (forgiveness) 145;

Shema (prayer) 40; Ten Commandments 17
prayer services: on-line 28–30, 144–5; internet mourning rituals 145; minyan.com 144
privacy 61
prophecy 16
Prophet Mohammed: Danish cartoon of 65
Protestant Church 7
Public Broadcasting Service (PBS) 188
Public Judaism 173, 175

rabbinical counselling: on-line 183–4, 225–6
rabbis 52, 108, 118–19, 129, 173, 230; and community 173; marketing of 172–85; and media effects 114–15, 224; and scandals 62–3
Rabin, Y. 206, 213, 215
Rabinowitz, S. 61
radio *xiii*, 27, 69, 78, 90–1, 100, 109, 116–18, 184
Radio Communaute Judaique (radio station) 197
Radio *Kol Chai* 80, 82, 90–4, 101, 111, 119, 128
Rahav-Meir, S. 40
Ramon, C. 80
rape 80, 81
Ravid, H. 150
Ravitzky, A. 131
readership patterns: in USA 190–4
Reagan, R. 191
Reform Jews 222; rabbis 63
Regev, U. 176
Reisner, A.I. 29
religion 3, 51–6, 202; audience interest in 116–20; commodification of 161; content analysis of 49–51; and foreign news 205–6; and media *xii-xiii*; and statehood 121; and symbols 46, 57; and US TV coverage 42
religion news 35–47, 38–41, 48–76, 208, 222
religious advertising 160–1; religious holiday advertising 161–4
religious broadcasting 90–1
religious identity 4, 111–13, 115, 124–5, 220; and Internet 152; in Jewish Diaspora 186; and media 109–10, 118–20, 163–4, 172, 223–6
religious journalism 85
religious media 55, 63, 77, 93–5, 98, 119, 128, 222–3

non-religious media 119
religious political parties 52, 66, 98, 123, 127, 215
reporter-editor relations 45–6
Revach, U. 40
right to know 19–22, 57, 96
right to privacy 20–1, 57
Rimon 139
Rokeach study 111–13, 116–20
Rosenblatt, G. 188
Rosh Yehudi (synagogue bulletin) 181
Rottenberg, A. 158
Rowan, D. 193–4
Rubin, N. 189
Ruge, M.: and Galtung, J. 52, 195, 202

Sabbath 6, 25–8, 46, 69–70; broadcasting on 4, 57, 66–72
Sarna, J. 188
Sasson, T.: Hecht, S. and Saxe, L. 202
Saxe, L.: Sasson, T. and Hecht, S. 202
Scharansky, B. 138
Schimmel, S. 152
Schlesinger, Y. 39
Schneersohn, Y. 177
Schwartz, M. 181
secular media 64, 83, 94, 104, 119, 129–30, 222–3
secular-religious tensions 103, 126, 130, 131, 216–17
Seeing the World (TV programme) 67
Sephardic Jews 41
Sex and the City (King): film screening 159
sexual modesty 18–19, 30, 80, 138, 141, 157, 230, 231
Shabbat Shalom (synagogue bulletin) 181
Shabbat V'Shabato (synagogue bulletin) 180
Shabbaton (synagogue bulletin) 182
Shahal, M. 70
Shalom Channel 188
Shapiro, A. 175
Shapiro, Y. 142
Sharon, A. 191
Shas Party 40, 53, 69, 79, 129, 139–41
www.shemayisrael.co.il 146
Sherlo, Y. 153, 182
Shilat, Y. 60
Shiloh, E. 99–100
www.shomershabes 26
Shragai, N. 39, 45

Siegel, J. 43, 44
Six Day War 206, 209, 214, 224
Sklar, M. 101–4, 105
source-reporter relations 41–5
speech: oral prayers 16–17
State of Israel *x*, *xi*; creation of 16
Stav, D. 142
stereotypes 125–9
synagogal bulletins 180–2, 231
synagogues 12, 51, 184, 219, 230
Syria 146

Takana 60
Talmud 17
talmudical colleges (*yeshivot*) 3
Techelet (TV channel) 102–3
Tehumin (law annual) 9
television 9, 49–51, 69, 100, 109, 110, 178; banning of 78, 110, 112; and Haredim 53; and the Sabbath 27
Temple Mount 72–4, 207, 215
Ten Commandments 17
Tennenbaum, I. 82
terrorism 84, 199, 208
Third Jewish Commonwealth 109–10
Torah 17, 219, 222, 231
Torah Communication Network 147–8
Torah educational websites 154
Torah Sheets (bulletin) 180
Torahnet 139
Tuchman, G. 37
Turkel, Y. 71–2
Tzenaya, S. 43
tzeniut (modesty) 19

United States of America (USA): foreign policy 190; readership patterns 190–4

Vatican 212
videos: banning of 78
virtual *minyan* (prayer) 28–30, 144–5
virtual rabbis 182–4
virtual synagogues 225–6
Vollman, I. 96

Walder, H. 80
Walla 37
Waller, D.: Fam, K.-S. and Erdogan, B.Z. 164
Washington Jewish Week 188–9
Washington Post 52, 127, 195

We have Reason to Believe (Jacobs) 191
Web Yeshiva 148–9
Western Wall 61, 64, 72–3, 92, 122–3, 145, 207, 212
Wikiyeshiva website 146–7
World Zionist Organisation 196

Y-NET 37, 38, 75
Yated Neeman (newspaper) 36, 41, 74, 78–83, 86–9, 111, 123, 165
Yediot Aharonot (newspaper) 35–8, 49, 60, 73, 93, 119, 127, 198
Yemen 146
Yeni, S.: and Keenan, K.L. 163
Yisrael Hayom (newspaper) 35, 38

Yisroel, A. 84
Y-Net 150
Yom Kippur: and media functioning 25
Yom Kippur War 199
Yom LeYom (newspaper) 36, 79, 87
Yosef, A. 27
Yosef, O. 41–5, 64, 175

Zadik, D. 57
Zilbershlag, D. 88
Zionism 84, 87, 106, 112, 113
Zisovitch, H. 45–6
Zulick, M. 16

Printed by Publishers' Graphics Kentucky